# *Invention and Method*

Society of Biblical Literature

Writings from the Greco-Roman World

John T. Fitzgerald, General Editor



Number 15

*Invention and Method*

Volume Editor
Cecil W. Wooten

# *Invention and Method*

## Two Rhetorical Treatises from the Hermogenic Corpus

The Greek Text, Edited by Hugo Rabe,
Translated with Introductions and Notes
by

George A. Kennedy

Society of Biblical Literature
Atlanta

INVENTION AND METHOD



---

**Library of Congress Cataloging-in-Publication Data**

Hermogenes, 2nd cent.

[Selections. English & Greek. 2005]

Invention and method in Greek rhetorical theory : two rhetorical treatises from the Hermogenic corpus / the Greek text, edited by Hugo Rabe, with introductions, English translations, and notes by George A. Kennedy.

p. cm. — (Writings from the Greco-Roman world ; v. 15)

Contains the Greek texts and English translations of two treatises, On invention, and On the method of forcefulness, once attributed to Hermogenes of Tarsus, but now believed to be by unknown authors.

The Greek texts are from Hermogenes, edited by Hugo Rabe, published in 1913 by B.G. Teubneri.

Includes bibliographical references and index.

ISBN-13: 978-1-58983-121-6 (alk. paper)

ISBN-10: 1-58983-121-7 (alk. paper)

1. Hermogenes, 2nd cent. — Translations into English. 2. Rhetoric—Early works to 1800. I. Kennedy, George Alexander, 1928– II. Rabe, Hugo. III. Title. IV. Series.

PA3998.H8E5 2005b

808–dc22 2005013283

---

05 06 07 08 09 10 11 12 — 5 4 3 2 1

Printed in the United States of America on acid-free, recycled paper conforming to ANSI/NISO Z39.48-1992 (R1997) and ISO 9706:1994 standards for paper permanence.

# Table of Contents

# Index of Short Titles Used in the Notes

| | |
|---|---|
| Felten | Josephus Felten, ed., *Nicolai progymnasmata*. Bibliotheca scriptorum Graecorum et Romanorum Teubneriana. Leipzig: Teubner, 1913. |
| Halm | Karl Halm, ed., *Rhetores Latini Minores*. Leipzig: Teubner, 1863. |
| Heath, "Apsines" | Malcolm Heath, "Apsines and Pseudo-Apsines," *AJP* 119 (1998): 89–111. |
| Heath, *Menander* | Malcolm Heath, *Menander: A Rhetor in Context*. Oxford: Oxford Univ. Press, 2004. |
| Heath, *On Issues* | Malcolm Heath, Hermogenes, *On Issues: Strategies of Argument in Later Greek Rhetoric*. Oxford: Clarendon, 1995. |
| Kayser | Carl Ludwig Kayser, ed., *Flavii Philostrati opera*. 2 vols. Leipzig: Teubner, 1870–71. Repr., Hildesheim: Olms, 1985. |
| Koerte | Alfred Koerte, ed., *Menandri quae supersunt*. 3rd ed. Edited by Andreas Thierfelder. 2 vols. Bibliotheca scriptorum Graecorum et Romanorum Teubneriana. Leipzig: Teubner, 1938. |
| Lausberg | Heinrich Lausberg, *Handbook of Literary Rhetoric: A Foundation for Literary Study*. Edited by David E. Orton and R. Dean Anderson. Leiden: Brill, 1998. |
| Lindberg | Gertrude Lindberg, "Hermogenes of Tarsus," *ANRW* 2.34.3 (1997):1978–2063. |
| Martin | Josef Martin, *Antike Rhetorik: Technik und Methoden*. Handbuch der Altertumswissenschaft 2/3. Munich: Beck, 1974. |
| Nauck[2] | August Nauck, *Tragicorum Graecorum fragmenta*. Edited by Bruno Snell. 2nd ed. Hildesheim: Olms, 1964. |

| | |
|---|---|
| Patillon, *ANRW* | Michel Patillon, "Le *De Inventione* du Pseudo-Hermogène," *ANRW* 2.34.3 (1997): 2064–2171. |
| Patillon, *Apsinès* | Michel Patillon, *Apsinès, Art rhétorique: Problèmes à faux-semblant.* Collection des universités de France, Série grecque 410. Paris: Belles Lettres, 2001. |
| Patillon, *L'Art rhétorique* | Michel Patillon, *Hermogène, L'Art rhétorique: Traduction française intégrale, Introduction et notes.* Collection *Idéa.* Paris: L'Âge d'homme, 1997. |
| Patillon, *Théorie du discours* | Michel Patillon, *Théorie du discours chez Hermogène le rhéteur: Essai sur les structures linguistiques de la rhétorique ancienne.* Collection d'Études Anciennes 117. Paris: Belles Lettres, 1985. |
| Psellos | Jeffrey Walker, "Michael Psellos on Rhetoric: A Translation and Commentary on Psellos' Synopsis of Hermogenes," *Rhetoric Society Quarterly* 31 (2001): 5–38. |
| Rabe | H. Rabe, ed., *Hermogenis opera.* Leipzig: Teubner, 1913; repr., Stuttgart: Teubner, 1969. |
| Rabe, "Rhetoren-Corpora" | Hugo Rabe, "Rhetoren-Corpora." *Rheinisches Museum* 67 (1912): 321–25 |
| Rutherford, Canons | Ian Rutherford, *Canons of Style in the Antonine Age.* Oxford: Clarendon, 1998. |
| Spengel | Leonard Spengel, ed., *Rhetores Graeci.* 3 vols. Bibliotheca scriptorum Graecorum et Romanorum Teubneriana; Leipzig: Teubner, 1853–56; repr., Frankfurt am Main: Minerva, 1966. |
| Spengel-Hammer | Leonard Spengel, ed., *Rhetores Graeci,* vol. 1, part 2. Revised by Caspar Hammer. Leipzig: Teubner, 1894. |
| Syrianus | Syrianus, *In Hermogenem commentaria.* Edited by Hugo Rabe. 2 vols. Bibliotheca scriptorum Graecorum et Romanorum Teubneriana. Leipzig: Teubner, 1892–93. |

| | |
|---|---|
| Usener-Radermacher | Hermann Usener and Ludwig Radermacher, eds., *Dionysii Halicarnasei Opuscula*. 2 vols. in 3. Bibliotheca scriptorum Graecorum et Romanorum Teubneriana. Dionysii Halicarnasei quae exstant 5–6. Leipzig: Teubner, 1899–1929. |
| Walz | Christian Walz, ed., *Rhetores graeci*. 9 vols. in 10. Stuttgart: Cottae, 1832–36. |
| Wooten | Cecil W. Wooten, *Hermogenes' On Types of Style*. Chapel Hill: University of North Carolina Press, 1987. |

# Note on the Greek Text

The Greek text and apparatus as printed here is, with minor changes and adaptation to a different pagination, that of Hugo Rabe in his edition of *Hermogenis opera*, Leipzig: Teubner, 1913. Rabe's page numbers are given in the margins.

Rabe based his text of *On Invention* primarily on five eleventh-century manuscripts, using the following abbreviations in the apparatus at the bottom of each page:

> Pa = Parisinus 1983; Pc = Parisinus 2977; Vc = Vaticanus Urbinas 130; Ac = Ambrosianus 523; and Ba = Basileensis 70. The accord of Pa and Pc is designated by **P**; that of Vc, Ac, and Ba is designated by **V**.

The text of *On Method* is based primarily on Pa, Pc, Vc, Ac, and two additional manuscripts:

> Sf = Scoriacensis (Escorial), of the twelfth century; and Ph = Parisinus 3032 of the tenth century.

In constructing his text of the Hermogenic works Rabe often gave preference to **P** over **V**, but in his edition of Aphthonius in 1926, dependent on the same manuscripts, he revised this view somewhat, stating (pp. vi-vii) his conclusion that corrections in **P** disguise faults in the texts which **V** (esp. Vc) reveals and allows for better emendation.

Rabe frequently cited readings of earlier editors. The most important of these are from the editions by Johannus Sturm (1555), Franciscus Portus (1569), Christianus Walz (1834), and Leonardus Spengel (1854).

For additional information see the *Praefatio* to Rabe's original text.

# On Invention

## INTRODUCTION

*Greco-Roman rhetoric was taught to students as consisting of five parts (also sometimes called "canons" or "functions of the orator") that provide a series of steps in composing a speech. The first of these parts is known in Greek as* heuresis, *or invention (Latin* inventio*), literally "finding," and listed a series of topics, with examples, that could suggest things to be said in the exposition of a subject and in support of an argument. Invention differs somewhat in each part of a speech. This treatise discusses three parts of a typical judicial or deliberative speech:* prooemion *or introduction,* diēgēsis *or narration of the facts, and* kataskeuē *or proof. There is no explicit discussion of epilogues. The fourth book of* On Invention *is largely devoted to matters of style and composition. It is throughout an unusual work, differing considerably from other discussions of its subject both in its teaching and its terminology.*

*The text of* On Invention *has survived as one part of a comprehensive "Art of Rhetoric" consisting of five separate works, probably assembled as a teaching text in the fifth or sixth century of the Christian era by some unknown rhetorician in Greece or Asia Minor. In late antiquity and the Byzantine period four of these works—*On Stases *(or* On Issues*),* On Invention, On Ideas *(or* On Types of Style*), and* On Method of Forcefulness*—were regarded as having been written by Hermogenes of Tarsus, who lived in the second half of the second century* C.E. *They were considered authoritative treatments of their subjects, overshadowing Aristotle's* Rhetoric *and other handbooks, and extensive commentaries were written to explicate them. Modern scholars regard only two of the works,* On Stases *and* On Ideas of Style, *as likely to be the work of Hermogenes of* Tarsus.[1]

[1] Whether Hermogenes, author of works on rhetorical theory, is to be identified with Hermogenes of Tarsus, an adolescent marvel at declamation described by Philostratus (*Lives of the Sophists* 2.7), has been recently called into question by Patillon, *Théorie du discours*, pp. 13–17. That the identification was accepted without question by late Greek, Byzantine, and Renaissance scholars

At the beginning of *On Stases* (perhaps originally called *On Divisions*), Hermogenes notes that the subject "is almost identical with the theory of invention, except that it does not include all the elements of invention" (p. 28 Rabe), and later (p. 53 Rabe) he promises to discuss differences between prooemia and epilogues in a future treatment of invention. Apparently he completed such a work, for in *On Ideas* (p. 378 Rabe), discussing *deinotēs*, he says, "This is a topic that is worthy of special treatment following our discussion of ideas, arranged separately on its own, just as our discussion of ideas followed the one on invention." Syrianus (2:3), writing in the fifth century, cites the first of these passages as evidence for the existence of a work on invention by Hermogenes in terms suggesting that he himself had not seen it. An anonymous treatise *On Figures of Speech* (vol. 3, pp. 110–60 Spengel) is perhaps the earliest extant work (fifth or sixth century C.E.) to draw directly on this treatise, referring to it as by Hermogenes and using some of its unusual terminology.

When the Hermogenic corpus was compiled, the editor may have searched in vain for Hermogenes' work on invention and come upon a treatment of the subject that seemed, at least in part, to fill the need. Alternatively, he may have preferred it to Hermogenes' work for some reason, just as he replaced the short treatise on progymnasmata attributed to Hermogenes by a fuller work by Aphthonius.[2] Perhaps *On Invention* was taken from another comprehensive treatment of rhetoric. Incorporation into the Hermogenic corpus probably involved some changes (omission of a preface to book 1 and of discussion of the epilogue? addition of discussion of figured and comparative problems?). An attraction of the source was perhaps that it bore the title *On Invention*,[3] whereas most other Greek works on the functions of the orator or parts of a political speech were usually entitled *Art of Rhetoric*.[4] The author refers (in 3.4 and 3.6, below) to his earlier work *On the Art of Division*, which could therefore be equated with the treatise by Hermogenes on stases. At the end of 4.6 (p. 194 Rabe) most manuscripts contain a short passage in which the author refers

is part of the evidence, but not quite conclusive.

[2] For English translations and discussion of these works, see George A. Kennedy, *Progymnasmata: Greek Textbooks of Prose Composition and Rhetoric* (SBLWGRW 10; Atlanta: Society of Biblical Literature; Leiden: Brill, 2003).

[3] *Peri heureseōs*.

[4] E.g., the treatises by Cassius Longinus and Apsines and the *Anonymous Seguerianus*.

to On Stases as his own work, but Hugo Rabe deleted this passage as being an interpolation. Arguments against Hermogenes' authorship are that On Invention does not discuss the differences between prooemia and epilogues, as Hermogenes had promised (On Stases, p. 53 Rabe), and differs significantly from Hermogenes' usual style and way of thinking (contrast, e.g., Hermogenes' prefaces with the preface to book 3 in this work). Perhaps conclusive, though not heretofore noticed, is the fact that Hermogenes and the author of On Invention each have a set of themes for declamation that are repeatedly cited, but the two sets do not overlap at all.[5] In addition, although some terms relating to stasis or to ideas of style that are found in the treatises regarded as genuine works by Hermogenes do occur in On Invention, there is no sign here of the unique Hermogenic classifications, and the author uses some Hermogenic terms in different senses from those found in the genuine works. Examples of these different uses include akmē and drimytēs.

On Invention is cited once by Syrianus (2:36) as the work of Apsines of Gadara, a famous rhetorician who taught in Athens in the mid-third century, and once by Lachares (Walz 7:931) as by Apsines (without specifying the Gadarean). Malcolm Heath has recently suggested that the author might indeed be Apsines of Gadara[6] and that the discussion of prokatastasis here is the origin of the much better discussion in the handbook traditionally ascribed to Apsines, a work that Heath thought may have been written by Apsines' student Aspasius, whom he identified with Aspasius of Tyre. Syrianus's citation, however, is from 4.13 (p. 208 Rabe), on figured problems, which was apparently not part of the original work and may indeed be by Apsines.[7] Lachares' citation concerns the difference between commata and cola as described in On Invention 4.4, which, if Apsines' name was not just a guess, might be derived from the same source used by Apsines. The passage does not occur in extant writings of Apsines of Gadara. Rabe had shown (Rabe, "Rhetoren-Corpora," 332) that Syrianus and Lachares probably used the same manuscript of On Invention, and it was his conclusion that reference to Apsines in it was a

[5] There is overlap in illustrations from Homer, Demosthenes, and other classical writers cited by the two authors, but many of these are traditional in rhetorical schools and cited by others.

[6] "Apsines and Pseudo-Apsines," *AJP* 119 (1998): 89–111; see also Heath, *Menander*, 53–60.

[7] Cf. the introductory note to 4.13 below.

*conjecture. Michel Patillon has proposed (*ANRW*, 2079–83) Aspasius of* Ravenna*, another famous rhetorician of the mid-third century, as the likely author. This attribution is dependent on a passage from a declamation cited in 4.14 quoted by an anonymous commentator on Hermogenes (Walz 7:951,24–27) as by Aspasius, but 4.14 is not likely to be a part of the original treatise on invention. It does not seem possible to identify the author of this treatise with any certainty. Heath may be right, however, that the discussion of* prokatastasis *in the rhetorical treatise traditionally attributed to Apsines reveals knowledge of the discussion of* prokatastasis *in* On Invention. *Ian Rutherford has argued that a development of the concept of* akmē *can also be traced from what is found here, where it is analyzed as performance, to its analysis as a textual feature in* On Ideas *1.10, and that Hermogenes was familiar with the discussion of* prokataskeuē *and the sequence of tropes as discussed in* On Invention.[8] *This suggests that* On Invention *might be based to a considerable extent on a work of the mid-second century* C.E.*, though largely written in the third or even fourth century and revised into its present form in the fifth or sixth when it was adapted to fill out the Hermogenic "Art of Rhetoric." A reason for regarding it as an adaptation of an earlier source is that the author does not claim originality for most of his unusual theories and terminology, although he does for a few matters of treatment, and his occasional use of the phrase "what is called" (e.g., in the first sentence of book 1), including its application to some of the unusual terms, suggests that he may be borrowing heavily from an earlier work. Rhetoricians of late antiquity often made extensive use of earlier works with vague words such as "they say" without naming the source. A few of the unusual Greek terms, identified in the notes below, can also be found in the Latin* Ars Rhetorica *by Fortunatianus, probably dating from the fourth or early fifth century* C.E. *They are probably not derived directly from* On Invention*, which like other works of the Hermogenic corpus was little known in the West, but from a common source dating perhaps from the second century.*

On Invention *is clearly intended to provide a system for rather elementary students in a school of rhetoric to learn the techniques of declamation, the practice exercises in public speaking on judicial or deliberative themes that were a major part of secondary education in the Greco-Roman world from at least the late fourth century* B.C.E. *Some*

[8] See Rutherford, *Canons*, 105–13.

*themes of declamation, assigned by teachers and practiced by students, are cited in the course of the work. In theory, declamation was preparation for actual public speaking in the lawcourts and assemblies of civic society, and it certainly contributed to that goal for some students.*[9] *Nevertheless, Greek teachers of rhetoric, known as "sophists" in the imperial period, show rather little interest in public address in contemporary life. They consistently imagine public speaking in the conditions of the Athenian democracy of the fifth and fourth centuries, rather than in the time of the* Roman Empire, *and their citations of actual speeches are almost entirely from works of the Attic orators, especially Demosthenes. Many themes of declamation on ostensibly historical subjects are quite unhistorical, invented as a challenge or for the sake of variety. For many students, practice in declamation probably helped to develop self-assurance, contributed to an ability to reason logically, imparted traditional moral values and familiarity with famous passages from classical oratory, encouraged the search for the right word in speaking and writing, and broadened a student's mind by suggesting there were two sides to most cases. Given a teacher who was not too much of a martinet, declamation could be fun and encouraged students to do their best in competition with others.*

*Although often ineptly written and even obscure,* On Invention *is important as a part of the Hermogenic corpus and thus as a treatment of rhetorical invention studied by many later Greek, Byzantine, and Renaissance students. From studying it, one could, in fact, learn how to construct a declamation on a conventional pattern. It is also of interest in that it differs radically from earlier discussions of its subject, omitting much traditional teaching (such as the functions and virtues of the parts of the oration), creating much new terminology, and giving traditional terms, including* epikheirēma *and* enthymēma, *unusual meanings. The author seems to have had little interest in, or possibly little knowledge of, earlier treatments of invention. Many of the innovations apparently resulted from a perceived need to teach students the composition of declamation at a very elementary, formulaic level.*[10] *Patillon (*ANRW, *pp. 2067, 2084–94, 2110–24) has argued that the author especially focused on extempore declamation, something in which his own candidate for author of the treatise, Aspasius*

9 Heath, *Menander*, 317–31, provides reason to believe that rhetorical training in late antiquity was of greater practical use than has been thought.

10 For a summary of the treatise, see Lindberg, 2057–61.

*of Ravenna, gained a considerable reputation, according to Philostratus (*On the Sophists *2.33), and that the author provides formulas, models, and topics that would be especially useful in extempore declamation on assigned themes.*[11] *School declamation in antiquity did not traditionally take the form of debate by opposing speakers on two sides of an issue, but the frequent references to arguments for or against a person or action in this work suggest that there may have been a rudimentary form of debate in the author's school.*

*The translation of* On Invention *offered here is based on the text in Hugo Rabe's edition of the Hermogenic corpus. I have also consulted Michel Patillon's* L'Art rhétorique, *which contains a French translation of the full Hermogenic corpus. There are commentaries on the treatise written in late antiquity and the Byzantine period, of which some were printed by Christian Walz in* Rhetores Graeci *5:363–436; 6:505–43; and 7:52–76 and 697–860. Between 1060 and 1067 the Byzantine scholar-statesman Michael Psellos made a 545-line versified synopsis of the four main Hermogenic works, dedicated to a student who later became the emperor Michael VII Doukas. Psellos's synopsis gives greater attention to* On Invention *than to other works in the collection, though at times (e.g., on hypolepsis in 1.1) Psellos misunderstands the meaning. His summary is principally of interest in showing how* On Invention *was understood in the Middle Byzantine period.*[12]

*Departing from the practice of Malcolm Heath in his translation of* On Issues *and that of Cecil W. Wooten in his translation of* On Types of Style, *the two major works in the Hermogenic corpus, and also from the practice of Michel Patillon in his French translations, I have transliterated unusual technical terms rather than tried to provide English equivalents. Few exact equivalents exist, and the interest of* On Invention *is to a considerable degree its strange terminology. Footnotes and a glossary at the end will provide explanations of the meanings of the terms. Some, but not all, can also be found in the English edition of Heinrich Lausberg's* Handbook of Literary Rhetoric.

[11] Cf., e.g., the reference to extemporaneity in 4.3 (p. 149). Extempore declamation is criticized in the treatise *On the Education of Children* found in Plutarch's *Moralia* (6F), especially on the part of young students, but the criticism implies that it was not unusual.

[12] English translation by Walker, "Psellos."

*In revising this work for publication within the Writings from the Greco-Roman World series, I am greatly indebted to John T. Fitzgerald, the General Editor, whose continued interest in the project I have much appreciated. He has encouraged me throughout and has facilitated many of the steps that have led to publication. Professor Cecil W. Wooten, the volume editor for the Society of Biblical Literature, has read the manuscript with patient care, contributed insights from his own extended study of Greek rhetoric and oratory, and saved me from errors and infelicities. Finally, I wish to thank Yannis Haralambous for his patient work in transcribing Rabe's Greek text and apparatus into the form used in this book.*

Fort Collins, Colorado
May 2005

# From the Corpus of Hermogenes:

# *On Invention*
## and
# *On Method of Forceful Speaking*

## Text and Translation

# ON INVENTION



## BOOK 1

*The treatise begins abruptly without preface, definition, or division of the subject, such as is usually found in rhetorical treatises on invention. The editor who added* On Invention *to* On Stases *and* On Ideas *may have dropped the beginning of his source as somehow unsuitable in terms of his objective to create a general art of rhetoric. The cumbersome first sentence of the treatise may be his inept way of providing a new beginning.*

*There are numerous other treatments of rhetorical invention that discuss the composition of the parts of a speech, beginning with the prooemion. Aristotle discusses the* proemion *in* Rhetoric *3.14. Latin discussions from the first century* B.C.E. *and first century* C.E. *include Cicero's early handbook,* On Invention *(1.20–26),* Rhetoric for Herennius *(1.5–11), Cicero's* On the Orator *(2.315–325), and book 4, chapter 1, of Quintilian's* Education of the Orator. *Greek examples, closer in time to this treatise, include the work known as* Anonymous Seguerianus *(§§1–39) and Apsines'* Art of Rhetoric, *chapter 1. [For text and translations of these works, see Mervin R. Dilts and George A. Kennedy,* Two Greek Rhetorical Treatises from the Roman Empire *(Leiden: Brill, 1997).] Characteristic of the treatment of the* prooemion *in all these works is the identification of its function as to create attention, receptivity, and goodwill on the part of an audience, with examples of how this can be done. [Cf. Anonymous Seguerianus §§1–39; Apsines, ch. 1.] The omission of any mention of this here is surprising and perhaps another indication that something has been dropped by the editor. An anonymous commentator, writing in the Byzantine period, summarizes the traditional definition and function of* prooemia *and says that "enough has been said about all these things by Hermogenes and Porphyry" (Walz 7.1:63).*

[93] # ΠΕΡΙ ΕΥΡΕΣΕΩΣ

## Α

## *Περὶ τῶν ἐξ ὑπολήψεως προοιμίων.*

*Ἡ πρώτη καὶ καλλίστη τῶν προοιμίων εὕρεσις καλλίστης καὶ πραγματικωτάτης εὑρέσεως τετύχηκε τῆς ἐκ τῶν ὑπολήψεων καλουμένης τῶν τε προσώπων καὶ τῶν πραγμάτων· ὅπως δὲ ταῦτα ἔχει, διελὼν ἐκθήσομαι καθ᾽ ἕκαστον ἐν μέρει. τεθείσης γάρτοι πάσης ὑποθέσεως ἀνασκοπεῖν ἄξιον πρῶτον τὸ πρᾶγμα τὸ γεγενημένον ὁποῖόν ἐστι, καὶ περὶ οὗ ἡ κρίσις ἢ τὸ βουλευτήριον συνέστηκεν· ἐν προβλήμασι γὰρ ἢ κρίνομεν ἢ βουλευόμεθα. δεῖ τοίνυν σκοπεῖν τὸ πρᾶγμα εἴτε καλόν ἐστιν εἴτε φαῦλον, εἶτα ἑξῆς τὰς περὶ τὸ πρόσωπον ὑπολήψεις ἑκάστου,*
[94] *τῶν δικαζόντων, τῶν κατηγο|ρούντων, τῶν ἀπολογουμένων, τῶν ἐχόντων αὐτὰ τὰ πράγματα καὶ τὰ ἐγκλήματα, τῶν ἔξωθεν ἐμφαινομένων· ἐμφαίνεται δὲ πολλάκις μὲν ἕν, πολλάκις δὲ πλείονα. τούτων ἕκαστον*

1 de titulo cf. Praef. || 2 περὶ προοιμίων· τόμος α′ **P**, (om. τόμος α′) Ac; om. (προοιμίων titulo l. 2 add.) Vc Ba || 3 προοιμίων om. **V** || 4 εὕρεσις vix san.; Dox.: τινὲς ... «ἡ ... προοιμίων ὑπὸ (ὑπόθεσις?) καλλίστης καὶ πραγματικωτάτης εὑρέσεως (μεθόδου supr. Vδ) τετύχηκεν» ... ἕτεροι δὲ ... «ἡ ... προοιμίων μέθοδος καλλίστης ὑποθέσεως τετύχηκεν» κτλ. || 5 πραγματικωτ[άτης m.po.] τετύχηκεν εὑρέσεως Pc || 6 ἔχ[ει m. 2] Vc || 8 [τὸ γεγενημένον] Spengel; cf. 6, 18 | καὶ om. Vl || 9 [ἢ] Vc; καὶ Vg || 14 δὲ καὶ πλείονα Ac | τούτων δὲ Le Md Oh Vx | ἕκαστ[ον] Ba

## CHAPTER I: ON PROOEMIA FROM HYPOLEPSIS (SUPPOSITIONS)[1]

The first and finest invention (*heuresis*)[2] of prooemia is that which has succeeded in finding the finest and most productive method of invention, which is called "from *hypolēpseis*[3] about the persons and actions." I shall explain what these are like by describing each variation separately.

Now when any hypothesis[4] has been proposed, it is right first to consider what sort of action has taken place and what the court or council has been convened to decide, for in problems[5] we are either making a legal judgment or advising a council. There is need, then, to consider whether the action in question is good or bad; then, in turn, hypolepses about the person of each of the following: the judges,[6] the prosecutors, | the defendants, those in- [94]
volved in the actions and indictments, those revealed from outside the case;[7] sometimes one is revealed, sometimes more than one. Each of the persons named is the object of hypolepses of some sort,

[1] The chapter headings are probably additions by a medieval scribe, not the work of the author.

[2] Here and elsewhere the author uses *heuresis* in the sense of the sources, topics, or techniques of finding what to say. The word *topos*, which might be expected, does not occur in books 1 or 2.

[3] "Called" seems to refer to some earlier treatise on which the author of the immediate source of *On Invention* will repeatedly draw. *Hypolēpsis*, although used to mean an assumption by Greek philosophers, is not a technical rhetorical term in any extant earlier text. Similar to what is called *doxa*, "opinion," as described by the author of Pseudo-Dionysius, *Art of Rhetoric* 2.13, it refers to previous beliefs or biases about persons or actions and might be roughly translated "suppositions" or "prejudices." Psellos (p. 21) seems to have misunderstood *hypolēpsis* to mean "a resumption of matters previously discussed" (Walker's n. 12).

[4] Here meaning a theme for declamation.

[5] I.e., themes for declamation.

[6] *Dikastai*, both judges and members of the jury. Declamation in the time of the Roman Empire usually assumed the conditions of the democratic courts and councils of Athens in the fourth century B.C.E.

[7] For example, enemies; see the end of this chapter and the anonymous commentator in Walz 7.1:701. In 4.1.6 Quintilian says that most writers on rhetoric consider only plaintiff, defendant, and judge; in 4.1.30 he suggests considering some persons not directly involved in the case; cf. Hermogenes, *On Stases* 46.24–47.7.

*ὁποίας ὑπολήψεις ἔχει καὶ ὅπως εἰς τὰ προοίμια παραληφθήσεται, τρανῶς διηγήσομαι.*

*Πρῶτον μὲν οὖν σκοπητέον τὸ πρᾶγμα ποταπόν ἐστι καὶ ποταπὸν ὑπείληπται, χρηστὸν ἢ φαῦλον, καὶ τίνα γνώμην ἔχουσιν οἱ δικασταὶ περὶ αὐτοῦ, καὶ ὅπως διετέθησαν ἐπὶ τῷ πεπραγμένῳ. εἰ μὲν οὖν χρηστὸν εἴη, χαίρειν αὐτοὺς εἰκὸς καὶ γεγηθέναι· καὶ τὸ προοίμιον οὖν ἔσται τὸν τρόπον τοῦτον «ὁρῶ μὲν ὑμᾶς, ὦ ἄνδρες δικασταί, χαίροντας ἐπὶ τοῖς πεπραγμένοις καὶ χάριν γινώσκοντας τῷ θεῷ», ὡς ἐπ' ἐκείνου τοῦ προβλήματος· ἐβοήθησάν ποτε φυγάδες πολεμουμένῃ τῇ πατρίδι καὶ νίκην εἰργάσαντο, καὶ γράφει τις αὐτοὺς κατάγειν· «τῷ μὲν θεῷ, ὦ ἄνδρες πολῖται, χάρις πολλὴ τῷ τὴν νίκην ἡμῖν κατὰ τῶν πολεμίων παρεσκευακότι καὶ τῆς παρούσης ἡδονῆς τὰς ἀφορμὰς ἐνδόντι· ἐπεὶ δὲ καὶ οἱ πολῖται μετά γε θεῶν γεγόνασιν ἡμῖν τῆς παρούσης θυμηδίας αἴτιοι, συμβουλεύσων παρελήλυθα κατάγειν αὐτοὺς καὶ ἀποδιδόναι τῇ πόλει, ἣν ἔσωσαν αὐτοί». τῆς δὲ κατὰ τὴν ἑρμηνείαν ἁπλότητος μὴ φροντίσῃς· διδασκαλικώτερον γὰρ ἐσπούδασα τὰς τέχνας ἀφηγήσασθαι, περιελὼν τὴν ἰσχὺν τοῦ λόγου καὶ γυμνὰ τιθεὶς* | [95] *τὰ νοήματα, ὡς εἶναι κατάδηλα μᾶλλον. Εἰ δὲ φαῦλον εἴη τὸ πρᾶγμα τὸ γεγενημένον, ἀνάγκη τοὺς δικάζοντας ἢ χαλεπαίνειν ἢ οἰκτείρειν ἢ ἑκάτερα πάσχειν ἐπὶ τοῖς αὐτοῖς, καὶ ὀργὴν καὶ λύπην· λέξομεν οὖν τὸ προοίμιον οὕτω λαμβάνοντες «ἐπειδὴ καὶ ὑμᾶς, ὦ ἄνδρες δικασταί, τῶν τετολμημένων ἕνεκεν ὁρῶ καὶ ἀχθομένους καὶ λελυπημένους, διὰ τοῦτο τὴν γραφὴν ἐνεστησάμην»· οἷον ἐνώπιόν τις τῆς μητρὸς ἀπέκτεινε τὸν υἱὸν κατὰ τὸν τῶν ἀκρίτων νόμον, ἐξέθανεν ἡ μήτηρ, καὶ κρίνεται αἰτίας θανάτου· «ἄχθεσθαι μὲν ὑμᾶς, ὦ ἄνδρες δικασταί, καὶ δυσχεραίνειν ἐπὶ τοῖς γεγενημένοις οὐδὲν ἀπεικός ἐστι, καὶ τούτῳ χαλεπαίνοντας ὑπὲρ ὧν ἐτόλμησε, καὶ ἐκείνους οἰκτείροντας ὑπὲρ ὧν ἔπαθον».*

3 cf. p. 4, 8 | πρᾶγμα ⌊I-II⌉ Vc || **5** αὐτοῦ ⌊VI-VII⌉ Pa | περὶ τῶι πεπραγμένὼ (= τὸ πεπραγμένον ?) Ac || **6** εἰκὸς αὐτούς Vc Ba | οὖν om. Ba || **7** τοῦτον τὸν τρόπον **V**; τοιουτότροπον Le | ὁρῶμεν **P** Vc Ba | ὑμᾶς post δικασταί Ba || **9** cf. 16, 1. 22, 26 sq. || **10** αὐτ⌊οὺ ex ὸ⌉ς Pc || **11** ⌊ὑ ex ἡ⌉μῖν Pa | ἐναντίων Pa || **13** γε om. Vc Ba | θεῶν Md Vb; θεὸν Pa Ac Ba; ⌊θεὸν⌉ Pc; τῶν θεῶν m. 1 Vc || **15** τῇ πόλει Ac; τὴν πόλιν Vc Ba, (ῆ et ει supr.) **P** | ἐσώσαντο αὐτοί Vc Ac || **20** ἐπὶ τούτοις αὐτοῖς Ba | λέξωμεν Ac || **22** λυπουμένους **V** || **24** κατὰ — νόμον Ba, m. 2 **P**, cf. 58, 17; om. Vc Ac, m. 1 **P**; γρ ἀπέκτεινε τὸν ἑαυτοῦ (ἑαυτῆς Pc) υἱὸν κατὰ τὸν τῶν ἀκρίτων νόμον καὶ κρίνεται **P** | ὁ πατὴρ post κρίνεται add. Vw, m. po. Pa || **25** ἄνδρες om. Pc

and I shall give a clear account of how these will be made to contribute to the prooemia.

First, then, one must look at what sort of thing the action is and what sort of thing it is supposed to be, good or bad, and what attitude the judges have about it and how they are disposed toward what has been done. Now if the action is good, it is likely that they are glad and rejoice, and thus the prooemion will be as follows: "I see that you are glad, men of the jury, at what has been done and are giving thanks to god," as in the following problem: Once some exiles came to the aid of their country in time of war and brought about a victory, and someone introduces a motion to restore them from exile, *(saying, "We owe)* much thanks, fellow citizens, to the god, who has supplied us with victory over our enemies and given us the source of our present happiness, but since these citizens have also been, with the help of the gods, the causes of our present rejoicing, I have come forward to advise you to bring them back from exile and restore them to the city that they themselves have saved." Don't worry about the simplicity of the style, for as a teacher does I have tried to bring out the technique, dispensing with the force of language and putting the bare thoughts | so they will be clearer. [95]

But if the action that has transpired is a bad thing, the judges necessarily either are annoyed or in grief or feel both at the same time, both anger and grief. We shall, therefore, start by speaking the prooemion thus: "Since I see that you are distressed and in grief, men of the jury, because of the awful things that have been done, for this reason I have introduced this action." For example, a man killed his son in the mother's presence in accordance with the law about the untried;[8] the mother died of shock, and he is brought to trial as responsible for her death: "That you are distressed and troubled at the things that have happened, men of the jury, is not surprising, and that you are angry at this man for what he dared to do and pity those in grief for what they suffered."

[8] In schools of declamation it was often assumed that fathers had a right to kill sons under certain conditions; here probably the son is suspected of incest; cf. 2.7 below, p. 59; Sopatros, *Dialexeis* 9 (Walz 8:313–15).

*αἱ δὲ ἀποδόσεις παντὸς προοιμίου αἱ ἀξιώσεις εἰσίν. ἀπὸ δὲ τῶν εὑρέσεων αἱ προτάσεις γίνονται, καὶ προοιμίου δριμύτης πρότασις.*

*Ἑξῆς τρεπτέον ἐπὶ τοὺς κατηγόρους καὶ τίνα τρόπον ἀπὸ τούτων εὑρίσκεται τὰ προοίμια· οἱ γὰρ κατηγοροῦντές τινος ὑπολήψεις ἔχουσι πολλάκις ἢ ἔχθρας ἢ φθόνου. τὸν μὲν οὖν φθόνον, εἴ τις ἐμφαίνοιτο τῷ προβλήματι, διακρουσόμεθα· δεινὸν γὰρ βασκανίαν ὁμολογεῖν καὶ ἐπίφθονον ἀεί. ἐμφαίνεται δὲ πολλάκις, ὅταν ἢ δόξῃ βασκαίνωμεν ἢ πλούτῳ, οἷον πρεσβεύων Αἰσχίνης παρὰ τὸν Φίλιππον ἐτραγῴδησε, νε-* [96] *νίκηκεν, ἐστεφάνωται, καὶ κρίνεται παραπρεσβείας ὑπὸ Δημο|σθένους· ὀρθῶς ἐρεῖ τὸ προοίμιον «μηδεὶς ὑμῶν, ὦ ἄνδρες Ἀθηναῖοι, νομίσῃ βασκαίνοντά με τοῦ στεφάνου καὶ τῆς νίκης Αἰσχίνῃ τὴν κατηγορίαν ἐνστήσασθαι κατ᾽ αὐτοῦ». ἢ πλούτῳ, οἷον ἀποκήρυκτος ᾔτησε τὸν πατέρα τροφάς, ὁ δὲ αὐτῷ ξίφος ἔδωκεν, ἐμισθοφόρησεν, ἐπανῆκε πλούσιος, ὁ πατὴρ δεόμενος τροφῶν προσῆλθε τῷ παιδί, ὁ δὲ αὐτῷ τὸ αὐτὸ ξίφος ἔδωκεν, ἀπέκτεινεν ἑαυτὸν ὁ πατήρ, καὶ κρίνεται ὁ παῖς αἰτίας θανάτου· ὕπεστι πλούτου τις πρόφασις, καλὸν οὖν διακρούσασθαι καὶ λέγειν ὅτι «οὐ τῆς περιουσίας αὐτῷ βασκαίνων τὸν ἀγῶνα ἐνεστησάμην».*

1 εἰσὶν suppl. m.2 Vc || 4 εὑρίσκονται Ac | γὰρ om. Vc Ba || 6 διακρουσώμεθα Vc Ac || 7-8 ἢ πλούτῳ om. Vn || 8 δόξῃ ante οἷον supr. Vg || 11 τὴν om. Vc || 12 πλούτου **V** (ω m. po. Ba) || 13 ἐπέδωκεν Ac || 14 ὁ δὲ πατηρ Ac | αὐτὸ om. Vc Ac || 15 ἐπέδωκεν Ac || 16 καὶ om. **P**

The apodoses of every prooemion are the speaker's *axiōseis* of the case.[9] The protases derive from inventions, and the protasis of a prooemion should be striking.[10]

Next, one should turn to the prosecutors and consider how prooemia are invented from them, for those prosecuting someone are often suspected of personal hatred or envy. Now we shall reject envy, if any is implied in the statement of the theme, for it is always a bad thing to admit to jealousy[11] and envy. It is, however, often implied whenever we are begrudging fame or wealth; for example, when on an embassy Aeschines acted in a tragedy at Philip's court, won the contest, was crowned, and is indicted for false embassy by Demosthenes.[12] | In the prooemion he[13] will rightly say, [96]
"Let none of you, men of Athens, think I instigated this accusation of Aeschines out of jealousy at his crown and victory." Or in the case of wealth; for example, a son who has been disowned sought to be supported by his father; the father gave him a sword; the son hired out as a mercenary; he returned rich; the father, falling into want, appealed to the son, who gave him the same sword; the father killed himself, and the son is brought to trial as responsible for his death. There is here an implication that the suit is brought because of the son's wealth; thus it is good to reject that and to say, "I did not initiate this contest out of jealousy of his wealth."[14]

[9] The protases are the circumstances of the case as the speaker has stated them, the apodosis the resulting conclusion. *Axiōsis* means something like "evaluation," the decision the speaker has made as a result of the facts he recounts. The term is not used in this sense in any earlier extant rhetorical treatise. In the first example quoted in the previous paragraph, "I have introduced this action" is the apodosis and is an *axiōsis*; in the second quotation the apodosis is left unexpressed.

[10] *Drimytēs*, or a striking turn of style, is frequently mentioned by the author; the term is discussed in Hermogenes, *On Ideas* 2.5, where Wooten (81–84) translates it as "subtlety." The word can also mean keenness or bitterness, which seems closer to the meaning here.

[11] *Baskania*, which may imply the "evil eye."

[12] Demosthenes' speech *On the False Embassy* is directed against Aeschines but says nothing about his acting in a tragedy at Philip's court. In *On the Crown* Demosthenes refers sarcastically several times to Aeschines as having been a third-rate actor on the Athenian stage.

[13] I.e., the declaimer taking the role of Demosthenes in this imaginary hypothesis.

[14] The speaker is either a member of the family, who might inherit the wealth, or a nonrelative who might receive a portion of the money, confiscated

*Τὰς δὲ ἔχθρας ποτὲ μὲν ὁμολογήσομεν, ποτὲ δὲ ἀρνησόμεθα, τοῦτο ποιοῦντες οὐχ ὅταν βουλώμεθα, ἀλλ᾽ ὅτε δεῖ ὁμόσε χωρεῖν ταῖς ἀρνήσεσι καὶ ταῖς ὁμολογίαις. ἔσται δὲ οὕτως· ἂν ἔχωμεν πρὸς ἔνδοξον πρόσωπον καὶ ὑπερέχον καὶ ἐπαινούμενον οἷον στρατηγὸν ἢ Περικλέα ἢ νομοθέτην, τότε ἀρνησόμεθα, ἢ πρὸς κοινὸν εὐεργέτην ἢ πρός τινα δι᾽ ἐξουσίαν ὠμὸν καὶ ἀπάνθρωπον. πρὸς νομοθέτην μὲν λέξομεν, ὅτι αἰσχρὸν ἀπεχθάνεσθαι κοινῷ εὐεργέτῃ, ὡς ὁ Δημοσθένης «μηδεὶς ὑμῶν, ὦ ἄνδρες Ἀθηναῖοι, νομίσῃ μήτε ἰδίας ἔχθρας ἐμὲ μηδεμιᾶς ἕνεκα ἄλλης ἥκειν Ἀριστοκράτους κατηγορήσοντα τουτουί». πρὸς δὲ ὑπερέχον πρόσωπον, ὅτι δέος τοῖς εὐδοκιμοῦσι προσκρούειν, οἷον ἠνέχθη σκη-*
[97] *πτὸς ἐπὶ τὴν | Περικλέους εἰκόνα, καὶ συμβουλεύει τις μηκέτι αὐτὸν Ὀλύμπιον καλεῖν, οἷον «οὐκ ἔχθρας ἕνεκεν, ὦ ἄνδρες Ἀθηναῖοι, τῆς πρὸς Περικλέα τὴν συμβουλὴν ταύτην ἐνεστησάμην, ἀλλ᾽ εὐνοίας πλέον, δεδοικώς, μή τι παρὰ τῶν θεῶν ἄνθρωπος ὢν πάθῃ». ἐξ ἀπονοίας δὲ ὠμὸν δι᾽ ἐξουσίαν, οἷον πένης καὶ πλούσιος ἐχθροί, ὑπέσχετο ὁ πλούσιος θρέψειν τοὺς πολίτας, εἰ λάβοι τὸν πένητα πρὸς ἀναίρεσιν, ἔδωκεν ὁ δῆμος, οὐκ ἔθρεψεν ὁ πλούσιος τοὺς τοῦ πένητος υἱεῖς, ἀπέθανον λιμῷ, καὶ κρίνεται φόνου· «οὐκ ἀπεχθανόμενος ἰδίᾳ τῷ πλουσίῳ τὴν ὑπὲρ τῶν πολιτῶν ἐνεστησάμην γραφήν, ἀλλ᾽ ἀγανακτῶν ἐπὶ τοῖς νόμοις καὶ τῇ πόλει». καὶ μυρίους τις ἂν εὕροι ἀριστεῖς ἢ πλουσίους ἢ στρατηγοὺς ἢ δημαγωγούς, οἷς ἀντιλέγοντας ἢ κατηγοροῦντας ἀναγκαῖόν ἐστι τὰς ἔχθρας τὰς ἰδίας παραιτεῖσθαι, καταφεύγειν δὲ ἐπὶ τὴν πόλιν καὶ τοὺς νόμους καὶ τοῦ κοινῇ τῇ πόλει συμφέροντος ἕνεκεν λέγειν ἐνίστασθαι τὸν ἀγῶνα. Ὁμολογεῖν δὲ δεῖ τὰς ἔχθρας, ἐὰν προαδικηθέντες ἀμυνώμεθα· ἀνεπίφθονον γὰρ τιμωρίαν κατὰ τῶν ἠδικηκότων λαμβάνειν, ὡς*

1 ὁμολογήσωμεν Vc | ἀρνησώμεθα Vc, (in ras.) Pa || **2** ὅτε βουλόμεθα **V** | ὅτ᾽ ἂν δεῖ **V** || **3** ἂν ἔχωμεν, sc. ἔχθρας; altera pars: p. 10, 24 sq. || **4** ἢ Περικλέα om. Vs; haec et **5** ἢ πρὸς κοινὸν εὐεργέτην del. Brinkmann || **5** πρὸς m. 2, ὡς m. 1 Vc || **7** Dem. 23, 1 || **8** μήτε μιᾶς **PV** || **8-9** ἄλλης ἕνεκα **V** || **9** κατηγορήσαντα Vc | τοῦ[τουί m. po.] Pa | τὸ ὑπερέχον Pc || **10** cf. Π. στ. 51, 8 || **11** εἰκόνα **PV**; οἰκίαν Vg, m. 1 Vl n | αὐτὸν μηκέτι **V** || **12** ὀλύμπιον καλεῖν, β et α supr. (m. 1 ?) Vc; καλεῖν ὀλύμπιον Ba || **16** ἐν λιμῷ θρέψειν Md Oh | cf. 259, 5 Sp. || **18** νὴ δία m. po. Ba || **19-20** ἐπὶ τῇ πόλει καὶ τοῖς νόμοις Vδ, cf. l. 22 || **23** κοινοῦ **V** | εἵνεκεν Ac | ἐνστήσασθαι Vδ, (γρ᾽ ἐνίστασθαι) Vk; haec v.l. in textum **P** irrepsit p. 12, 8 || **25** κατὰ om. v.l. Dox; παρὰ Og, m. po. Pa

As for feelings of hostility, sometimes we shall admit and sometimes deny them, not doing this whenever we want but when it is necessary to confront the denials and admissions head on. This will be as follows: if our hostilities are directed at a person who is well-regarded and distinguished and admired, such as a general or Pericles or a lawgiver, then we shall deny the feelings; also in regard to a common benefactor or someone cruel and inhumane in use of power. In regard to a lawgiver we shall say that it is shameful to be hostile to a common benefactor, as Demosthenes says (23.1), "Let none of you, men of Athens, think that I have come to accuse this man, Aristocrates, out of any private hatred."[15] In regard to a distinguished person, (*we shall say*) that we fear giving offense to people who are well-thought-of; for example, a thunderbolt struck | the statue of Pericles and someone advises [97] to cease calling him "Olympian," saying something like, "Not out of any hatred of Pericles, men of Athens, have I introduced this proposal, but rather out of goodwill, fearing lest he suffer something from the gods since he is but a man." Against a man cruel in use of power one speaks out of desperation; for example, a poor man and a rich man are enemies; the rich man promised to pay for the support of the citizens if he can take the poor man and get rid of him. The people granted this. The rich man did not support the poor man's sons; they died of starvation, and the rich man is accused of murder. "Not out of private hatred for this rich man did I introduce this suit on behalf of the citizens but because I am distressed for the laws and the city." In replying to or prosecuting military heroes or rich men or generals or demagogues one can find many cases in which it is necessary to deny any hatred of a private sort and to take refuge in the claim of having instigated the trial in the interest of the city and the laws and for the sake of what will benefit the city in general.

On the other hand, it is necessary to acknowledge hatreds if we are defending ourselves when we have previously been done an injustice, for there is no reproach against taking vengeance from those who have wronged us, as Demosthenes did in the speech *Against Androtion* (22.1): "I shall try to do, if I can, what Eucte-

by the state, for bringing the prosecution.

[15] Nothing is known about Aristocrates except for what little Demosthenes says in the speech, and there is no reason to think he was regarded as a "common benefactor" by the Athenians.

*καὶ ὁ Δημοσθένης ἐν τῷ Κατ' Ἀνδροτίωνος ἐποίησε λόγῳ «ὅπερ Εὐκτήμων, ὦ ἄνδρες δικασταί, παθὼν ὑπ' Ἀνδροτίωνος κακῶς ἅμα τῇ τε πόλει βοηθεῖν ᾤετο δεῖν καὶ δίκην ὑπὲρ αὑτοῦ λαβεῖν, τοῦτο κἀγὼ πειράσομαι ποιεῖν, ἐὰν ἄρα οἷός τε ὦ»· καὶ ἐν τῷ Κατὰ Νεαίρας πάλιν ὁμοίως.*

[98] | *Καὶ περὶ τοὺς ἀπολογουμένους ὑπέρ τινος ὑπόληψις εὑρίσκεται πολλάκις εὐνοίας ἢ κέρδους. τὸ μὲν οὖν κέρδος ἀεὶ παραιτητέον καὶ τὸν μισθόν, πλὴν εἰ μὴ πιθανῶς λέγοιμεν μισθὸν ἔχειν [παρὰ] τῶν βοηθουμένων τὴν σωτηρίαν, οἷον ἐὰν ὑπὲρ ἀριστέων λέγωμεν ἢ ὑπὲρ τυραννοκτόνων ἢ καθάπαξ δημοσίᾳ τὴν πόλιν εὖ ποιησάντων· οἷον ἐπὶ τῶν τριάκοντα τυράννων ἐξετίθεσαν Ἀθηναῖοι τὰ γένη, Μεγαρεῖς ἀναιρούμενοι ἔτρεφον, παυσαμένης τῆς τυραννίδος ἥκουσιν ἀποδιδόντες τὰ γένη, καὶ γράφει τις τὸ κατὰ Μεγαρέων ἀνῃρῆσθαι πινάκιον· ἄριστον γὰρ ἐνταῦθα διομολογήσασθαι μισθὸν ἔχειν τὴν τῶν φιλτάτων σωτηρίαν λέγοντα οὕτως «μισθὸν μὲν οὖν, ὦ ἄνδρες Ἀθηναῖοι, παρὰ Μεγαρέων αὐτός τε ὁμολογῶ μέγιστον εἰληφέναι τῶν παρόντων λόγων καὶ ὑμεῖς δ' ἂν ὁμολογήσαιτε, τὴν σωτηρίαν τῶν φιλτάτων». Τὴν δὲ εὔνοιαν φανερῶς ἔστιν ὁμολογεῖν ἄνευ κέρδους, ὅταν ὑπὲρ τῶν δημοσίᾳ τὴν πόλιν εὐεργετησάντων λέγωμεν, οἷον μελλόντων μονομαχεῖν ἀδελφῶν δύο κατὰ τὸν νόμον τὸν περὶ τῶν ἀριστέων περὶ τοῦ γέρως ἐξέλιπεν ὁ ἥλιος, καὶ γράφει τις λελύσθαι τὸν νόμον· οἷον «φιλεῖν μὲν*
[99] *τοὺς ἀδελφοὺς οὐκ ἂν ἀρνηθείην ἔγωγε κοινοὺς σω|τῆρας τῆς πόλεως γεγενημένους». ἢ ἂν ὑπὲρ συγγενῶν ποιώμεθα τοὺς λόγους· ἀνεπίφθονος γὰρ ὁ ὑπὲρ τῶν προσηκόντων λόγος· ὡς καὶ ὁ Δημοσθένης ἐν τῷ*

1 ὁ om. Ac Ba | πεποίηκε Ba || **2-3** τε τῆι Ac || **3** οἴεται **V** Dem. 22, 1 || **4-5** Dem. 59, 1 || **6** καὶ suspect. | πρὸς (pro περὶ) Ac || **7** τὸ . . . κέρδος Vc, v.l. **P**; τοῦ . . . κέρδους **P** Ac, m. 1 Ba || **8** καὶ Vc, v.l. **P**; ἐνστήσασθαι **P**, (κυρῶσαι καὶ m. po. supr.) Ba; om. Ac | μισθὸν, m. 2 ἀγῶνα supr., Pb | παρὰ om. Om || **9** γρ τὴν τῶν φιλτάτων σωτηρίαν **P** || **10** (δημοσίᾳ om.) τῆι πόλει, m. 2 δημοσία τὴν πόλιν, Vc | εὐεργετησάντων Vt || **13** cf. Thuc. 1, 139; Plut. Pericl. 30; cf. p. 24, 9 (ubi καθαιρεῖν; at ἀναιρεῖν etiam Diod. XII 39, 4) || **15** οὖν om. Pc || **17** ὁμολογήσητε Vc Ba, (αι with η supr.) **P**; ὁμολογήσετε Ac | πάντες ante τὴν add. Ac, πάντως Vc Ba, εἰκότως Od || **18** ἄνευ κέρδους suspecta || **19-20** cf. Aps. I 2 p. 234, 15 Sp.-H. || **20** τῶν om. Pc || **20-21** cf. 44, 19 || **22** κοιν⌊οὺ ex ὀ⌉ς σωτηρ⌊Ι⌉ας Pa || **23-24** ἀνεπίφθονος (ν supr.) Pa

mon did, men of the jury, when after suffering at the hands of Androtion he thought it right at one and the same time to go to the aid of the city and to get justice for himself." And similarly again in *Against Neaera* (59.1).[16]

| A hypolepsis of acting out of favoritism or for profit is often [98] invented against those speaking in someone's defense. Now one should always reject motivation of profit or pay (*misthos*), unless we can persuasively claim that the safety of those who are being aided constitutes pay; for example, if we are speaking on behalf of military heroes or tyrannicides or those who once benefited the city entirely in a public way; for example, under the Thirty Tyrants Athenians sent their families into exile; the Megarians received and cared for them; when the tyranny was over, they came to restore the families, and someone introduces a motion to rescind the decree against the Megarians.[17] Here it is best for the speaker to acknowledge that there was "pay" in the form of the safety of their dear ones, saying, "I myself, men of Athens, acknowledge that I have received the greatest pay from the Megareans, the safety of our loved ones, in return for the present speech, and you would acknowledge it as well." It is possible openly to acknowledge favoritism without profit whenever we are speaking about those who have benefited the city publicly; for example, when two brothers were about to engage in single combat for a prize in accordance with the law about military heroes,[18] there was an eclipse of the sun, and someone introduces a motion to rescind the law. Thus, "For my part, I would not deny loving these brothers who have both | been saviors of the city." Or if we are giving a speech [99] for family members, for a speech on behalf of relatives is not open to reproach. Thus Demosthenes in *Against Leptines* said (20.1), "Men of the jury, I agreed to speak with others in this case, to

[16] Not a genuine work by Demosthenes. The speaker begins by revealing his hostility to Neaira's lover, Stephanus.

[17] The Megarean Decree of 432, prohibiting trade by Megara in Aegean and Black Sea ports; cf. Thucydides 1.139; Plutarch, *Pericles* 30; Diodorus 12.39.4.

[18] The law is imagined to provide that the greatest hero in a battle is entitled to whatever prize he demands. Here two brothers contend for the prize. Cf. Pseudo-Quintilian, *Minor Declamations* 258; S. F. Bonner, *Roman Declamation in the Late Republic and Early Empire* (Berkeley and Los Angeles: University of California Press, 1949), 88–89.

*Πρὸς Λεπτίνην εἶπεν «ἄνδρες δικασταί, μάλιστα μὲν εἵνεκα τοῦ νομίζειν συμφέρειν λελύσθαι τὸν νόμον, εἶτα καὶ τοῦ παιδὸς εἵνεκα τοῦ Χαβρίου ὡμολόγησα τούτοις, ὡς ἂν οἷός τε ὦ, συνερεῖν». Οὕτω περὶ τῶν κατηγορούντων καὶ τῶν ἀπολογουμένων.*

*Περὶ δὲ τοὺς τὰ ἐγκλήματα ἔχοντας ἢ χρησταὶ ὑπολήψεις συνίστανται ἢ πονηραί. ἐὰν μὲν οὖν κατηγορῶμεν, τὰς φύσει προσούσας φαύλας βεβαιώσομεν, οἷον «τὴν μὲν ἀσέλγειαν, ὦ ἄνδρες δικασταί, καὶ τὴν ὕβριν, ᾗ πρὸς ἅπαντας ἀεὶ χρῆται Μειδίας, οὐδένα οὔθ᾽ ὑμῶν οὔτε τῶν ἄλλων πολιτῶν ἀγνοεῖν οἴομαι»· τὰς δὲ χρηστὰς προσούσας ὑπολήψεις διαλύσομεν, οἷον «οὐκ ἀγνοῶ μέν, ὦ ἄνδρες Ἀθηναῖοι, ὅτι τὸν Χαρίδημόν τινες εὐεργέτην οἴονται· ἐγὼ δὲ ἐάνπερ ἃ βούλομαί τε καὶ οἶδα τούτῳ πεπραγμένα δυνηθῶ πρὸς ὑμᾶς εἰπεῖν, οἴομαι δείξειν οὐ μόνον οὐκ εὐεργέτην, ἀλλὰ καὶ κακονούστατον καὶ πολὺ τἀναντία ἢ προσῆκεν ὑπειλημμένον». Ἐὰν δὲ ἀπολογώμεθα, τοὐναντίον ποιήσομεν, τὰς μὲν χρηστὰς βεβαιοῦντες ὑπολήψεις, τὰς δὲ φαύλας διαλύοντες, οἷον δέκα νέοι τὴ?ν τάξιν λιπόντες ἔφυγον, τῷ ἑνὶ ἀπαντήσασα ἡ μήτηρ ἀπέκτεινεν αὐτόν, οἱ ἐννέα στραφέντες ἠρίστευσαν, καὶ κρίνεται ἡ*
[100] *γυνὴ φόνου· ἐνταῦθα γὰρ μία μὲν ὑπόληψις περὶ τὴν | γυναῖκα χρηστή, ὅτι τῆς νίκης αἰτία, ἣν χρὴ βεβαιῶσαι κατὰ τὰ προοίμια λέγοντα οὕτως «ὅτι μὲν οὐκ ἄλλος τις ἡμῖν τῆς νίκης αἴτιος μᾶλλον τῆς γυναικὸς ἐγένετο, πάντας ὑμᾶς ἐλπίζομεν ἐγνωκέναι»· μία δὲ φαύλη, ἡ τοῦ δοκεῖν παιδοκτόνον αὐτὴν εἶναι, ἣν χρὴ θεραπεῦσαι λέγοντα οὕτως «εἰ μὲν οὖν τοῖς κατηγόροις πειθόμενοι τὴν γυναῖκα ταύτην παιδοκτόνον ὑπολήψεσθε, οὐκ ὀρθῶς ποιήσετε· εἰ δὲ τὰ πεπραγμένα σκοπήσετε καὶ τὰ τοῦ τετελευτηκότος δίκαια ἐγκλήματα, φανεῖται ἡ γυνὴ οὐκ ἀγαθὸν υἱὸν ἀλλὰ προδότην πονηρὸν ἀποκτείνασα».*

*Ἐμφαίνεται δὲ καὶ ἔξωθεν πρόσωπα, ὡς ἔφαμεν, πολεμίων μάλιστα πολλάκις, ἀφ᾽ ὧν οὕτω ληψόμεθα τὰ προοίμια ζητοῦντες ἐπὶ τῇ παρούσῃ κρίσει, τί ἂν βούλοιντο τέλος οἱ πολέμιοι γενέσθαι, λέγοντες*

**1** ἕνεκα **P** || **2** λελύσθαι τῆι πόλει τὸν Vc, v.l. **P**, Dem. 20, 1 | καὶ supr. Pa; δὲ καὶ Vb || **6** φύσει⌊Ι⌉ Pc || **7-8** Dem. 21, 1 || **8** πάντας **V** || **10** μὲν οὖν Ac, Dem. 23, 6 | ὦ ἄνδρες δικασταὶ **P**; om. Dem. || **12-13** αὐτὸν m. 2 supr. post δείξειν Vc || **16** καὶ τῷ Vc || **20** ὑμῖν **P** Vc Ac | μᾶλλον ἢ τῆς Ba || **24** ὑπολήψεσθε **V**, (αι supr.) Pc; ὑπολήψα[ε]ισθε Pa | σκοπήσετε **V**, (αι supr.) Pc; σκοπήσα[ε]ιτε Pa || **27** καὶ om. m. 1 Vc | p. 4, 13 || **28** γρ′ πολλάκις δὲ καὶ συμμάχων **P** (at coniungendum ἐμφαίνεται . . . πολλάκις)

the best of my ability, mostly because of thinking that it is advantageous for the law to be rescinded, and then too for the sake of Chabrias's son." Hypolepses about prosecutors and defendants are treated in this way.

Hypolepses about those under indictment are either favorable or unfavorable. If we are prosecuting, we shall insist on the natural wickednesses of the defendant; for example (Dem. 21.1), "The wantonness, men of the jury, and the insolence that Meidias always shows toward everybody, I think none of you nor any other citizens fail to recognize." Hypolepses about the existence of good qualities we shall refute; for example (Dem. 23.6), "I am not unaware, men of Athens, that some people think Charidemus is a benefactor; but as for me, if I can say to you what I want and what I know has been done by him, I think I shall show not only that he is no benefactor but that he is very ill-disposed to us and exactly the wrong conclusion has been drawn about his character." If we are, on the other hand, speaking for the defense, we shall do the opposite, strengthening favorable hypolepses and rebutting unfavorable ones; for example, ten young men deserted their military post; the mother of one encountered him and killed him; the other nine, having been turned back, performed with heroism, and the woman is tried for murder. Here one hypolepsis about the
| woman is favorable, that she is the cause of the victory,[19] and it is [100]
necessary to emphasize this in the prooemia, speaking as follows: "That no other person was the cause of our victory more than this woman, we hope that all of you know." But there is one bad hypolepsis, that she seems to be the murderer of her son, which needs to be remedied by saying, "If then you are persuaded by the prosecutors and suppose this woman is the murderer of her son, you will not do rightly; but if you look at what has been done and the just charges against the one who has died, the woman seems to have killed a wicked traitor, not a good son."

Persons from outside the case are also revealed (*to have suppositions about the case*), as we said, most often in the case of enemies. We shall derive prooemia from them by asking in the present crisis what outcome the enemy would want, speaking as follows in the case mentioned earlier: Some exiles came to the aid

[19] The argument would be that the killing served as a warning to the other deserters.

*οὕτως ὡς ἐν ἐκείνῳ τῷ προβλήματι· φυγάδες πολεμουμένῃ τῇ πατρίδι ἐβοήθησαν καὶ νίκην εἰργάσαντο, καὶ γράφει τις αὐτοὺς κατάγειν· «τοῖς μὲν οὖν πολεμίοις δι' εὐχῆς ἐστι μὴ καταδέξασθαι τοὺς πολίτας ἡμᾶς ἐνθάδε, ἵνα ὦμεν αὐτοῖς ληφθῆναι ῥᾴδιοι· ἡμᾶς δὲ οὐκ ἄξιον ποιεῖν, ἃ δοκεῖ τοῖς πολεμίοις».*

*Ταῦτά σοι περὶ τῶν ἐξ ὑπολήψεως προοιμίων πεπλήρωται, τοῦτον εὑρισκόμενα τὸν τρόπον ἁπανταχῇ.*

## [101] | *Περὶ τῶν ἐξ ὑποδιαιρέσεως προοιμίων.*

*Ἑξῆς λεκτέον περὶ τῶν ἐξ ὑποδιαιρέσεως προοιμίων πάνυ παγκάλην καὶ ποικίλην ἐχόντων τὴν τέχνην. εὑρίσκεται δὲ καὶ ταῦτα ἀπὸ τῶν ἑξῆς μαθημάτων, οὐκ ἐν πᾶσι δὲ προβλήμασιν οὐδὲ πάντα ἐν πᾶσιν· εὔθικτα μὲν γάρ ἐστιν εὑρεθέντα καὶ δριμέα, πολλάκις δὲ φαίνεται τῶν ἐξ ὑπολήψεως ἡ ἀρετή, διότι πανταχῇ φαίνεται.*

*Ἔστι δὲ τῶν ἐξ ὑποδιαιρέσεως εἴδη τρία, ὧν καὶ τὰ παραδείγματα θήσομεν. καὶ πρῶτον ἔστιν ὅτε δύο πεπραγμένων ἀδικημάτων, ὧν καὶ τὸ ἕτερον ἀναδέξασθαι δύναται κρίσιν, ὑποδιαιροῦντες ποιήσομεν προοίμιον οὕτως· οἷον κατέσκαψάν τινες πόλιν ἐν πολέμῳ καὶ ἐγεώργησαν αὐτήν, οὐκ ἀνῆκεν ἡ γῆ καρπούς, καὶ κρίνονται ἀσεβείας· ἐνταῦθα δύο ὄντων ἀδικημάτων ἰσοστασίων, τοῦ τε κατασκάψαι τὴν πόλιν καὶ τοῦ γεωργῆσαι, ποιήσομεν ἐξ ὑποδιαιρέσεως προοίμιον οὕτως «εἰ μὲν οὖν καὶ διὰ τὸ κατασκάψαι τὴν πόλιν ἔδοσαν αὐτοὶ δίκην, ὀρθῶς ἂν ἐγένετο· νῦν δὲ πολλῷ πλέον, ὅτε καὶ γεωργῆσαι διέγνωσαν ἣν κατέσκαψαν*

1 cf. 6, 9 || 2 καλεῖν m. 1 Ba, (γρ καταγειν) Vc || 2-3 οἷον τοῖς Ba, W VI 542, 15 || 3 καταδέχεσθαι Ba || 4 cf. 260, 5 Sp. || 10 καὶ supr. Vδ, om. We || 11-12 εὔθικτα (η supr.) **P** Vc; εὔθηκτα praeferunt Dox., schol. **P** (W VII 710, 8) || 12 μὲν om. Pc | πλεονάκις Ald.; πλειστάκις m. po. Vc | ⌊φαίνεται δὲ πολλάκις m. po.⌉ Pc | ἐμφαίνεται Ba || 13 φαίνεται (ε ρ supr.) **P** || 14 ὑπο⌊διαιρέσεως m. po.⌉ Pc | τὰ om. Vc Ba || 15 ad ὅτε mg.: γρ ἢ γὰρ δύο πεπραγμένων Pa, (ἤτοι) Pc || 15-16 ὅτἂν ... ποιήσωμεν Ac || 15 καὶ om. Vc || 18 τοὺς καρποὺς Ac; cf. 24, 12 | δὲ δύο Pc || 19 ὄντων τῶν Vδ || 21 δίκας **V**

of their country in time of war and brought about a victory, and someone introduces a motion that they be recalled: "Now it is the prayer of the enemy that we not bring these citizens back home, in order that it may be easier for them to capture us, but it is not right for us to do what seems best to our enemies."

You have here everything there is to say about prooemia from hypolepses, since they are invented in this way everywhere.

## | CHAPTER 2: ON PROOEMIA FROM HYPODIAERESIS (SUBORDINATION) [101]

Next we must speak of prooemia from *hypodiairesis,*[20] having quite a fine and varied art. These are found by applying the following procedures (*mathēmata*),[21] but each is not applicable in every problem nor all in any one. They are indeed effective (*euthikta*) and striking (*drimeia*) when invented, but often the superiority of prooemia from hypolepsis is evident, because these are seen in every case.

There are three species of (*proemia*) from hypodiaeresis, of which we shall give examples. The first is when two wrongs have been done and it is equally possible to submit the second to judgment. By subordinating one to the other we make a prooemion in this way; for example, some men destroyed a city during a war and plowed up the ground, the ground failed to produce crops, and the men are tried for impiety.[22] Since there are two wrongs of equal weight here, having destroyed the city and having plowed it up, we shall make a prooemion from hypodiaeresis as follows: "Now if they had been punished for destroying the city, it would have been rightly done; but now much more so, since they determined to plow up the city that they had destroyed." Cutting up one thing into small bits, however, is not a prooemion from

[20] *Hypodiaireō* and *hypodiairesis* are terms of Stoic logic meaning "subdivide, subdivision"; cf. Diogenes Laertius 7.84. But *hypodiairesis* does not occur as a rhetorical term in any earlier extant text.

[21] The author uses *mathēma* in this chapter to mean something the student has learned; other rhetoricians spoke of topics, theorems, or starting points for invention. Maximus Planudes (Walz 5:376) defines *mathēmata* in this context as "the methods and hypotheses from which propositions (*protaseis*) are found."

[22] I.e., they had offended the tutelary divinities of the city.

*πόλιν». οὐ μέντοι ἡ ἑνὸς πράγματος εἰς λεπτὸν τομὴ προοίμιόν ἐστιν ἐξ ὑποδιαιρέσεως, ἀλλὰ τῶν ἀπ᾽ ἀρχῆς ἄχρι τέλους ἐξ ὑποδιαιρέσεως κατασκευή· οἷον ἔπεισεν ἐν λιμῷ καὶ πολιορκίᾳ ῥήτωρ τὴν ἄχρηστον* [102] *ἡλικίαν ἀποκτεῖ|ναι, γέρων λαθὼν ἠρίστευσεν, αἰτεῖ εἰς τὸ γέρας τὸν ῥήτορα· ἐνταῦθα τὸ ἀδίκημα ἕν, τὸ τὰ γένη διαφθαρῆναι, ἐξ ὑποδιαιρέσεως δὲ εἰ λέγοι «εἰ γὰρ μόνους τοὺς πατέρας ἔπεισεν ἀποκτεῖναι ἢ μόνας τὰς γυναῖκας, ἄξιος ἦν θανάτου», οὐ προοίμιον λέγει, ἀλλὰ κατασκευάζει τὰ ἀπ᾽ ἀρχῆς ἄχρι τέλους.*

*Δεύτερον ἐξ ὑποδιαιρέσεως μάθημα οὕτως εὑρίσκεται, ἐν ᾧ ποιοῦμεν προοίμιον. ἐνίοτε τοῖς προσώποις καὶ πρὸ τῶν πραγμάτων ἴδιαι παρακολουθοῦσιν ὑπολήψεις, οἷον Αἰσχίνῃ, Δημοσθένει, δεύτεραι δὲ αἱ ἐπισυμβαίνουσαι ἀπὸ τῶν πραγμάτων. ὅταν οὖν εὕρωμεν ἐν προβλήματι τὰς ὑπολήψεις ἑκατέρας περὶ τὸ ἓν πρόσωπον, τήν τε φύσει προσοῦσαν καὶ τὴν ἐπιγενομένην, ὑποδιαιροῦντες λέγομεν ὡς ἐν ἐκείνῳ τῷ προβλήματι· Δημάδης πρεσβεύσας παρὰ τὸν Φίλιππον, καὶ ἐρομένου ποταπαί εἰσιν αἱ Ἀθῆναι τοῦ Μακεδόνος, ἐπὶ τῆς τραπέζης αὐτὰς κατέγραψε καὶ ἐπανελθὼν ὕβρεως κρίνεται· οἷον «καὶ διὰ τὸν ἄλλον μὲν βίον, ὦ Ἀθηναῖοι, τὸν προσόντα Δημάδῃ καὶ τὴν προδοσίαν ἄξιον ἦν κολάσαι τοῦτον, οὐχ ἥκιστα δὲ καὶ διὰ τὰ νῦν αὐτῷ γεγενημένα, ἐξ ὧν αἰσχύνην ὁμοῦ καὶ ζημίαν περιῆψε τῇ πόλει». γίνεται δὲ καὶ ἐπὶ τῶν ἰδιωτικῶν τοῦτο πολλάκις, ἂν ἔχωμεν ἢ μάγον ἢ τελώνην ἢ πορνοβοσκόν· οἷον πορνοβοσκὸς τὰ τῶν Μουσῶν ὀνόματα ταῖς ἑταίραις τίθεται καὶ κρίνε-* [103] *ται ἀσεβείας· λέγομεν | γὰρ οὕτως «ἄξιον μὲν ἦν τὸν πορνοβοσκὸν καὶ διὰ τὸν ἄλλον μισεῖσθαι βίον πονηρὸν ὄντα καὶ δὴ καὶ τιμωρίας ἄξιον, οὐχ ἥκιστα δὲ νῦν, ὅτε καὶ ἠσέβησεν εἰς τὰς θεάς».*

1 λεπτὸν: cf. p. 222, 24 Sp. || 4 καὶ αἰτεῖ Ba || 5 ἐνταῦθα δ⌊ὲ⌋ Pa || 6 δὲ εἰ Ac, (εἰ supr.) Vc; οὖν εἰ Pc Ba; οὖν (δὲ εἰ supr.) Pa | λέγ⌊ο ex ε⌋ι Pa || 7 οὖν add. ante λέγει Pc Ac, supr. Pa || 9 ἐν ὧι **PV**; ἐν om. m. 1 Vδk; ὃ (om. ἐν) v.l. **P** || 10 ἐνίοτε δὲ **V** || 11 καὶ post αἰσχίνηι add. (m. 1 ?) Vc || 11-12 αἱ ἐπισυμβαίνουσαι Ac Ba, v.l. **P**; ἐπισυμβαίνουσιν (om. αἱ) **P** Vc || 12 πλασμάτων m. 1 Vc Ac || 14 ἐπιγινομένην **V** || 15 τὸν om. Pc | [καὶ] Spengel || 17-18 ὦ ἄνδρες ἀθηναῖοι Ac || 18 ἦν om. Pc || 19 γινόμενα Pc || 25 καὶ om. Pc

hypodiaeresis; it is using hypodiaeresis to construct an argument from-beginning-to-end;[23] for example, during a famine and siege an orator persuaded a city to kill those useless because of their age; | one old man escaped notice and performed a deed of valor; he [102] demands the orator as his prize.[24] Here there is only one crime, destroying families, and if someone should say by hypodiaeresis, "for if he persuaded you to kill only the fathers or only the women, he would be deserving of death," he is not speaking a prooemion but constructing an argument from-beginning-to-end.

A second precept from hypodiaeresis that is used to make a prooemion is as follows. Sometimes specific hypolepses are attributed to persons in advance of their actions—for example, to Aeschines or Demosthenes—and a second set is derived from the actions. Whenever, then, we find each of these hypolepses about one person in a problem, one belonging to him by nature and the other acquired, we utilize hypodiaeresis, as in the following problem: Demades went on an embassy to Philip, and when the Macedonian asked what sort of place Athens was, he drew (*an image of* ) it on the table, and after he returned home he is indicted for hybris.[25] Thus, "Demades deserved to be punished, Athenians, both for his conduct throughout his life and his treason, but not least for what he has now done, as a result of which he has brought shame and loss on the city." This occurs often in the case of character types, if we are dealing with a charlatan or tax collector or brothel keeper; for example, a brothel keeper gave the names of the Muses to his girls and is charged with impiety. We can say, | "The brothel keeper deserved to be hated because of his [103] life in general, for he is a wicked man deserving punishment, but not least now when he has also committed an act of impiety toward the goddesses."

[23] On this term, see 3.10 below. It occurs repeatedly in Hermogenes' *On Stasis*, where it is translated by Heath as "sequence of events."

[24] To kill or enslave him; cf. n. 18 above.

[25] If it was a question of giving Philip geographical information, the indictment would have been for treason. Since, however, the charge is hybris, aggravated insult, drawing a small picture or map is regarded as belittling Athens.

*Τρίτον ἐξ ὑποδιαιρέσεως μάθημα εἰς προοιμίων εὕρεσιν, ὃ καλεῖται τοῦ ἀθρόου πρὸς τὸ μέλλον [ὑποδιαίρεσις]· γίνεται δέ, ὅταν κακοῦ τινος τολμηθέντος λέγῃς δεῖν τὸν εἰργασμένον δοῦναι τιμωρίαν καὶ διὰ τὸ τετολμημένον καὶ ἵνα μὴ πάλιν τολμηθῇ. δεῖ δὲ τὸ τοῦ ἀθρόου πρὸς τὸ μέλλον ποιεῖν τότε, ὅταν ἢ τὸ μηδεπώποτε γεγονὸς τοῦτο συμβὰν παθεῖν πάλιν φυλαττώμεθα ἢ ὅταν τὸ αὐτὸ πράττηται πολλάκις. τὰ δὲ παραδείγματα σαφεστέραν ποιεῖ τὴν τέχνην· πολλοὶ τυραννοῦσιν ἐκ τοῦ αὐτοῦ γένους, καὶ γράφει τις ἐλαύνειν τὸ γένος· ἐνταῦθα καλλίστην χώραν ἔχει τὸ προοίμιον, ἐὰν λέγωμεν οὕτω «καὶ τῶν γεγενημένων μὲν εἵνεκα τυραννίδων καλῶς ἂν ἔχοι μισοῦντας τὸ γένος τῆς πόλεως ἐκβάλλειν τιμωροῦντας αὐτοὺς ὑπὲρ ὧν ἐπάθομεν, οὐχ ἥκιστα δὲ καὶ τοῦ μέλλοντος πρόνοιαν ποιουμένους, ἵνα μὴ τοῖς ὁμοίοις περιπίπτωμεν ἀεί». καὶ πάλιν· ἐμίχθη τις ταριχευομένῳ σώματι, καὶ γράφει τις λελύσθαι τὸν τῆς ταριχείας νόμον· καὶ γὰρ ἐκεῖ δυνάμεθα λέγειν «ἵνα μὴ πάλιν γένηται».*

## [104] | Περὶ τῶν ἐκ περιουσίας προοιμίων.

*Τὰ ἐκ περιουσίας καλούμενα προοίμια ἰδίαν εὕρεσιν ἔχει ἐν ταῖς κατηγορίαις καὶ ἐν ταῖς ἀπολογίαις, σαφῆ δὲ αὐτὰ ἐν ἑκατέροις ποιήσω. ἐὰν γὰρ κατηγοροῦντές τινος φόνου δυνώμεθα λέγειν ὅτι «ἠδυνάμην αὐτὸν καὶ δημοσίων ἀδικημάτων κρίνειν», ἐκ περιουσίας ποιοῦμεν τὸ*

1 ἐξ — εὕρεσιν om. Mr || **1-2** καλεῖται τὸ τοῦ Ac Mr || **2** [ὑποδιαίρεσις] Spengel || **3** τινὸς m. 2 suppl. Vc | δεῖ Vδ || **4** τολμηθῆι πάλιν **V** || **6** μὴ m. po. supr. ante παθεῖν Va | φυλαττώμεθα παθεῖν (om. πάλιν) Pc; (πάλιν add. m. 2) παθεῖν ⌊πάλαι del. m. 2⌋ φυλαττώμεθα Vc || **7** οἷον πολλοὶ Ac || **8** ἐκβάλλειν Ac; cf. Aps. I 2 p. 241, 7 Sp.-H. || **9** ἔχει χώραν Pc || **10** μὲν om. **P** | εἵνεκεν Vc Ac || **11** αὐτοὺς Ac; αὐτοῖς **P** Vc; ? m. 1 Ba || **13** pr. καὶ om. Ba | cf. Herod. 2, 89. Demetr. De eloc. 239 | τεταριχευμένωι Ac | καὶ γράφει τίς suppl. m. 2 Pc || **17** εὕρεσιν, m. po. ὑπόθεσιν, Vc || **18** αὐτὰ suppl. (m. 1 ?) Vc

A third precept from hypodiaeresis in the invention of prooemia is what is called *tou athroou pros to mellon.*[26] This occurs whenever some evil deed has been dared and you say that the perpetrator should be punished both for what he dared to do and in order that it not be done again. We should use *tou athroou pros to mellon* either whenever we are preventing something that has never happened before from ever happening or when the same thing is done often. Some examples will make the technique clearer. Many members of the same family become tyrants and someone introduces a motion to expel the family. Here the prooemion is given the best commonplace[27] if we speak as follows: "Because of the tyrannies that have occurred, it would be good for us to expel this hated family from the city, punishing them for what we suffered, but not least now because we would be exercising foresight for the future in order that we may never incur anything similar." And again: someone has intercourse with an embalmed body,[28] and someone introduces a motion to rescind the law permitting embalming; for here we can say, "that it may not happen again."

## | CHAPTER 3: ON PROOEMIA FROM PERIOUSIA (SUPERFLUITY) [104]

Prooemia called "from *periousia*"[29] take specific forms of invention in prosecutions and in defenses, and I shall make clear what this is in each case. If when prosecuting someone for homicide we can say, "I could have brought him to trial also for wrongs to the state,"[30] we are creating a prooemion from periousia, and if

[26] Literally, "from the collected (or the crowd) to what is going to be," thus "to prevent the same thing being tried again," another example of the author's unusual technical terminology, but note "what is called." Patillon (*L'Art rhétorique*, 218) translates the phrase "pour en finir une fois pour toutes," "to finish with it once and for all."

[27] *Khōra*, used to mean *topos*; cf. 3.15 below, p. 133.

[28] Cf. Herodotus 2.89.

[29] Although a common Greek word with a variety of applications, often meaning "abundance," *periousia* is not used as a technical rhetorical term in any earlier text. To translate it "abundance" here would invite confusion with *peribolē*, abundance as a feature of style. Patillon (*ANRW*, 209 n. 112) translates it as "a fortiore."

[30] Cf. 2.6 below.

*προοίμιον, κἂν δημοσίων ἀδικημάτων κρίνοντες δυνώμεθα λέγειν ὅτι «ἠδυνάμην αὐτὸν καὶ ἀσεβείας κρίνειν», ἐκ περιουσίας προοιμιαζόμεθα· οἷον ἀριστεὺς ἄχειρ προσῆλθε στρατηγῷ δεόμενος τροφῶν, ὁ δὲ εἶπεν «ἀχρήστους ἡ πόλις οὐ τρέφει», κατὰ κρημνοῦ ὦσεν ἑαυτὸν ὁ ἀριστεύς, καὶ κρίνεται ὁ στρατη γὸς αἰτίας θανάτου· λέγομεν γὰρ ἐκ περιουσίας ὅτι «ἠδυνάμην αὐτὸν καὶ δημοσίων ἀδικημάτων εἰσαγαγεῖν γραψάμενος, ὅτι κοινὸν εὐεργέτην τῆς πόλεως ἀπώλεσεν». ἢ ἐκεῖνο τὸ πρόβλημα· ἡ Φύη μετὰ τὴν κατάλυσιν τοῦ Πεισιστράτου κρίνεται δημοσίων ἀδικημάτων· λέγομεν γὰρ «ἠδυνάμην μὲν οὖν καὶ ἀσεβείας αὐτὴν γραψάμενος εἰς ὑμᾶς ἀγαγεῖν, ὅτι τὸ σχῆμα τῆς Ἀθηνᾶς ἀσεβῶς ὑπεκρίνατο». Ἰστέον δέ, ὅτι μικροτέρου κρίνοντας δεῖ λέγειν ὅτι «καὶ μείζονος ἠδυνάμην», μὴ μέντοι μείζονος κρίνοντας λέγειν ὅτι «καὶ τοῦ μικροτέρου ἠδυνάμην»· ἄτεχνον γὰρ τὸ τοιοῦτον.*

[105] *Ἐν δὲ ταῖς ἀπολογίαις εὐκαταληπτότερον τὸ ἐκ περι|ουσίας μάθημα· πᾶς γὰρ ὁστισοῦν μετὰ τὴν εὐεργεσίαν κρινόμενος ἄριστα ποιήσει προοίμιον ἐκ περιουσίας λέγων «ἐγὼ μὲν καὶ γέρας ὑπελάμβανον ἐπὶ τοῖς πεπραγμένοις λήψεσθαι, μή τί γε δὴ καὶ κρίσεις ὑπομενεῖν», οἷον ὁ στρατηγὸς ὁ τὰς τριήρεις νικώμενος καταφλέξας καὶ νικήσας καὶ κρινόμενος δημοσίων ἀδικημάτων, ἢ ὁ ῥίψας ἀπὸ τοῦ τείχους τὴν ἀσπίδα καὶ ἀποκτείνας τὸν πολέμιον. καὶ καθάπαξ ῥᾳδίου τοῦ μαθήματος ὄντος χρειώδους δὲ ἀνθεκτέον.*

## *Περὶ τῶν ἀπὸ καιροῦ προοιμίων.*

*Τὸ δὲ ἀπὸ καιροῦ καλούμενον προοίμιον ἄφατόν τινα τὴν ὑπερβολὴν τῆς δυνάμεως ἔχει, ἐὰν εὑρεθῇ. ἔστι δὲ τοιοῦτον τῇ δυνάμει, ἐὰν δυνώμεθα τὴν ἀξίωσιν, ἣν εἰσφέρομεν, τρόπον τινὰ ἤδη δεῖξαι καὶ γεγενημένην. ἔστι δὲ αὐτοῦ τὸ τῆς ἰσχύος τοιοῦτον· οἷον ἐφυγαδεύθη-*

3 τῷ στρατηγῷ Ba || 4 οὐ suppl. m. po. Pc || 6 εἰσαγ⌊ω⌉[α]γ⌊ή⌉[εῖν]ν γραψά⌊σθαι⌉[μένος] Vc || 7 ἢ ὡς **V** (cf. 40, 19) || 8 ἡ φυλή m. 2 mg. Ba, v.l. Dox.; ἡ φύ⌊Ι⌉η Vc || 9 γὰρ οὕτως ὅτι Ba | αὐτ⌊ή⌉ν Pa, (η m. 2 ex ο) Pc; δίκην v.l. **P**; δίκην αὐτὴν Vc Ba; αὐτὴν καὶ ἀσεβείας δίκην Ac || 10-11 ὑπεκρίνατο[ε] Vc || 11 καὶ om. Vc Ac; καὶ τοῦ Ba || 16 ἐν (pro ἐπὶ) Ac || 22 om. Vc || 25 καὶ om. Vc || 26 αὐτοῦ ex τούτου Vc

when bringing someone to trial for wrongs to the state we can say, "I could have brought him to trial also for impiety," we are making a prooemion from periousia; for example: a military hero who had lost a hand came to seek support from a general, but the latter said, "The city does not feed the useless." The hero threw himself down a cliff, and the general is brought to trial as responsible for his death. Using periousia, we say that "I could also have brought an indictment against him for wrongs to the state because he destroyed a common benefactor of the city." Or the following problem: After the fall of Peisistratus, Phya is brought to court for wrongs to the state.[31] We say, "Now I could have brought her in to you under a charge of impiety, because she impiously acted the figure of Athene." You should understand that when bringing to court on a lesser charge one ought to say, "and I could have brought a greater charge," but not to say, "and I could have brought a lesser charge" when bringing a greater one, for such a thing would be lacking in art.

In defenses, the precept from periousia is more easily comprehended, | for everyone who is brought to trial after some good [105] deed will best use a prooemion from periousia, saying, "I even supposed I would receive a prize for what I have done, certainly not have to undergo trials"; for example, the general who set fire to some ships when being defeated and after victory was tried for wrongs to the state; or the man who threw his shield from the wall and killed an enemy soldier. And one should cultivate a precept that is quite easy and useful.

## CHAPTER 4: ON PROOEMIA FROM KAIROS (OCCASION)

What is called prooemion "from *kairos*"[32] has an indescribably great power whenever it has been employed. It has power of this sort if we are able to show that the axiosis[33] that we propose has in some way already taken place. Its force is of the following sort; for example, some people had been banished and had established

[31] She was six feet tall and impersonated Athene restoring Peisistratus to Athens in 559 B.C.E.; cf. Herodotus 1.60.

[32] *Kairos* generally refers to a specific moment of time, an occasion, but here it means something already done in the past.

[33] Cf. n. 9 above.

*σάν τινες καὶ ἔκτισαν ἐπὶ τοῖς ὁρίοις τῆς πατρίδος ἑτέραν πόλιν, ἐν ᾗ ᾤκουν, πολέμου ἐνστάντος ἐκείνοις, ὅθεν ἐξεβλήθησαν, ἐπανελθόντες ἐβοήθησαν αὐτοῖς, καὶ γράφει τις αὐτοὺς καταδέχεσθαι· λέγομεν γὰρ «τὸ μὲν δοκεῖν ἐγὼ γράφω τὸ ψήφισμα τήμερον τοὺς πολίτας καταδέχεσθαι, τὸ δὲ ἀληθὲς ἤδη τούτους δεδέγμεθα, ὅτε συμμάχους ὄντας αὐτοὺς κατελθεῖν εἰάσαμεν». ἀλλὰ καὶ Μεγαρεῖς ἐπὶ τῶν τριάκοντα τυράννων ἐκτιθέντων Ἀθηναίων τὰ γένη ἀναιρούμενοι ἔτρεφον αὐτά,* [106] *καταλυθείσης τῆς τυραννίδος | ἥκουσιν ἀποδιδόντες τὰ γένη, καὶ ἀξιοῖ τις καθαιρεῖν τὸ περὶ τῶν Μεγαρέων πινάκιον. καὶ ἔτι ἐν τοῖς τὴν πόλιν κατασκάψασι καὶ σπείρασιν αὐτήν· θέλοντες γὰρ αὐτοὺς ἀσεβεῖς ἀποδεῖξαι φαμὲν ὑπὸ τῶν θεῶν ἐληλέγχθαι καὶ πρὸ τῶν ἡμετέρων λόγων, ὅτι εἰσὶν ἀσεβεῖς, ἐξ ὧν ὡς ἐναγεστάτοις οὐδὲ τοὺς καρποὺς ἀνῆκεν ἡ γῆ. καλεῖται δὲ τοῦτο καὶ ἀγχίστροφον ἐπιχείρημα.*

*Τὸ δὲ ἐπὶ τῶν ἐπιπεπλεγμένων προβλημάτων οὐκ ἀναγκαῖον ἐνόμισα προσθεῖναι μάθημα· ἢ γὰρ καλόν ἐστι καὶ τῶν ἐξ ὑπολήψεως ὂν φαίνεται, ἢ προκατάστασις ὂν διηγηματικόν, οὐ προοίμιον εὑρίσκεται.*

## *Περὶ παντὸς προοιμίου, καὶ ἐκ πόσων μερῶν συνέστηκεν.*

*Σύγκειται δὲ πᾶν προοίμιον ἐκ προτάσεως, ἥτις ἐστὶν ἐκ τῶν μαθημάτων εὑρισκομένη τῶν προκειμένων, ἐξ ὧν δή τοι καὶ γίνεται, ἐκ*

1 ⌊τοῖς ὁρίοις, ex τοῦ ὅρους ?⌉ Vc || 2-3 cf. 6, 9 || 4 τήμερον τὸ τοὺς Ba || 5 τότε ὅτε ὡς συμμάχους Ba || 5-6 αὐτοὺς ante ὄντας Vc, et ante ὄντας et post 23 εἰάσαμεν Pc || 6 ἄλλο, sc. πρόβλημα, Sturm (potius καὶ ἄλλο) | p. 12, 11 || 8 ἥκουσιν (α supra ου) Pa || 9 τὸ περὶ τῶν μεγαρέων καθαιρεῖν Ba | p. 16, 17 || 10 ἀσεβεῖς αὐτοὺς Pc || 10-11 ἐπιδεῖξαι Vc Ac || 11 τοῦ θεοῦ Ba || 12 ἀσεβεῖς εἰσίν Pc || 14 ἐπὶ Pa, (? m. 1) Pc; κατὰ **V**, v.l. Pc, W VII 62, 30 || 16 cf. 34, 6 || 17 καὶ om. Vc, (m. 2 suppl.) Pa (sed in titulo marg. καὶ m. 1 Pa) | συνίσταται Ba || 18 πρῶτον μὲν ἐκ in lemmate Mr (lectionum l. 17 δεύτερον ἐκ .. τρίτον ἐξ .. 18 τέταρτον ἐκ unum testem Ma novi) | ἐκ ⌊II—III⌉ τῶν Pa

another city on the boundaries of their native country and dwelt there; when a war befell those by whom they had been expelled, they went back to aid them, and someone introduces a motion to restore them. Here we say, "It looks as though I am introducing a decree today to restore citizens, but the truth is we had already received them back when we allowed them to return as our allies." Another example is that of the Megarians who received and cared for families sent to them by Athenians during the rule of the Thirty Tyrants; after the tyranny was dissolved | they came [106] to restore the families, and someone thinks it right to rescind the decree against the Megareans.[34] And further, in the case of those who destroyed the city and sowed the ground,[35] for when wanting to show that they were impious, we say that they have been shown to be impious by the gods, even before our speeches, ever since the earth refused to bear fruit for them, as being under a very heavy curse. This epikheireme[36] is also called an *ankhistrophon.*[37]

I do not think it necessary to add a precept for cases of mutual allegation,[38] for either what is claimed is good and seems to be derived from hypolepsis, or being a prokatastasis[39] it belongs to the invention of narrations, not of prooemia.

## CHAPTER 5: ON ALL PROOEMIA, AND OF HOW MANY PARTS THEY ARE COMPOSED

Every prooemion is composed of (1) a protasis, which is invented from the precepts laid down above, from which you can certainly

[34] On the Megarean Decree, see n. 17 above. The argument here would be that the decree has already effectively been rescinded since the Megareans received the families.

[35] Cf. 1.2 above, p. 17.

[36] On epikheiremes, see 3.5 below.

[37] A sudden transition; cf. *On Sublimity* 9.13 and 27.3.

[38] *Epipeplegmena problēmata;* Maximus Planudes (Walz 5:380) cites a situation in which Aeschines and Demosthenes are imagined as bringing an accusation for false embassy against each other, each claiming that he himself has shown goodwill toward the city and has a good reputation. In so far as the hypolepses relate to the past, they belong to the prooemion; if to the present, they belong to the narration.

[39] A preliminary statement or demonstration; see 3.2 below.

*κατασκευῆς, ἐξ ἀποδόσεως, ἥτις ἐστὶν ἀξίωσις, ἐκ βάσεως, ἣ συνάγει τὴν πρότασιν καὶ τὴν ἀπόδοσιν.*

*Ἐὰν μὲν οὖν θελήσωμεν πολιτικώτερον στῆσαι τὸ προοίμιον, εἰς τὴν ἀξίωσιν ψιλὴν αὐτὸ στήσομεν. ἐὰν δὲ προστιθῶμεν καὶ τὴν αἰτίαν* [107] *τῆς ἀξιώσεως ἁπτόμε|νοι τοῦ πράγματος αὐτοῦ, πανηγυρικωτέρα γίνεται ἡ βάσις, καὶ μάλιστα, ἂν μὴ τὰ ἀπ' ἀρχῆς ἄχρι τέλους ἁπλῶς εἴπωμεν ἀλλ' ἐπιφωνηματικῶς. ποιεῖ δὲ πανηγυρικὴν τὴν βάσιν καὶ ἡ εὐρυθμία, ἵνα τὸ πανηγυρικὸν ᾖ διπλοῦν, ἢ ἐν τῷ λόγῳ διὰ τὴν εὐρυθμίαν ἢ ἐν τῷ νῷ διὰ τὴν ἐν τοῖς ἀπ' ἀρχῆς ἄχρι τέλους φιλοτιμίαν. Δεῖ δὲ τὸ προοίμιον ἐν μὲν τοῖς πολιτικοῖς ἡρμηνεῦσθαι μακροτέροις τοῖς κώλοις καὶ σχοινοτενέσιν, ἐν δὲ τοῖς παθητικοῖς συνεστραμμένοις καὶ εὐκόλοις μᾶλλον. Περιβολὴ δὲ αὐτάρκης προοιμίων διπλασιάσαι ὄνομα καὶ διπλασιάσαι κῶλον καὶ προτάσεως ἀπὸ αἰτίας κατασκευή.*

**1** ἡ ἀξίωσις Pa Vc Ba || **3** ἐθελήσωμεν Pc Ac, (o) Ba || **6** τὸ Vc Ac || **7** δὲ πολλάκις **V**, v.l. **P** || **8** διὰ Pa **V**; κατὰ Pc || **9** ἐν τοῖς **P** Vc; εἰς τὰ m. 2 Vc; εἰς τὸ Ac Ba; om. v.l. **P** || **10** ἑρμηνεύεσθαι Mr || **12** εὐκόλοις, ω supra κ (m. po. ?), Pa || **13** pr. καὶ om. Ba | ἀπὸ τῆς Ac; ἐξ Vc Ba | κατασκευή⌊Ι⌉ **P**; κατασκευήν **V**; de utraque lect. cf. Dox.

find one; (2) a *kataskeuē*;[40] (3) an apodosis, which is an axiosis; and (4) a *basis*,[41] which joins together the protasis and the apodosis.[42]

If we want to make the prooemion more characteristic of political oratory,[43] we shall limit it to a plain axiosis.[44] If we add the reason for the axiosis, | touching upon the action itself, the basis becomes more panegyrical, and especially if we do not state the sequence of events[45] in a simple way but speak sententiously (*epiphōnēmatikōs*).[46] Another thing that makes the basis panegyrical is harmonious rhythm, so it becomes panegyrical in two ways, verbally by means of the rhythm, and in thought by means of the distinction[47] given to the sequence of events. [107]

The prooemion in political speeches should be expressed in longer, extended (*skhoinoteneis*)[48] cola, but in emotional oratory[49] in more compressed (*synestrammena*)[50] and simpler ones. To secure expansion (*peribolē*)[51] in prooemia it is sufficient to double the words and repeat the colon and offer support for the protasis by

[40] Here meaning a supporting statement; elsewhere often "proof" as a part of a speech.

[41] I.e., a summation or conclusion; see the example in the last sentence of this chapter.

[42] The examples offered below may make these parts clearer. The author's theory and terminology of parts of a prooemion are not found in any earlier text. Although it is not true that "every" prooemion consists of these parts, the author is offering novices a formula for beginning speeches in a way he will approve. Compare the formula for a prooemion offered here with the more complex formula to be followed in invention of a proof in 3.4–10 below.

[43] I.e., make the prooemion of the declamation more like what is appropriate to deliberative or judicial oratory. The author regards panegyric as more emotional than political oratory; sometimes it is, sometimes it is not.

[44] E.g., "I have come forward to recommend a plan" or to prosecute or defend someone.

[45] *Ta ap' arkhēs akhri telous*, "from beginning to end"; see the discussion in 3.10 below.

[46] I.e., express or imply a personal opinion, exclamation, or value judgment; cf. 4.9 below; Pseudo-Dionysius, *Art of Rhetoric* 2.10.1 and 18; Julius Rufianus §29, p. 45 Halm.

[47] *Philotimia*; Patillon (*L'Art rhétorique*, 221 n. 5) paraphrases it as "un certain intérêt."

[48] Cf. 4.4 below, p. 157.

[49] I.e., panegyric.

[50] Cf. Martin, 73.

[51] In the sense of "abundance" this is one of Hermogenes' "ideas" of style; cf. *On Ideas* 1.11; but the meaning here seems somewhat more limited.

*καὶ ὄνομα μέν, ἂν λέγωμεν «πρῶτον μέν, ὦ ἄνδρες Ἀθηναῖοι, τοῖς θεοῖς εὔχομαι πᾶσι καὶ πάσαις, τῇ τε πόλει καὶ πᾶσιν ὑμῖν» καὶ «ὑπὲρ ὑμῶν καὶ τῆς ὑμετέρας εὐσεβείας καὶ δόξης». κῶλον δὲ ὡς ἐν τῷ Κατὰ Ἀριστοκράτους «ὑπὲρ τοῦ Χερρόνησον ἔχειν ὑμᾶς ἀσφαλῶς καὶ μὴ παρακρουσθέντας ἀποστερηθῆναι πάλιν αὐτῆς». προτάσεως δὲ ἐξ αἰτίας κατασκευή, ἂν λέγωμεν πολλαχῇ δὲ δυνάμεθα εἰπεῖν «τὰ μὲν τούτῳ τετολμημένα λέληθεν ὑμῶν οὐδένα» τοῦτο ἡ πρότασις, ἡ δὲ κατασκευὴ ἐξ αἰτίας «ἐπεὶ μηδὲ οὕτως ἐστὶ μικρὰ τὰ τετολμημένα, ὡς δύνασθαι καὶ λαθεῖν». λεκτέον δὲ καὶ ἐπὶ παραδείγματος·* | [108] *πωλοῦσι τὰ τέκνα οἱ νησιῶται, καὶ γράφει τις παρὰ Ἀθηναίοις ἐπανεῖναι τὸν φόρον· «οἷα μὲν οὖν, ὦ Ἀθηναῖοι, πάσχουσιν οἱ νησιῶται κακὰ προφάσει τῶν φόρων, λέληθεν οὔτε ὑμᾶς οὔτε τῶν ἄλλων Ἑλλήνων οὐδένα» τοῦτο ἡ πρότασις· «καὶ γὰρ οὐδὲ οὕτως ἐστὶ μέτριον, ὃ τολμῶσι περὶ τὰ φίλτατα, ὥστε λαθεῖν ἐνεῖναι δύνασθαι» τοῦτο ἡ κατασκευὴ τῆς προτάσεως· εἶτα ἡ ἀπόδοσις «ὑμᾶς δὲ προσήκει πρόνοιαν ποιουμένους τῆς ὑμετέρας εὐδοξίας ἐπανεῖναι τοῖς ἀθλίοις τὸν φόρον καὶ μηκέθ᾽ οὕτως ὀχληροὺς καθίστασθαι». ἐὰν μὲν οὖν πολιτικῶς ἐθελήσῃς στῆσαι, οὕτω στήσεις τὴν ἀξίωσιν· εἰ δὲ βούλει, πρόσθες καὶ τὴν τῆς ἀξιώσεως αἰτίαν, τουτέστιν αὐτὸ τὸ πρᾶγμα, αὐτὸ λέγω τὸ ἀπ᾽ ἀρχῆς ἄχρι τέλους γυμνόν· καὶ ἐὰν θελήσωμεν εἰπεῖν τὸ ἀπ᾽ ἀρχῆς ἄχρι τέλους τολμῶντες ἐπιφωνηματικώτερον, ἔσται καὶ οὕτως πανηγυρικὴ ἡ βάσις «δι᾽ ὃν ἀναγκαζόμεναι δυστυχοῦσιν ἀπαιδίαν αἱ νῆσοι».*

1 καὶ om. Vc Ac | ὀνόματος Ac, v.l. Dox. | Dem. 18, 1 | ἄνδρες om. Vc Ba | δικασταὶ Ac Ba || 2 αἰτῶ Ac, m. 1 Vc | πάσαις ὅσην εὔνοιαν ἔχων ἐγὼ διατελῶ Dem. || 3 εὐσεβείας τε καὶ **V**, Dem. | κώλων Ac; κώλου v.l. Dox. || 4 Dem. 23, 1 | ὑμᾶς ἔχειν Pc **V** | ἀσφαλῶς ὑμᾶς ἔχειν Ba || 6 κατασκευὴ Sc; κατασκευὴν **PV** || 6-7 πεπραγμένα Pc || 8-9 ὡς ⌊μηδὲ del.⌉ δύνασθαι (καὶ er.) Vc || 9 ἐπὶ ⌊III⌉ παραδείγματος Vc || 9-10 cf. Pollux Naucrat. apud Philostr. V. S. II 12. Aps. I 2 p. 261, 20 Sp.-H. || 10 αὐτοῖς ante τὸν add. Ba, m. 2 suppl. Vc || 11 οὖν om. **V** || 12 ἄλλον m. 1, τῶν ἄλλων m. 2, Vc || 15 ποιουμένους post 9 εὐδοξίας Vc Ac || 17 οὖν om. **V** | γρ καὶ στῆναι **P** || 18 τῆς om. Ba || 19-20 καὶ ἐὰν δὲ Ba, (καὶ om.) Vc || 20 ἐθελήσωμεν Ac Ba | τὰ Vc || 20-21 cf. 26, 7 || 21 πανηγυρικὴ καὶ οὕτως Ba | ὃν **P**; οὓς **V**; Dox.: γράφεται καὶ «δι᾽ ὅντινα», φόρον δῆλόν γε ὅτι || 22 ἀπ⌊αι m. po.⌉δίαν Pa | subscr. τέλος τοῦ α´ τόμου **P**; τόμος α´ Vc; om. Ac Ba

giving a reason. In the case of words, if we say (Dem. 18.1), "First, men of Athens, I pray to the gods, both gods and goddesses, for our city and all of you," and "for your sake and your reverence and fame"; in the case of cola, as in *Against Aristocrates* (Dem. 23.1): "For the sake of your holding the Chersonese securely and not being deprived of it again by being misled."[52] There is kataskeuē for the protasis from a reason if we say—and we can often say this—"None of you has forgotten the things this man has dared to do," that is the protasis, and the kataskeuē from a reason is, "since the things he dares are not so negligible as to be able to be forgotten." We should mention an example: | The islanders are selling [108]
their children into slavery, and someone introduces a motion in the Athenian assembly to abolish the tribute.[53] The protasis is, "What sort of evils the islanders, for their part, are suffering, O Athenians, because of this tribute, none of you nor any of the other Greeks has failed to notice." The kataskeuē for the protasis is, "for what they dare to do with their loved ones is not so trivial that it can go unnoticed." Then comes the apodosis: "For your part, it is right for you to take thought for your good name and to remove the tribute from these wretched folk and no longer to be so importunate." This, then, is how you state your axiosis if you want to do it in the political style. But if you want, add the reason for the axiosis, that is, the action itself, what I am calling the plain form of the sequence of events. If we want to state the sequence of events in a venturous and more sententious style, the basis will be panegyrical if we say, "Because of this the islands have the misfortune of being forced to become childless!"

[52] This is the figure *kata arsin kai thesin* ("by negation and affirmation"), used for abundance as described in *On Ideas,* pp. 293–94 Rabe.

[53] Philostratus (*Lives of the Sophists* 2.12, p. 593 Kayser) quotes part of a declamation by Pollux on this theme.

## BOOK 2

*Book 2 discusses* diēgēsis, *the narration or statement of facts in a speech, giving special attention to what the author calls* prokatastasis, *the beginning, usually the first sentence, of the narration. Diegesis (literally "a leading through") is the word used for narration by both Plato (*Phaedrus *266e) and Aristotle (*Rhetoric *3.16), as well as most later Greek rhetoricians until the third century* C.E., *when it began to be replaced by* katastasis *(a "setting down, or statement"). Although Apsines usually refers to narration as diegesis, he uses katastasis as well (*Art of Rhetoric *2.1 and repeatedly in ch. 3); in 3.3 he makes a distinction between* aphēgēsis, *a "recounting" of incidents, and katastasis, which "lays the basis for proof from personal intent of the speaker" and also "rebuts objections arising from the assumptions of the hearers."*[54] *Some writers (e.g., Theon, vol. 2, p. 60 Spengel) use* diēgēma *instead of diegesis, a more general word for narrative of any kind. Aristotle (*Rhetoric *3.13.5) attributed to the school of Theodorus of Byzantium a division into prodiegesis (preliminary narration), diegesis, and epidiegesis (supplementary narration), also mentioned in* Anonymous Seguerianus *(§57). According to the latter (§112, probably derived from a lost work by Alexander Numeniou, a rhetorician of the mid-second century), "Diegesis differs from katastasis in that in katastasis we set out what the judges know, while in diegesis we describe what they do not know." This distinction did not prevail but suggests a stage by which katastasis began to refer to narration.*

*A prokatastasis as understood in* On Invention *is the opening statement of the narration, providing some background for it, such as in looking back to past actions that help to explain present circumstances. Heath ("Apsines," 103–5) explains the initial emphasis on this preparation for the narration and relative neglect of actual narration until the end of the book on the ground that there seemed more scope for artistic invention in introducing a narration than in composing the narration itself. The emphasis is, however, consistent with the author's interest in showing elementary students of declamation how to get started with each part of a speech, and in declamation the narration is almost identical to the problem as assigned by the teacher. It*

[54] See the discussion by Heath, *On Issues*, 83.

*is something the student can develop but not, or not usually, something he is expected to invent.*

*The only other extended discussion of prokatastasis is found in the second chapter of Apsines'* Art of Rhetoric. *Early in that discussion Apsines says, "We create a prokatastasis in questions for declamation either by a scrutiny of intention—and this is threefold, for we scrutinize either our own intention or that of the hearers or that of the opponents—or from a removal of an objection or from a preliminary statement of the question at issue or from a preliminary prejudicial attack or preliminary division or a contrast of circumstances of the past and those now existing; or else the first heading is introduced as a statement of the case—and this is done in detail and with narrative—or we introduce an epigrammatic thought from the heading, separating it out as a statement of the case (katastasis)—many such are found in speeches of Aristeides—or we bring in a trope, or start from a promise" (2.1). Each of these types is then discussed and illustrated in the course of the chapter. Heath argues ("Apsines," 103–5) that Apsines' chapter may be a further development of what is found in* On Invention. *More likely it is a development, adding other sources, of a prokatastasis, from what was found in an earlier work (perhaps by Apsines' teacher Basilicus?) from which the discussion in* On Invention *is borrowed with little change. Other occurrences of prokatastasis are found in* Anonymous Seguerianus *(§244), derived from Harpocration (second century), where it is applied to the prooemion, and with the meaning "introductory statement of the narration" in Rufus (§16); Troilus (*PS *52,11 Rabe); Syrianus (2:64–65 and 127); and Maximus Planudes (Walz 5:384). See also Martin, 54, 78, 219, 223; Lausberg, §§279 and 339.*

*In chapters 2–6 the author considers the invention of the prokatastasis in five categories of declamation. Patillon (*L'Art rhétorique, *87–89) plausibly suggests that the author regarded all declamation themes as capable of being assigned to one of these five types.*

*As in the account of the prooemium, the author, or possibly the editor that created our text, omits traditional teaching about narrations, such as dividing them into types and showing how to secure the virtues of clarity, brevity, and persuasiveness. Quintilian (4.2.32) says that the doctrine of the virtues of narration originated with the school of Isocrates. Cf.* Anonymous Seguerianus *§§63–104; Lausberg, §§293–95; and the introduction to 2.7 below.*

# Β

## *Περὶ καταστάσεως ἤγουν διηγήσεως.*

*Διήγησίς ἐστι παντὸς μὲν προβλήματος αὐτὸ τὸ πρᾶγμα, ἐξ οὗ*
[109] *συνέστηκεν ἡ ὑπόθεσις. καὶ διὰ τοῦτο | διήγησιν μὲν εὑρεῖν οὐ δύσκολον· φαίνεται γὰρ τοῦ πράγματος πλατυνομένου τοῖς τρόποις, οἷς ἐκθήσομαι· τὴν δὲ προκατάστασιν τῆς διηγήσεως τὴν καὶ προδιήγησιν καλουμένην ἄξιον ἐξετάσαι, πόθεν ληφθήσεται καὶ ἀπὸ τρόπων ὁπόσων, καὶ εἰ ὁμοίως ἐν πᾶσι προβλήμασιν ἡ αὐτὴ ἢ καθ᾽ ἕκαστον εἶδος ζητήματος ἰδία τις εὕρεσις προκαταστάσεως γίνεται.*

*Ὡς ἐν κεφαλαίῳ μὲν οὖν εἰπεῖν πάσης διηγήσεως ἐν παντὶ προβλήματι ζητητέον τὰ πρεσβύτερα μέν, χρήσιμα δὲ τῇ ὑποκειμένῃ ἀξιώσει ἢ κρίσει, κἀκεῖθεν λαμβάνειν ἄξιον, καὶ προκαταστήσαντας ὡς προσήκει τὴν προδιήγησιν οὕτως εἰς αὐτὴν χωρῆσαι τὴν ἐμφαινομένην ἐν αὐτῷ τῷ προβλήματι διήγησιν· ἄτεχνον γὰρ καὶ ἰδιωτικὸν τὸ τῆς διηγήσεως αὐτόθεν ἄρχεσθαι, ὅθεν καὶ τὸ πρόβλημα λέγει. ἀλλ᾽ ἐπεὶ τῶν προβλημάτων εἴδη ποικίλα καὶ τῶν πραγμάτων αἱ ζητήσεις διάφοροι, ποικίλας καὶ τὰς εὑρέσεις παραδώσομεν, ὥστε τεθείσης ὑποθέσεως αὐτίκα εἰδέναι, ἐφ᾽ ὃ τρεπτέον ἐστὶν εἰς εὕρεσιν τῆς προκαταστάσεως τεχνικόν.*

## *Περὶ μετοικιῶν καὶ τῆς ἐν τούτοις εὑρέσεως.*

*Οἱ περὶ μετοικίας βουλευόμενοι δυοῖν τούτοιν ἕνεκεν θατέρου τὴν*
[110] *βουλὴν ἔχουσιν· ἢ γὰρ προσόντος | ἀγαθοῦ καὶ ἀφανισθέντος λύπῃ τῶν ἀπολωλότων βουλεύονται μετοικεῖν, οἷον Λυδοὶ μὴ ῥέοντος τοῦ Πακτωλοῦ τὸν χρυσὸν ἢ Αἰγύπτιοι μὴ ὑπερβαίνοντος τοῦ Νείλου καὶ ἄρδοντος*

**1** τόμος β′ περὶ εὑρέσεως **PV** || **1-2** τόμος β′ περὶ διηγήσεως Mr || **2** προκαταστάσεως Ac Ba | ἤγουν διηγήσεως om. **V** || **3** μέν ἐστι παντὸς Ba || **4** μὲν om. **V** || **5** p. 50, 4 || **6** καὶ om. m. 1 Pa || **9** καὶ οὐχ ἡ αὐτὴ add. ante γίνεται Ac; Dox.; τινὲς ἐσφαλμένον ἐνόμισαν εἶναι τὸ παρὸν χωρίον· καὶ δεῖ (sic Vδ) μᾶλλον εἶπον οὕτως αὐτὸ ἀναγιγνώσκεσθαι «καὶ εἴ τις εὕρεσις προκαταστάσεως καὶ οὐχὶ αὐτὴ γίνεται» ἢ οὕτως «καὶ εἰ ὁμοίως ἐν πᾶσι προβλήμασιν ἡ αὐτὴ εὕρεσις προκαταστάσεως γίνεται ἢ καθ᾽ ἕκαστον εἶδος ζητήματος ἰδία τις» || **12-13** προσῆκε **V** || **13** διήγησιν Pa || **14** γὰρ om. m. 1 Ac || **15** λέγειν Vc Ac; λέγεται Va || **16** πρ⌊οβλημά m. po.⌉των Pc || **17** τῆς ὑποθέσεως Vc || **19** τεχνικήν Vc; schol. **P**: εφ᾽ ὃ τεχνικὸν τρεπτέον ἐστί, δηλονότι θεώρημα κτλ. || **20** τούτοις, i.e. τοῖς προβλήμασι || **21** μετοικεσίας Mr || **23** οἷον suppl. m. 2 Vc

## CHAPTER 1: ON KATASTASIS OR DIEGESIS[55]

The diegesis of every problem is (*a statement of*) the action itself from which the hypothesis has been constructed. As a result, | [109]
it is not difficult to invent a diegesis, for it becomes evident when the action is developed in the ways I shall set out, but (*first*) it is worthwhile to examine the prokatastasis of the diegesis, which is also called the prodiegesis, asking from what it will be derived and in how many different ways, and if it is the same in all problems or if there is a specific invention of prokatastasis in each species of question.

Now to speak in general of every diegesis in every problem, one should seek out prior events useful for the evaluation or judgment to be made in the case, and they are the right things to start from, and after first setting out an appropriate prodiegesis, then to move on to the actual diegesis itself that appears in the particular problem; for it is inartistic and simplistic for the diegesis to begin directly with what is stated in the problem.[56] But since there are various kinds of problems, and investigations of subjects are different, we shall describe varied forms of invention, so that when a hypothesis is proposed it will be immediately[57] evident where one should turn for artistic invention of the prokatastasis.

## CHAPTER 2: ON EMIGRATIONS AND INVENTION IN DECLAMATION ABOUT THEM

People debating about emigrating take council for one or the other
of the two following reasons: either | because of the disappear- [110]
ance of some existing good, in distress at what has been lost they debate emigrating—for example, the Lydians because the Pactolus River ceases to carry gold, or the Egyptians because the Nile is not flooding and watering the earth—or some unexpected evil

[55] The chapter heading is not part of the original text and was added by a scribe in late antiquity or the Byzantine period when katastasis was the common term for narration. The author of *On Invention* does not use *katastasis* to mean narration.

[56] I.e., the problem as set forth by the teacher.

[57] I.e., in extempore debate; cf. Patillon, *ANRW*, 2085.

*τὴν γῆν· ἢ προσεπιγενομένου κακοῦ ἀπροσδοκήτου, οἷον σείεται Σικελία συνεχῶς καὶ βουλεύονται μετοικεῖν, ἢ πάλιν ῥεῖ ἐπὶ τὴν Κατάνην ἀπὸ τῆς Αἴτνης τὸ πῦρ καὶ βουλεύονται μετοικεῖν.*

*Εἰ μὲν οὖν ἀγαθοῦ τινος ἐπιλείποντος βουλευόμεθα μετοικεῖν, τὴν προκατάστασιν λέξομεν λαβόντες ἐντεῦθεν «οἱ πρόγονοι τὰς πόλεις ἔκτισαν ἢ τὴν πόλιν ἐνταῦθα οὐδενὶ τῶν ἄλλων ἐπαρθέντες ἢ τούτῳ τῷ ἀγαθῷ. μέχρι μὲν οὖν πάγιον ἦν καὶ βέβαιον, εἰκότως ἐμένομεν· καὶ γὰρ ἀπελαύομεν τῶν ἀγαθῶν· ἐπεὶ δὲ οἴχεται, μετοικισθῆναι δίκαιον». εἰ δὲ κακὸν ἐπιγένηταί τι, λέξομεν τὴν προκατάστασιν ὡς «οἱ πρόγονοι μηδεμιᾶς ἐλπίδος ἐμφαινομένης τοιούτου κακοῦ ἔκτισαν ἐνταυθοῖ τὴν πόλιν· εἰ γὰρ ᾔδεσαν, οὐκ ἂν ἔκτισαν». ὁ δὲ ἀξιῶν μένειν ὁμοίως καὶ αὐτὸς ἀναβήσεται ἐπὶ τὰς κτίσεις τῶν προγόνων, ὧν πρεσβύτερον οὐδέν, λέξει δὲ ἀγαθοῦ μέν τινος λείποντος ὡς «οὐ διὰ τοῦτο ἔκτισαν ἐνταυθοῖ τὴν πόλιν οἱ πρόγονοι οὐδὲ τούτῳ μόνῳ ἐπαρθέντες, ἀλλὰ καὶ ἄλλοις πολλοῖς, ὧν προσόντων οὐ δεῖ τὴν ἀπουσίαν τοῦ ἑνὸς ὀδύ-*
[111] *ρεσθαι». ἐὰν δὲ κακοῦ ἐπιγενομένου, λέξει ὅτι «οὐχ ὡς ἀπαθῆ καὶ | ἀθάνατον ἔκτισαν οἱ πρόγονοι τὴν πόλιν, ἀλλ᾽ ὡς ὑποκειμένην καὶ αὐτὴν πάθεσιν ἀνθρωπίνοις».*

*Θῶμεν δὲ καὶ ἐπὶ παραδείγματος· βουλεύονται Αἰγύπτιοι μετοικεῖν τοῦ Νείλου μὴ ἐπαναβαίνοντος ἔτι· ἐρεῖς οὕτω «δοκῶ τοι καὶ τοὺς προγόνους οὐδενὶ τῶν ἄλλων ἐπαρθέντας τὴν Αἴγυπτον οἰκῆσαι, ἐπεὶ μήτε ὀρῶν ἀσφάλεια μήτε ποταμῶν ἄλλων κάλλος ἐν Αἰγύπτῳ φαίνεται μήτε πρὸς φυτείαν ἐπιτήδειος οὔτε γάρ εἰσιν ἐλαῖαι παρ᾽ ἡμῖν οὔτε ἄμπελοι, τῇ δὲ τοῦ ποταμοῦ χαίροντας φορᾷ καὶ τῇ παραδόξῳ γεωργίᾳ». ὁ δὲ ἀξιῶν μένειν ἐρεῖ ὡς «οὐ διὰ τὸν ποταμὸν μόνον οἱ πρόγονοι τὸν οἰκισμὸν ἐποιήσαντο τῆς Αἰγύπτου, ἀλλὰ πολλὰ αὐτῆς καὶ ἄλλα θαυμάσαντες, τὴν κρᾶσιν τὴν τῶν ἀέρων, τὸ τῶν πεδίων εὐήλατον, τὸ εἰς τὰ ἄλλα τῆς γῆς εὔφορον, τὴν τῆς θαλάσσης γειτνίασιν καὶ τὴν τοῦ ποταμοῦ πρὸς τὰ ἄλλα χρείαν, καὶ οὐ διὰ τὴν ἀρδείαν μόνον, ἣν καὶ αὐτὴν*

**1** προσεπιγινομένου Pc **V** | ἀδοκήτου, γρ ἀπροσδοκή^τ^, **P**; ἀπροσδοκήτως Ac || **2** cf. Thuc. 3, 116 | cf. p. 228, 14 Sp.; Aps. I 2 p. 255, 7 Sp.-H. || **4** γρ᾽ ἐπιλιπόντος **P** || **5-6** οἱ πρόγονοι τὴν πόλιν ἔκτισαν ἐνταῦθα? || **9** ἐπιγίνεταί Vc Ac || **10** ἐκφαινομένης Ac || **12** εἰς Vc Ac | τῶν προγόνων om. **V** || **13** ἐπιλιπόντος Ac Ba | οὐ om. Pc || **16** ἐπιγινομένου Vc Ac | schol. **P**: λείπει τὸ δημηγορῆ καὶ προσεπακουστέον || **19** οἱ αἰγύπτιοι Pa Ac Ba || **20** ἐρεῖ οὕτως **V** | τι Pa; μοι Sc (cf. p. 38, 4) || **21** εἰς τὴν αἴγυπτον κτίσαι Vc, (om. εἰς) Ba || **22** mg. m. 1 ἄλλον Pa, γρ᾽ καὶ ἄλλο Pc || **23** ἐπιτήδειον Vc, (ut vid.) m. 1 Ba || **24** χαίροντας Sc.; χαίροντες Pv || **25** νοτισμὸν? cf. l. 17 || **26** καὶ ἄλλα om. **V** || **27** τὴν om. **V** || **29** alt. καὶ — | μόνον om. Pc

has come upon them; for example, Sicily continually experiences earthquakes and the inhabitants consider emigrating, or fire flows down on Catania from Etna and the inhabitants consider emigrating.[58]

Now if we are debating about emigrating because of the loss of something good, we shall speak our prokatastasis by starting from the following: "Our ancestors established cities—or this city—here, moved by nothing other than this resource;[59] for as long as it was steady and secure, we rightly stayed here, for we were enjoying the benefits. But since it is gone, it is right to emigrate." If, on the other hand, something bad has befallen them, we shall state our prokatastasis thus: "Our ancestors founded the city here at a time when no expectation of any evil such as this was manifested, for if they had known it, they would not have founded the city." Someone who, nevertheless, thinks it right to remain will also reach back to the foundation by the ancestors, than which nothing is more venerable, and he will say that if some good thing is gone, "It was not for this that our ancestors founded the city here, nor were they moved by this alone but by many other reasons. Since these still exist, there is no need to be distressed at the loss of one thing." If some evil has come upon them, he will say,
| "Our ancestors did not found this city to be unaffected by suf- [111]
fering and immortal, but knowing that it too would be subject to human sufferings."

Let us provide an example. The Egyptians are debating about emigrating since the Nile is no longer rising. (*In favor of migrating*) you will speak thus: "I really think that our ancestors were moved by no other reason when they settled Egypt (*than the benefits of the river*), since neither the protection of mountains nor the beauty of other rivers is to be found in Egypt nor land suitable for plantations—there are neither olives nor vines in our country—but they were pleased by the produce of the river and by the incomparable conditions for agriculture here." He who thinks they should remain will say, "Our ancestors did not make the settlement of Egypt solely because of the river but because they admired many other things about the country: the temperate climate, the open plains, the easy access to other parts of the earth,

58 Cf. Apsines 3.15. The theme was drawn from Thucydides 3.116.

59 I.e., the benefit that has now been lost.

*ἔχειν ἔστιν ἀνθρώποις γε οὖσι καὶ παρὰ τοῦ θεοῦ· οὐ γὰρ ἔξω που τῶν ὅρων οὐρανοῦ τὰς πόλεις ὑπετίθεσαν». Καὶ πάλιν· ῥεῖ τὸ πῦρ ἐπὶ τὴν Κατάνην ἀπὸ τῆς Αἴτνης καὶ βουλεύονται μετοικεῖν· ὁ μὲν ἀξιῶν μετοικεῖν ἐρεῖ τὸν τρόπον τοῦτον «οὐδὲ γὰρ τοὺς προγόνους μοι δοκῶ κτίσαι τὴν Κατάνην ὑπὸ τὴν Αἴτνην φέροντας, εἰ τοιαύτας ἔσεσθαι συμφορὰς προσεδόκησαν, ἀλλὰ νομίζοντας ἐν ὁρίοις στήσεσθαι τὸ πῦρ. μέχρι μὲν* [112] *οὖν | ἐφύλαττε τοὺς ὅρους, καὶ ἡμεῖς ἐμένομεν· ἐπεὶ δὲ ὑπερβαίνει καὶ κατατρέχει τὴν πόλιν, μετοικιζώμεθα». ὁ δὲ ἀξιῶν μένειν οὕτως «οὐδὲ γὰρ τοὺς προγόνους τοὺς κτίσαντας τὴν Κατάνην ἐνταῦθα ἔλαθε πλησίον οὖσα ἡ Αἴτνη, καὶ ὡς πυρὸς ἔχει ῥύακας, καὶ ὡς φύσις αὕτη πυρὸς ὑπερβαίνειν τε τοὺς ὅρους, ἐν οἷς ἂν ἑστήκῃ, καὶ ῥεῖν· ἀλλ' οὐχ ὡς ἀθάνατον οὐδ' ὡς ἀπαθῆ κακῶν ἐσομένην καὶ ἀπείρατον πυρὸς ἔκτιζον τὴν Κατάνην· πολλοῖς γάρτοι καὶ μὴ Κατάνην οἰκοῦσιν ἠνώχλησε πῦρ τοῖς μὲν αὐτόματον, τοῖς δὲ ἐξ ἐπιβουλῆς, τοῖς δὲ καὶ ἐξ οὐρανοῦ».*

## *Περὶ νόμων εἰσφορᾶς.*

*Αἱ δὲ τῶν νόμων εἰσφοραὶ μετὰ περιστάσεως καὶ αἱ λύσεις τῶν νόμων μετὰ περιστάσεως προδιηγήσεις ἕξουσι τοιαύτας καὶ λαμβανομένας οὕτως· ἐὰν μὲν λύωμεν τὸν νόμον, λέγοντες ὅτι «τοῦτον ἐχρῆν μηδὲ γεγράφθαι τὸν νόμον τὴν ἀρχήν»· οὐδὲ γάρ ἐστι τούτου τι πρεσβύτερον οὐδὲ τῇ ἀξιώσει μᾶλλον ἁρμόδιον τοῦ φάσκειν λελύσθαι τὸν νόμον τοῦ μηδὲ τὴν ἀρχὴν αὐτὸν γεγράφθαι. κατασκευασθήσεται δὲ*

**1** ἐν ἀνοις Pc || **2** ὑπε⌊I—II⌉⌊τ⌉ίθεσαν Vc || **3** ἀπὸ τῆς αἴτνης om. Vc Ac || **6** ὅροις Pc || **7** οὖν om. Pc || **8** μετοικιζόμεθα Ac, (ώ over ό) Vc, (ό over ώ) Pc || **9** alt. τοὺς om. Vc | τὴν om. **V** || **10** cf. Thuc. 3, 116 | φύσις πυρὸς ἐστὶν αὕτη (mg. σις αὕτη πυρὸς, m. 2 ?) Vc || **11** ἑστήκει **P** Ac, (ει in ras.) Vc | οὐκ, om. ὡς, **V** || **13** τὸ πῦρ Vc || **14** καὶ om. Vc Ba || **15** add. καὶ θέσεως ἢ διαθέσεως Pa, (er.) Pc ; add. καὶ θέσεως ἢ διαλύσεως Va ; add. (sic) περὶ νόμων θέσεως ἢ διαθέσεως Ac || **16-17** αἱ ante μετὰ m. po. supr. Ac || **17-18** ἃς λαμβάνομεν οὕτως ? || **19** τὸν νόμον post 16 ἐχρῆν Ac | τι τούτου Pc || **20** τὸ (οῦ m. po.) Pa ; τ⌊ῶ m. 2⌉ Pc | δεῖν ante λελύσθαι add. Pe, εἰς τὸ add. mg. m. po. Pa || **21** τοῦ (ω over οῦ), sed ω er., Pa ; τὸ Vc Ac ; ἢ τὸ Ba | δεῖν γεγράφθαι Pe

the proximity of the sea, and the utility of the river for other things and not only for irrigation, which is one of the things human beings can have from God; for surely they did not establish their cities beyond the limits of heaven." And again: Fire is flowing on Catania from Mount Etna and the inhabitants debate emigrating. One who favors emigration will speak in this way: "I do not think our ancestors would have established Catania, putting it under Etna, if they had expected there would be such disasters, but they thought the fire would be stopped within its boundaries. Now so long | as it kept to the mountains we were remaining here. But [112] since it overflows and runs down on the city, let us emigrate." One thinking it best to remain will say, "Our ancestors who established Catania here did not fail to see that Etna was nearby and that it has fiery eruptions and that it is natural for fire to overflow the boundaries in which it has been held and to flow downward. But they did not found Catania to be immortal and free from suffering and untouched by fire, for fire has troubled many even though they do not inhabit Catania, some of its own accord, some by intrigue, some from heaven."[60]

## CHAPTER 3: ON PROPOSALS ABOUT LAWS

Proposals for (*new*) laws, with an account of the circumstance (prompting need for them), and proposals to repeal (*old*) laws, with an account of the circumstance, will have prodiegeses of the following sort and be treated as follows.[61] If we are arguing to repeal the law, we say that "this law should never have been written in the first place"—for there is nothing more fundamental than this nor more in harmony with our recommendation to repeal the law than (*to say*) that it <ought> not have been written

[60] I.e., from spontaneous or unknown combustion, from foreign or domestic attack, or from lightning strikes.

[61] Cf. the progymnasmatic exercise on proposals for laws as described in the handbooks of Theon, Pseudo-Hermogenes, Aphthonius, and Nicolaus; these exercises do not provide for identification of specific circumstances as do declamation problems. The word here translated "repeal" is in Greek *lysis* (noun) or *lysein* (verb), the regular terms used by rhetoricians for "refutation" or "refute." Refutation was regarded as an easier exercise than proof and thus taught first. Similarly, the author here treats repeal of an old law before introduction of a new one as perhaps easier to argue.

[113] *προχωρῶν ὁ λό|γος ἐκ τῶν συμβάντων «οὐ γὰρ ἂν τοιῶνδε καὶ τοιῶνδε ἐπειράθημεν κακῶν· ἐπεὶ δὲ ἐτέθη καὶ ἐπάθομεν τὰ καὶ τά, λῦσαι δίκαιον». δῆλον γάρ, ὡς λύσει τις νόμον ἐν προβλήματι κακοῦ τινος ἀπαντήσαντος ἐξ αὐτοῦ τοῦ νόμου, καὶ ὡς ἂν μηκέτι τοῦτο γίγνοιτο σκοπούντων τινῶν· οἷον Λακεδαιμόνιοι μετὰ τὰ ἐν Μαραθῶνι βουλεύονται λύειν τὸν τῆς πανσελήνου νόμον, οἷον «ἔδει μηδὲ κεῖσθαι τοῦτον τὴν ἀρχὴν ἐν Λακεδαίμονι τὸν νόμον· οὐ γὰρ ἂν δόξης ἀπεστερήμεθα τοιαύτης καὶ τροπαίων καὶ κατορθωμάτων καὶ τῶν συμβεβηκότων». δεῖ γάρ, ὡς ἔφην, περίστασιν ἔχειν τὰς λύσεις τῶν νόμων ἢ τὰς εἰσφοράς· αἱ γὰρ ἄνευ αἰτίας καὶ περιστάσεως εἰσφοραὶ νόμων ἢ λύσεις γυμνάσματά ἐστι μόνα, ὅθεν οὐδὲ διηγήσεις ἔχει.*

*Ἐὰν δὲ γράφωμεν νόμον καὶ εἰσφέρωμεν, ἡ προκατάστασις τῆς διηγήσεως γενήσεται ἡ αὐτή, οἷον «τοῦτον ἐχρῆν πάλαι κεῖσθαι τὸν νόμον, ἐξ ἀρχῆς. οὐ γὰρ ἂν τούτου κειμένου ταῦτα ἡμᾶς συνέβη παθεῖν, ἃ πεπόνθαμεν μὴ κειμένου τοῦ νόμου»· οἷον Ἀλκιβιάδης μετὰ τὰ κατὰ Κύζικον εἰσφέρει νόμον μηδένα στρατηγὸν ἀπὸ στρατοπέδου ἀνακαλεῖσθαι· φήσει γὰρ «τὸν νόμον τοῦτον ἐχρῆν πάλαι γεγράφθαι καὶ γεγενῆσθαι κύριον· οὐ γὰρ ἂν ἔβλαψε μὴ ἀνακαλουμένους ὑμᾶς Ἀλκιβιάδην ἐκ Σικελίας». ἢ ὡς ἐκεῖνο τὸ πρόβλημα· τοὺς μοιχοὺς χρήματα ἐκτιν-*
[114] *νύναι, πολλοὶ μοιχεύουσι | καὶ καταβάλλουσι χρήματα, καὶ γράφει τις κτείνειν τοὺς μοιχούς· ἐνταῦθα γὰρ καὶ εἰσφορὰ νόμου καὶ λύσις ἐστί· καὶ προκατάστασις γενήσεται τῆς διηγήσεως, ὅτι μήτε ἐκεῖνον ἐχρῆν γεγράφθαι τὸν νόμον τὸν περὶ τῶν χρημάτων καὶ ὅτι τοῦτον ἐχρῆν*

3 γὰρ, supr. δὲ, **P**; δὲ Ac || 4 μη⌊κέτι m. 2 supr.⌋ Vc || 5 ἡμῶν Ac || 6 μὴ, om. δὲ, Pc || 7 τὴν ἀρχὴν om. **V** || 8 ⌊καὶ τῶν συμβεβηκότων⌋ ? (fort. v.l. aberravit, quae ad l. 1 ascripta erat) || 11 cf. Prog. p. 26, 14 Rabe | εἰσίν (om. μόνα) Dox. II 554, 10 W. || 12 ἡ κατάστασις Vc || 12-13 γενήσεται τῆς διηγήσεως **V** || 13 αὕτη m. 2 ex ἡ αὐτή Pc | οἷον om. **V** || 13-14 τὸν νόμον κεῖσθαι Pc || 17 φησὶ Ac || 18 ἔβλαψε ex ἔβλεψα Pa | μὴ om. m. 1 Ac || 20 καταβάλλονται (supr. ουσι) Vc || 21 γὰρ om. Vc Ac || 22-42.1 sic Pa, (ἀρχῆθεν om.) Pc, (γράφεσθαι τὸν περὶ τῶν χρημάτων νόμων; 5 ὅτι om.) Ba; ὅτι μήτ' ἐκεῖνον ἐχρῆν γεγράφθαι τὸν νόμον ἀρχῆθεν . . . μοιχούς· καὶ ὅτι τοῦτον ἐχρῆν γεγράφθαι τὸν περὶ τῶν χρημάτων νόμον m. 1 Vc; ὅτι μήτε ἐκεῖνον ἐχρῆν γεγράφθαι τὸν περὶ τῶν χρημάτων νόμον ἀρχῆθεν τὸν ἀξ. κτ. τ. μοιχούς m. 1 Ac

in the first place.[62] Continuing on, the argument will be supported | from the results: "For we would not have experienced [113] such and such evils. But since the law was imposed and we suffered this and that, it is right to repeal it." Clearly one will attack a law in a problem on the ground that some evil has arisen because of the law and that some people are seeking that this may no longer be the case. For example, the Lacedaimonians, after the events at Marathon, are debating whether to repeal the law about the full moon,[63] saying, for example, "This law should not have been laid down in Lacedaimon in the first place, for we would not have been deprived of great glory and trophies and victories and all that has resulted." As I said, speeches against and for laws should be related to some circumstance, for without a reason and a circumstance, proposals for or against laws are only exercises (*gymnasmata*) and thus do not have narrations.[64]

If we draft a law and introduce it, the prokatastasis of the diegesis will be similar; for example, "This law ought to have been laid down long ago, right from the beginning, for if it had been in effect, we would not have suffered the things we have suffered because the law was not in effect." For example, after the events at Cyzicus,[65] Alcibiades introduces a law that no general is to be recalled from an expedition. He will say, "This law ought to have been drafted and ratified long ago, for it would have prevented the harm to you of recalling Alcibiades from Sicily." Or consider this problem: (The law requires) adulterers to pay a fine; many men are committing adultery | and paying down their money, and some- [114] one drafts a law to put adulterers to death. Here there is both a proposal for a law and one to repeal a law, and the prokatastasis of the diegesis will be that that law about fines ought not to have been drafted and that this law authorizing the killing of adulterers ought to have been drawn up from the beginning.

[62] There seems to be a corruption in the Greek. Read *dein gegraphthai* with Pe; see above, *app. crit.* p. 38, 21.

[63] The law prohibited taking the field for war before the full moon; cf. Herodotus 6.106.

[64] Cf. the Hermogenic *Progymnasmata*, ch. 12, p. 26, 14–15 Rabe, which draws a similar distinction.

[65] Where Alcibiades had won a decisive battle over the Peloponnesian fleet in 410 B.C.E., thus recovering the prestige he lost in being recalled from Sicily. There is no evidence that such a law was considered.

*γεγράφθαι τὸν νόμον ἀρχῆθεν τὸν ἀξιοῦντα κτείνειν τοὺς μοιχούς.*

## ***Περὶ πολέμου καὶ εἰρήνης.***

*Ὁμοίως κἂν πολεμεῖν γράφωμέν τισιν ἢ καταλύειν πόλεμον, χρησόμεθα ταῖς προκαταστάσεσιν οὕτως· ἂν μὲν γράφωμεν πολεμεῖν τισιν, εἰς τὰ πρεσβύτερα τῶν ἐγκλημάτων ἀνατρέχοντες καὶ λέγοντες ὅτι «τούτοις πάλαι ἐχρῆν πολεμεῖν· ἐχθροὶ γὰρ καὶ πρὸ τούτων τῶν ἀδικημάτων ἄλλα εἰς ἡμᾶς πολλὰ εἰργασμένοι», εἶτα καταβαίνοντες εἰς τὰ νῦν γεγενημένα. τὰ μὲν γὰρ πρεσβύτερα τῶν ἀδικημάτων προκατάστασίς ἐστι τῆς διηγήσεως, ἃ δὲ νῦν διὰ τὸν πόλεμον γράφεις, ἡ διήγησις· οἷον ἔχρησεν ὁ θεὸς τῷ Κροίσῳ τοὺς ἀρίστους ἑλέσθαι τῶν Ἑλλήνων συμμάχους, εἵλετο Λακεδαιμονίους, καὶ συμβουλεύει τις Ἀθηναίοις Κύρῳ συμμαχεῖν «ἔδει Κροίσῳ καὶ πάλαι πολεμεῖν· ἐξ οὗ γὰρ τὴν ἀρχὴν διεδέξατο παρὰ Ἀλυάττου τοῦ πατρός, καὶ τοῖς Ἕλ-*
[115] *λη|σιν ἐπεβούλευε, καὶ τοῖς ἐν τῇ Ἀσίᾳ Δωριεῦσι καὶ Ἴωσι καὶ Αἰολεῦσι· πρὸ γὰρ τῆς Κροίσου ἀρχῆς πάντες Ἕλληνες ἦσαν ἐλεύθεροι», καὶ τοῦτο πλατυνόμενον προκατάστασις ἔσται καὶ προδιήγησις· εἶτα ἡ διήγησις «ἐπεὶ δὲ καὶ νῦν, χρήσαντος αὐτῷ τοῦ θεοῦ τοὺς ἀρίστους τῶν Ἑλλήνων ἑλέσθαι συμμάχους, εἵλετο Λακεδαιμονίους καὶ τὴν πόλιν ἡμῶν ὕβρισε, πολεμῶμεν αὐτῷ συμμαχοῦντες Κύρῳ». Καὶ πάλιν ἅρματι νικήσας Ἀλκιβιάδης Ὀλύμπια, ἐρομένων Ἠλείων ὅθεν εἴη, «τῆς ἀρίστης» ἔφη «πόλεως», ἐμαστίγωσαν αὐτόν, ἐπανελθὼν γράφει στρατεύεσθαι ἐπὶ τοὺς Ἠλείους· ἡ προκατάστασις τῆς διηγήσεως «ἐχρῆν Ἠλείοις πάλαι πολεμεῖν· ἐχθροὶ γὰρ ἡμῶν εἰσι καὶ βοηθοῦντες ἀεὶ Λακεδαιμονίοις καὶ Κορινθίοις, καὶ ναῦς διδόντες καὶ χρήματα εἰς τὸν καθ᾽*

2 om. Ac || 3 καὶ m. 1 Pa || 5 ἀνατρέχοντες ante 4 εἰς **V** || 6 τούτους Ac || 7 πολλὰ om. Pc || 9 ἐστι om. **V** | δια supr. (m. 1 ?) Pa || 10 cf. Herod. 1, 53 || 10-11 τῶν ἑλλήνων ἑλέσθαι Pc, cf. l. 18 || 11 καὶ om. Pc || 12 οἷον ἔδει Vc || 13 ἀλυάττου[εω] **P**, ἀλυάττεω **V** (-άτεω Ac); ex Herod. 1, 6, de eodem exemplo cf. Dion. Hal. De c. v. 4 II 1 p. 18 Us. | τοῦ τούτου πατρὸς Ac || 14 ἐπεβούλευσε **V** || 15 γὰρ **PV**; δὲ Herod. | ἕλληνες ἦσαν Ac Ba, Herod.; ἦσαν ἕλληνες **P** Vc || 16 ἐστι[αι] Pc | καὶ ⌊προ m. 2 supr.⌋ διήγησις Vc || 19 ὑμῶν m. 1 Pa || 21 ἔφη[τῶν] πόλεως[ων] Pa | καὶ ἐπανελθὼν Vc | γράφει ἐπανελθὼν Pc || 23 ἡμῶν om. Ba

## CHAPTER 4: ON WAR AND PEACE

Similarly, if we introduce a motion to go to war with someone or to end a war, we shall use prokatastases as follows. If we are introducing a motion to go to war with someone, we shall run over earlier complaints and say that "we ought to have gone to war with these people long ago, for they are enemies and have committed many other wrongs against us before these," then coming to what has now happened. The earlier wrongs provide a prokatastasis of the diegesis, and (*an account of*) the present wrongs, for which you propose the war,[66] constitutes the diegesis; for example, the god in an oracle told Croesus to choose the best of the Greeks as allies;[67] he chose the Lacedaimonians, and someone advises the Athenians to make an alliance with Cyrus: "We ought long ago to have made war on Croesus, for ever since he inherited power from his father Alyattes | he has been plotting against the Greeks and the Do- [115]
rians and Ionians and Aeolians in Asia, for before Croesus came to power all the Greeks were free." When this is extended it will provide a prokatastasis and prodiegesis. Then the diegesis: "But since now, after the god told him to choose the best of the Greeks as allies, he chose the Lacedaimonians and insulted our city, let us join with Cyrus in making war on him." Or again, when Alcibiades won the chariot race at Olympia, the Eleans asked where he came from,[68] and he said, "From the best city." They flogged him, and he went home and introduces a motion to make an expedition against the Eleans. The prokatastasis of the diegesis: "We should long ago have gone to war with the Eleans, for they are our enemies, going to the aid of Lacedaimonians and Corinthians and giving ships and money for the war against us."[69] Then the die-

[66] Accepting Patillon's emendation of the text to read *ta de nun di' ha*.

[67] The declamation is developed from the report in Herodotus 1.53.

[68] So that the name of his city could be proclaimed: "Alcibiades, an Athenian." Alcibiades entered seven teams in the Olympic games, probably in 416 B.C.E., and won first, second, and third prize with them. See Thucydides 6.16; Isocrates 16.34; Plutarch, *Alcibiades* 11; David Gribble, *Alcibiades and Athens* (Oxford: Clarendon, 1999), 16. The story about his refusal to name his city and the resulting beating is a fabrication, probably by a teacher creating novel themes for declamation.

[69] Rabe here deletes the following: "Whence Thucydides said (1.27), 'They asked the Eleans for hulls and money.'" On the alliance of the Eleans and

*ἡμῶν πόλεμον». [ὅθεν καὶ Θουκυδίδης εἴρηκεν «Ἠλείους δὲ ναῦς ᾔτησαν κενὰς καὶ χρήματα».] εἶτα ἡ διήγησις «ἐπεὶ δὲ καὶ νῦν ἐνίκησα τὸν ἀγῶνα καὶ ἠρώτησαν ὅθεν εἴην, ἐγὼ δὲ τὰ βέλτιστα ἀπεκρινάμην, οἳ δὲ ἐμαστίγωσάν με τὴν πόλιν ὑβρίζοντες, στρατεύειν ἐπ' αὐτοὺς ἄξιον».*

*Ἐὰν δὲ καταλύωμεν πόλεμον, ἡ προκατάστασις γενήσεται τῆς* [116] *διηγήσεως ὅτι «μηδὲ τὴν ἀρχὴν ἐχρῆν κε|κινῆσθαι τοῦτον τὸν πόλεμον», καὶ προσχρησόμεθα ταῖς ἀπὸ τῆς ἱστορίας αἰτίαις, ἐὰν ἔχωμεν· οἷον σείεται ἐν τῷ πολέμῳ τῷ Πελοποννησιακῷ Δῆλος, καὶ γράφει τις καταλύειν τὸν πόλεμον ἐν τοῖς Ἕλλησι λέγων ὅτι «μηδὲ τὴν ἀρχὴν ἐχρῆν κεκινῆσθαι τοῦτον τὸν πόλεμον ἐν ἡμῖν συμμάχους γε ὄντας καὶ φίλους καὶ τοῖς βαρβάροις ἀεὶ μαχομένους πρότερον, ἀφ' οὗ καὶ ἐνδοξότεροι διατελοῦμεν ὄντες πολέμου», τοῦτο ἡ προκατάστασις· εἶτα ἡ διήγησις «ἐπεὶ δὲ καὶ νῦν Δῆλος σείεται χαλεπαίνοντος τοῦ θεοῦ ἐπὶ ταῖς ἡμετέραις διαφοραῖς, καταλύσωμεν τὸν πόλεμον». Ἐὰν δὲ μὴ βοηθώμεθα ἀπὸ τῆς ἱστορίας, ἡ προκατάστασις διαβολὴν ἕξει τοῦ πολέμου ὅτι «οὐκ ἐχρῆν οὐδὲ τὴν ἀρχὴν τὸν πόλεμον τοῦτον ἄρασθαι καταλιπόντας εἰρήνην· χαλεπὸν γὰρ πρᾶγμα πόλεμος καὶ δύσκολον» καὶ ὅσα ἔχει ἐν αὐτῷ κακά, «ἡ δὲ εἰρήνη καλόν» καὶ ὅσα ἔχει ἐν αὐτῇ καλά· οἷον πολεμούντων τινῶν ἐξέλιπεν ὁ ἥλιος, καὶ γράφει τις λελύσθαι τὸν πόλεμον· ἐνταῦθα γὰρ ὃν ὑπεθέμην τρόπον προδιηγούμενοι κακίσομεν τὸν πόλεμον καὶ τὴν εἰρήνην ἐπαινεσόμεθα, εἶτα χωρήσομεν εἰς τὴν διήγησιν, τὴν ἔκλειψιν διηγούμενοι τοῦ ἡλίου καὶ ὅτι διὰ τοῦτο προσήκει καταλῦσαι τὸν πόλεμον.*

1-2 delevit Rabe (ut p. 90, 2–4) || 1 ὅθεν **P**; οὕτω **V**, v.l. **P**; ἔνθεν v.l. Dox. | Thuc. 1, 27 || 2 κενὰς (αι supra) Pa; [ε m. po.] Pc Vc Ba | ἡ om. (καὶ supr.?) Vc || 3 ἂν εἴην Pa || 4 στρατεύεσθαι (ειν supra) Vc; cf. p. 42, 20–21 || 5 ἡ om. Ac; [I] Vc || 5-6 τῆς διηγήσεως supr. (m. 1?) Ac || 7 χρησόμεθα Pc || 7-8 cf. Thuc. 2, 8 || 9 τὸν om. Ac || 10-11 συμμάχοις γε οὖσι καὶ φίλοις . . . μαχομένοις Ba, m. po. Pc Vc || 11-12 ἔνδοξοι Vcδ Ac; γρ καὶ ἔνδοξοι διατελοῦμεν ὄντες· τὸ (sic) πολέμου δηλονότι μὴ προκειμένου Pc, (προ[I]κειμένου) Pa; γρ' καὶ ἐν δόξῃ (ο) διατελοῦμεν ὄντες πολέμου Dox. || 12 ὄντες Pa; ὄντ[ες m. po.] Pc | πολέμου **P**; [circ. VII] Vc; om. Ac Ba Vδ || 14 καταλύσομεν Ac || 15 τῆς om. Ba || 16 ἄρασθαι v.l. **P**; αἱρεῖσθαι **PV** || 17 μὲν γὰρ **V** | δύσκολος Pc || 19 ὁ ἥλιος ἐξέλιπεν Ac Ba; cf. 12, 21 || 20 διηγούμενοι Pa | κακίσ[ο]μεν Vc || 21 ἐπαινεσ[ό]μεθα Vc | χωρήσ[ο]μεν Vc

gesis, "But now when I won the contest and they asked where I came from, and when for my part I gave the best answer, for which they flogged me, insulting the city, it is right to make an expedition against them."

If, on the other hand, we are for putting an end to a war, the prokatastasis of the diegesis will be that "not even in the first place should we | have set this war in motion," and we shall use [116]
historical reasons if we have any; for example, Delos suffers an earthquake during the Peloponnesian war,[70] and someone[71] introduces a motion to end the war among the Greeks, saying that "we ought not to have set this war in motion in the first place, in that we have been allies and friends among ourselves and have previously always fought barbarians, as a result of which war we are even more glorious." This is the prokatastasis; then the diegesis: "Since now Delos has been shaken by an earthquake, the god being angry at our differences, let us put an end to the war." But if we have no support from history, the prokatastasis will contain an attack on the war, to the effect that "we should not have raised this war in the first place, abandoning peace, for war is a difficult thing and unpleasant," listing the evils in it, "and peace is good," listing the good things in it. For example, when some cities were at war there was an eclipse of the sun,[72] and someone introduces a motion to end the war. Here, giving a prodiegesis in the way I laid down, we shall castigate war and praise peace; then we shall go on to the diegesis, describing the eclipse of the sun and saying that it is, for that reason, appropriate to put a stop to the war.

the Lacedaimonians, see Thucydides 5.31.

[70] In 431 B.C.E.; cf. Thucydides 2.8, who says it was the first earthquake there in memory.

[71] In schools of declamation the venue was often assumed to be Athens if none other was specified.

[72] Cf., e.g., Herodotus 1.74.

[117] ## | *Περὶ ἀσεβείας ἢ φόνου.*

*Ἐὰν δὲ ἀσεβείας κατηγορῶμέν τινος, πρὸ τοῦ κατηγορουμένου ἐγκλήματος τὰ πρεσβύτερα ζητοῦντες ἀδικήματα προδιηγησόμεθα, καὶ εἴ τι ἀσεβὲς φθάνοι ἄλλο προειργασμένος. κἂν μὲν ἱστορίαν ἔχωμεν, ἀπ᾽ ἐκείνης ζητήσομεν· ἂν δὲ ἰδιωτικὸν ᾖ τὸ πρόβλημα, κατὰ παράλειψιν διασύροντες φήσομεν «ἐγὼ τὸν μὲν ἄλλον βίον παραλιμπάνω λέγειν ὡς ἀσεβὴς καὶ ἐναγὴς καὶ κατὰ πάντα ἀποτρόπαιος, ὡς ἂν μὴ δοκοίην ἐνοχλεῖν ὑμᾶς μάτην, περὶ ὧν νῦν οὐ δικάζετε, περὶ τούτων ἀκούοντας, ἀλλὰ τὸ τελευταῖον αὐτῷ τολμηθὲν ἀσέβημα διέξειμι πρὸς ὑμᾶς»· οἷον μυούμενός τις ἐμάνη καὶ ἀσεβείας κρίνεται· ἡ αὐτὴ γὰρ προδιήγησις ἁρμόσει τῷ προβλήματι, εἶτα καταβησόμεθα εἰς τὴν διήγησιν «ἐπειδὴ γὰρ ὁ καιρὸς ἐνέστη τῶν μυστηρίων καὶ ἔδει μυεῖσθαι καθαροὺς εἰσιόντας εἰς τὸ ἀνάκτορον, τηνικάδε καὶ οὗτος οὔτε καθηράμενος ἀπὸ τῶν ἀσεβημάτων οὔτε ἁγνεύσας οὕτω» καὶ τὰ ἑξῆς. ἐν δὲ τοῖς ἀπὸ ἱστορίας οὕτω· κρίνονται Ἀθηναῖοι ἀσεβείας ἐπὶ Ποτιδαίᾳ· ὅτι Ἀθηναῖοι ἀρχῆθεν ἀσεβεῖς, καὶ ὅτι Λακεδαιμόνιοι διὰ τοῦτο πρὸς αὐτοὺς* [118] *τὸν πόλεμον ἐξενηνόχασι, καὶ ὅτι πρῶτον μὲν τὸ Κυλώνειον ἄγος οὐκ | ἠθέλησαν ἐλάσαι, εἶθ᾽ ὅτι τὰς τριακοντούτεις σπονδὰς ἔλυσαν, εἶθ᾽ ὅτι πόλεις ἀσεβῶς Ἑλληνίδας τὰς μὲν ἀνέστησαν τὰς δὲ ἐξώρισαν. εἶτα καταβησόμεθα εἰς τὴν διήγησιν «καὶ νῦν Ποτίδαιαν ἄποικον Κορινθίων οὖσαν» καὶ τὰ ἑξῆς.*

*Ἐὰν δὲ ἀπολογώμεθα, ἀνάπαλιν ποιήσομεν, εἴ τι πρεσβύτερον ἔχοιμεν τῆς κρίσεως βοηθοῦν ἡμῖν ἀπὸ ἱστορίας εὐσεβῶς πεπραγμένον, λέγοντες, εἰ δὲ ἰδιωτικὸν εἴη τὸ πρόβλημα, κατὰ παράλειψιν εἰσάγοντες, ὥσπερ ἐν ταῖς κατηγορίαις ἔφαμεν.*

1 καὶ (ἢ supr.) Vc | ἢ φόνου om. Ba || 3 ἀδικήματα Pa **V**; ἐγκλήματα Pc | προηγησόμεθα Pa || 4 φθάνοι .. προειργασμένος Ba, (φθάνει) Vδ, φθάνουσιν .. προειργασμένοι **P** Vc Ac || 5 εἴη Pc || 8 δοκιμάζετε Ac || 9 τολμηθὲν αὐτῶι Ac | ἀδίκημα Ba || 10 καὶ αὕτη (αὐτὴ Ac Ba) γὰρ ἡ **V** Vδ; Dox.: τονὲς παρέλκειν ἐνόμισαν τὸν «καὶ» ... ἔνιοι δὲ ... «καὶ τούτῳ γὰρ τῷ προβλήματι ἁρμόσει ἡ παροῦσα προδιήγησις» || 13 τηνικαῦτα δὲ καὶ Vc || 14 οὕτω om. Ba || 15 cf. Aps. I 2 p. 230, 4 Sp.-H. | οἱ ἀθηναῖοι Ba | ποτίδαιαν m. 1 Vc Ac || 15-16 ⌊ἀθηναῖοι m. po.⌉ Vc || 16 sq. Thuc. 1, 66 126 cet. || 17 τὸν supr. Vc; om. **P** Ac || 19 τὰς ἑλληνίδας τὰς Pc | ἀνέσκαψαν, γρ ἀνέστησαν, Pc || 22 εἴ τι, supr. ὅτι, Pa || 23 τῆς ἱστορίας Ac | εὐσεβὲς Vc Ac || 25 ὥσπερ καὶ Sc | p. 46, 6

## | CHAPTER 5: ON IMPIETY OR HOMICIDE [117]

If we are prosecuting someone for impiety (*asebeia*), before specifying the complaint as charged we shall provide a prodiegesis by looking for earlier wrongs and whether he previously committed some other impiety. If there is a historical record, we shall seek evidence from that; but if the problem concerns a private individual, we shall disparage him by paraleipsis, saying, "I pass over saying how impious and polluted and abominable in all ways his previous life has been,[73] that I may not seem to trouble you in vain if you hear things about which you are not now making judgment, but I shall describe to you in detail the most recent impiety he has dared to commit." For example, when someone was being initiated into the mysteries he suddenly went mad and is being tried for impiety. The same prodiegesis will fit this problem; then we shall go on to the diegesis: "For when the time of the mysteries arrived and it was necessary for those to be initiated to go in a state of purity into the temple, at that time this man was neither purified from unholy things nor thus cleansed," and so on. In prodiegeses from history as follows: The Athenians are being tried for impiety for their action at Potidaea.[74] (*We shall say that*) the Athenians were impious from the beginning, and that the Lacedaimonians went to war with them for that reason, and that first they were unwilling to expel the Cylonian pollution |, then that they broke the thirty [118]
years' truce, then that they impiously transplanted (*the inhabitants of*) some Greek cities and banished others. Then we shall go on to the diegesis, "And now they have mistreated Potidaea, being a colony of Corinth," and so on.

If we are speaking for the defense, we shall do the opposite, if we have anything to help us in the trial from the history of something done reverently before the trial, speaking about that, and if the problem concerns a private individual, proceeding by paraleipsis, as we said in describing prosecutions.

73 The example of Demosthenes and Aeschines and the fact that declamations dealt with fictitious cases, often hundred of years in the past, perhaps seemed to excuse the advice to slander the defendant as given here and in the next chapter.

74 Cf. Apsines 1.54. For the incident in 430 B.C.E. on which the declamation is based, see Thucydides 2.70.

Ὁμοίως κἂν φόνου κατηγορῶμεν ἢ βίας ἢ τοιούτων ἀδικημάτων, τὸν αὐτὸν τρόπον τὰ πρεσβύτερα βίαια ζητήσομεν, εἰ ἔχοιμεν, ἀπὸ ἱστορίας, εἰ δὲ μή, κατὰ παράλειψιν τιθέντες· καὶ ἐν ταῖς ἀπολογίαις ὁμοίως τὰς ἐπιεικείας ἢ ἀπὸ ἱστορίας βοηθούμενοι τιθέντες ἢ κατὰ παράλειψιν εἰσάγοντες. ποιοῦσι δὲ τὰς τοιαύτας προδιηγήσεις ἐπὶ μὲν τῶν πόλεων αἱ πράξεις, ἐπὶ δὲ τῶν ἀνδρῶν οἱ βίοι προχωροῦντες εἰς τὰς τῆς διηγήσεως χρείας.

## Περὶ δημοσίων ἀδικημάτων.

Κἂν δημοσίων ἀδικημάτων κατηγορῶμεν, ἀπὸ τῶν πρεσβυτέρων ληψόμεθα· οἷον τριακόσιοι νύκτωρ τὰ δεσμὰ ῥήξαντες αἰχμάλωτοι ἀπὸ τῶν πολεμίων φυγόντες ἦλθον εἰς τὴν πατρίδα, νόμου κελεύον-
[119] τος νύκτωρ μὴ ἀνοίγεσθαι τὰς πύλας οὐκ ἀνέῳξεν αὐτοῖς ὁ στρατη|γὸς καὶ κρίνεται δημοσίων ἀδικημάτων· ἐνταῦθα γὰρ καὶ ὁ κατήγορος ἀπὸ πρεσβυτέρων ἀδικημάτων ἄρξεται λέγων ὅτι «ἡμεῖς μὲν αὐτὸν ἐχειροτονήσαμεν στρατηγὸν πάντων προτιμήσαντες, ὃ δὲ δύσνους ὢν ἀρχῆθεν περὶ τὴν πόλιν ἐπέδειξε τοῦτο καὶ ἐν τῇ στρατηγίᾳ· οὕτω γοῦν φαύλως ἐστρατήγησεν, ὥστε καὶ ἡττήθημεν καὶ ἧτταν βαρεῖαν, ἐν ᾗ τριακοσίους πολίτας αἰχμαλώτους συνέβη γενέσθαι μετὰ τὸν τῶν ἄλλων φόνον»· εἶτα ἐπὶ τὴν διήγησιν χωρήσομεν «ἀλλ' ἐπειδὴ ἡ τύχη παρέσχε τοῖς πολίταις τόλμαν ῥῆξαι τὰ δεσμὰ δυνηθῆναι καὶ λαθεῖν» καὶ τὰ ἑξῆς.

Ἐὰν δὲ ἀπολογώμεθα· «οὕτως ἐγὼ περὶ τὴν πόλιν εὔνους ἀρχῆθεν ἐγενόμην, ὥστε καὶ τοῦ πολέμου καταλαβόντος ὑμᾶς τῆς ἐμῆς εὐνοίας ἔχοντες δείγματα πάντας παραλιπόντες τοὺς ἄλλους ἐμὲ στρατηγὸν ἐχειροτονήσατε».

Τυραννοκτόνοι δὲ πάντες καὶ ἀριστεῖς ὁμοίως προδιηγήσεις ἕξουσι τοὺς βίους, ἀφ' ὧν χωροῦμεν ἐπὶ τὰς διηγήσεις τῶν πραγμάτων, ἐφ' οἷς αἱ κρίσεις.

**2** βίαια om. Sc; βία, m. po. σ add., Pa || **3** θέντες **PV**; correxit Rabe || **4** βοηθούμενα m. 1 Pc; βοηθουμένας Pa **V**; correxit Rabe || **5** διηγήσεις m. 1 Pa || **6** χωροῦντες Vc || **8** om. Vc Ba || **10** cf. 52, 15 || **11** φεύγοντες Vc || **12** θύρας Ba || **13** καὶ ὁ κατήγορος: pergit l. 21 || **14** τῶν πρεσβυτέρων Ba || **15** στρατηγεῖν Ac Ba, v.l. **P**, m. 2 Vc; cf. l. 24–25, p. 52, 18 || **16** γὰρ (pro γοῦν) Ac || **19** χωρήσ⌊ο⌉μεν Vc || **20** λαθεῖν: exsp. φυγοῦσιν ἐπανελθεῖν || **22** ἀπολογώμεθα πρὸς αὐτὸν Ac | οὕτως etiam ante εὔνους **P** || **23-24** ὑμᾶς πολλὰ τῆν ἐμῆς εὐνοίας Sc; ὑμᾶς τῆς εὐνοίας (m. 2 πολλὰ et ἐμῆς supr.) Vc || **24** παραδείγματα Pc | παραλιπόντ⌊ε ex α⌉ς Pa || **24-25** στρατηγεῖν (ὸν supr.), m. 1, **P** || **27** χωρῶμεν Vc || **28** ἐφ' αἷς ἡ κρίσις Ac

Similarly, if we are prosecuting a case of homicide (*phonos*) or violence (*bia*) or some such wrongdoing, in the same way we shall look to see if we have any earlier strong points from history, and if not, proceed by paraleipsis. And similarly in defenses, going to the aid of the accused either by citing good actions from history or introducing them by paraleipsis. In the case of cities, their actions will provide such prodiegeses, in the case of men their lives, contributing to the needs of the diegesis.

## CHAPTER 6: ON WRONGS TO THE STATE

If we are prosecuting a charge of wrongs to the state (*dēmosia adikēmata*), we shall derive the prokatastasis from earlier actions; for example, one night three hundred prisoners broke their bonds and having escaped from the enemy came to their native city. Since the law required that the gates not be opened at night, the general did not open the gates for them, | and he is tried for pub- [119]
lic wrongs.[75] Here the accuser will begin with earlier wrongdoings (*by the general*), saying that "we elected him general, preferring him to all others, but he was from the beginning ill-disposed toward the city and has shown this even in his military command. He was such a bad general that we were defeated at heavy loss in a battle where the result was that three hundred citizens were taken prisoner after the death of many others." Then we shall go on to the diegesis: "But since fortune provided our fellow citizens the courage to be able to break their bonds and escape notice," and what follows.

If we are speaking for the defense: "I was so well-disposed to the city from the beginning that when war came upon you, having indications of my goodwill and passing over all the others, you elected me general."

All speeches about tyrannicides and military heroes[76] will, similarly, draw on their lives in the past, from which we proceed to diegeses of the actions with which the trials are concerned.

[75] Cf. *Anonymous Problemata*, no. 53 (Walz 8:411).

[76] In cases where they seek a prize for their actions; see D. A. Russell, *Greek Declamation* (Cambridge: Cambridge University Press, 1983), 24–25.

## *Περὶ διηγήσεως.*

*Ταυτὶ μὲν οὖν περὶ τῶν προκαταστάσεων τῶν ἐν ταῖς διηγήσεσι καὶ ὅθεν δεῖ ἀρχομένους μὴ ἀκεφάλως ἐμβάλλειν τοῖς πράγμασι. Ῥη-*
[120] *τέον δὲ ἑξῆς, τίσι πλατύ|νεται ἡ διήγησις τρόποις. ἡμεῖς μὲν οὖν φαμεν πρῶτον χρῆναι τῶν λεγομένων ἕκαστον καὶ τρισὶ καὶ τέτρασι κώλοις πλατύνεσθαι ἢ καὶ πλείοσιν ἐκφέρεσθαι πολλάκις· οὐ γὰρ ἐστενοχώρηται τῆς διηγήσεως ἡ δύναμις ῥητῷ μέτρῳ, καθάπερ καὶ τὸ προοίμιον, ἀλλ᾽ ἐξουσίαν ἔχει καὶ μέτρον τὴν βούλησιν ἢ τὴν δύναμιν τοῦ λέγοντος οἷον «ἐγὼ περὶ τὴν πόλιν εὔνους οὐ τήμερον, οὐδὲ νῦν ἠρξάμην ἀγαπᾶν τὰ κοινά, ἀλλὰ τῆς πρὸς ὑμᾶς εὐνοίας πάλαι καὶ πρόπαλαι πολλὰ ἐξενήνοχα δείγματα· καὶ ὅτι τὰ πρὸς ὠφέλειαν ὑμῖν ἀνασκοπῶ, μυριάκις δηλῶσαί μοι δοκῶ»· τὸ γὰρ αὐτὸ πρᾶγμα πολλάκις ἑρμηνευθὲν κόσμον ἐνεδείξατο τοῦ λόγου. τρέφει δὲ καὶ τὴν δύναμιν τοῦ ῥήτορος*

2 ταῦτα Ac Ba, m. 2 Vc || 3 λέλεκται ante καὶ add. Vc || 4 μὲν om. **V** | ὅτι post φαμεν add. **P** || 5 χρὴ m. po. ex χρῆναι Pc || 6 ἢ om. Vc || 9 cf. 48, 22 || 11 ὑμῶν Pc | ἀνασκοπῶ[ν m. po.] Pc; ἀνασκοπ$\overset{ω}{ῶ}$ν Pa; ἀνασκοπῶν **V**

## CHAPTER 7: ON DIEGESIS

*The author's insistence in this chapter on verbal amplification of a statement of facts is an unusual doctrine, presumably related to his desire to provide formulary techniques for elementary students of declamation, but inconsistent with the traditional teaching that a narration should be clear, concise, and credible, a doctrine that Quintilian (4.2.31) associated with the school of Isocrates. Aristotle criticizes it in* Rhetoric *3.16.4–6. Among later Greek writers the best discussion of the virtues of the narration is found in* Anonymous Seguerianus *§§63–104. Apsines (3.1) notes that there is special need in diegeses for persuasiveness and clarity. He adds in passing that there are two kinds—one a simple statement of the facts, the other an examination of intentions and the arguments that are being set out—and reports that others have made a division into the kind of narrative found in historical writing and that found in political oratory. See also Theon's extended discussion of narrative* (diegema) *as a progymnasmatic exercise (vol. 2, pp. 78–96 Spengel).*

So much then about prokatastases in diegeses and about where one should begin so as not to enter on the subject "without giving it a head" (*akephalōs*). Next we must say in what | [120]
ways a diegesis is extended (*platynetai*).[77] Now, first, we say that each of the things said should be extended in three or four phrases (*kōla*) or often continued in even more,[78] for the possibilities of the diegesis are not narrowly confined by a stated limit, as in a prooemion, but the will or the ability of the speaker is its resource and limit; for example, "Not only today am I well-disposed toward the city, nor have I just now begun to love the commonwealth, but for a long time, even for a *very* long time, I have shown signs of my goodwill toward you, and I think that I have shown a thousand times that I am looking to your advantage."[79] For the same thing, repeatedly expressed, has revealed the ornament of

[77] The more traditional terms for "amplify" and "amplification" would be *auxanō* and *auxēsis*.

[78] According to the anonymous commentator in Walz 7.2:725, this "is called *hermēneia*," varying the same thought with different words that make the language ornate and foster the power of the speaker.

[79] The theme is that of the general prosecuted for wrongs to the state; cf. 2.6 above.

μάλιστα ἐν ταῖς περιγραφαῖς τοῦτο ἀσκούμενον· ἐξ ἀνάγκης γὰρ ποικίλων ὀνομάτων καὶ διαφόρων εὐποροῦμεν ζητούντων ἡμῶν ποικίλοις καὶ πολυτρόποις ὀνόμασι μεταποιεῖν τὰ κῶλα.

Πρῶτον μὲν οὕτω μηκύνεται ἐξ ἑρμηνείας. ἔπειτα δὲ καὶ τὸ παραλειφθὲν ζητήσαντες λέξομεν κἀκεῖνο ἐν κώλοις ὅσοις ἂν δυνώμεθα, οἷον «τόδε μὲν οὐκ ἐποίησα οὐδὲ εἰργασάμην, ἐκεῖνο δὲ οὐ διεπραξάμην».

Ἔπειτα μέντοι καὶ τοῦ πεπραγμένου τὴν αἰτίαν ζητήσομεν, καὶ
[121] ὅταν εὕρωμεν, ὅσοις ἂν δυνώμεθα κώλοις | ἕκαστα ἀφηγησόμεθα· οὐδεὶς γὰρ νοῦς οὕτω καλὸς εἰς κατασκευὴν διηγήσεως ὡς αἰτία.

Πλατύνουσι δὲ διήγησιν καὶ οἱ λογισμοί, εἰ πρὸ τῶν πράξεων λέγοιμεν βεβουλεῦσθαι, ὡς, εἰ μὲν τόδε ποιήσαιμι, τόδε ἀπαντήσεται, καὶ προστιθέναι τὰς αἰτίας· εἰ δὲ τόδε ἐργασαίμην, τόδε ἀπαντήσεται.

Καὶ παραδείγματος ἕνεκεν καὶ σαφηνείας τῶν θεωρημάτων καὶ ἐπὶ προβλήματος λέξομεν· ἔστω δὲ ὁ στρατηγὸς ὁ μὴ ἀνοίξας τὰς πύλας. ἀπὸ τοῦ παραλειφθέντος πρῶτον «ἡμεῖς γὰρ ἐνστάντος τοῦ πολέμου καὶ καταρραγείσης τῆς μάχης καὶ κινηθείσης ἡμῖν πρὸς τοὺς ἐχθροὺς φιλονεικίας ἄλλον μὲν οὐδένα τῶν πάντων στρατηγὸν ἐχειροτονήσαμεν οὐδὲ ἐπεστήσαμεν τοῖς πράγμασιν οὐδὲ τὸ στρατόπεδον ἐπιστεύσαμεν», εἶτα τὸ πραχθὲν «τοῦτον δὲ στρατηγεῖν ἠξιώσαμεν καὶ τὸ ἀξίωμα τῆς πόλεως ἐπιστεύσαμεν καὶ πᾶσαν τὴν δύναμιν ἔχειν καὶ τάττειν ὅπως ἐθελήσειεν ἐπετάξαμεν», εἶθ' ἡ αἰτία «οὐχ ὡς μὰ τὴν ἀλήθειαν προδώσοντος αὐτοῦ τὴν πόλιν καὶ τοὺς ἐχθροὺς ἀγαπήσοντος, ἀλλ' ὡς εὐνοϊκῶς προστησομένου τῶν ἡμετέρων πραγμάτων. ὃ δὲ

1 μάλιστα om. Mr | γρ ἐν ταῖς γραφαῖς **P**; γρ καὶ συγγραφαῖς καὶ γραφαῖς Ba; ἔνια τῶν βιβλίων «περιγραφαῖς» ἔχει· ἔνια δὲ «συγγραφαῖς»· καὶ ἄλλα «γραφαῖς»· ὁ μὲν οὖν ἐξηγητὴς «περιγραφαῖς» ἀναγνοὺς κτλ. Dox. || **2** mg. m. 1 εὐπορήσομεν Pa; ⌊I-II⌉εὐπορ⌊οῦ m. po.⌉μεν Vc || **4** οὖν οὕτως Ba || **5** δυν⌊ώ m. po. ex ησό⌉μεθα Ba || **6** δὲ οὐδὲ Ac || **9** ἂν om. Vc || **10** οὕτω νοῦς **V** || **11** οἱ Pc, (supr.) Pa; om. **V** || **13** τάδε ἀπαντήσεται Ba || **14** ἕνεκα Ba | τῆς σαφηνείας Vc || **15** p. 48, 12 || **16** συστάντος Sturm || **17** τῆς om. Ba || **18** ἀπάντων Ac || **22** θελήσειεν Vc Ba | αἰτία τοῦ πραχθέντος Ac, v.l. **P** || **22-23** μὰ τὴν ἀθηνᾶν Ac

the speech. When this is practiced it most fosters the ability of the orator in *perigraphae*,[80] for we necessarily make plentiful use of different and varied words when we are seeking to recast the clauses in varied and manifold ways.

First, then, the diegesis is lengthened by the style of expression (*hermēneia*). Then, having looked for something that has been omitted, we state that also in as many clauses as we can; for example, "I did not do this, on the one hand, nor bring it about, nor, on the other hand, did I carry through that undertaking."

Then surely we shall look for the cause (*aitia*) of what has been done, and when we find it, we shall describe each thing in as many cola as we can, | for there is no thought so fine for the [121]
construction of a diegesis as cause.

Calculations (*logismoi*) also extend a diegesis, if we were to claim that there had been planning before the actions took place; for example, "if I were to do one thing, this result will follow,"[81] and add the causes; and "if I had done something else, this other result will follow."

For an example and clarification of these rules,[82] we shall discuss a problem, and let it be the general who did not open the gates.[83] First, from what has been omitted: "For[84] when the war had begun and the battle was raging and our rivalry with the enemy had been excited, we elected no other person out of all the possible ones to be our general, nor did we put them in charge of events, nor did we entrust the army to them"; then what *was* done: "We thought it right for this man to be general, and we entrusted the reputation of the city to him and ordered that he have all power and make what arrangements he wished"; then the cause: "Certainly not because he was betraying the city and loving its enemies, but because with all goodwill he took charge of our affairs. But

[80] Explained by Patillon (*L'Art rhétorique*, 233 n. 1) as language in which several successive cola form a certain system, such as antithesis or parallelism. A period is a type of *perigraphē*. The word does not seem to be used in this sense elsewhere.

[81] *Apantēsetai*; the word frequently implies encountering a difficulty.

[82] *Theōrēmata*, a term found repeatedly in ch. 1 of the rhetorical handbook attributed to Apsines but rare elsewhere of rhetorical practice.

[83] Cf. 2.6 above.

[84] The particle *gar* (Latin *enim*) regularly marks the beginning of a narration; cf. e.g., Lysias 1.6; 3.5; 7.4, etc.

*ταῦτα πιστευθεὶς» πάλιν ἐκ τῶν παραλειφθέντων «οὔτε ἐστρατήγει
καλῶς οὔτε ἐξηγεῖτο τῶν πραγμάτων σεμνῶς»· εἶθ' ἡ αἰτία τοῦ παραλειφθέντος «δύσνους γὰρ ἦν περὶ τὴν πόλιν καὶ ἄδικος πάνυ· ἀλλὰ
καὶ αἴτιος ἡμῖν ἥττης ἐγένετο. ἐπεὶ δὲ ὁ θεὸς καλῶς ποιῶν καὶ κηδό-*
[122] *μενος τῶν τῆς πόλεως πραγμάτων καὶ ἐπαν|ορθούμενος τὰ τῆς πόλεως
πταίσματα κατὰ νοῦν ἐποίησε τοῖς πολίταις ῥῆξαι τὰ δεσμὰ καὶ φυγεῖν
δυνηθῆναι καὶ σωθῆναι πρὸς ἡμᾶς», εἶτα ἀπὸ τῶν λογισμῶν «ἐνταῦθα ὁ στρατηγὸς ἐλογίσατο, ὡς, εἰ μὲν ἀνοίξει τὰς πύλας, σωθῆναί τε
παρασκευάσει τοὺς τριακοσίους καὶ οὐδὲν ὄφελος αὐτῷ τῆς προδοσίας
ἔσται καὶ τῆς ἥττης ἡμῖν ἀπαντήσει παραμυθία, εἰ δὲ μὴ ἀνοίξειεν, ὡς
πληρώσει τε τὴν ἐπιθυμίαν καὶ πάντες τεθνήξονται καὶ εἰς στενὸν κο-
μιδῇ καταστήσεται τὰ ἡμέτερα τοῦτο, ὃ καὶ πράττειν προείλετο». καὶ
παρατηρητέον, ὅτι καὶ τὰ πραττόμενα καὶ τὰς αἰτίας τῶν πραττομένων καὶ τὰ παραλειπόμενα καὶ τὰς αἰτίας τῶν παραλειπομένων καὶ τοὺς
λογισμοὺς καὶ πάντα ἐν πολλοῖς κώλοις καὶ ποικίλοις λέγειν δυνάμεθα.*

*Εἰ δὲ τρόπος ἐν διηγήσει τῶν πεπραγμένων πλατύνοιτο, διασκευά-
ζεται τὸ πρόβλημα, οὐ διηγεῖται· αἰτία μὲν γὰρ διήγησιν, τρόπος δὲ
διασκευὴν κατασκευάζει. τρόποι δὲ διηγήσεως τρεῖς, ἁπλοῦς, ἐγκατά-
σκευος, ἐνδιάσκευος. ὅταν μὲν οὖν ᾖ τὰ πράγματα πολλὰ καὶ ποικίλα
καὶ ἱκανὰ καὶ βαρῇ τοὺς ἀντιδίκους, ἡμῖν δὲ βοηθῇ, ἁπλῇ χρησόμε-*
[123] *θα τῇ διηγήσει· οὐ δεῖται γὰρ | ἰσχυρῶν λόγων τὸ αὐτομάτως ἰσχῦον
πρᾶγμα. ἐὰν δὲ σύντομος ᾖ καὶ πολιτικὴ ἡ διήγησις, τῷ ἐγκατασκεύῳ*

**2** σεμνῶς Ba, m. 2 Vc Ac; om. Vc Ac; ὀρθῶς **P** || **4** post ἐγένετο Vc m. 1 mg.: ἡ διήγησις αὐτ⌊mg. decurt.⌉ || **5-6** ταύτης τὰ πταίσματα Ac || **6** τοῖς πολίταις om. Vc Ba || **6** ῥῆξαι τὰ δεσμὰ τοὺς πολίτας Ac || **7** ὑμᾶς Vc | τῶν om. Pa || **10** ἀπαντήσοι Vc || **12** ἡμέτερα <πράγματα>? cf. p. 52, 19. 24 | ὃ Pa, (er.) Pc; om. **V** | προείλ⌊ε (το) m. po.⌉ Pc || **15** ⌊λο m. po. ex παραλο⌉γισμούς Pc | πλείοσι Ba | καὶ ποικίλοις om. Vc || **16** πραττομένων Vc || **17** οὐ **P** Ac; καὶ οὐ Vc; οὐχ ἁπλῶς Ba Vδ; καὶ οὐχ ἁπλῶς Sc; Dox.: ἔν τισι τῶν βιβλίων οὐ τέθειται τὸ «οὐχ ἁπλῶς» κτλ. || **17-18** γρ καὶ οὕτως (om. καὶ οὕτως Pc)· αἰτία μὲν γὰρ διήγησιν ἐγκατάσκευον· τρόπος δὲ διήγησιν ἐνδιάσκευον (Pc hic quoque ἐγκατάσκευον) κατασκευάζει mg. **P**, cf. Dox. v.l.; cf. p. 56, 6 || **18** διηγήσεων **V** || **19** ἢ post ποικίλα Pc || **20** ἱκανὰ ἢ καὶ Ac | βαρ⌊ῆ m. po.⌉ Vc || **22** ὅταν Ba | ἡ om. Mr | τῷ om. Vc Ac

when he was trusted with these things," taking up again what was left undone, "he did not perform well as general, nor did he exercise leadership over affairs in a responsible way"; then the cause of what was left undone: "for he was ill-disposed toward the city and altogether unjust, and he became the cause of our defeat. When the god, favoring us and caring for the affairs of the city and | lifting the city up from its fall, set it in the mind of the citizens (*who were held prisoners*) to break their bonds and to be able to flee and come safely to us," then from reasoning, "at that time the general reasoned that if he opened the gates, he would provide opportunity for the three hundred to be saved, and there will be no profit for him in treason, and we will get consolation for the defeat, but if he were not to open the gates he will fulfill his desire, and all will be killed, and our affairs will be reduced to the final extremity—this is what he chose to do." Observe carefully that we are able to say the things done and the causes of the things done and the things omitted and the causes of the things omitted and the reasonings and everything in many and varied cola. [122]

If the manner (*tropos*)[85] of what has been done is extended in a diegesis, the problem is being artistically developed (*diaskeuazetai*), not being narrated (*diēgeitai*), for giving a cause contributes to narration, while (*other rhetorical*) treatment contributes to artistic development (*diaskeuē*).[86] There are three manners of treating a diegesis: simple (*haplous*), argued (*enkataskeuos*), highly developed (*endiaskeuos*).[87] Now when the facts are numerous and varied and sufficient and weigh against the opponent and help our case, we shall use a simple diegesis, for | something that is sufficiently strong in itself has no need of strong words. But if the diegesis is brief and of a political sort, we shall use the argued manner, [123]

[85] By use of vivid description, personifications, and other figures of speech; on this use of *tropos*, cf. 3.15 below, p. 129.

[86] On *diaskeuē*, cf. 3.15 below. Maximus Planudes (Walz 5:390) explains that this is a matter of the quality (*poiotēs*) in contrast to the quantity (*posotēs*) of what is said.

[87] Translated by Lindberg (2058) as "the simple, the explanatory, and the depictive narration." Patillon (*L'Art rhétorique*, p. 234) translates "simple, avec confirmation, avec représentation." *Enkataskeuos* is used by Dionysius of Halicarnassus, Demetrius, and other writers on rhetoric to mean an elaborated style; *endiaskeuos* is not found earlier, nor is the division into three tropes of narration. The tropes identified here correspond roughly to the traditional division into three *genera dicendi*: plain, middle, and grand styles.

*χρησόμεθα τρόπῳ ταῖς αἰτίαις κατασκευάζοντες αὐτήν, ἵνα γένηται ῥητορικωτέρα τῇ προσθήκῃ τῶν αἰτιῶν εἰς τὴν κατασκευὴν βοηθουμένη. ἐὰν δὲ ᾖ σύντομος καὶ φαιδροτέρα, τῷ ἐνδιασκεύῳ χρησόμεθα τρόπῳ μὴ φειδόμενοι μηδὲ τῶν ἀπὸ τοῦ τρόπου κατασκευῶν· ἐνδιάσκευος γάρτοι διὰ τοῦτο κέκληται, ὅτι τοῖς ἀπὸ τῆς διασκευῆς μέρεσι βοηθεῖται. ἔφαμεν δὲ ἤδη φθάσαντες, ὅτι αἰτία μὲν κατασκευάζει, τρόπος δὲ διασκευάζει.*

*Ἁπλῆ μὲν οὖν διήγησις παρὰ Δημοσθένει ἐν τῷ Κατὰ Κόνωνος αἰκίας «ἐξήλθομεν εἰς Πάνακτον ἔτος τουτὶ τρίτον. καὶ μεθ' ἡμῶν ἐσκήνωσαν οἱ Κόνωνος υἱεῖς καὶ προσούρουν τε ἡμῖν καὶ τὰς ἀμίδας κατερρήγνυον»· οὐ γὰρ εἶχε μᾶλλον δεινῶσαι τῷ λόγῳ ἢ τὰ πράγματα λέγων αὐτὰ ὁ ῥήτωρ ψιλά, ἃ ἔπραττον ἐκεῖνοι· γυμνὰ γάρτοι λεγόμενα πλέον ἰσχὺν ἔλαβεν, ἢ εἴ τις αὐτὰ ἐκόσμει λόγοις.*

*Ἐγκατάσκευος δέ ἐστιν ἡ Κατὰ Ἀριστοκράτους. φάσκων γὰρ* [124] *Χερρόνησον κινδυνεύειν τῇ πόλει τὰς αἰτίας | λέγει, δι' ἃς ἐσῴζετο, καὶ τὰς αἰτίας, ἐξ ὧν ἀπολεῖται· «ἔστι γὰρ τοῦτο, τελευτήσαντος Κότυος Βηρισάδην καὶ Ἀμάδοκον καὶ Κερσοβλέπτην τρεῖς ἀνθ' ἑνὸς Θρᾴκης γενέσθαι βασιλέας· συμβέβηκε γὰρ ἐκ τούτου αὐτοῖς μὲν ἀντιπάλους εἶναι τούτους, ὑμᾶς δὲ ὑπέρχεσθαι καὶ θεραπεύειν». καὶ καθάπαξ ἡ διήγησις πᾶσα διὰ τῆς θεωρίας πεπλήρωται ταύτης.*

*Ἐνδιάσκευον δὲ ἐκεῖνο τὸ μέρος τῆς διηγήσεως ἐν τῷ Περὶ τῆς παραπρεσβείας παρὰ τῷ Δημοσθένει «θέαμα δεινόν, ὦ ἄνδρες Ἀθηναῖοι, καὶ ἐλεεινόν· ὅτε γὰρ νῦν ἐπορευόμεθα εἰς Δελφούς, ἐξ ἀνάγκης ἦν ὁρᾶν ταῦτα πάντα, οἰκίας κατεσκαμμένας, τείχη περιῃρημένα, χώραν ἔρημον τῶν ἐν ἡλικίᾳ, γύναια δὲ καὶ παιδάρια ὀλίγα καὶ πρεσβύτας ἀνθρώπους οἰκτρούς».*

**3** σφοδροτέρα Dox. || **4** διασκευῶν Ba, (δι m. po. in ras.) Pc || **4-5** γάρτοι καὶ Vc || **6** διήγησιν κατασκευάζει Vc; γρ' καὶ οὕτως (om. καὶ οὕτως Pa)· ὅτι αἰτία μὲν διήγησιν ἐγκατάσκευον· τρόπος δὲ διήγησιν ἐνδιάσκευον κατασκευάζει mg. **P**, cf. Dox. v.l.; cf. p. 54, 16 || **8** ἡ διήγησις Pa | Dem. 54, 3. 4 | ⌊ἀριστ m. po.⌉ωνος Pa || **10** ἀρίστωνος **PV** (κόνωνος m. 2 Vc Ba, m. po. **P**); Dox.: ἔν τισι τῶν βιβλίων «οἱ τοῦ κόνωνος υἱοὶ» γέγραπται κτλ. | pr. καὶ om. **P** || **11** δηλῶσαι$^{ειν}$, ειν m. 2, Vc | τὸν λόγον **P**, m. 2 Vc || **12** ὁ ῥήτωρ post ψιλὰ Pc, post 11 εἶχεν Ba || **13** mg. πλείονα m. po. Ma | ἰσχύος Portus | λόγος$^{οις}$ Pa; λόγοις$^{ο}$ Pc || **14** δὲ διήγησις ἐστιν Ba | ἡ vix san. || **15** τὴν πόλιν Vc | ἃς m. 2 ex ὧν Vc || **16** αἰτίας om. Vc | ἐξ ὧν Pc **V**, v.l. Pa; δι' ἃς Pa | ἔστι τοίνυν ὦ ἄ. Ἀθ. τοῦτο, τὸ τελευτήσαντος Dem. 23, 8 || **20** ταύτης πεπλήρωται Pc || **20** Dem. 19, 65 || **21** περὶ τῆς **P**; om. Vc; περὶ om. Ba (cf. 64, 8. 18 cet.); τῆς om. Ac || **22** δεινὸν post ἀθηναῖοι Ac | ἄνδρες om. Ba

supporting what we say with the causes in order that the diegesis may become more rhetorical,[88] the proof being helped by addition of the causes. If the facts are few and rather clear (*phaidrotera*), we shall use the highly developed manner, not sparing any of the supports from the manner of treatment. It is called *endiaskeuos* because it is helped by features of *diaskeuē*. We have already said earlier that a cause provides support (*kataskeuazei*), while the manner of treatment provides artistic development (*diaskeuazei*).

A "simple" diegesis, then, among Demosthenes' works is that in the prosecution of Conon for assault: "This is the third year since we went out to Panactus. The sons of Conon shared a tent with us and urinated on us and broke chamber pots over our heads."[89] The orator could not have made the speech more striking than he does by stating the plain facts of what they did, for stated nakedly they have more force than if one fancied them up with words.

An "argued" diegesis is that in *Against Aristocrates*. Claiming that the Chersonese was a source of danger to the city, | he [124]
mentions the causes through which it was saved and the causes from which it was ruined:[90] For the reason is this: "When Cotys died, Berisades and Amadocus and Cersobleptes became kings of Thrace, three kings instead of one. The result of this was that they became rivals of each other, and you flattered and courted them." And briefly stated, the whole diegesis is concerned with this topic.[91]

The following part of the diegesis in *On the False Embassy* by Demosthenes is "highly developed." "An awful sight, men of Athens, and piteous. For when recently we were on our way to Delphi, we could not help seeing it all—houses razed to the ground, walls dismantled, the land destitute of men in their prime, only a few weak women and mere boys and miserable old men."[92]

What is best and most necessary to know is that most diege-

88 I.e., persuasive, as in a real speech by a rhetor.

89 Demosthenes 54.34, with much omitted.

90 Demosthenes 23.8.

91 The narration occupies §§8–17 of the speech.

92 Demosthenes 19.64.

*Τὸ δὲ ἄριστον καὶ ἀναγκαιότατον εἰδέναι, ὅτι τῶν διηγήσεων αἱ μὲν πλεῖσται πᾶσιν ὑποπίπτουσι τοῖς τρόποις, ὥστε τινὰ μὲν αὐτῶν μέρη ἁπλᾶ εἶναι, τινὰ δὲ ἐγκατάσκευα, τινὰ δὲ ἐνδιάσκευα, ὡς φαίνεται ἡ διήγησις αὕτη παρὰ τῷ Δημοσθένει, μᾶλλον δὲ αἱ πλείους· τὸ μὲν γὰρ λέγειν «ὑμεῖς τοῦτον ἐχειροτονήσατε πρεσβευτὴν οὐχ ὡς τῶν ἀποδωσομένων τὰ ὑμέτερα, ἀλλ᾽ ὡς τῶν φυλαξόντων τοὺς ἄλλους» τῆς ἐγκατασκεύου μέρος ἐστί, τὸ δὲ λέγειν «ὁ δὲ τῇ πρώτῃ τῶν ἐκκλησιῶν πάντα εἰπὼν κατὰ Φιλοκράτους, τῇ δ᾽ ὑστεραίᾳ μεταβαλόμενος δῆλός*
[125] *ἐστι προδιδόναι» ἁπλῶς | λέγει καὶ ἁπλῶς διηγεῖται, ἐπὶ τέλει δὲ ἐδείξαμεν ὅτι ἐνδιασκεύως τὰ περὶ Φωκέας διηγεῖται.*

*Ἀκμὴ δὲ διηγήσεως τριχῶς γίνεται, ἤτοι τοῦ πράγματος αὐτοῦ ἢ τῆς ἀξιώσεως ἢ τῆς αἰτίας τῆς ἀξιώσεως συνεχῶς διαφόροις κώλοις καὶ ποικίλοις λεγομένης, ἢ καὶ τῶν δύο ἢ καὶ τῶν τριῶν πολλάκις ὁμοίως παραλαμβανομένων· οὕτω γὰρ ἡ ἀκμὴ μείζων γίνεται καὶ ποικίλη μᾶλλον, ἐὰν τὸ πρᾶγμα τρισὶ κώλοις ἢ τέτρασιν εἴπωμεν, ἐπὶ τέλει δὲ καὶ τὴν ἀξίωσιν καὶ τῆς ἀξιώσεως τὴν αἰτίαν. οἷον ἐνώπιόν τις τῆς μητρὸς ἀπέκτεινε τὸν υἱὸν κατὰ τὸν τῶν ἀκρίτων νόμον, ἐξέθανεν ἡ μήτηρ, καὶ κρίνεται ὁ πατὴρ αἰτίας θανάτου· «καὶ συλλαβὼν τὸν υἱὸν ἔπαιεν, ἐτίτρωσκεν, ἐφόνευεν ὁμοῦ τῇ γυναικί, ὡς ἀλλοτρίους, ὡς ἐχθρούς, ὡς ἔκ τινος τῶν πολεμίων γεγονότας» τὸ πρᾶγμα τοῦτο· εἶτα ἡ ἀξίωσις «τίς οὐκ ἀγανακτεῖ, τίς οὐκ ὀργίζεται, τίς οὐ χαλεπαίνει τοῖς γεγενημένοις; τίς οὐκ ἀπαιτεῖ τὴν προσήκουσαν τιμωρίαν», εἶτα ἡ αἰτία «δι᾽ ὃν πεπλήρωται μιασμάτων ἡ οἰκία, δι᾽ ὃν ἄθεσμοι φόνοι, δι᾽ ὃν ἀσεβεῖς σφαγαί, δι᾽ ὃν γένος ὅλον ἔρριπται πεφονευμένον, παρ᾽ οὗ ἥκιστά τις ἂν προσεδόκησεν;»*

**3** τὰ (pro alt. τινὰ) Vc | τινὰ Pa Ba; τὰ Vc Ac | τινὰ δὲ ἐνδιάσκευα om. Pc || **5** cf. Dem. 19, 12 || **6** τῶν om. Ba || **7** τῷ Ba | λέγειν suspect. | cf. Dem. 19, 15 || **8** μεταβαλλόμενος **V** || **9** λέγει[ν] . . . διηγε[σθ]ῖται Pa | p. 56, 21 || **12** τῆς ἀξιώσεως **P** Ba, (ex τῶν ἀξιώσεων) Ac; om. Vc | κώλοις om. Pc || **13** καὶ ποικίλοις om. Vc Ba | γινομένης Ac || **14** μείζων ἡ ἀκμὴ γενήσεται Vc Ba, (γίνεται) Ac || **15** ἔνθα (pro ἐὰν) Vc | ⌊τρί⌋σὶ Pa | εἴπωμεν (ω m. 2 ex ο Vc) ἢ τέτρασιν (τέσσαρσιν Ba) **V** || **16** pr. καὶ om. Ac | τὴν τῆς ἀξιώσεως αἰτίαν Vc | cf. 6, 23 || **22** ἀπαιτεῖ <τοῦτον> . . . δι᾽ ὃν? || **22-23** αἰτία τῆς ἀξιώσεως Vc || **23-24** ὃν ex ὧν Vc || **25** subscr. τέλος τοῦ β´ τόμου **P**; om. **V**

ses fall under one of these manners of treatment, with the result that some instances of them are simple, some argued, some highly wrought, as this diegesis by Demosthenes seems to be, and many others, for to say, "You did not elect this man an ambassador in the belief that he was one of those who were going to sell out your interests but as one of those who were going to keep an eye on the others,"[93] is an instance of one that is argued, and to say (cf. 19.15), "At the first meeting, having spoken against Philocrates, and at the later one changing his tune, he clearly betrayed you,"[94] is simply | spoken and simply narrated, and finally we showed that [125]
the diegesis about the Phocians is highly wrought.

The *akmē*[95] of a diegesis occurs in three ways: either when (1) the action or (2) the axiosis[96] or (3) the cause of the axiosis is stated repeatedly in different and varied cola, or often two or three of these are combined, for the akme gains in effect and becomes more varied if we state the action in three or four cola and then at the end add the axiosis and the cause of the axiosis; for example, a man killed his son in the presence of his mother in accordance with the law about those not brought to trial.[97] The mother dropped dead, and the father is being tried as responsible for her death: "And finding him with her, he struck, he wounded, he murdered his son together with his wife, as though they were strangers, as personal enemies, as born from some enemy of the state." This is the action. Then the axiosis: "Who is not outraged, who is not infuriated, who is not angered at what has been done? Who does not demand condign punishment?" Then the cause: "Has not the house been filled with pollution, (*have there not been*) unlawful killings, impious slaughter, a whole family murderously snatched from life, by the very person whom one would least expect?"

93 Demosthenes 19.12.

94 Demosthenes 19.15.

95 For the author's understanding of *akmē*, literally "peak," see 3.13, 4.4, and 4.9 below. *Akmē* is otherwise found as a rhetorical term only in Hermogenes, *On Ideas* 1.10, where it is the name for florescence in style, a mixture of aggressive attack and amplifying exposition. Cf. Rutherford, *Canons*, 105–12, who defines *akmē* in *On Invention* as "a sort of culminating effort, associated with the heat of debate, with amplifying language, with the impetus of the speaker which makes the audience rise. The author ... associates it particularly with panegyrical *epikheirēmata*" (107–8).

96 On axiosis, the speaker's "evaluation," see n. 9 above.

97 On the law, see n. 8 above.

## | BOOK 3 [126]

*Book 3 discusses* kataskeuē, *the "confirmation" or proof as the third major division in a speech after the prooemion and diegesis: everything before it is preparatory. The importance of the subject is here emphasized by a formal dedication and catalogue of the contents of the book. If there was a dedication and introduction to book 1, it was omitted when our editor adapted the work for its present function in the Hermogenic corpus. Rabe pointed out (p. ix) that there are examples of dedications elsewhere than at the beginning of a work. Varro prefixed dedications to later books of* De Lingua Latina *and* Rerum Rusticarum Libri, *and Phrynichus added dedications in his Attic lexicon. Julius Marcus is unknown; he was apparently a student and probably from a prominent family; cf. the dedication to a student named Postumius Terentianus by the author of the treatise* On Sublimity, *traditionally attributed to Longinus.*

*The term kataskeuē, meaning "confirmation," largely replaced the Aristotelian term* pistis *during the time of the Roman Empire and occurs repeatedly in Apsines'* Art of Rhetoric, *though pistis (described as* kataskeuastikos*) is retained in* Anonymous Seguerianus *(cf. §143). Kataskeuē had been earlier used by Dionysius of Halicarnassus to mean "artistic treatment" (Latin* ornatus*; cf.* On Composition, *vol. 2, pp. 70,4; 156,13; 160,19; 164,12 Usener-Radermacher). It perhaps first came into common use to mean confirmation as a progymnasmatic exercise (cf.* anaskeuē *to mean "refutation") and is found in this sense in Theon's treatises on the exercises (e.g., vol. 2, pp. 64,32; 66,32; 69,21 Spengel), usually dated to the first century* C.E.*; cf. also Quintilian 2.4.18; Suetonius,* On Rhetoricians *24,5. The term kataskeuē in the sense of confirmation appears once in Hermogenes'* On Stases *(65,16) and once in* On Ideas *(398,10). Forms of the verb* kataskeuazein, *meaning "to confirm, to prove," are more common in the Hermogenic corpus and elsewhere in Greek of the imperial period.*

*Other technical terms mentioned in chapter 1 will be discussed in notes on the chapters devoted to their subjects later in this book.*

[126] | Γ

*Τὸ τρίτον μοι σύνταγμα τουτὶ γέγονεν, ὦ κράτιστε Ἰούλιε Μᾶρκε, περὶ ὧν ἤδη σοι φθάνω καὶ δι᾽ ἐμαυτοῦ πολλάκις τεχνολογήσας, τοῦ κορυφαίου τῆς ῥητορικῆς μέρους· ἔστι δὲ ἥ τε τῶν κεφαλαίων εἰσαγωγὴ καὶ οἱ τρόποι τούτων καὶ δι᾽ ὅσων γίνονται, εἶτα περὶ τῶν λύσεων καὶ ἐξ ὅσων συνίστανται, εἶτα ἐπιχειρημάτων καὶ τῶν τόπων, ἐξ ὧν λαμβάνονται, εἶτα ἐργασιῶν, αἳ καθ᾽ ἕκαστον τῶν ἐπιχειρημάτων ἐκλαμβάνουσαι ἐργάζονται, καὶ μὴν καὶ τῶν ἐπὶ τούτοις ἐνθυμημάτων ἐμοὶ παρευρεθέντων, ἀφ᾽ ὧν τὸ ἀκρότατον τῆς δριμύτητος καὶ παρὰ τοῖς ἀρχαίοις εὑρίσκεται· περαιτέρω δὲ τούτων προβαίνουσαν τὴν ῥητορικὴν οὐχ εὑρήκαμεν, ἀνακυκλουμένην δέ γε. πρὸ δὲ τούτων βραχέα μοι περὶ προκατασκευῆς εἰπεῖν ἔδοξεν.*

## *Περὶ προκατασκευῆς.*

*Ἡ προκατασκευὴ πρεσβύτερόν ἐστι μέρος λόγου τῆς κατασκευῆς, ὡς δηλοῖ καὶ τοὔνομα. ἔργον δὲ αὐτῆς τὸ προεκτίθεσθαι τὰ κεφάλαια καὶ τὰ ζητήματα, οἷς περιπλακεὶς ὁ λόγος συμπληρώσει τὴν ὑπό-*

1 τόμος γ΄. περὶ εὑρέσεως **P** Vc Ac; περὶ εὑρέσεως· τόμος τρίτος Ba; τόμος γ΄ περὶ τῆς τῶν κεφαλαίων εἰσαγωγῆς **Pπ** || 2-3 ἰούλιε μάρκε **P** Ba; μάρκε ἰούλιε, mg. m. 2 γρ καὶ μάρκε αἴλιε, Vc; μάρκε m. 1, ἰούλιε m. 2 suppl. Vbδ; θεόφιλε Ac || 3 τινὰ τῶν βιβλίων προσκείμενον ἔχει τὸ «καὶ δι᾽ ἐμαυτοῦ» κτλ. Dox. || 5 τινὰ τῶν βιβλίων «καὶ οἱ τούτων τρόποι καὶ δι᾽ ὅσων γίνεται» ἔχει . . . ἀλλ᾽ ἄμεινον «καὶ οἱ τρόποι ταύτης» κτλ. Dox. || 6 γίνονται Ba | περὶ ἐπιχειρημάτων Sc; ⌊circ. III⌉ ἐπιχειρημάτων Vc || 10 ἀρχαιοτέροις **P** || 12 ἔδοξεν εἰπεῖν Pc || 14 ἢ om. Pc | εἶχε τὸ παλαιὸν «πρεσβύτερόν ἐστι μέρος τῆς διηγήσεως τοῦ λόγου τῆς κατασκευῆς ὡς δηλοῖ» Dox. || 15 δὲ ⌊II-III⌉ αὐτῆς Vc

## CHAPTER 1: PROOEMION

This is the third book of my work, most excellent Julius Marcus, dealing with artistic matters that I have already discussed with you many times, the most important part of rhetoric. It concerns the introduction of the headings (*of the argument*) and their manner of treatment and from what they are derived, then discussion of refutations and from what they are composed, then epikheiremes and the topics[98] from which they are taken, then the elaborations that are taken up and worked out in the case of each of the epikheiremes, and also, as you will see, an account of enthymemes in support of them that I have discovered along the way,[99] by which the highest degree of striking effect (*drimytēs*) is invented by the ancients. We have not found that the art of rhetoric, although often inclusive, extends beyond these matters.[100] But before taking up these subjects, I think it best to say a few words about prokataskeuē.

## CHAPTER 2: ON PROKATASKEUĒ

*Prokataskeuē*,[101] as the name indicates, is the earlier part of the confirmation (*kataskeuē*) of a speech. Its function is to set out in advance the headings and the questions by which the speech,

[98] This, 68,8, and 106,12 below seem to be the only instances of *topos* to mean "topic" in *On Invention*. Elsewhere the word usually means a "place" (e.g., Athens).

[99] This seems to refer to the unusual meaning of enthymeme as described in ch. 8 below. The author attributes his discovery to his study of the ancient orators.

[100] The author's summary of book 3 includes only chs. 1–9. Possibly the editor has added chs. 10–15 from another part of the original work. On the basis of style and terminology, it could be by the same author, but the limitation of rhetoric to invention is strange, ruling out not only delivery and memory (often neglected by later Greek writers) but style as well, in which the author clearly has some interest.

[101] Cf. Rutherford, *Canons*, 112–13, comparing Hermogenes, *On Ideas* 235,8ff. and 236,21ff., where, however, the term *prokataskeuē* does not occur. It is found in prolegomena to the Hermogenic corpus, where it is probably derived from this chapter, and occurs twice in the *Rhetores Latini Minores*: Julius Rufinianus §2 and Fortunatianus 2.5, pp. 60 and 110 Halm.

[127] *θεσιν, οἷόν ἐστιν | ἐκεῖνο παρὰ τῷ Δημοσθένει «δίκαιον δέ ἐστιν ἴσως ἐμὲ τρία ὑμῖν ὑπεσχημένον, ἓν μὲν ὡς παρὰ τοὺς νόμους τὸ ψήφισμα εἴρηται, δεύτερον δὲ ὡς ἀσύμφορόν ἐστι τοῦτο τῇ πόλει, τρίτον δὲ ὡς ἀνάξιός ἐστι τούτων τυχεῖν Χαρίδημος, ἁπάντων τούτων ὑμῖν αἵρεσιν δοῦναι, τί πρῶτον ἢ τί δεύτερον ἢ τί τελευταῖον βουλομένοις ὑμῖν ἐστιν ἀκοῦσαι»· ταῦτα γάρτοι προειπὼν πᾶσαν ἡμῖν ἐπὶ κεφαλαίου τὴν τομὴν ἐσήμανε τοῦ λόγου, εἶτα καθ᾽ ἕκαστον αὐτῶν λαβὼν διεπεράνατο ταῖς κατασκευαῖς τὰς ἁρμοττούσας ἑκάστῳ τῶν ἐπιχειρήσεων προσαγαγὼν δυνάμεις. καὶ μὴν καὶ ἐν τῷ τῆς Παραπρεσβείας λόγῳ προκατασκευῆς ἔχει χώραν καὶ δύναμιν τὸ λέγειν αὐτὸν «σκέψασθε παρ᾽ ὑμῖν αὐτοῖς, τίνων προσήκει λόγον παρὰ πρεσβευτοῦ λαβεῖν· πρῶτον μὲν τοίνυν ὧν ἀπήγγειλε, δεύτερον δὲ ὧν ἔπεισε, τρίτον δὲ ὧν προσετάξατε αὐτῷ, μετὰ ταῦτα τῶν χρόνων· ἐφ᾽ ἅπασι δὲ τούτοις, εἰ ἀδωροδοκήτως ἢ μὴ ταῦτα πάντα πέπρακται»· καὶ γὰρ ἐνταῦθα ἐπὶ κεφαλαίων τὰ ἐγκλήματα προὔθηκεν, ὧν καθ᾽ ἕκαστον ἐξελέγξει καὶ ἀποδείξει. εἰ δὲ ζητοίης, εἰ τούτοις τέτμηκε τοῖς κεφαλαίοις τὸν λόγον ἢ εἰ τούτοις μόνοις ἢ εἰ τῇ τάξει ἐχρήσατο τῆς ἐπαγγελίας ἐν τῇ κατασκευῇ, λόγον ἴδιον ζητεῖς θεωρίας καὶ τέχνην τοῦ τῆς Παραπρεσβείας καὶ οἰκονομίαν, οὐκ*
[128] *ἀναιρεῖς τὸ μὴ οὐ προεκτίθεσθαι τὰ | κεφάλαια τὸν ῥήτορα, ὃ τῆς προκατασκευῆς ἐστιν ἴδιον· πολὺ δὲ δήπουθεν διενήνοχε τεχνολογῆσαι διδασκαλικὴν θεωρίαν ἢ θεωρῆσαι δικανικὴν ἀνάγκην λόγου· πρὸς τὸ χρήσιμον τῶν ζητουμένων διοικονομουμένου· ἐπεὶ κἀκεῖνό σοι ἀστεῖον καὶ χάριεν προειρῆσθαι, ὡς τετηρήκαμεν τὴν προκατασκευὴν ταύτην οὐ μιᾷ χώρᾳ συνεζευγμένην ἀλλὰ διπλῇ· ποτὲ μὲν γὰρ μετὰ τὰ προοίμια τάττει τὴν προκατασκευήν, ὡς ἐν τῷ τῆς Παραπρεσβείας λόγῳ, ποτὲ*

**1** ἐκείνω m. 1 Pa | Dem. 23, 18 || **2** ὑπεσχημένον εἰπεῖν Ba || **3** δὲ om. Pc | ἔσται Vc Ac || **4** alt. ἐστι om. Vc Ac | τούτου Ac Ba || **5** ἡμῖν Pc Ac || **6** κεφαλαίων Spengel, cf. l. 14 || **8** ἑκάστωι (ηι supra) Pa || **9** alt. καὶ om. Pa || **10** τὸ ⌊I⌉ Vc | cf. Π. ἰδ. p. 281, 22 sq. Sp.; Aps. I 2 p. 247, 12 Sp.-H. || **11** τῇ πόλει post προσήκει add. Ba, Dem. 19, 4 || **13** τὸν χρόνον **V** || **14** πάντα om. Pc || **15** ⌊ἀ m. 1 ex ὑ⌉ποδείξει Pc || **16** τετ′⌊I⌉μηκε Pa || **18-19** ἀναιρεῖς m. po. Pc; ἂν ἐρεῖς **PV** Mr (οὐκ ἂν m. 1, οὔκουν m. 2 Vc Ba) || **20** κατασκευῆς Pc || **22** τῶι ζητουμένω Ac | ἀστεῖόν σοι Ac || **23** προσειρῆσθαι Spengel

when woven together, will fulfill the hypothesis,[102] as does | this [127] passage in Demosthenes (23.18): "Since I have promised to discuss three things—first, how the decree is worded contrary to the laws; second, how this is inexpedient for the city; and third, how Charidemus is unworthy of obtaining these things—it is probably right for me to offer you a choice among them as to what you want to hear discussed first, what second, and what last." By these introductory words he signaled to us the division by heading in the speech; then having taken them one by one he continued with the confirmations, bringing forward effective arguments suited to each of the epikheiremes. In the speech *On the False Embassy* (19.4) as well, the following statement has the place and function of a prokataskeuē: "Consider among yourselves what are the points on which it is proper to expect an account from an ambassador: first, then, what he reported; second, what he persuaded you to do; third, what instructions you gave him; after this an account of the dates; and in addition to all these things, whether all these things have been done with or without taking bribes." Here he has set out in headings the complaints that he will prove and demonstrate one by one. If you ask whether he has divided the speech into these headings or if into only these or if he used the announced order in the confirmation, you are seeking a specific account of theory as found in the art and arrangement of *On the False Embassy* and you are not considering whether or not | the [128] orator set out the headings in advance, which is the property of the prokataskeuē. There is certainly a lot of difference between an artistic account of theoretical teaching and seeing the constraints in a judicial speech that is arranged for the utility of what is under consideration. You (*Julius Marcus*) have perceptively and gracefully remarked earlier that we have found such a prokataskeuē not only attached to one context but to two, for sometimes he puts the prokataskeuē after the prooemia,[103] as in the speech *On the False Embassy*, sometimes after the diegesis, as in the speech *Against*

[102] The *prokataskeuē* thus performs the functions of what in Latin is called the *partitio*; cf. Cicero, *On Invention* 1.31–32.

[103] Late Greek rhetoricians often use prooemion in the plural, regarding separate points made as each constituting one prooemion; cf. *Anonymous Seguerianus* §37; Apsines 1.14–15.

*δὲ μετὰ τὴν διήγησιν, ὡς ἐν τῷ Κατὰ Ἀριστοκράτους λόγῳ.*

*Καὶ τοῦτο μὲν ἐξήρκεσεν ἂν εἰπεῖν ἄλλῳ, ὅτι διττὴν ἔχει χώραν, σοὶ δὲ οὐκ ἀποκρύψομαι παραστῆσαι, τί ποτε τῷ ῥήτορι ἐνενόησα. καὶ γὰρ οὖν καὶ αὐτῷ διαπορῆσαί μοι παρέστη γενομένῳ τοῦ πράγματος ἐν ἐπιστάσει καὶ εὗρον τὸν ῥήτορα, εἰ μὲν ἀπατήσειν μὴ μέλλοι τοὺς δικαστάς, ἀλλὰ πληρώσειν τὴν ἐπαγγελίαν καθαρῶς, μετὰ τὴν διήγησιν τιθέντα τὴν προκατασκευὴν καὶ ἅμα συνάπτοντα καὶ ἐπάγοντα τὴν κατασκευήν, ὥστε ἔτι τῆς μνήμης οὔσης ἐναύλου τῆς κατὰ τὴν ἐπαγγελίαν μηδὲν ψεύδεσθαι δοκεῖν, ἀλλ᾽ ὡς ἐπηγγείλατο τιθέντα τὴν κατασκευὴν οὕτως· ὅταν δὲ μέλλῃ δικαίως μὲν δοκεῖν ἐπαγγέλλεσθαι, τὴν ἐπαγγελίαν δὲ παρ᾽ οὐδὲν τίθεσθαι, τηνικαῦτα μετὰ τὰ προοίμια προκατασκευάζοντα καὶ μεταξὺ τὴν διήγησιν τάττοντα, εἶθ᾽ οὕτω τῆς μνήμης διὰ τῆς διηγήσεως ἐξελόντα τὴν ἐπαγγελίαν κατασκευάζοντα*
[129] *ὕστερον, ὡς βούλεται· καθά|περ οὖν ἐν τῷ τῆς Παραπρεσβείας ἑάλωκε λόγῳ· καὶ γὰρ ἐνταῦθα φήσας δεῖν πρῶτον εὐθύνας ἀπαιτεῖν ὧν ἀπήγγειλε, τὸ «ἀνεύθυνος ἐπὶ λόγοις» μετὰ πολλὰ τέθεικε κεφάλαια, καὶ ὅλως τὴν τάξιν τῆς ἐπαγγελίας συγχέας οὐχ ὡς ἐπηγγείλατο κατεσκεύασεν. εἰ δὲ εἰς τὸν λόγον αὐτὸν δέοι λέγειν, καθ᾽ ἕκαστον τῶν μερῶν ἰδίας ἔχει τέχνας καὶ ἀπορρήτους, οὐ μέντοι τὰ τῆς οἰκονομίας ἐκείνης ἴδια κοινὰ διδασκαλίας τεχνῶν τοιούτων δύναται γενέσθαι.*

**2** ἄλλ⌊ωι, ex οις?⌉ Vc || **4** πάρεστι **V** | γενομέν⌊ῳ m. po.⌉ Ba || **7-8** pr. καὶ — κατασκευήν om. Pc || **9** τιθέναι? || **12** καὶ μὴν καὶ ὡς ὅτι δύναται μηκίστην ταύτην ποιεῖ post τάττοντα add. Ac, (ποιοῦντα) v.l. **P** || **14** τῆς **P** Vc Ac; περὶ Ba | p. 64, 9. 18 || **14-15** ἐφωράθη m. 2 Ba, v.l. **P** || **16** Dem. 19, 182 (cf. p. 90, 21); cf. Aesch. 3, 205 | ἀνεύθυνον Ac, ? m. 1 Vc || **17** cf. schol. Demosth. p. 351, 19 Dind. || **19** ἰδίας τὰς τέχνας ἔχει Ac, (om. τὰς) Ba; ⌊III⌉ ἰδίας ἔχει τέχνας Vc

*Aristogeiton.*[104]

It would be enough to say to somebody else that a prokataskeuē has two possible places, but I shall not hide from presenting to you what I once noticed in the Orator.[105] For when I was at a loss about the matter and stymied, I discovered that if the Orator was not going to deceive the judges but to fulfill his initial statement of the case in an honest way, he put the prokataskeuē right after the diegesis and immediately brought in the confirmation, so that, memory of what was said earlier still being fresh, he does not seem to be lying but to provide the confirmation in accordance with his claim; but when he intended to seem to make a claim rightly but was not going to give serious attention to it, in this case he put the prokataskeuē after the prooemia and between them and the diegesis, letting memory of the claim be lost because of the diegesis and later confirming what he wants.[106] | [129]
This is exactly what he did in the speech *On the False Embassy*, for saying there (19.4) that it was first necessary to demand scrutinies of what the ambassador reported, he put the phrase "subject to scrutiny for his words" (19.182) after many headings, and completely rearranging the order of his initial claim, he confirmed it but not in the form he had announced. If there should be need to speak about the speech itself, (*I could point out that*) it has its own special and unusual techniques in each of the parts; however, the special characteristics of that arrangement cannot become general rules for the teaching of such arts.[107]

[104] Dionysius of Halicarnassus had rejected the authenticity of the two speeches (Demosthenes 25–26) *Against Aristogeiton* (cf. *Opuscula*, I p. 292 Usener-Radermacher), and modern scholars have generally agreed, but the work remained of interest to the rhetoricians; cf., e.g., Apsines 2.13; 2.19; 3.11; 8.11.

[105] A regular term used by rhetoricians to refer to Demosthenes and only Demosthenes.

[106] The author's observation does not seem to apply to speeches other than *On the False Embassy*. Demosthenes' usual custom was to insert a prokataskeuē (i.e., a *partitio*) after the diegesis and before the proof; cf., e.g., *Against Meidias* 21; *Against Aristocrates* 18; *Against Timocrates* 19; but in *On the Crown*, *Against Androtion*, and several other speeches there is no prokataskeuē.

[107] The author views the function of his handbook as supplying practical suggestions for students in composing their declamations and not as the appropriate place for a rhetorical analysis of Demosthenes' speech. It may be that in this passage he is counteracting the claims of some other rhetorician.

*Εὗρον καὶ ἄλλο προκατασκευῆς εἶδος παρευρεθὲν τοῖς ἀρχαίοις, ὃ κεφαλαίων μὲν ἐπαγγελίαν οὐκ ἔχει, ἀπόδειξιν δὲ παρίστησι τοῦ κατὰ τοὺς νόμους δοκεῖν εἰσέρχεσθαι τὴν κρίσιν. προκατασκευὴ δ' ἂν καλοῖτο καὶ τοῦτο εἰκότως, ὅτι λόγος ἐστὶ πρὸ τῶν κεφαλαίων λεγόμενος εἰκόσι λογισμοῖς πᾶσαν τὴν κατασκευὴν προκαλούμενος. καὶ τούτῳ κέχρηνται πολλοὶ τῶν ἀρχαίων, ἀλλὰ καὶ Δημοσθένης ἐν τῷ Κατὰ Μειδίου. τῆς γὰρ στάσεως οὔσης ὁρικῆς, καὶ τεμνομένων τῶν ὅρων οἷς ἴσμεν τόποις, κέχρηται νοήμασι τοῖς διδοῦσι κατὰ τῶν οὕτως ἀδικησάντων περὶ τὴν ἑορτὴν ἐξουσίαν εἶναι προβολῆς τοῖς κατηγορεῖν ἐσπουδακόσιν, εἰ παρὰ τὰ διωρισμένα τις ἐκ τῶν νόμων ἐν τοῖς Διονυσίοις ποιεῖ, καὶ τοῦτο ἀποδείξας καὶ ἀναγνοὺς ἐκ νόμων οὕτως ἐχώρησεν εἰς τὴν μελέτην τοῦ ὅρου· καίτοι τό γε τὴν κατηγορίαν ἐκ νόμων εἰσιέναι [130] ταύτην οὐδὲν ἔμελλε | διοίσειν οὔτε τῇ κατασκευῇ τοῦ ὅρου οὔτε τῇ νίκῃ τοῦ τὸ πραχθὲν ἀσέβειαν εἶναι δοκεῖν, οὐχ ὕβριν. Καὶ μέντοι καὶ Αἰσχίνης ἐν τῷ Κατὰ Τιμάρχου λόγῳ τῷ αὐτῷ τρόπῳ τῆς προκατασκευῆς ἐχρήσατο. καὶ γὰρ ἐκεῖνος πορνείας γραφὴν ἐνστησάμενος καὶ τοῦ τὰ πατρῷα κατεδηδοκέναι τὸν Τίμαρχον προκατασκευῇ κέχρηται τῇ διδούσῃ κατὰ τῶν ἀσελγῶς ζησάντων ἐξουσίαν εἶναι κατηγορίας καὶ γραφῆς· καίτοι τοῦτο οὔτε τοῦ στοχασμοῦ τῶν κεφαλαίων ἅπτεται οὔτε πρὸς τὴν νίκην αὐτῷ τοῦ τὸν κρινόμενον αἱρήσειν συναγωνίζεται· καὶ γὰρ εἰ τὰ μάλιστα διδόασιν οἱ νόμοι τὴν ἐξουσίαν τοῖς βουλομένοις κατηγορεῖν κατὰ τῶν οὕτω ζησάντων, οὐδέν τι παρὰ τοῦτο μᾶλλον ὁ Τίμαρχος ἐλήλεγκται τοιοῦτος ὢν ἐκ τούτων τῶν νοημάτων, οἷον αὐτὸν ἐν τοῖς κεφαλαίοις ἀποδείξει, ἀλλ' ἔστιν ἀπηλλοτριωμένη τῶν ζητημάτων ἡ τοιάδε προκατασκευή. Εἰ δέ μοι λέγοι τις, ὡς ὁ Δημοσθένης ἐν τῷ Κατὰ Τιμοκράτους λόγῳ μεταξὺ τῶν δύο νομίμων, τοῦ τε παρανόμως εἰσενηνοχέναι τὸν νόμον <Τιμοκράτην δεικνύντος καὶ τοῦ τὸν*

**3** τούς om. Ac Ba || **4** λεγόμενος Pa **V**; καλούμενος Pc || **6** Dem. 21, 9 || **8** τόποις **PV**; κεφαλαίοις ascript. m. po. **V** | γρ καὶ οὕτως· τοῖς διδοῦσιν ἐξουσίαν κατὰ τῶν οὕτως ἀδικησάντων **P** || **9** ἐξουσίαν etiam ante 8 κατὰ (er.) Vc || **13** ⌊συν m. 2⌉οίσειν Vc Ba; cf. schol. **P**: συνοίσειν ὠφελήσειν || **14** καὶ m. po. add. ante οὐχ Pa || **15** Aesch. 1, 13 sq. || **18** τῆι δηλούσῃ m. 1 Vc, v.l. **P** | et 13 ζη⌊τη er.⌉σάντων Pa || **19** cf. 70, 8 || **20** αὐτῶι Pc **V**; αὐτὸν Pa || **22** τοῦτο m. 2 (ex τούτων?) Vc || **25** λέγει **V** || **27-70.1** addidit Portus, (παράνομον εἶναι) m. po. Pa

I have found another kind of prokataskeuē invented by the ancients, one that does not contain a statement of headings but provides a demonstration tending to show that the trial has been undertaken in accordance with the laws. This might rightly be called a prokataskeuē because it is an account given before the headings, anticipating all the kataskeuē with probable reasonings. Many of the ancients have used this, among them Demosthenes in *Against Meidias* (21.9). Since the stasis there is one of definition,[108] and definitions are divided into the topics[109] with which we are familiar, he has used considerations (*noēmata*) granting to those eager to prosecute people who have committed wrongs relating to a festival the right of preliminary appeal (*probolē*) (*to the Assembly*) if someone acts at the Dionysia contrary to what is specified by the laws; and having demonstrated this and read from the laws, he proceeded to a careful treatment of the definition. Yet, surely, to enter on this prosecution on the basis of these laws was not going | to help confirmation of the definition nor contribute [130]
to victory in showing that what was done was impiety (*asebeia*), not personal insult (*hybris*). Aeschines, also, in the speech *Against Timarchus* used the same kind of prokataskeuē. He had filed a civil charge of prostitution and of squandering his patrimony against Timarchus, and in a prokataskeuē (9–36) claims there is a right of prosecution and indictment against those living licentiously; yet this neither fits the conjectural stasis of the headings nor contributes to his victory over the defendant. For even if the laws have, to a considerable extent, granted the right to those wanting to prosecute people living in that way, Timarchus has not the more been convicted of being such a person from these considerations, something Aeschines will show in the headings, but such a prokataskeuē is a departure from the questions at issue.

If someone were to say to me that in the speech *Against Timocrates,* in between the two questions of legality, one showing that the procedure Timocrates followed in introducing his law was illegal <and one that this law introduced by Timocrates was illegal,>

108 Hermogenes (*On Stases,* p. 63 Rabe) cites *Against Meidias* as an example of stasis of definition, but he does not comment on this aspect of the argument and throughout uses *probolē* to mean a brief, initial statement of the actions with which a case is concerned rather than in the legal sense of appeal to the Assembly.

109 See note 98 above, p. 63.

εἰσενηνεγμένον εἶναι παράνομον> τὸν ὑπὸ Τιμοκράτους γραφέντα, μέσῳ κέχρηται τούτῳ τῷ νοήματι ἐν τοῖς κεφαλαίοις, ὅτι κατὰ τῶν μὴ [131] ποιησάντων, ἃ προστάττουσιν οἱ νόμοι, νομοθετοῦντες καὶ | τὸ πῶς, διδόασιν ἐξουσίαν κατηγορίας τοῖς βουλομένοις, ἐρῶ τὰς αἰτίας, καθ' ἃς ἐκεῖ μὲν κεφαλαίων μέρος ἐγένετο, προκατασκευῆς δὲ ἐνταῦθα. ὅταν μὲν γὰρ ἄλλης στάσεως ὁ λόγος ᾖ κεφαλαίοις ἄλλοις διαιρουμένης, τῷ νομίμῳ δὲ οὐ κατασκευασθησομένης, τότε προκατασκευὴ τὸ νόμιμον γίνεται, ὡς ἐν τῷ Κατὰ Τιμάρχου στοχασμοῦ τῆς στάσεως οὔσης προκατασκευὴ τὸ νόμιμον ἐγένετο καὶ ἐν τῷ Κατὰ Μειδίου ὅρου οὔσης τῆς στάσεως ἀπὸ τῆς προκατασκευῆς τὸ νόμιμον ἐγένετο· οὔτε γὰρ ὅρος οὔτε στοχασμὸς τούτῳ τῷ κεφαλαίῳ τέμνονται. ὁ δὲ Κατὰ Τιμοκράτους λόγος πραγματικῆς ὢν τῆς κατὰ νόμον εἰσφορᾶς ὀφείλων τῷ νομίμῳ κατασκευασθῆναι τὸ ἐκ τοῦ νόμου βοηθοῦν μέρος αὐτῷ τετήρηκε τῷ νομίμῳ. ἄξιον δὲ κἀκεῖνο τηρῆσαι τῶν ῥητόρων ἐν τούτοις, ὅτι καινοὺς ἀγῶνας εἰσιόντες ὃ μὲν πορνείας, ὃ δὲ τῆς περὶ τὰ Διονύσια προβολῆς, οἷς οὐκ ἦσαν Ἀθηναῖοι συνειθισμένοι τῷ μηδένα τοιοῦτον πρότερον εἰσελθεῖν, ἀναγκαίως ἐχρήσαντο ταύτῃ τῇ προκατασκευῇ, ὡς ἂν μὴ προσκρούοιεν τοῖς δικασταῖς ἐκ τοῦ τὰ πρὸς μηδενὸς ἄλλου γενόμενα τολμᾶν εἰσάγειν, ἀλλὰ προσεκτικὸς καὶ διδασκαλικὸς τῆς κατηγορίας ὁ λόγος γένοιτο τοῖς δικασταῖς μαθοῦσιν, ὅτι, περὶ ὧν πρῶτον δικάζουσιν, ἐκ νόμων ὥρμηνται καὶ ἀπὸ τῆς τῶν νόμων βουλήσεως.

1 τὸν ὑπὸ τιμοκράτους γραφέντα del. m. po. Pa, om. Portus | τοῦ τιμοκράτους Vc Ac | post γραφέντα mg. m. po. Ba: καὶ τοῦ ὅτι ἐναντίος ἐστὶν ὁ νόμος τούτου τοῖς πάλαι κειμένοις (cf. Dem. 24, 32) || 2 cf. Dem. 24, 18 || 3 ποιησάντων m. 1, ποιεῖν m. po., Pc | καὶ post νόμοι add. m. 2 Ba | νομοθετοῦντες Pa Ac; νομοθετόυντων Pc Vc Ba | νομοθετοῦντες — πῶς om. Portus, del. (ὀρθῶς supr.) m. po. Pa | καὶ τοῦ πῶς del. m. po. Ba | τὸ scripsit Rabe coll. schol. **P** (W VII 742, 1); τοῦ **P** Ba; om. Ac, m. 1 Vc || 5 ἐγένετο Pa **V**; εἰσάγεται Pc || 7 νόμιμον m. po. (ex νόημα ?) Vc || 13 αὐτῶι μέρος Vc || 14 νόμωι Pc || 14-15 sic Dem. 19, 120 ἀγῶνας καινούς (cf. schol. Dem. 255a Dilts) || 15 cf. Dem. 21, 1 || 16 οἱ ἀθηναῖοι Vc Ac | εἰθισμένοι Ba; συν⌊ει ex η⌋θισμένοι Vc | τοιο⌊ῦτο⌋ν Pc; τῶν τοιούτων Vc Ac || 17 ἐχρήσατο Pc || 18 γινόμενα Vc || 20 ὧν **P**; οὗ **V** || 21 ὥρμηται Ac Ba; (ν er.) Vc | κολάσεως, m. 1 βουλή supr., Pc

Demosthenes used, in the midst of the headings, the consideration that legal provisions, directed against those who do not do what the laws enjoin and | not in the way specified, grant the right [131] of prosecution to those who wish (cf. Dem. 24.18)—(*if someone were to say this to me*,) I shall explain the reasons why the part with the headings is where it is and the prokataskeuē is elsewhere. Whenever a speech is a matter of another stasis divided into other headings, and confirmation is not going to rest on the issue of legality, then the question of legality becomes a prokataskeuē, as in *Against Timarchus*, where, since the stasis is conjectural, consideration of legality has become a prokataskeuē, and in *Against Meidias*, where the stasis being that of definition, consideration of legality is handled by the prokataskeuē, for neither stasis of definition nor of conjecture are divided into this heading.[110] Since the speech *Against Timocrates* deals with the legality of the introduction of a law—thus is a matter of pragmatic stasis[111] and needs to be confirmed by a legal consideration—the part about coming to the aid of the law has looked to the issue of legality. It was right for the orators to keep to that treatment in these speeches, because when undertaking novel cases, in one case prosecution for prostitution, in the other of an appeal to the assembly (*probolē*) about the Dionysiac festival—cases the Athenians had not previously been accustomed for anyone to undertake—they necessarily used this kind of prokataskeuē so as not to startle the judges because no one else had dared to make an indictment, yet the speech would interest and inform the judges about the charge, knowing that the issues on which they were for the first time making a decision arose from laws and from the intent of the laws.[112]

*The order of chapters 3–6 given here follows the rearrangement in Rabe's edition.*

[110] I.e., the validity of laws applicable to a case are not a necessary heading in stasis of fact or definition.

[111] Cf. the scholion on Demosthenes 24.1b, p. 314,14–15 Dilts: "Every prosecution of a document creates pragmatic stasis." Pragmatic stasis is a subdivision of stasis of quality and concerned with the future, e.g., that a proposed law will not prove advantageous to the city; cf. Hermogenes, *On Stases*, p. 38,4–5, and pp. 76–79 Rabe.

[112] I.e., concerned the legality of the law, not its interpretation.

[132] ## | *Περὶ κεφαλαίων.*

*Περὶ μὲν τῆς τῶν κεφαλαίων εὑρέσεως κατὰ τὴν διαιρετικὴν ἐξεθέμεθα τέχνην, καὶ ὅσα ἑκάστης τῶν στάσεων ἴδια καὶ ὅσα κοινὰ καὶ τὰ τούτων διάφορα· νυνὶ δὲ πρόκειται δεῖξαι, πῶς τῆς διαιρετικῆς τέχνης ὑποβαλλομένης τῶν κεφαλαίων ἕκαστον ἡμεῖς ἐκλαβόντες αὐτὸ κατασκευάσομεν· τὸ γὰρ πᾶν τῆς ῥητορικῆς ἰσχυρὸν ἐν τούτοις ἵσταται καὶ τὸ τῆς νίκης κράτος ἐν τῇ κατασκευῇ τῶν κεφαλαίων διαφαίνεται.*

*Κεφάλαιον τοίνυν ἤτοι παρ᾽ ἡμῶν αὐτῶν εἰσάγομεν, ὃ δεῖται κατασκευῆς, ἢ παρὰ τῶν ἐχθρῶν τίθεται, ὃ δεῖται λύσεως. οἷον ἐὰν μὲν ἀπολογώμεθα ἐν τοῖς στοχασμοῖς, τὴν τῶν ἐλέγχων ἀπαίτησιν ἡμεῖς εἰσάγομεν λέγοντες «ἐλέγχους πάρασχε», εἶτα κατασκευάζομεν ἐκ τῶν ἐπιχειρημάτων συνιστάντες ὅτι «δεῖ παντὸς πράγματος ἐλέγχους παρέχεσθαι καὶ παντὸς ἐγκλήματος». ἐὰν δὲ κατηγορῶμεν, ἀνάγκη τοῦ ἐχθροῦ τὸ κεφάλαιον τιθέντος καὶ λέγοντος «ἐλέγχους πάρασχε» ἡμᾶς*
[133] *λύειν | λέγοντας «οὐ δεῖ ἐλέγχους παρέχεσθαι παντὸς πράγματος» καὶ εἰς τοῦτο κατασκευῆς εὐπορῆσαι τῆς ἀπὸ τῶν ἐπιχειρημάτων, ἵνα δείξωμεν, ὅτι μὴ δεῖ τοὺς ἐλέγχους ἀπαιτεῖν. καὶ ἐν ταῖς πραγματικαῖς, εἰ τύχοι, ἢ τιθέμεθα κεφάλαιον λέγοντες «οὐ δεῖ καινοτομεῖν» ἢ «οὐ δεῖ παρὰ τὰ δόξαντα λέγειν» ἢ «οὐ δεῖ ἔθος καταλύειν», καὶ ὅ τι ἂν τούτων εἰσάγωμεν, ἐκ τῶν ἐπιχειρημάτων εἰς τὰς κατασκευὰς βοηθούμεθα δεικνύντες, ὅτι μηδὲν τούτων δεῖ ποιεῖν, ἢ καινοτομεῖν ἢ τὰ δόξαντα λύειν ἢ ἔθος παραβαίνειν· ἢ τεθὲν παρὰ τῶν ἀντιδίκων λεγόντων, ὅτι*

1 — 96, 19 ordinem commentarii Mr secutus est Rabe; cf. Spengel, Praef. p. XI, *Münchener Gel. Anzeigen* 1835 p. 265. Ordo Ba: π. κεφαλαίων, π. βιαίου, π. ἐπιχειρημάτων, π. ἐνστάσεως καὶ ἀντιπαραστάσεως. **P** Vcδ Ac: π. βιαίου, π. κεφαλαίων, π. ἐπιχειρημάτων, π. ἐνστάσεως κ. ἀντ.; Dox.: μήπω τοίνυν ἄμεινον ἦ (ἦν Vδ) λέγειν λήθῃ τῶν ἀντιγράφων τὸ περὶ βιαίου προταγῆναι τοῦ περὶ τῶν κεφαλαίων, ὀφεῖλον ὑπὸ τὴν ἔνστασιν <καὶ> ἀντιπαράστασιν ταχθῆναι μετὰ τὸν περὶ κεφαλαίων λόγον. Portus: π. εἰσαγωγῆς κεφαλαίων, π. ἐπιχειρημάτων, π. εἰσαγωγῆς καὶ λύσεως κεφαλαίων κατ᾽ ἔνστασιν καὶ ἀντιπαράστασιν, π. λύσεως κεφαλαίων κατὰ βίαιον ὅρον || **2-3** ἐξεθέμην Ac Ba, v.l. Pa, W VII 55, 10 || **3** μέθοδον (pro τέχνην) W VII | liber ille deperditus est; cf. etiam Π. στ. p. 28, 12; 36, 3. 43, 15 sq. || **4** τούτ⌊ων ex οις⌋ Pc || **8** αὐτῶν om. Ac | εἰσαγεται v.l. **P**, m. 2 Vc Ba || **9** μὲν οὖν Ac || **11** cf. 88, 8 sq. || **12** συνιστάντες (ω supr.) Pa; συνιστῶντες Pc Ac, (άν m. 2 supr.) Vc, (ex cr. m. po.) Ba || **12-13** παρασχέσθαι m. 2 ex παρέχεσθαι Vc (cf. l. 15) || **13-14** τὸ κεφάλαιον τοῦ ἐχθροῦ Vc || **15** παρασχέσθαι Vc || **16** εὐπορήσομεν Ba, v.l. Pa || **18** cf. 80, 5 || **18-19** ἢ — λέγειν m. po. suppl. Ac || **19** γρ᾽ παραβαίνειν **P** || **21-22** pr. ἢ — παραβαίνειν suspecta || **22** ὅτι om. **V**

## | CHAPTER 4: ON HEADINGS [132]

We have published a discussion of the invention of headings (*kephalaioi*) in our *Art of Division*, explaining the properties of each of the forms of stasis and how much is common and what is different among them.[113] Now it is our purpose to show how, when the art of division is presumed, we take up and confirm each of the headings, for the whole strength of rhetoric rests on these things, and the power of victory is revealed in the confirmation of the headings.[114]

We introduce a heading either from our own case, which is in need of confirmation, or one is taken from the case of our opponents, which requires refutation. For example, if we are speaking for the defense in cases where the facts are at issue, we introduce a demand for evidence, saying, "Provide evidence." Then we support this from epikheiremes,[115] maintaining that "there is need to provide evidence of every fact and for every complaint." But if we are prosecuting and the opponent is stating a heading and saying, "Provide evidence," we must refute this, | saying, "There is [133] no need for evidence of every fact," and we must have an abundance of argument from epikheiremes in order to show that there is no need to demand evidence. And in pragmatic cases,[116] if that happens to be the situation, either we state the heading, saying, "There is no need to make innovations" or "There is no need to speak contrary to common opinion" or "There is no need to depart from custom," and whichever of these we introduce, we support the argument by adding epikheiremes, showing that there is no need to do any of these things, neither to innovate nor to contradict common opinion nor to depart from custom. If it is claimed by the

[113] This was wrongly understood by later readers to refer to Hermogenes' *On Stases*. Headings (Heads in Heath's translations) include the major categories of stasis (conjecture of fact, definition of act, quality of act, etc.), the so-called "final headings": the legal, the just, the advantageous, the honorable, and the possible (cf. Apsines ch. 9), and more generally any proposition to be supported by argument.

[114] As usual, the author is primarily interested in providing formulas that an elementary student of declamation can apply to an assigned topic.

[115] A supporting argument. On the author's conception of an epikheireme, see ch. 5 below.

[116] As when new laws are in question; cf. n. 111 above.

*οὐ δεῖ ταῦτα ποιεῖν, ἡμεῖς αὖθις δεόμεθα λύσεως, ἵνα δείξωμεν, ὅτι δεῖ καινοτομεῖν καὶ τὰ δόξαντα λύειν καὶ ἔθος παραβαίνειν, καὶ εἰς τὴν τούτων κατασκευὴν βοηθούμεθα τοῖς ἐπιχειρήμασι.*

*Πολλῶν δὲ πολλὰ ἐκθεμένων περὶ ἐπιχειρήματος καὶ πολὺν ἀναλωσάντων λόγον καὶ μηδενὸς δυνηθέντος σαφῶς παραστῆσαι, πειράσομαι ὅτι μάλιστα σαφέστατα διακρῖναι, τίς εὕρεσις ἐπιχειρήματος, ὃ κατασκευάζει τὸ κεφάλαιον ἢ τὴν λύσιν, καὶ τίς εὕρεσις ἐργασίας, ἣ κατασκευάζει τὸ ἐπιχείρημα, καὶ τίς εὕρεσις ἐνθυμήματος, ὃ κατασκευάζει τὴν ἐργασίαν. ἐὰν μὲν οὖν ἡμεῖς εἰσάγωμεν κεφάλαιον, ἁπλῆς δεήσει τῆς θέσεως καὶ τῆς εἰς τοῦτο κατασκευῆς εὐπορήσομεν ἀπὸ τῶν ἐπιχειρημάτων μετὰ προτάσεως. τὸ δὲ ἐντελέστερον, ἐὰν τιθῆται ἀπὸ τῶν ἐχθρῶν καὶ εἰσάγηται· τότε γὰρ δεῖ κοσμῆσαι τὸ κεφάλαιον προ-*
[134] *τάσει, ὑποφορᾷ, ἀντιπρο|τάσει, λύσει τῇ καὶ ἀνθυποφορᾷ καλουμένῃ. ὃ δὲ τούτων ἕκαστόν ἐστι, σαφῶς παραστήσω· πρότασις μὲν γάρ ἐστιν ἡ ἐπαγγελία τῆς ὑποφορᾶς, ὑποφορὰ δὲ ὁ τοῦ ἐχθροῦ λόγος, ἀντιπρότασις δὲ ἡ τῆς λύσεως ἐπαγγελία, εἶτα ἡ λύσις, ἣν ποιούμεθα ἐκ τῆς τῶν ἐπιχειρημάτων κατασκευῆς. οἷον εἰ τύχοι κατατρέχει Χερρόνησον Φίλιππος, γράφει Δημοσθένης διορύξαι τὸν Ἰσθμόν· «τάχα τοίνυν καὶ*

4 ἐπιχειρήματος Pc Ac, (ων m. 1 supr.) Pa; ἐπιχειρημάτων Vc Ba || 7 τὸ κεφάλαιον ἢ m. po. suppl. Pc || 10 καὶ τὴν τούτου κατασκευὴν εὑρήσομεν Vc || 11 ὑπὸ Ba || 17 συνεχῶς κατατρέχει p. 92, 1 (Aps. I 2 p. 226, 19. 233, 18. 254, 20. 255, 10 Sp.-H.)

opponent that there is no need to do these things, we need refutations in turn, in order to show that there is a need to innovate and to contradict common opinion and to depart from custom, and we support the argument about these things with epikheiremes.

Since many have published much about epikheiremes,[117] and wasted their words because none of them has been able to give a clear description, I shall try in the clearest possible way to explain how to invent an epikheireme that confirms the heading or the refutation (*lysis*), and how to invent an elaboration (*ergasia*) that confirms the epikheireme, and how to invent an enthymeme that confirms the elaboration. Now, then, if we ourselves introduce a heading, we shall fill the need for a simple proposition (*thesis*) and confirmation (*kataskeuē*) of it by epikheiremes with an introductory statement (*protasis*). This takes a more complete form, however, if a proposition has been stated and introduced by our opponents,[118] for in that case there is need to adorn the heading with a protasis, a hypophora, an antiprotasis, | and a lysis, [134]
which is also called an anthypophora.[119] I shall clearly state what each of these is. A protasis is the introduction of the hypophora, and a hypophora is the proposition of the opponent, and an antiprotasis is the introduction of the lysis, followed by the lysis, which we make from the confirmation of the epikheiremes. For example, let us say that Philip is overrunning the Chersonese and Demosthenes is introducing a motion to dig a canal through the

[117] The fullest earlier discussion in Greek is that by Minucianus in Spengel-Hammer, 340–51; see Prentice A. Meador, "Minucian, *On Epicheiremes*: An Introduction and a Translation," *Speech Monographs* 31 (1964): 54–63. Minucian (341) defined an epikheireme as "whatever is taken for proof of the question at hand," and he divides epikheiremes into example and enthymeme. Apsines (8.1) uses epikheireme in this same sense. In *Anonymous Seguerianus,* on the other hand, derived from Neocles (second century?), an epikheireme is a reason in support of a heading or premise; cf. §§36, 158, 216, and 248. See further the introductory note to ch. 5 below.

[118] That is, if it involves refuting an objection imputed to the opponent.

[119] These terms might be translated "introduction, proposition of the opponent, denial of the proposition, refutation of the proposition," the latter requiring supporting arguments. *Hypophora*, *anthypophora,* and *antiprotasis* are not elsewhere found in pre-Byzantine Greek texts, but they do occur in Latin; cf. Fortunatianus 2.27, pp. 117–18 Halm; Martianus Capella, *On Rhetoric* §52, pp. 490–91 Halm. The author is providing beginning students with a technique to develop propositions logically.

*τοιοῦτος ἥξει λόγος παρὰ τῶν ἀντιδίκων» τοῦτο ἡ πρότασις, «ὡς χαλεπὸν διορύξαι Χερρόνησον» τοῦτο ἡ ὑποφορά, «ἔστι δὲ τοῦτον αὐτῶν οὐ χαλεπὸν διαλῦσαι τὸν λόγον» τοῦτο ἡ ἀντιπρότασις, «τὸ γὰρ διορύσσειν πρᾶγμα ῥᾴδιον» τοῦτο ἡ λύσις, ἥτις δεῖται ἐπιχειρημάτων. Τὸ μὲν οὖν πλῆρες κεφάλαιον οὕτω. Λείπει δὲ πολλάκις ἡ πρότασις οὐδὲν βλάπτουσα τὴν ὑποφοράν κόσμος γάρ ἐστι τοῦ λόγου καὶ πλέον οὐδὲν πολλάκις· ἔσθ᾽ ὅτε γὰρ καὶ θεωρίας ἐνδείγματα καλλίστης ἐμφανίζουσιν ἥ τε πρότασις καὶ ἡ ἀντιπρότασις, εἰ τῆς ἑρμηνείας τοῖς ὀνόμασι προσέχοιμεν, ἐξ ὧν τὸ εἶδος τῆς ὑποφορᾶς ὅπως διασύρεται καὶ διαδείκνυται θεωροῦμεν, οἷον «ἀγανακτήσει τοίνυν αὐτίκα δὴ μάλα, ὡς ἐγὼ πυνθάνομαι, εἰ μόνος τῶν ἐνταυθοῖ πολιτευομένων λόγων εὐθύνας ὑφέξει». εἰ μὲν γὰρ ἔλεγε «πυνθάνομαι τοίνυν αὐτὸν περιάγοντα κατὰ τὴν ἀγορὰν λέγειν, ἃ καὶ νῦν ἴσως πρὸς ὑμᾶς ἐρεῖ ἀγανακτῶν, εἰ μόνος τῶν ἐνταυθοῖ πολιτευομένων λόγων εὐθύνας ὑφέξει», μετὰ προτάσεως* [135] | *ἔκειτο· ἐν οἷς γὰρ λόγοις ἐλπίζεται ἡ ὑποφορά, τοῦτό ἐστιν ἡ πρότασις· τὸ δὲ λέγειν «ἀγανακτήσει τοίνυν, εἰ μόνος τῶν ἐνταυθοῖ πολιτευομένων λόγων εὐθύνας ὑφέξει» τοῦτό ἐστιν ἡ ὑποφορά. Ποτὲ δὲ ἡ ἀντιπρότασις λείπει, τουτέστιν ἡ τῆς λύσεως ἐπαγγελία, οἷον «ἔστι δὲ οὐκ ἄδηλον, ὦ Ἀθηναῖοι, τοῦθ᾽, ὅτι Λεπτίνης, κἄν τις ἄλλος ὑπὲρ τοῦ νόμου λέγῃ, δίκαιον μὲν οὐδὲν ἐρεῖ περὶ αὐτοῦ» μέχρι τούτου ἡ πρότασις· «φήσει δὲ ἀναξίους τινὰς ἀνθρώπους εὑρομένους ἀτέλειαν ἐκδεδυκέναι τὰς λειτουργίας» τοῦτο ἡ ὑποφορά· «ἐγὼ δὲ ὅτι μὲν τινῶν κατηγοροῦντα πάντας ἀφαιρεῖσθαι τὴν δωρεὰν τῶν ἀδίκων ἐστίν, ἐάσω» τοῦτο εὐθέως ἡ λύσις. λείπει δὲ ἡ ἀντιπρότασις· ἦν δὲ ἂν πλῆρες, εἰ ἔλεγε «χρὴ δὲ ὑμᾶς, ὦ Ἀθηναῖοι, μηδαμῶς ἀποδέχεσθαι τοῦτον τὸν λόγον· τὸ γὰρ τινῶν κατηγοροῦντα πάντας ἀφαιρεῖσθαι τὴν δωρεὰν ἄδικον». Καὶ ἡ ἀντιπρότασις μέντοι λείπουσα οὐδὲν τῷ νοήματι λυμαίνεται, ἀλλὰ τὴν αὐτὴν ἔχει δύναμιν τῇ προτάσει, ἥτις μόνον κόσμος ἐστὶ τῷ λόγῳ· ἐπεὶ πολλάκις καὶ χωρὶς προτάσεως καὶ ἀντιπροτάσεως*

**2** χερρόνησον m. 1, τὸν ἰσθμόν m. po. Pa | τούτων Vc Ac | αὐτὸν Ba || **4** τοῦτό ἐστιν Ac || **5** οὕτω m. po. ex τοῦτο Ba || **6** cf. l. 28–29 || **8** ἡ om. Pc || **10** Dem. 19, 182 || **10-11** ὡς ἐγὼ πυνθάνομαι m. po. suppl. Ba || **11** ἐνταῦθα Ba || **13** κατὰ m. po. suppl. Vc | ἡμᾶς Ba || **14** ἐνταῦθα Pc Vc Ac || **16** λέγειν ὅτι Pc | ἐνταῦθα Vc || **19** Dem. 20, 1 | ὦ ἄνδρες ἀθηναῖοι Ba || **21** εὑραμένους Vc Ba || **23-24** τῶν — ἐάσω om. **V** || **24** εὐθέως Pa **V**; ἐκ τοῦ εὐθέος Pc || **24-25** πληρες (ἧς supra) Pa; (ε m. 2 ex η) Vc; πλήρης Ac || **25** ἔλεγες Pc; ἔλεγε⌊Ι⌉ Vc || **26** πάντων Ac || **27** ἡ m. 2 suppl. Vc | τῶν νοημάτων τί m. 1 Vc || **28** αὐτοῦ Pc | μόνος m. 2 suppl. Vc || **28-29** l. 6 || **29** καὶ **PV**; κεφάλαια? | προτάσεως καὶ om. m. 1 Vc

isthmus. (*He can say:*) "Probably some such argument will come from my opponents," which is the protasis, "about how difficult it is to dig through the Chersonese," which is the hypophora, "but it is not difficult to refute this argument of theirs," which is the antiprotasis, "for the excavation is an easy thing," which is the lysis and needs epikheiremes (*to support it*). A full heading takes this form.

But often the protasis is omitted with no harm to the hypophora, for it is an ornament of the speech and often nothing more. Sometimes the protasis and antiprotasis are manifestations of the finest art (*theōria*), if we pay attention to the words in the expression, from which we observe how the appearance of the hypophora is disparaged and revealed; for example (Dem. 19.182): "He intends then to express immediately, as I understand, his indignation if he alone of those in public life here will have to render account of his words." If he had said, "I understand that he is going around the marketplace saying what probably he will say now to you, expressing indignation if he alone of those in public life here will have to render account of his words," it would be stated with a protasis, | for the protasis consists of words that arouse ex- [135]
pectation of the hypophora. This is the hypophora: "He intends to express his indignation if he alone of those in public life here will have to render account of his words."

Sometimes the antiprotasis—that is, the introduction of the lysis—is omitted; for example (Dem. 20.1): "It is not unclear, Athenians, that Leptines, and anyone else that may speak in favor of the law, will have nothing right to say about it." Up to this point it is a protasis; then the hypophora: "He will say that some unworthy men, having acquired immunity, have shirked performing liturgies." Then the lysis follows immediately: "But I leave aside the objection that it is unjust for one who prosecutes some to take away the grant from all." The antiprotasis is lacking. It would be complete if he had said, "But it is necessary, Athenians, for you in no way to accept this argument, for it is unjust, by accusing some, to deprive all of the grant." Omission of the antiprotasis does no harm to the thought, for the antiprotasis has the same function as the protasis, which is only an ornament of the speech. We often find omission of both protasis and antiprotasis in ancient writers;

*εὑρίσκομεν παρὰ τοῖς ἀρχαίοις, οἷον «ἀλλ᾽ ἀδίκως, φησίν, ἦρξας» ἡ
ὑποφορὰ χωρὶς προτάσεως· «εἶτα παρών, ὅτε με εἰσῆγον οἱ λογισταί,
[136] οὐ κατηγόρεις;» ἡ λύσις χωρὶς ἀντι|προτάσεως. Τὸ δὲ πλῆρες ἀπὸ τῶν
ἀρχαίων οὕτω «Φίλιππος γὰρ ἄρχεται μὲν περὶ Ἁλοννήσου λέγων, ὡς
ὑμῖν δίδωσιν ἑαυτοῦ οὖσαν, ὑμᾶς δὲ οὔ φησι δικαίως αὐτὸν ἀπαιτεῖν· οὐ
γὰρ ὑμετέραν οὖσαν οὔτε λαβεῖν οὔτε νῦν ἔχειν. ἔλεγε δὲ καὶ πρὸς ἡμᾶς
τοιούτους λόγους, ὅτε πρὸς αὐτὸν ἐπρεσβεύομεν» τοῦτο ὅλον πρότασις·
εἶτα ἡ ὑποφορὰ «ὡς λῃστὰς ἀφελόμενος ταύτην τὴν νῆσον κτήσαιτο,
καὶ προσήκει αὐτὴν ἑαυτοῦ εἶναι», τοῦτο ἡ ὑποφορά· «τοῦτον δὲ τὸν
λόγον, ὡς οὐκ ἔστι δίκαιος, οὐ χαλεπόν ἐστιν αὐτοῦ ἀφελέσθαι» τοῦτο ἡ ἀντιπρότασις· «ἅπαντες γὰρ οἱ λῃσταὶ τοὺς ἀλλοτρίους τόπους
καταλαμβάνοντες καὶ τούτους ἐχυροὺς ποιούμενοι ἐντεῦθεν τοὺς ἄλλους
κακῶς ποιοῦσιν. ὁ δὴ τοὺς λῃστὰς τιμωρησάμενος καὶ κρατήσας οὐκ ἂν
δήπου εἰκότα λέγοι, εἰ φαίη, ἃ ἐκεῖνοι ἀδίκως καὶ ἀλλότρια εἶχον, ταῦτα ἐᾶν ἑαυτοῦ γίνεσθαι» τοῦτο ἡ λύσις· καὶ ἡ τοῦ κεφαλαίου εἰσαγωγὴ
ἐκ τῶν τεττάρων πεπλήρωται, προτάσεως, ὑποφορᾶς, ἀντιπροτάσεως,
λύσεως.*

## *Περὶ ἐνστάσεως καὶ ἀντιπαραστάσεως.*

*Ἰστέον, ὅτι τὴν ἔνστασιν καὶ ἀντιπαράστασιν ἐναντία κεφάλαια
τῆς ἀντιλήψεως ἡ διαιρετικὴ παρέδωκε τέχνη· οἷον «ἐξῆν μοι κτεῖ-
[137] ναι τὸν υἱόν» τὸ κεφάλαιον, | εἶτα ἡ ἔνστασις «οὐκ ἐξῆν», εἶτα ἡ
ἀντιπαράστασις «εἰ δὲ καὶ ἐξῆν, ἀλλ᾽ οὐκ ἐνώπιον τῆς μητρός». καὶ
πάλιν «ἀνεύθυνος ἐπὶ λόγοις» τὸ κεφάλαιον, «ἀλλ᾽ οὐκ ἀνεύθυνος» ἡ
ἔνστασις, «εἰ δὲ καὶ ἀνεύθυνος, οὐχ ἵνα ὑβρίζῃς τὴν πόλιν» ἡ ἀντιπαράστασις.*

1 Dem. 18, 117 (ἦρξα; om. φησίν) || **2-3** εἶτα — ἀντιπροτάσεως m. po. suppl. Ac || **2** μὲν (pro με) Ba || **3** διὰ τί ante οὐ add. Ba, m. 2 Vc, m. po. Ac; cf. 96, 17 || **3-17** τὸ — λύσεως potius p. 76, 5 tractanda erant || **4** Dem. 7, 2. 3 || **6** πρότερον post δὲ add. Ba || **7** ἡ πρότασις Ba || **9** προσ⌊ῆκο m. po.⌉ν Ba; προσήκειν Sc, Dem. | τοῦτο **P** Vc Ac; μέχρι τούτου Ba, mg. **P** || **10** οὐδὲ (pro οὐ) Vc | (alt.) ἐστι Ac; om. Pc || **12** ἐχυροὺς Pc Vc Ac, (ὁ m. po.; ex ε?) Pa; ὀχυροὺς Ba || **13** κακ⌊ῶς m. 2, ex ὰ⌉ Vc || **14** λέγηι Vc || **15** τοῦτο m. po. ex τούτου Pa || **19** sq. cf. Π. στ. 67, 2. 4 | τὴν post καὶ supr. m. 2 Ba || **20** τῆς om. Vc Ba || **20-21** cf. 58, 16. 6, 23 || **21** ἀντιληπτικῶς ante τὸ add. Sc, mg. (vix v.l.) **P**; ἀντιληπτικὸν m. po. Pa Vc | ⌊I⌉ οὐκ Vc; ἢ οὐκ Ac Ba; εἰ οὐκ Sc || **21-22** εἶτα ἡ ἀντιπαράστασις **P**, suppl. m. 2 Vc; (om. εἶτα) ἡ ἀντιπαράστασις post 22 μητρός add. **V** || **23** cf. 90, 21 | ἐπ᾽ ὀλίγοις m. 1 Vc Ba || **24** ἀλλ᾽ οὐχ Pc; cf. Π. στ. 48, 18. 73, 13 ann.

for example (Dem. 18.117): "'But' he says, 'you performed your office wickedly'"; this is a hypophora without a protasis. "Then you were there when the auditors brought me in and you did not accuse me?" The lysis lacks an antiprotasis. | An example of the [136] full form from one of the ancients is the following (Dem. 7.2–3): "Philip begins by saying about Halonnesus that he is giving you what belongs to him and denies that you are rightly demanding it 'back,' for it was never yours to take nor to keep now. He was saying something of the same sort to us when we went on the embassy to him." All this much is a protasis. Then the hypophora: "Since he acquired this island by taking it from pirates, it is fair for it to be his." "But it is not difficult to deprive him of this argument as not just"; this is the antiprotasis. The lysis follows: "For all pirates who take over places that do not belong to them and make these places a secure base, from there do harm to others. But someone who punished the pirates and overpowered them would certainly not be speaking credibly if he said we should let a place be his that the pirates wrongly held when it was not theirs." The introduction of the heading is made complete from the four parts of protasis, hypophora, antiprotasis, and lysis.

## CHAPTER 6: ON ENSTASIS AND ANTIPARASTASIS

You should know that the *Art of Division* described enstasis and antiparastasis as headings opposed to a counterplea (*antilēpsis*);[120] for example, if the heading (*of the counterplea*) is "I had a right to kill my son," | then the enstasis is "You had no such right," and [137] the antiparastasis is "Even if you did have a right, it was not in the presence of his mother."[121] And again, if the heading is "I am not liable for what I said,"[122] the enstasis is "But you are not without liability," and the antiparastasis is "Even if you are not liable, it is not so you can insult the city."

[120] Cf. the opening of 3.4 above, and Hermogenes, *On Stases*, pp. 65–71 Rabe. Lindberg (2058) translates enstasis and antiparastasis as "direct and indirect refutation." Patillon (*L'Art rhétorique*, 246) transliterates *antiparastasis* as "antiparastase" and *enstasis* as "instance"; an enstasis is often an objection to a claim in a particular instance.

[121] On the theme, cf. pp. 7 and 59 above.

[122] Cf. Demosthenes 19.182.

*Χρὴ δὲ ἡμᾶς καθ᾽ ἕκαστον τῶν κεφαλαίων ἐν πάσῃ στάσει πειρᾶσθαι τὰς μάχας καὶ τὰς κατασκευὰς κατ᾽ εἰκόνα τῆς ἐνστάσεως καὶ ἀντιπαραστάσεως εἰσάγειν· πάντως γὰρ δυοῖν θάτερον, ἢ τὸ τῆς ἐνστάσεως ἢ τὸ τῆς ἀντιπαραστάσεως, βιαιότατον τὸν ῥήτορα ἀποδείξει, οἷον ἐὰν λέγωμεν ὅτι «δεῖ καινοτομεῖν», κεφάλαιον, εἶτα λέγωμεν ὅτι «καινοτομεῖν προσήκει ἐπὶ τῷ συμφέροντι»· τοῦτο γὰρ ἀντιπαραστατικῶς εἰσάξομεν· εἶτα ὅτι «μηδὲ καινόν», τοῦτο ἐνστατικῶς. καὶ πάλιν ὅτι «δύσκολον τόδε ποιῆσαι», κεφάλαιον· «ἀλλ᾽ οὐ δύσκολον», ἐνστατικῶς· «εἰ δὲ καὶ δύσκολον, ποιητέον», ἀντιπαραστατικῶς. Ἅμα γάρτοι καὶ ἡ εὐπορία τῶν νοημάτων καὶ τῶν ἐπιχειρημάτων ἀμύθητος καὶ πολλὴ γίνεται ζητούντων ἡμῶν, εἴτε τὴν ἔνστασιν πρώτην θείημεν εἴτε τὴν ἀντιπαράστασιν, καὶ εἰς ἐκείνην πρῶτον τὴν προκειμένην ἀπὸ τῆς περιστάσεως ζητούντων τὰ ἐπιχειρήματα, εἶτα εἰσαγόντων τὴν ἑτέραν καὶ πάλιν εἰς ἐκείνην ἀπὸ τῆς αὐτῆς περιστάσεως ζητούντων τὰ [138] ἐπιχειρήματα, καὶ εἰς ἄπειρον οὗτος ὁ λογισμὸς τὰ | νοήματα ἐξάγει· εἰ γὰρ ἡ ἔνστασις εὕροι δύο ἐπιχειρημάτων πίστεις καὶ ἡ ἀντιπαράστασις δύο καὶ εἰς ἕκαστον ἐπιχείρημα ἐργασίαν δῶμεν καὶ καθ᾽ ἑκάστην ἐργασίαν αὖθις ἐνθύμημα, τῷ ὄντι εἰς ἄπειρον ὁ τοιοῦτος λογισμὸς τὰ νοήματα ἐξάγει. τοῦτο δὲ ἀπορήσασα ὀλιγάκις ἡ τέχνη πάσχει. ἤδη δὲ ἠρκέσθησαν οἱ παλαιοὶ πολλάκις καὶ δίχα τῶν ἐπιχειρημάτων ἐν ταῖς λύσεσιν αὐτῷ τῷ ἐνστατικῷ καὶ ἀντιπαραστατικῷ χρήσασθαι μόνοις, ὡς μυριάκις ἐν τοῖς ἀρχαίοις ἐπιδείξομεν. τάξιν δὲ οὐκ ἀεὶ τὴν αὐτὴν ἔχει, τί πρῶτον θετέον, ἔνστασιν ἢ ἀντιπαράστασιν, ἀλλὰ τὸ παραδοξότερον αὐτῶν καὶ βιαιότερον δεύτερον τάττεται, πάσχει δὲ τοῦτο ποτὲ μὲν ἡ ἔνστασις, ποτὲ δὲ ἡ ἀντιπαράστασις.*

**4** ἀποδείξει τὸν ῥήτορα **V** || **5** cf. 72, 18 cet. | εἴτε(?) m. 1 Vc Ba | λέγομεν m. 1 Vc | ὅτι om. Ac || **6** ἀλλ᾽ ante ἐπὶ add. Sc, m. po. Vc || **7** εἰσάξωμεν Ba | καινόν **P** Ac; καινοτομεῖν Vc Ba || **9** καὶ om. Pc || **10** καὶ τῶν ἐπιχειρημάτων om. Vc || **13** ζητητέον **V**; om. Sc || **18** ἐργασίαν om. Vc Ba | ἐνθυμήματα Vc Ba | ὡς ἔφθην εἰπὼν ante τὰ add. Ac || **19** ἀπορήσασα post ὀλιγάκις **V** Mr; del. ? || **20** δί⌊χα⌋ Vc; ex διὰ Ac; διὰ ex δίχα Ba || **21** ″χρήσασθαι ′καὶ ἀντιπαραστατικῶι ⁼μόν⌊οις⌋ Vc || **22** παλαιοῖς Pc || **23** τί — ἀντιπαράστασιν suspecta (σημ mg. **P**; fort. nota mg. irrepsit; σημείωσαι· τί πρῶτον κτλ.) || **23-24** παραδοξότατον Pc || **24** δεύτερον **P**, v.l. Vc; πρῶτον **V** (ἁρμοζόντως m. 2 supr.) Vc | αὐτὸ **V**

In each of the headings in all forms of stasis we must try to introduce objections (*makhai*) and confirmations (*kataskeuai*) in the form of enstasis and antiparastasis, for it is always strongest for the orator to demonstrate one or the other, either an enstasis or an antiparastasis; for example, if we say, "There is need to innovate,"[123] that is a heading; then let us say that "to innovate contributes to what is advantageous," for we shall introduce this like an antiparastasis;[124] then, like an enstasis, "It is nothing new." Again, "to do this is disagreeable" is a heading, "but it is not disagreeable" takes the form of an enstasis, "and even if it is disagreeable it must be done" takes the form of an antiparastasis. At the same time, the supply of thoughts and epikheiremes is untold, and many are found when we seek them, whether we put the enstasis first or the antiparastasis, seeking from the circumstances epikheiremes for the one put first, then introducing the other and again seeking epikheiremes for it from the same circumstance, and this reasoning will lead our thoughts to limitless possibilities; | for if enstasis [138] provides the proofs of two epikheiremes and antiparastasis of two more and we supply an ergasia[125] to each epikheireme and an enthymeme in turn to each ergasia, such reasons will in fact lead our thoughts to limitless possibilities. The art rarely suffers a lack in this respect. Old writers often made sufficient use of enstatic and antiparastatic statements alone and without epikheiremes in their refutations, as we shall very often show in the case of the ancients. The order of what should be put first, enstasis or antiparastasis, is not always the same, but the more unexpected and stronger is put second, and sometimes this is enstasis and sometimes antiparastasis.

123 Unnecessarily emended by Patillon (*L'Art rhétorique*, 247) to become an enstasis: i.e., "There is no need to innovate."

124 I.e., in answer to the opponent's objection. The full sequence would be: A. There is need to innovate. B. There is no need to innovate. A. This is nothing new (enstasis). B. It is new, and innovation is not advantageous. A. Innovation contributes to what is advantageous (antiparastasis). But the order can be rearranged so that when B objects to innovation A can reply with the antiparastasis rather than the enstasis, leaving the latter for possible use later. Note the parallel to stasis of fact and to stasis of quality.

125 An "elaboration"; see ch. 7 below.

## *Περὶ βιαίου.*

*Ἔστι καὶ τρίτον εἶδος λύσεως, τὸ παραδοξότατον καὶ ἰσχυρότατον καὶ νικητικώτατον, ὃ καὶ βίαιον κέκληται· γίνεται δέ, ὅταν εἰς τὸ ἐναντίον περιιστάναι δυνώμεθα τὸν λόγον ἐξ αὐτῶν αἱροῦντες τὸν ἀντίδικον, οἷς θαρρῶν εἰσέρχεται, ὡς ὁ Δημοσθένης «ἀλλὰ ἀγανακτήσει Φίλιππος, ἐὰν τῶν πρεσβευσάντων τὴν εἰρήνην καταψηφίσησθε». δι' ἃ γὰρ ἐκεῖνος οἴεται σωθήσεσθαι, διὰ ταῦτα δείκνυσιν αὐτὸν ἀπολωλέναι* [139] *δίκαιον· ὃ μὲν γὰρ φήσει δεῖν φυλάττεσθαι τοὺς Ἀθηναίους, | μὴ εἰς ὀργὴν προκαλέσωνται Φίλιππον, ὃ δὲ δείκνυσιν αὐτὸν τιμωρίας ἄξιον ἐξ αὐτοῦ τούτου μάλιστα, διότι τοῖς Ἀθηναίοις τοιαῦτα ψηφίσασθαι παρακελεύεται, δι' ἃ μὴ χαλεπαίνει Φίλιππος· ἐπιφέρει γὰρ οὕτως «ἐγὼ δέ, εἰ τοῦτό ἐστιν ἀληθές, οὐκ ἔχω σκοπούμενος εὑρεῖν, ὅ τι μεῖζον τούτου κατηγορήσω. εἰ γὰρ ὁ τῆς εἰρήνης χρήματα ἀναλώσας ὥστε τυχεῖν αὐτῆς, οὗτος οὕτω νῦν γέγονε φοβερὸς καὶ μέγας, ὥστε τῶν ὅρκων καὶ τῶν δικαίων ἀμελήσαντας ὑμᾶς ἤδη τί Φιλίππῳ χαριεῖσθε σκοπεῖν, τί παθόντες ἂν οἱ τούτων αἴτιοι τὴν προσήκουσαν δίκην δεδωκότες εἶεν;» ἢ ὅταν ἐναντία δείξῃ ποιοῦντα τὸν ἀντίδικον, ὧν φησὶν εἰργάσθαι, ὡς ἐπ' ἐκείνης τῆς ὑποφορᾶς «ἂν τοίνυν ἀντὶ Πυλῶν καὶ Φωκέων ὡς Χερρόνησος περίεστι τῇ πόλει λέγῃ, μὴ ἀποδέξησθε, ὦ Ἀθηναῖοι, μηδὲ πρὸς οἷς ἐκ τῆς πρεσβείας ἠδίκησθε, καὶ ἐκ τῆς ἀπολογίας ὄνειδος προσκατασκευασθῆναι τῇ πόλει»· καὶ γὰρ ἐκεῖ κεχρημένος τῇ ἐνστάσει φανερῶς, ὅτι μὴ διὰ Φωκέας Χερρόνησος σῴζεται ἡ πρὸ τεττάρων μηνῶν σῳζομένη, μέτεισιν ἐπὶ τὸ βίαιον δεικνὺς τὸ ἐναντίον, οὗ φησιν ὁ ἀντίδικος, ὅτι μὴ μόνον αὐτὴν οὐκ ἔσῳζε διὰ Φωκέας, ἀλλ' ὅτι καὶ κινδυνεύειν αὐτὴν ἐποίησε διὰ Φωκέας ἀπολωλότας «εἶτα καὶ νῦν ἐν μείζονι κινδύνῳ τὴν Χερρόνησον εὑρήσετε ἢ τότε· πότερον γὰρ*

2 δὲ καὶ Vc || 4 τὸν λόγον δυνώμεθα Ac || 5 Dem. 19, 134 || 7 ἐκεῖνο[ς] Vc; ἐκεῖνον Ac || 8 φησι Ac, (ει supr.) Pa Vc || 9 ἐκκαλέσωνται Pc | τὸν φίλιππον **V** || 11 χαλεπαίνεῖ [α], m. po. supr., Ba | Dem. 19, 134 || 13 ἕνεκα post εἰρήνης add. v.l. **P** || 15 [τι m. po.] Ba; om. Sc | φιλίππου Ba | χαριεῖσθαι **P** Ba || 17 ἂν εἶεν Pc || 18 εἰργάσασθαι sic Pa || 19 χερρόνησος ὡς **V**, Dem. 19, 78 || 20 μηδὲ om. m. 1 Vc; μηδ' ὑπομείνητε Dem. | παραπρεσβείας Ba || 21 προκατασκευασθῆναι m. 1 Pc Vc || 24 μὴ **P** Vc Ac; οὐ Ba || 24-25 ἀλλά τι, m. 2 ὅτι supr., Vc || 25 Dem. 19, 79 || 26 πρότερον Ac, m. 2 Vc

## CHAPTER 3: ON BIAION

There is a third species of refutation,[126] the most unexpected and strongest and most effective, which has been called *biaion.*[127] It occurs when we can turn around the argument and catch the opponent with the very things he has boldly asserted,[128] as Demosthenes did (19.134): "But (*Aeschines will say that*) Philip will be antagonized if you (*the Athenian jury*) vote to condemn those who arranged the peace." He shows him rightly destroyed by the very arguments by which he thinks to be saved, for Aeschines will say that the Athenians should beware | lest they provoke Philip [139] to anger, but Demosthenes shows that Aeschines deserves to be punished especially for this very reason, because he is urging the Athenians to vote in such a way that Philip will not be offended, for he continues as follows: "For my part, if this is true, I can imagine, on consideration, no more serious charge I shall make than this. If he who spent money so as to get this peace is now become so fearsome and great that having forgotten your oaths and justice you are considering how you can please Philip, what penalty would be appropriate for those responsible for this to suffer?" Or when he shows the opponent doing the opposite of what he says he has done, as in the following hypophora[129] (19.78): "But if now he (*Aeschines*) says that Chersonnesus belongs to the city in return for Thermopylae and the Phocians, do not, Athenians, accept the argument, and do not allow shame to be prepared for the city from his defense in addition to the wrong that you suffered from his embassy." Here, after clearly making use of the enstasis that Chersonnesus, saved four months earlier, was not saved because of the Phocians, he goes straight on to the biaion, showing the opposite of his opponent's claim, that not only did he not save it because of the Phocians, but he caused it to be in danger because the Phocians had been destroyed: "You will find that Chersonnesus is in

[126] In addition to simple refutation and the use of enstasis and antiparastasis.

[127] I.e., forcible or violent refutation. *Biaion* is not found as a rhetorical term in any earlier text, but "has been called" here as elsewhere points to the author's reliance on some lost source.

[128] Cf. Aristotle, *Rhetoric* 2.23.7.

[129] Hypophora is the proposition of the opponent; cf. 3.4 above, n. 119.

[140] εὐπορώτερον | ἂν δίκην ἔδωκε Φίλιππος ἐξαμαρτὼν εἰς αὐτήν» καὶ τὰ ἑξῆς· πλὴν ὅτι τῆς ἐνστάσεως πολὺ διαφέρει τὸ βίαιον· ἡ μὲν γὰρ ἔνστασις ἀναιρεῖ τὸ λεγόμενον ὡς οὐκ ὄν, τὸ βίαιον δὲ παρίστησι τοῦ λεγομένου τὸ ἐναντίον. ἐναργῶς δὲ ἐμήνυσεν ἐνταῦθα ἑκάτερα, τῷ μὲν εἰπεῖν, <ὅτι> οὐ διὰ Φωκέας Χερρόνησος σῴζεται τὴν ἔνστασιν πληρώσας, τῷ δὲ εἰπεῖν, ὅτι καὶ κινδυνεύει διὰ Φωκέας Χερρόνησος, τὸ βίαιον παραστήσας.

## *Περὶ ἐπιχειρημάτων.*

1 ἂν om. Ba || 4 ἐνταῦθα ἐμήνυσεν **V** || 5 addidit Rabe | σώιζεται χερόννησος Pc || 6 καὶ om. **V**

greater danger now than then, for | would Philip would have more [140]
easily been punished for trespass against it (*then or now*)?" and so on. Nevertheless, biaion is much different from enstasis, for enstasis counters what is being said on the ground that it is not true, while biaion sets out the opposite of what is being said. Clearly he employed both here: by saying that Chersonnesus was not saved because of the Phocians he completes an enstasis, and by saying that Chersonnesus is in danger because of the Phocians he provides a biaion as well.

## CHAPTER 5: ON EPIKHEIREMES

*An* epikheirēma *is literally "a laying hands on, a grasping." The term does not occur in Aristotle's* Rhetoric, *where its place is taken by* enthymēma, *but is found in the* Topics *(8.162a16) meaning a dialectical, as opposed to an apodeictical, syllogism, that is, an inductive argument that is probable but not certain. Diogenes Laertius's list (5.43) of the works of Theophrastus includes eighteen books of epikheiremes. Possibly he used the word of a rhetorical syllogism, possibly that development was the work of Stoic philosophers and grammarians. In any event, by the early first century* B.C.E. epikheirēma *had come to refer to a five-part argument, consisting of a proposition, supporting reason, proof of the reason, embellishment, and conclusion; cf.* Rhetoric for Herennius *2.2 (where* epicheiremata *appears as a Latin word) and 2.28; also Cicero,* On Invention *1.61 (where the term is attributed to the followers of Aristotle and Theophrastus). Quintilian says (5.10.1) that* enthymemata, epicheiremata, *and* apodeixis *are distinguished by the Greeks but have much the same general meaning. Subsequently (5.10.5–6) he says some regarded an* epicheirema *as a completed proof and that it has at least three parts. Among Greek authors, Minucian regarded an* epikheirēma *as the general term for an "artificial" proof and divided it into example and enthymeme (cf. n. 117 above), a meaning used also by Apsines (8.1). In* Anonymous Seguerianus *§§36, 158, 216, and 248, derived from Neocles, an* epikheirēma *is a reason in support of a heading or premise, which is the meaning here in* On Invention. *Byzantine commentators express surprise at the use of* epikheirēma *in* On Invention, *and the anonymous commentator of Walz 7.2:752 and Maximus Planudes (Walz 5:395) cite Neocles'*

*Εἴτε οὖν εἰσάγοιμεν ἡμεῖς κεφάλαιον εἴτε τεθὲν λύοιμεν, δεῖ ζη-
τεῖν τὰ ἐπιχειρήματα ὅθεν εὑρεθήσεται καὶ ἀπὸ τρόπων ὁπόσων. εἴτε
γὰρ κατασκευάζοιμεν εἴτε λύοιμεν, ἀπὸ τῶν αὐτῶν αἱ γενέσεις τῶν
νοημάτων τοῖς ἐπιχειρήμασι καὶ παρὰ ταῦτα οὐδεὶς ἂν εὑρεῖν ἕτερον
δύναιτο. εὑρίσκεται τοίνυν πᾶν ἐπιχείρημα γινόμενον ἀπὸ τῆς περιστά-
σεως· περίστασις δέ ἐστι τὸ πᾶν ἐν ἡμῖν καὶ λόγοις καὶ πράγμασι καὶ
δίκαις καὶ ὑποθέσεσι καὶ βίῳ, τόπος, χρόνος, τρόπος, πρόσωπον, αἰ-
[141] τία, πρᾶγμα· προστιθέασι δὲ οἱ φιλόσοφοι καὶ ἕβδο|μόν τι, τὴν ὕλην,
ἣν ὁ ῥήτωρ οὐκ ἰδίᾳ χωρίσας ἔχει, πιθανῶς δὲ ἐπιμερίζει τῶν ἄλλων
ἑκάστῳ, ὅτῳ ἂν καὶ δύνηται. εἴτε οὖν ἀξιοῖμεν γενέσθαι τι, φήσομεν
ἐπιχειροῦντες δεῖν αὐτὸ γενέσθαι, καλὸν γὰρ εἶναι ἢ διὰ τὸν τόπον ἢ
διὰ τὸν χρόνον ἢ διὰ τὸν τρόπον ἢ διὰ τὸ πρόσωπον ἢ διὰ τὴν αἰτίαν ἢ
διὰ τὸ πρᾶγμα· εἴτε ἀντιλέγοιμεν ἀξιοῦντες μὴ δεῖν γενέσθαι, φήσομεν
μὴ δεῖν αὐτὸ πραχθῆναι, φαῦλον γὰρ εἶναι ἢ διὰ τὸν τόπον ἢ διὰ τὸν
χρόνον ἢ διὰ τὸν τρόπον ἢ διὰ τὸ πρόσωπον ἢ διὰ τὴν αἰτίαν ἢ διὰ τὸ
πρᾶγμα· εἴτε ἐπὶ τοῦ παρελθόντος εἴτε ἐπὶ τοῦ μέλλοντος· «πραχθήσεται τόδε διὰ τὸν τόπον ἢ χρόνον» καὶ τὰ ἑξῆς ἢ «οὐ πραχθήσεται
διὰ τὸν τόπον ἢ χρόνον» καὶ τὰ ἑξῆς.*

1 εἴτε τεθὲν **P**; εἴτε καὶ θέντες Ac; εἴτε θέντες Sc, (ex ἢ τεθέντος) Mr; ⌊I-II⌉ εἴτε θέντες (m. po. γρ′ εἴτε τεθὲν) Vc; ⌊ἢ m. po.⌉τεθ⌊ὲ⌉ν ⌊III⌉ Ba; Dox.: ἓν τισι τῶν βιβλίων «ἢ τεθέντος» εὗρον, ἐν ἑτέροις δὲ «εἴτε θέντες», ἐν ἄλλοις δὲ «ἢ εἰ τεθέντες», ἐν ἐνίοις δὲ «ἢ εἰ τεθὲν λύομεν» κτλ. | λύομεν Pc || 2 ἀπὸ τρόπων ὁπόσων (γρ καὶ ἀπὸ τινων) **P**, (τρ in ras.) Ba; ἀπὸ τίνων (om. τρόπων) Ac, m. 1 Vc || 2-3 εἴτε γὰρ ἀνασκευάζοιμεν εἴτε κατασκευάζοιμεν Sc || 3 γὰρ m. po. suppl. **V** | εἴτε λύοιμεν om. Vc Ba | alt. τῶν om. v.l. Dox. || 6 τὸ — ἡμῖν vix sana || 6-7 καὶ πράξεσι καὶ βίῳ καὶ δίκαις καὶ ὑποθέσεων περιστάσεσι Dox. W II 215, 1 || 7 cf. Π. στ. 43, 1 || 8 schol. **P** (in Herm. Π. ἰδ. p. 276, 9 sq. Sp.) W VII 921, 2: ὁ φιλόσοφος Πορφύριος . . . ἑπτά || 12 ἢ διὰ τὸν τρόπον om. Vc Ba; supr. post τόπον m. 2 Vc || 13 [δεῖν] γενέσθαι? || 13-14 φήσομεν ἐπιχειροῦντες μὴ δεῖν Sc, v.l. Pc, (φήσομεν καὶ) v.l. Pa; cf. l. 10 || 14-15 ἢ διὰ τὸν χρόνον ἢ διὰ τὸν τρόπον post 10 αἰτίαν Vc Ba || 16 εἴτε — μέλλοντος suspecta || 17 ἢ διὰ τὸν τρόπον ἢ Ba | τὸν om. Pc | ἢ οὐ om. Ac || 18 διὰ — ἑξῆς om. Ac

*definition of an* epikheirēma *as a syllogism. The description in chapters 5, 7, and 8 below of an argument consisting of epikheireme, ergasia of the epikheireme, enthymeme, and epenthymeme seems to be a variant of the five-part argument of Hellenistic times.*

Whether we are introducing a heading ourselves or refuting one proposed (*by an opponent*), there is need to ask where epikheiremes will be found and how many modes (*tropoi*) of them are there; for whether we are confirming or refuting arguments, the sources of the epikheiremes are from the same ideas (*noēmata*), and no one could find any other beyond these. Now every epikheireme is derived from the circumstances (*peristasis*), and circumstances as a whole are found in what concerns us: our words and actions and judicial processes and speeches and life, including place, time, manner, person, cause, and action.[130] The philosophers add a seventh, | the material (*hylē*),[131] which the orator does [141]
not deal with separately but divides up in a persuasive way among each of the others however he can. If, then, we think something was rightly done, we shall construct epikheiremes to say that it was necessary for it to have been done, for it is good, either because of the place or because of the time or because of the manner or because of the person or because of the cause or because of the action; and if we are speaking in opposition, claiming it ought not to have been done, we shall say that it should not have been done, for it is bad, either because of the place or the time or the manner or the person or the cause or the action, whether in the past or in the future: "This will have been done because of the place or time" and so on, or "This will not have been done because of the place or time" and so on.

Let us consider some examples from which all will become clear. In a case of conjectural stasis, for instance, the first head-

[130] This list of topics, found in some form in all rhetorical handbooks, originated with Aristotle's ten categories of substance, quantity, quality, relation, place, time, possession, position, activity, and passivity (*Categories* 4 and *Topics* 1.9). Cf. Hermogenes, *On Stases*, p. 46,1–2 Rabe: person, act, place, manner, time, and cause.

[131] Cf. Troilus Sophista in Hugo Rabe, ed., *Prolegomenon Sylloge* (Bibliotheca scriptorum Graecorum et Romanorum Teubneriana; Rhetores Graeci 14; Stuttgart: Teubner, 1931), 52,1.

*Καταμάθωμεν δὲ καὶ ἐπὶ παραδειγμάτων, ἀφ᾽ ὧν πάντα σαφῆ γίνεται. οἷον ἐπὶ τοῦ στοχασμοῦ πρῶτον ἐμπίπτει κεφάλαιον παραγραφικόν, εἶτα ἡ τῶν ἐλέγχων ἀπαίτησις, εἰ μή τι πρὸ αὐτοῦ παραδόξως ἕτερον εὑρεθείη, καθὰ συμβαίνει πολλάκις· ἔστω δὲ πρόβλημα ὁ Περικλῆς ὁ κρινόμενος προδοσίας, ὅτι μὴ ἐδῄωσεν αὐτοῦ τοὺς καρποὺς Ἀρχίδαμος. εἴτε γὰρ ἀπαιτοίη τοὺς μάρτυρας ὁ Περικλῆς, ἐπιχειρήσει λέγων τῇ τῶν ἐλέγχων ἀπαιτήσει πρῶτον μὲν ἀπὸ τοῦ πράγματος* [142] *ὅτι «δεῖ ἐλέγχους παρέχεσθαι προδοσίας» τὸ κεφάλαιον ὁρί|σας, εἶτα ἐπιφέρων ἐπιχείρημα «παντὸς γὰρ πράγματος κρινομένου δεῖ τοὺς ἐλέγχους παρέχεσθαι· δίκαιον γὰρ τοῦτό γε»· εἶτα ἀπὸ τοῦ προσώπου ὅτι «καὶ δεῖ Περικλέα μὴ ἄνευ μαρτύρων κρίνεσθαι προδοσίας»· εἶτα ἀπὸ τοῦ τόπου ὅτι «καὶ μὴ δεῖ ἐν δημοκρατίᾳ ἄνευ μαρτύρων τὰς κρίσεις γίνεσθαι»· εἶτα ἀπὸ τῆς αἰτίας ὅτι «καὶ διὰ τοῦτο δεῖ μάρτυρας παρέχεσθαι τοῦ Περικλέους τῆς προδοσίας καὶ ἀπαιτεῖν, ἵνα τοῦτο προεγνωκότες οἱ κατήγοροι μὴ συκοφαντῶσι προπετῶς, γινώσκοντες ὅτι συκοφαντίας ἁλώσονται προπετῶς κατηγοροῦντες, ἐὰν μὴ παρέχωσι μάρτυρας». εἰ δὲ ἀντιλέγοιμεν μὴ δεῖν μάρτυρας παρέχεσθαι, καὶ τότε ὁμοίως ἐπὶ τὴν περίστασιν βαδιούμεθα λέγοντες καὶ πρῶτον μὲν τὸ κεφάλαιον ὁρίζοντες «οὐ δεῖ μάρτυρας παρέχεσθαι τῆς προδοσίας τῆς Περικλέους», εἶτα <ἐπιφέροντες> ἐπιχείρημα ἀπὸ τοῦ πράγματος «πᾶν γὰρ πρᾶγμα, ᾧ πρόσεστιν ἀδίκημα, κρύφα πράττεται πρὸς τῶν πονηρῶν, ἵνα μὴ κατάφωροι γινόμενοι διδῶσι τιμωρίας»· εἶτα ἀπὸ τοῦ προσώπου ὅτι «καὶ μαρτυρεῖν οὐδεὶς ἐθελήσει κατὰ Περικλέους φοβούμενος τὸ ἀξίωμα τοῦ ἀνδρός»· εἶτα ἀπὸ τῆς αἰτίας ὅτι «καὶ μὴ δεῖ μάρτυρας ζητεῖν πάντων τῶν ἀδικημάτων, ἀλλὰ καὶ ἀπὸ τῶν εἰκότων κρίνειν· εἰ δὲ μή, πειράσονται πάντες ἄνευ* [143] *| μαρτύρων ἐπιτίθεσθαι τοῖς ἀδικήμασιν ὡς ἐξ οὐδενὸς ἄλλου ἁλωσόμενοι πλὴν τούτου»· εἶτα*

**2** cf. Π. στ. 43, 18 | κεφάλαιον om. Vc Ba || **3** εἶτα om. Vc Ba || **3-4** παραδοξότερον εὑρεθείη Mr || **4-5** cf. 94, 1 || **5** τοὺς καρποὺς αὐτοῦ Pc, m. 1 Vc || **6-7** cf. 72, 10 sq. || **7** ἀπὸ τοῦ πράγματος post 88, 9 ἐπιχείρημα transp. 8 τὸ κεφάλαιον ὁρίσας post 7 μὲν ? cf. 88, 19 sq. 90, 5 || **8** παρασχέσθαι **V** (m. 1 Pa ?) || **10** παρασχέσθαι Vc Ba || **13** δεῖ post μάρτυρας Ac ; supr. Pa || **14** παρασχέσθαι Ac | τῆς προδοσίας τῆς περικλέους **V** | καὶ ἀπαιτεῖν om. Ac || **15** προπετῶς, φανῶς m. 2 supr. Vc || **16-17** εἰ δὲ μὴ εὐποροῦμεν μαρτύρων καὶ τότε Ac, v.l. **P**, (μάρτυρας) m. 1 Vc Ba ; εἰ δὲ μὴ εὐποροῦμεν μαρτύρων καὶ ἀντιλέγοιμεν Sc || **18** τὴν om. Ac | λέγοντες — μὲν om. Vc Ba || **19** τὸ κεφάλαιον λέγοντες (om. καὶ πρῶτον μὲν et ὁρίζοντες) Ac | παρασχέσθαι μάρτυρας Ac | παρασχέσθαι **V** || **20** alt. τῆς om. Ac | addidit Rabe | ἐπιχείρημα post πράγματος Vc Ba || **22** γενόμενοι Pc || **24** καὶ om. Ac || **25** ἀπὸ add. ante πάντων Pa | καὶ om. Vc Ba

ing[132] is to question the legality of the prosecution (*paragraphē*); then comes a demand for evidence, unless unexpectedly something else is put earlier, as often happens. Let us take the problem of Pericles being tried for treason because Archidamus did not burn his crops.[133] If Pericles were to demand witnesses, he will first construct an epikheireme from the act with a demand for evidence, saying, "It is necessary to provide evidence of treason,"
thus defining the heading; | then bring in an epikheireme, "for [142]
when any act is being judged, it is necessary for evidence to be provided, for this is just"; then an argument from the person, saying that "Pericles should not be judged guilty of treason without witnesses"; then from the "place," saying, "and trials in a democracy should not take place without witnesses"; then from the cause, saying, "for this reason too witness should be furnished and demanded of Pericles' treason, in order that prosecutors may learn from the start not to be in a hurry to play the informer, knowing that they will be caught playing the informer by prosecuting hurriedly if they do not provide witnesses."

If, on the other hand, we are arguing on the other side that there is no need for witnesses to be provided, we shall then proceed similarly, speaking on the basis of the circumstances and first defining the heading as "There is no need to provide witnesses of the treason of Pericles," then <adding> an epikheireme from the act, "For every act in which there is a wrong is done by wicked men in secret, in order that they may not be detected and punished"; then from the person, saying that "no one will want to give testimony against Pericles, fearing the man's reputation"; then from the cause, that "there is no need to seek for witnesses of all crimes, but one should judge on the basis of probabilities;
otherwise, everyone will try, without | any witnesses, to attempt [143]
crimes, expecting to be caught by nothing other than this"; then

[132] When speaking for the defense; cf. Hermogenes, *On Stases*, pp. 43–45 Rabe.

[133] Cf. Thucydides 2.13. Pericles gave his farms to the state for fear that the Spartan king, Archidamus, would spare them on his invasion of Attica in 431 B.C.E.

*ἀπὸ τοῦ τόπου ὅτι «καὶ ἐν Ἀθήναις, ὅπου καὶ ἡ ἀλήθεια τῶν πραγμάτων πλέον ἰσχύει τῶν μαρτύρων». [ὡς ἐν τῷ Κατὰ Τιμάρχου φησὶν Αἰσχίνης, ὅτι καὶ τοὺς ξένους οὐκ ἀπὸ τῶν μαρτύρων ἐν τοῖς δήμοις, ἀλλ᾽ ἀπὸ τῆς ἀληθείας εὑρίσκετε.] καὶ ἐπὶ τῆς βουλήσεως ὁμοίως τὸ κεφάλαιον ὁρίσαντες ὅτι «οὐκ εἰκὸς ἐθελῆσαι προδοῦναι Περικλέα» τρεψόμεθα πάλιν ἐπὶ τὰ ἐπιχειρήματα ἀπὸ τοῦ πράγματος «οὐκ εἰκὸς ἐθελῆσαι προδοῦναι Περικλέα· φαῦλον γὰρ πρᾶγμα ἡ προδοσία καὶ ὃ μηδεὶς ἂν ἡδέως ὑποσταίη νοῦν ἔχων», καὶ ὅτι «ἀντὶ πολλῶν καὶ μεγάλων ἀγαθῶν οὐκ ἂν πονηρὸν πρᾶγμα εἱλόμην»· εἶτα ἀπὸ τοῦ προσώπου «οὐκ ἂν ἠθέλησα προδοῦναι, Περικλῆς ὤν, φιλόπολις ἀεὶ καὶ φιλαθήναιος καὶ κρείττων χρημάτων»· εἶτα ἀπὸ τῆς αἰτίας «οὐκ ἂν ὑμᾶς προὔδωκα· οὐ γὰρ ἐδεόμην χρημάτων πλούσιος ὤν, οὐδὲ ἐμισούμην παρ᾽ ὑμῶν ἀλλ᾽ ἐθαυμαζόμην»· εἶτα ἀπὸ τοῦ χρόνου ὅτι «μηδὲ προδοῦναι ἂν ἠθέλησα νῦν, ἔχων τηλικαύτην δόξαν καὶ τοσαύτην». καὶ ἡ δύναμις ὅτι «οὐκ ἂν ἠδυνήθην προδοῦναι», καὶ πρῶτον μὲν ἀπὸ τοῦ πράγματος ὅτι «προδοσία πρᾶγμα δύσκολον καὶ οὐ ῥᾳδίως πραχθῆναι δυνάμενον»· εἶτα ἀπὸ τοῦ προσώπου ὅτι «καὶ Περικλεῖ δύσκολον, ὃς* [144] *ἐν | προσχήματι τιμῆς ἀεὶ πρὸς Ἀθηναίων φυλάττεται, κρύφα μηδὲν πρᾶξαι δυνάμενος»· εἶτα ἀπὸ τοῦ χρόνου ὅτι «καὶ τότε δύσκολον, ὅτε ἡ πόλις ἐφυλάττετο, μήτε εἰσιόντος τινὸς μήτε ἐξιόντος». Καὶ ὁ Δημοσθένης ἐν τῷ Περὶ παραπρεσβείας «ἀνεύθυνος, φησίν, ἐπὶ λόγοις», εἶτα «οὐκ ἀνεύθυνος», καὶ πρῶτον ἔλαβεν ἀπὸ τοῦ πράγματος «οὐδὲν γὰρ πρᾶγμα ἀνεύθυνον, ᾧ πρόσεστιν ἀδίκημα»· εἶτα ἀπὸ τοῦ προσώπου ὅτι «καὶ ῥήτωρ ἀνεύθυνος ἐν λόγοις οὐκ ἂν εἴη· ἕκαστος γὰρ ὧν ἐστι κύριος, τούτων τὰς εὐθύνας δίδωσιν»· εἶτα ἀπὸ τοῦ τόπου ὅτι «καὶ ἐν δημοκρατίᾳ οὐδεὶς ἀνεύθυνος ἐν λόγοις», «οἷς γάρ ἐστιν ἐν λόγοις ἡ πολιτεία, πῶς, ἂν οὗτοι μὴ ὦσιν ἀληθεῖς, ἀσφαλῶς ἔστι πολιτεύεσθαι;» καὶ καθάπαξ, ὡς ἔφαμεν, πάντα τὰ κεφάλαια οὕτω καὶ*

1 alt. καὶ om. Vc Ba || **2-4** delevit Rabe | verba ab Aeschine aliena (nec 1, 153 nec 1, 89 sq. conferri possunt) declamationem sapiunt || **4** καὶ ἡ βούλησις Vc Ba | cf. Π. στ. 46, 8 | ὁμοίως om. Pa || **5** ὅτι — Περικλέα om. Ac || **6** τρεψώμεθα **P** | τὸ ἐπιχείρημα Ac | πρῶτον ἀπὸ Ac | ὅτι οὐκ Ac || **7** περικλέα om. **P** Ac || **8** ἡδέως om. Pc || **9** ἄν τι Ac | τοῦ om. Ac || **10** cf. Thuc. 2, 60 || **13** ὑμῶν Ac, (ι supr.) **P**; ὑμῖν Vc Ba | οὐδὲ Vc Ba || **15** alt. καὶ om. **V** || **15-16** τὸ πρᾶγμα (om. ἀπὸ) **V** || **17** καὶ om. Ac || **18** ἀθηναίων v.l. **P**, m. po. **V**; ἀθηναίους ὢν **PV** || **20** Dem. 19, 182; cf. 66. 16 || **21** φησὶν om. Vc Ba || **22** εἶτα **P** Ac; ἢ Vc Ba || **24** ἐν Vc Ba, Dem., (m. 1 ἐπὶ supr.) Pa; ἐπὶ Pc Ac || **26** pr. ἐν (ἐπὶ supr.) Pa; ἐπὶ (ἐν supr.) Pc | Dem. 19, 184 || **26-27** ἐν λόγοις ἐστὶν Pc || **27** ἔστι om. v.l. **P** || **28** p. 86, 3 sq. | οὕτως τὰ κεφάλαια **V**

from the place, that "and in Athens, where the truth of actions has more strength than testimony of witnesses."[134] And similarly, after defining a heading on the basis of intent, saying that "it is not probable that Pericles wanted to be a traitor," we shall turn back to epikheiremes from the act: "It is not probable that Pericles wanted to be a traitor, for treason is a bad thing and something that no one in his right mind would undertake with pleasure," and (*personifying Pericles*) that "I would not have chosen a wicked thing rather than many great good things"; then from the person: "I would not have wanted to be a traitor, being Pericles, always a lover of the city and philathenian and superior to money"; then from the cause: "I would not have betrayed you, for I had no need of money since I was rich, nor was I detested by you but admired"; then from the time, saying, "I would not have wanted to be a traitor now when I have so fine and great a reputation." Facility also: "I could not have committed treason," arguing first from the act, saying that "treason is an unpleasant business and something that cannot be easily done"; then from the person, that "it is also unpleasant for a Pericles, who | has always kept an honorable basis in his dealings [144]
with Athenians, being unable to do anything in secret"; then from the time, that "it would also have been difficult then, when the city was guarded, no one going in or out." And Demosthenes in *On the False Embassy* (19.182): "He (*Aeschines*) says he is not accountable for his speeches," then "He is not unaccountable," and first he took an argument from the act: "for no action is not accountable in which there is crime"; then from the person, that "an orator would not be unaccountable for his speeches, for each person is accountable for the things that are in his control"; then from the place, that in a democracy no one is unaccountable for his speeches (19.184): "For where government is based on speeches, how is it possible to be carried on safely if the speeches are not true?"

Once again, as we said, all headings can be refuted and con-

[134] The text continues, "As Aeschines says in *Against Timarchus*, that you discover strangers in towns not from witnesses but from the truth," but the clause is rejected by Rabe since it is not found in that speech.

*ἀνασκευασθήσεται καὶ κατασκευασθήσεται. οἷον συνεχῶς κατατρέχει Χερρόνησον Φίλιππος, καὶ γράφει Δημοσθένης διορύξαι τὸν Ἰσθμόν. κεφάλαιον «καινὰ γράφεις, καινοτομεῖν δὲ οὐ δεῖ»· πρῶτον ἀπὸ τοῦ πράγματος «πονηρὸν γὰρ ἡ καινοτομία»· εἶτα ἀπὸ τοῦ προσώπου ὅτι «καὶ μὴ δεῖ καινοτομεῖν Ἀθηναίους, τοὺς συνετοὺς καὶ τοῖς ἀρχαίοις ἀεὶ καὶ νόμοις καὶ ἔθεσι χρωμένους»· εἶτα ἀπὸ τοῦ καιροῦ ὅτι «καὶ μὴ δεῖ ἐν πολέμῳ καινοτομεῖν· ἀγαπητὸν γάρ, εἰ καὶ τὰ συνήθη φυλάτ-*
[145] *των τις ἐν ἐκείνῳ σωθήσεται». καὶ πάλιν «δεῖ | καινοτομεῖν», ἡ λύσις ἀπὸ τοῦ πράγματος «καλὸν γὰρ τὸ καινοτομεῖν καὶ ὁ βίος ἀεὶ καινοτομεῖται τοῖς πράγμασι καὶ διὰ τοῦτο βελτίων γίνεται»· εἶτα καὶ ἀπὸ τοῦ προσώπου «δεῖ καινοτομεῖν Ἀθηναίους· ὡς νεωτεροποιοὶ γὰρ καὶ παρὰ τοῖς ἐχθροῖς ἐπαινούμεθα»· εἶτα ἀπὸ τοῦ καιροῦ ὅτι «καὶ δεῖ ἐν πολέμῳ καινοτομεῖν· καινοτόμον γὰρ πρᾶγμα ὁ πόλεμος καὶ ἀφ᾿ ἑαυτοῦ τεχνᾶται τὰ πολλά». κεφάλαιον ἕτερον ἐμπίπτει πάλιν ὅτι «δύσκολον διορύξαι Χερρόνησον»· ἀπὸ τοῦ πράγματος «αὐτὸ γὰρ τὸ διορύσσειν δύσκολον»· εἶτα ἀπὸ τοῦ προσώπου ὅτι «καὶ? Ἀθηναίοις δύσκολον τοῖς ἀήθεσιν»· εἶτα ἀπὸ τοῦ τόπου ὅτι «καὶ μακρὰν τῆς πατρίδος δύσκολον»· εἶτα ἀπὸ τοῦ καιροῦ ὅτι «καὶ ἐν πολέμῳ δύσκολον ταῦτα ποιεῖν». ἡ λύσις «οὐ δύσκολον· τό τε γὰρ πρᾶγμα ῥᾴδιον καὶ ἐν τῇ ἡμετέρᾳ χώρᾳ», εἶτα ὅτι «καὶ Ἀθηναίοις πάντα ῥᾴδια». Αἱ μὲν οὖν γενέσεις τῶν ἐπιχειρημάτων αὗται.*

*Πολλάκις δὲ ἀπὸ μιᾶς γενέσεως καὶ δύο καὶ τρία εὑρίσκεται ἐπιχειρήματα, οἷον ἀπὸ τοῦ προσώπου, ὅτι μὴ ὁ δεῖνα τόδε ἐποίησεν· ἔστι γὰρ τοῦτο τοῦ ποιοῦντος. εἶτα, ὅτι μηδὲ κατὰ τῶνδε ἐποίησεν· ἔστι γὰρ ἀπὸ προσώπου, καθ᾿ ὧν δοκεῖ πεποιηκέναι. εἶτα, ὅτι μηδὲ ὑπὲρ τῶνδε*
[146] *ἐποίησεν· ἔστι γὰρ ἀπὸ προσώπου | τῶν, δι᾿ οὓς κρίνεταί τις. οἷον ἐπὶ*

1 γρ καὶ πάλιν οἷον συνεχῶς Pa, (οἱ pro οἷον) Pc | cf. 74, 17 || 2 ⌊Ι⌉ φίλιππος Vc || 3 τὸ κεφάλαιον Vc Ba | cf. 98, 18 sq. || 5 τοῖς **P**; τοὺς **V** || 6 καὶ om. Vc Ba || 8 καὶ πάλιν m. 2 Vc Ac, v.l. **P**; om. **PV** | δεῖ **V**, v.l. Pa; δεῖν **P** || 9 εἶτα ἐπιχείρημα ante ἀπὸ add. **V**, v.l. Pa || 10-11 εἶτα ὅτι καὶ δεῖ καινοτομεῖν ἀθηναίους ἀπὸ τοῦ προσώπου ὡς **V** || 12 τοὺς ἐχθροὺς Vc | καὶ om. Vc Ba || 13 ἀπ᾿ αὐτοῦ Vc Ba, at 142, 13 || 14 καὶ κεφάλαιον **V** | ἕτερον om. Vc Ba || 15 εἶτα ante ἀπὸ add. Ac, m. 2 Vc || 16 εἶτα καὶ Ac || 17 μακρὰν ἀπὸ τῆς **V** || 19 τὸ γὰρ διορύσσειν πρᾶγμα ῥᾴδιον p. 76, 3 | καὶ om. **V** || 20 ῥάιδιον ποιεῖν Ac | οὖν **P**; om. Vc Ba; γὰρ Ac || 23 τοῦ om. Vc Ba || 24 τοῦτο **P**; τὸ πρόσωπον v.l. **P**, m. 2 Vc; ἀπὸ προσώπου Sc; om. **V** | μὴ (om. δὲ) Pc || 25 καὶ ἀπὸ προσώπου τῶν καθ᾿ Vc Ba || 26 πεποίηκεν Pc

firmed in this way. For example, Philip has continually been overrunning the Chersonese, and Demosthenes introduces a motion to dig a canal through the isthmus.[135] (*His opponent's*) heading is "You are proposing a novelty, and there is no need to innovate." (*This is supported*) first from the act, "for innovation is a bad thing"; then from the person, that "there is no need for Athenians to innovate, since wise men always keep to ancient laws and customs"; then from the occasion, "and there is no need to innovate in time of war, for it is agreeable if one is saved then while defending the ordinary." And in reply, "There is need | to innovate," the [145]
lysis from the act, "for innovation is a good thing, and life is always being changed by events and in this way becomes better"; then from the person: "There is need for Athenians to innovate, for we are praised even among our enemies for doing new things"; then from the occasion, "and there is need to innovate in time of war, for war is an innovating thing and many things are taught by it." Another heading applies again, that "it is troublesome to dig through the Chersonese," supported from the act, "for digging a canal is in itself troublesome"; then from the person, "and it is troublesome to Athenians who are unfamiliar with excavation"; then from the place, "and it is troublesome that it is far from home"; then from the occasion, "and it is troublesome to do this in time of war." The lysis is "It is not troublesome, for the thing is easy and in our territory," then "and all things are easy for Athenians." These are the sources of epikheiremes.

Often two or three epikheiremes are found from one source; for example, from the person, saying that so-in-so did not do this; this is arguing from the doer. Then, saying that he did not do it against these men; this is from the person of those against whom he seems to have acted. Then, that he did not do it for the sake of these people; this is from the person | of those because of whom [146]

[135] There is no historical basis for such a proposal.

*παραδειγμάτων ὅτι «οὐκ εἰκὸς ἐθελῆσαι προδοῦναι Περικλέα, τὸν συνετόν, τὸν οὕτω λαμπρὸν καὶ μέγαν καὶ στρατηγὸν ἔνδοξον», ἀπὸ τοῦ Περικλέους τοῦτο· ὅτι «μηδὲ εἰκὸς ἐθελῆσαι προδοῦναι Ἀθηναίους, τοὺς τιμῶντας αὐτόν» ἄλλο πρόσωπον· ὅτι «μηδὲ εἰκὸς ἐθελῆσαι προδοῦναι Λακεδαιμονίοις, τοῖς ἐχθροῖς, τοῖς ἐπιβουλεύσασιν αὐτῷ» καὶ τοῦτο ἄλλο πρόσωπον. καὶ πάλιν «δεῖ καινοτομεῖν Ἀθηναίους» ἀπὸ τοῦ προσώπου, «ἀεὶ γὰρ Ἀθηναῖοι καινοτόμοι», καὶ «δεῖ καινοτομεῖν κατὰ Φιλίππου τι ποιοῦντας· καινοτόμος γὰρ καὶ Φίλιππος, δεῖ δὲ μιμεῖσθαι τὰς τῶν πολεμίων ἐπιτηδεύσεις ἐν τῷ πολέμῳ» καὶ ταῦτα ἄλλα πρόσωπα. καὶ πάλιν ὅτι «χαλεπὸν διορύσσειν Χερρόνησον», καὶ λήψῃ ἀπὸ τοῦ τόπου ἐπιχείρημα «μακρὰν γὰρ Ἀθηναίων Χερρόνησος» καὶ πάλιν «χαλεπὸν διορύξαι Χερρόνησον· μέγας γὰρ ὁ τόπος, ὃν ἀξιοῦσι διορύξαι, πέντε καὶ τετταράκοντα σταδίων». εὑρίσκεται δὲ πολλάκις οὕτω καὶ ἐπὶ τῆς αἰτίας, οἷον συμβουλεύει ὁ Θεμιστοκλῆς ἐν τῇ θαλάττῃ μυεῖν, «ἀλλὰ δέος, μὴ ἐπιστήσηται βασιλεὺς μυοῦσιν ἡμῖν». «ἀλλ᾽ οὐκ ἐπιστήσεται», ἀπὸ τῆς αἰτίας, «ἵνα μὴ δόξῃ περὶ τοὺς θεοὺς ἀσεβὴς εἶναι, κωλύων γενέσθαι μυστήρια»· καὶ πάλιν «οὐκ ἐπιστήσεται, ἵνα μὴ ἀσεβήσας ἡττηθῇ»· ἔστι γὰρ ἴδιον μὲν τὸ «ἵνα μὴ δόξῃ ἀσεβὴς*
[147] *εἶναι», ἴδιον δὲ «ἵνα μὴ ἀσεβήσας ἡττηθῇ», ἐπεὶ καὶ ἐν εἰρήνῃ | φυλάξεταί τις ἀσεβὴς εἶναι δοκεῖν, κἂν μηδὲν διὰ τοῦτο φανερὸν ἤδη φοβῆται κακόν. καὶ ὅλως εὑρίσκεται ἐπὶ πάντων, πλὴν οὐκ ἀεί, σπανιάκις δέ γε.*

*Ὥσπερ τοίνυν τοῦτο ἴσμεν, ὅτι πολλάκις ἡ μία γένεσις τοῦ ἐπιχειρήματος δύο καὶ τρία παρατυχὸν εὑρίσκει ἐπιχειρήματα, οὕτως ἰστέον, ὅτι καὶ πολλάκις ἓν ἐπιχείρημα εὑρίσκεται κοινὸν καὶ δύο καὶ τριῶν γενέσεων, ὡς δύνασθαι τὸ αὐτὸ δοκεῖν εἶναι καὶ καιροῦ καὶ τόπου ἢ αἰτίας καὶ πράγματος ἢ προσώπου καὶ τόπου, οἷον ὅτι «μὴ δεῖ τῶν κρίσεων ἐλέγχους παρέχεσθαι παρ᾽ ὑμῖν τοῖς δημοκρατουμένοις»· τοῦτο γάρ ἐστι κοινὸν καὶ τοῦ προσώπου τῶν δημοκρατουμένων καὶ τοῦ τόπου, ἔνθα ἐστὶν ἡ δημοκρατία· καὶ πάλιν «δεῖ λόγων εὐθύνας εἶναι*

1 cf. 88, 4 | τὸν συνετόν om. Ac Ba (sed ad λαμπρὸν mg. m. 1 : συνετὸν ⌊καὶ m. po.⌉ Ba) || **1-2** post συνετόν add. Vc, v.l. **P**: ἀθηναίους τοὺς φίλους λακεδαιμονίοις τοῖς ἐχθροῖς || **2** ⌊II-IV⌉ τὸν Vc | τοῦ om. v.l. Pc || **5** ἐπιβουλεύουσιν Sc || **6** cf. 72, 8 cet. || **9** τοῦτο **V** || **9-10** ἄλλο πρόσωπον Vc Ba; ἄλλου προσώπου Ac, m. 2 Vc || **10** cf. 92, 14 || **11** τῶν ἀθηναίων Ac || **15** ἐπιστήσεται **V** | ὑμῖν Pc || **18** ἡττηθῆι καὶ διατοῦτο· ἔστι γὰρ ἄλλο μὲν Vc Ba || **19** δὲ τὸ ἵνα Pc || **21** ˝εὑρίσκεται ˊἐπὶ πάντων (m. 2 corr.) Vc || **22-23** τοῦ νοήματος? || **23** παρὰ τυχὸν v.l. **P**, v.l. Dox. (cf. 158, 6); παρὰ τὸ τυχὸν **PV** || **24** καὶ om. Vc Ba || **26** μὴ Ba, m. po. Pa; καὶ **P** Ac; ⌊II-III⌉ Vc; cf. 88, 8. 88, 17. 90, 1 | cf. 90, 26 || **28** καὶ κοινὸν καὶ Pc || **29** cf. 90, 26

someone is being tried. Some examples: "It is not probable that Pericles wanted to be a traitor, a man who is intelligent, so glorious and great and a respected general." This is from the person of Pericles; another person is involved in saying, "It is not probable that he wanted to betray Athenians, who honor him," and still another person is brought in as follows: "It is not probable he wanted to betray to Lacedaimonians, to enemies, to those who plotted against him." And again, "There is need for Athenians to innovate" argues from the person, "for Athenians are always innovative," and "There is need to innovate by doing something against Philip, for Philip too is innovative, and there is need to imitate the practices of enemies in war," introducing other persons. And again, when arguing that it is difficult to dig through the Chersonese you will take an epikheireme from the place: "for Chersonese is far from Athens" and "it is difficult to dig through the Chersonese, for it is a large distance they propose to excavate, one of forty-five stades." Arguments are often found from the cause; for example, Themistocles recommends holding initiations into the mysteries at sea. "But there is fear that the king may attack us when initiating." "But he will not attack," from the cause, "in order not to seem to be irreverent toward the gods by preventing the celebration of the mysteries." And again, "He will not attack in order not to be defeated because of irreverence." "In order not to seem to be irreverent" is one thing and "in order not to be defeated because of irreverence" is something different, since also in peace time | one guards against seeming to be irreverent, even if [147]
one is afraid of no clear evil because of this. Generally, techniques of invention apply to all cases, but not always; there are rare exceptions.

Now just as we understand that often one source of epikheiremes suggests two or maybe three epikheiremes, similarly you should understand that often one epikheireme is invented in common from two and three sources, so that the same can seem to be derived from occasion and place or cause and action or person and place; for example, "There is no need to provide evidence for trials among you who live in a democracy." This combines person—those living in a democracy—and place, where the democracy is. Again, "There is need for accountability of words among you who

*παρ᾽ ὑμῖν τοῖς δημοκρατουμένοις»· κοινὸν γάρ ἐστιν, ὡς ἔφην, ἀμφοῖν.*

*Ταῦτα δὲ πάντα ἐξεθέμην, ὅπως εἰδείημεν καὶ τὰς εὐπορίας μὴ περιττὰς εἶναι δοκεῖν, ἃς ὑποβάλλει τὰ ἐπιχειρήματα, ὅταν ἐξῇ πολλὰ λαβεῖν, καὶ τὰς ἀπορίας, καὶ ὅτι μὴ παρ᾽ ἡμᾶς ἀπαντᾶν τὰ νοήματα προσήκει νομίζειν, καὶ μάλιστα ὅταν ἓν νόημα καὶ ἓν ἐπιχείρημα ἐπικρατῇ πολλῶν γενέσεων. τὸ πρᾶγμα γάρ ἐστι τὸ πάσχον τὴν ἀπορίαν ἢ δεχόμενον τὴν εὐπορίαν, ὁ μέντοι τεχνίτης εἰς τὴν θεωρίαν ἀποβλέπων*
[148] *εἴσεται, περὶ τί συμβαίνει ἡ ἀνάγκη· ὥστε εἰδέναι τοῦτο καὶ | μὴ λυπεῖσθαι αὐτὸν καθάπερ ἀνόητον, εἰ μὴ δυναμένης τῆς τέχνης ὑποβαλεῖν τῷ πράγματι ἐπιχειρήματα αὐτός ἐστιν ἐν στενῷ κομιδῇ τῆς εὐπορίας τῶν νοημάτων. ἔστι δὲ τῷ τρόπῳ τῆς μεταποιήσεως καὶ τὰ πλήθη συστεῖλαι τῶν νοημάτων καὶ τὰ ἄπορα ἐκτεῖναι καὶ πολλὰ ποιῆσαι ταῖς κατὰ τὴν ἑρμηνείαν θεωρίαις· ἐπεὶ μηδὲ Δημοσθένης ᾐδέσθη πολλάκις ἑνὶ χρησάμενος ἐπιχειρήματι καὶ ποτὲ μὲν αὐτὸ τρέψας καὶ μεταποιήσας, ὡς ἐν τῷ τῆς Παραπρεσβείας πρώτῳ μεταστατικῷ, ποτὲ δὲ μηδὲ ἐργασάμενος, ὡς ἐν τῷ Περὶ τοῦ στεφάνου «ἀλλ᾽ ἀδίκως, φησίν, ἦρξας. εἶτα παρών, ὅτε με εἰσῆγον οἱ λογισταί, διὰ τί οὐ κατηγόρεις;» ἠρκέσθη γὰρ τῷ ἀπὸ τοῦ χρόνου ἐπιχειρήματι νικῆσαι τὴν ὑποφορὰν «νῦν οὖν κατηγορεῖς, δέον ὅτε ἐκρινόμην καὶ τὰς εὐθύνας ἐδίδουν;»*

4 μὴ **P**; μηδὲ Ac; μὴ δεῖ Vc Ba | ἀπαντᾶν **P**; ἅπαντα **V**, v.l. Pc || 5 προσήκει om. Vc Ba || 5-6 ἐπικρατῆι **P**, (-τεῖ) Ac; κοινὸν ἧι Vc (γρ ἐπικρατεῖ) Ba; mg. m. 1 καὶ ἓν ἐπιχείρημα κοινὸν ἢ πολλῶν γενέσεων Pa, (γρ´ καὶ; πολλῶν ἣν κοινὸν) Pc || 7 ἀναδεχόμενον **V**; γρ καὶ ἀναδεχόμενον καὶ ἐπιδεχόμενον mg. **P** || 8 συμβαίνειν ἀνάγκη Ac || 9 ὑποβάλλειν Ac || 10 ἀπορίας vulg. || 15 cf. Dem. 19, 8 cet. (schol. **P** = W **V** 400, 6) | ἐν er. Ba | πρώτωι μεταστατικῶι Vc Ba; τῶι πρώτω τὸ μεταστατικόν **P** Ac | μὴ Vc || 16 Dem. 18, 117 || 17 εἰσήγαγον Pc | διατί **P**; om. **V**, Dem. (cf. 78, 3) || 19 ἐδίδουν m. 1 Ba; ἐδίδων **P** Ac; ?m. 1 Vc

live in a democracy"; both are combined, as I said.

*In the following passage the author tells students not to be discouraged if there seem too many things that could be said or if there are too few. In the latter case it is possible to state the same argument in different words. The advice, however, is so cumbersomely stated that it might confuse rather than encourage a student. It seems possible that this is an addition by the editor who created* On Invention *out of an earlier account and not part of the source, which is otherwise closely followed.*

I have explained all this in order that we may understand that the resources that epikheiremes supply in abundance may not seem excessive whenever it is possible to get many and that the lack of them may not seem so either, [*and*] because it is not appropriate to think to encounter ideas by ourselves,[136] and especially whenever one idea and one epikheireme exploits many sources. The subject may be one suffering from lack or one admitting an abundance (*of things to say*), but the expert (*tekhnitēs*), looking to the theory, will know why the constraint exists, and so he will know also | not to be distressed as if he were ignorant if [148]
he finds himself lacking a supply of ideas when his art is not able to supply an abundance of epikheiremes for the subject. By using metapoiesis[137] it is possible both to contract the number of ideas as well as to fill up a lack and to do many things by a knowledge of forms of expression (*hermēneia*). Not even Demosthenes was ashamed to use one epikheireme repeatedly, both sometimes turning it one way and sometimes altering it, as in the first part of *On the False Embassy* (19.8), but sometimes not elaborating it, as in *On the Crown* (18.117): "'But,' he says, 'you exercised your office wrongly.' Since you were present when the accountants brought me in, why did you not bring a charge?" The epikheireme from time was sufficient to defeat the hypophora: "You are bringing a charge now, when you should have done so at the time I was being examined and giving my accounts."

[136] I.e., spontaneously, to be able to make up arguments without training in rhetoric.

[137] I.e., by stating things in different ways.

## *Περὶ ἐργασίας ἐπιχειρημάτων.*

*Ὥσπερ τοίνυν τῆς λύσεως εὑρεθείσης καθ' ἕκαστον κεφάλαιον
ἤτοι ἐκ τῆς ἐνστάσεως ἢ ἀντιπαραστάσεως δεόμεθα τῶν ἐπιχειρημάτων εἰς κατασκευὴν τῆς λύσεως, οὕτω δεησόμεθα πάλιν ἐργασίας εἰς
τὴν κατασκευὴν τοῦ ἐπιχειρήματος. ἐργάζεται δὲ πᾶν ἐπιχείρημα ἀπὸ
τούτων, ἃ δοκοῦσιν εἶναι τινὲς ἐπιχειρήματα, οἷον ἀπὸ παραβολῆς, ἀπὸ*
[149] *παραδείγματος, ἀπὸ μικρο|τέρου, ἀπὸ μείζονος, ἀπὸ ἴσου, ἀπὸ ἐναν-
τίου. καὶ ἡ μὲν γένεσις τῶν ἐπιχειρημάτων ἀπὸ περιστάσεως, ταῦτα
δὲ οὐ καθ' ἕκαστον κεφάλαιον ζητηθήσεται, ἀλλὰ καθ' ἕκαστον ἐπιχείρημα. ὥσπερ δὲ κεφαλαίου τεθέντος εἰς τὴν λύσιν ἢ κατασκευὴν
πολλάκις μὲν πολλῶν εὐποροῦμεν ἐπιχειρημάτων, πολλάκις δὲ ὀλίγων,
οὕτω καὶ ἐπὶ τοῦ ἐπιχειρήματος πολλάκις μὲν ἀπὸ τῆς ἐργασίας εἰς
κατασκευὴν εὑρέθη τοῦ ἐπιχειρήματος πλείονα, πολλάκις δὲ ἐλάττο-
να. οἷον τὸ ἐπιχείρημα ἔστω εἰ τύχοι ἀπὸ προσώπου· πολλάκις μὲν εἰς
κατασκευὴν τοῦ ἐπιχειρήματος τοῦ ἀπὸ τοῦ προσώπου εὕρηται ἐργασία ἐκ παραδείγματος μόνον, πολλάκις δὲ καὶ ἐκ παραδείγματος καὶ
ἐκ παραβολῆς, πολλάκις δὲ καὶ ἐκ τούτων καὶ ἐκ τοῦ ἐναντίου, πολλάκις δὲ καὶ ἐκ πλειόνων. Θῶμεν δὲ καὶ ἐπὶ παραδείγματος. «οὐ δεῖ
καινοτομεῖν», κεφάλαιον. ἡ λύσις ὅτι «δεῖ καινοτομεῖν, εἰ συμφέρει»·
ἐπιχείρημα ἀπὸ τοῦ προσώπου ὅτι «καὶ δεῖ καινοτομεῖν Ἀθηναίους
ὄντας· καινοτόμοι γάρ ἐσμεν»· εἶτα ἐργασία ληφθεῖσα ἐκ παραδείγματος εἰς κατασκευὴν τοῦ ἐπιχειρήματος τούτου ὅτι Ἀθηναῖοι καινοτόμοι
«καὶ οἱ πατέρες ἡμῶν ἐκαινοτόμησαν τόδε καὶ τόδε»· καὶ πολλάκις οὐχ
ἓν εὑρίσκεται παράδειγμα ἀλλὰ πλείονα, καὶ τοῖς μὲν ἀπείροις ἔδοξε
πολλὰ εἶναι ἐπιχειρήματα, ἡμῖν δὲ οὐκ ἐπιχειρήματα ἀλλ' ἐργασία, καὶ*
[150] *| ἐργασία ἀπὸ παραδείγματος μία, κἂν ᾖ τὰ παραδείγματα πολλά. καὶ
ὁ Δημοσθένης εἶπέ που λέγων «οὐ δὴ θαυμαστόν, εἰ στρατευόμενος*

**2** vix san. | τῆς post ἢ add. Ac, supr. Pa || **3** ἢ Pa **V**; καὶ Pc || **4** τὴν κατασκευὴν Ac || **6** schol. **P**: Μινουκιανὸν λέγει· καὶ Μητροφάνην (de interpretis auctoritate dubitat Glöckner, Quaest. rhet. 44) || **8** περιστάσεως **P** || **10-14** et πολλάκι **P** || **12** ἐπὶ τοῦ ἐπιχειρήματος **P** Ba, m. 1 Vc; ἐπιχειρήματος εὑρεθέντος (om. ἐπὶ τοῦ) Ac, m. 2 Vc, v.l. **P** || **15** alt. τοῦ om. Vc Ba || **16** μόνου Vc Ba || **16** καὶ om. Pc || **18** cf. 80, 5. 92, 3 || **19** ὅτι καὶ δεῖ **V** | ἐὰν συμφέρηι **V** || **20** τοῦ om. Pc | καὶ om. Pc || **22** τοῦ[του]? || **23-24** sic **V** Vδ; ἓν παράδειγμα οὐχ εὑρίσκεται **P**; Dox.: τὰ πλείω τῶν βιβλίων ἀντὶ τοῦ «εἰς ἓν εὑρίσκεται ἐπιχείρημα» «οὐχ ἓν εὑρίσκεται παράδειγμα» ἔχει || **24** ἀλλὰ καὶ πλείονα Pc || **25** cf. 98, 5–6 | ἐργασίαι Vc Ba || **27** Dem. 2, 23

## CHAPTER 7: ON ERGASIA OF EPIKHEIREMES

Now just as after a lysis has been invented for each heading we need epikheiremes either from enstasis or antiparastasis for confirmation of the lysis, so we shall need in turn an ergasia[138] for confirmation of the epikheireme. Every epikheireme is elaborated from these things that some think to be epikheiremes;[139] for example, from comparison, from example, from a lesser, | from [149]
a greater, from an equal, from an opposite. The source of the epikheiremes is from the circumstances, but these will not have been sought for each heading but for each epikheireme. Just as when a heading has been postulated, on the one hand we sometimes have an abundance of many epikheiremes for its refutation or confirmation but sometimes, on the other hand, only a few, so for an epikheireme: sometimes, on the one hand, from the ergasia many things are found for the confirmation of the epikheireme, and sometimes, on the other hand, few things. For example, let there be an epikheireme, say from a person. Often for confirmation of the epikheireme from a person an ergasia is invented from an example alone, but often also from an example and from a comparison and often from these and from the opposite, and often from even more things.

Let us propose the following as an example: "There is no need to innovate." That is a heading. The lysis is "There is need to innovate, if it is advantageous." An epikheireme from a person is "and there is need to innovate since we are Athenians, for we are innovators." Then comes an ergasia taken from an example for confirmation of this epikheireme that Athenians are innovators: "and our ancestors made this and that innovation." Often not only one but many examples are invented, and to the inexperienced in these matters there seem to be many epikheiremes, but to us they are an ergasia, not epikheiremes, and | they make up a single erga- [150]
sia from example, even if there are many examples. Demosthenes said somewhere (2.23), "There is no wonder if he (*Philip*), going

[138] The author uses *ergasia* (literally, "a working") with the meaning of an "elaboration" to provide support for an epikheireme; cf. Fortunatianus 2.29, p. 119 Halm.

[139] A scholiast in Parisinus 1983 identifies "some" as Minucianus and Metrophanes, but this may not be reliable; see the apparatus on p. 98, 6.

*ἐκεῖνος καὶ παρὼν ἐφ᾽ ἅπασιν ἡμῶν μελλόντων καὶ ῥᾳθυμούντων περιγίνεται», τοῦτό ἐστιν ἐπιχείρημα ἀπὸ τοῦ πράγματος· εἶτα ἐργασίᾳ κέχρηται ἀπὸ τοῦ ἐναντίου «τοὐναντίον γὰρ ἦν θαυμαστόν, εἰ μηδὲν ὧν δεῖ ποιοῦντες ἡμεῖς τοῦ πάντα ἃ προσήκει ποιοῦντος περιῆμεν». ἂν δὲ λέγῃς «καλὸν τὸ τιμᾶν γονέας», ἐπιχείρημα ἀπὸ τοῦ πράγματος, ἐπιφέρῃς δὲ «καὶ γὰρ τὰ θηρία τοῦτο ποιεῖ», ἐκ παραβολῆς ἐργασίαν τῷ ἐπιχειρήματι δίδως. κἂν λέγῃς ἐπιχείρημα πάλιν «ἔξεστι τῇ πόλει παρ᾽ ἑαυτῇ ποιεῖν, ἃ βούλεται», εἶτα ἐπιφέρῃς «καὶ γὰρ ἐν ταῖς οἰκίαις ἔξεστιν ἑκάστῳ δεσπότῃ ποιεῖν, ἃ βούλεται», ἐργασίαν ἀπὸ τοῦ μικροτέρου λέγεις.*

## *Περὶ ἐνθυμήματος.*

*Τὸ δὲ ἐνθύμημα δόξαν δριμύτητος ἀποφέρεται μείζονα γνωσθέν, ὅ τί τέ ἐστι καὶ ὅπως εὑρίσκεται καὶ ὅπου. καὶ γὰρ ἡ τάξις αὐτὴ τὴν τῆς δριμύτητος δόξαν ἐξ ἀνάγκης αὐτῷ προστίθησι· δεῖ γὰρ τεθέντος κεφαλαίου λῦσαι πρῶτον ἀπὸ τῆς ἐνστάσεως ἢ ἀντιπαραστάσεως, εἶτα προσλαβεῖν τὸ ἐπιχείρημα εἰς κατασκευὴν ἀπὸ τῆς περιστάσεως, εἶτα*
[151] *ἐργάσασθαι ἀφ᾽ ὧν τὴν | ἐργασίαν ἔφαμεν γίνεσθαι τοῦ ἐπιχειρήματος, εἶτα τὸ ἐνθύμημα ἐπενεγκεῖν τῇ ἐργασίᾳ. οἷον κεφάλαιον ὑποκείσθω «χαλεπὸν διορύξαι Χερρόνησον», εἶτα ἡ λύσις ἀπὸ τῆς ἐνστάσεως ὅτι «οὐ χαλεπὸν τὸ διορύξαι», εἶτα ἐπιχείρημα ἀπὸ τοῦ πράγματος «γῆν γὰρ ὀρύξομεν, παιδιὰ δὲ τὸ ὀρύσσειν», εἶτα ἐργασία ἐκ παραδείγματος ὅτι «καὶ βασιλεὺς Περσῶν δεηθείς ποτε διώρυξε τὸν Ἄθω», εἶτα ἐνθύμημα εἰς τοῦτο «καίτοι ἐκεῖνος μὲν διώρυσσεν ὄρος, ἡμεῖς δὲ γῆν ὀρύξομεν»· ὥσπερ γὰρ ἡ ἐργασία κατασκευάζει τὸ ἐπιχείρημα, οὕτω καὶ τὸ ἐνθύμημα κατασκευάζει τὴν ἐργασίαν, καὶ πάλιν ὥσπερ καθ᾽ ἕκαστον ἐπιχείρημα ζητοῦμεν ἐργασίαν, οὕτω καθ᾽ ἑκάστην ἐργασίαν*

**2** τοῦ om. Pc || **5** ὅτι. καλὸν Pc | τοῦ om. Pc || **6** ἐπιφέρεις **V** || **7** τῇ om. Vc Ba || **8** ὃ **V** | ἐπιφέρεις **V** || **9** ὃ **V** | τοῦ om. Ac || **11** capita π. ἐνθυμήματος, (π. ἐπενθυμήματος,) π. τῶν ἀπ᾽ ἀρχῆς ἄχρι τέλους (100, 11–120, 1) post caput π. διασκευῆς (126–134) transp. Mr | ἐνθυμημάτων Ac || **12** cf. Aps. I 2 p. 289, 18 Sp.-H. | δὲ om. Mr | ἐν ἑαυτῷ ἀποφέρεται v.l. **P** || **13** αὕτη **PV** || **15-16** εἶτα — περιστάσεως m. 2 suppl. Vc || **16** τῆς λύσεως post κατασκευὴν add. Ba, (m. 2) Vc, v.l. **P** || **17** ἐργάζεσθαι Vc Ba | p. 98, 5 || **19** cf. 94, 12 | ἡ om. Ac | τῆς om. Vc | ὅτι om. Vc Ba || **23** διώρυξεν Portus || **23-24** ὀρύξομεν γῆν Pc || **25** καὶ om. **V**

on campaigns and appearing everywhere, should get the better of us who delay and take our ease"; this is an epikheireme from the act. Then he has used an ergasia from the opposite: "The wonder would be the opposite, if we who do nothing that is needed were to get the better of one who does everything that is appropriate." If you say "It is a good thing to honor parents," it is an epikheireme from an act, and if you add "for even wild beasts do this," you are giving an ergasia from a comparison in support of the epikheireme. If you state the epikheireme "It is permitted to the city to do what it wants with its own" and then add "for it is permitted to each master to do what he wants in his own house," you state an ergasia from the lesser.

## CHAPTER 8: ON ENTHYMEME

Enthymeme *(literally, "something in the mind") is the name in Aristotle's* Rhetoric *(e.g., 1.2 and 2.22) for a rhetorical syllogism, often with one term implied. It thus can take the form of a statement (the conclusion) with a supporting reason (the major premise), or the form of a condition: if something is the case (and it is), then something else follows. Enthymeme in Aristotle is one of the two forms of artistic proof, the other being example. Quintilian reports (5.10.1–2) that the term enthymeme was used to mean anything conceived in the mind or a proposition with a reason or a way of completing an argument from consequents or conflicts.* Anonymous Seguerianus *(§§146, 157) and Apsines (ch. 8) echo the Aristotelian concept, but the former also reports (§158) that "according to some, an enthymeme is a conclusion of an antecedent epikheireme related to the question at issue in one period." This seems similar to the view found below. An anonymous commentator on this passage (Walz 7.2:761–67) lists twenty-one kinds of enthymemes (from the opposite, from the included, from the related, etc.) and continues with mention of more traditional definitions of enthymemes made by Neocles, Harpocration, and Alexander (who were the sources for* Anonymous Seguerianus*).*

The enthymeme has a reputation for striking effect (*drimytēs*), greater when it is understood what it is and how it is invented and where, for it is the arrangement itself that necessarily gives it the reputation of striking effect. When a heading has been proposed, one should refute it first from the enstasis or antiparastasis,

*ζητοῦμεν ἐνθύμημα. ὥστε εἰς ἄπειρον προχωρεῖν δύνασθαι τὴν δριμύτητα, εἰ ἡ λύσις μὲν εὐπορήσειεν ἐνστάσεώς τε καὶ ἀντιπαραστάσεως, τούτων δὲ ἑκάστη πάλιν ἐπιχειρημάτων δύο ἢ τριῶν, τῶν δὲ ἐπιχειρημάτων ἕκαστον ἐργασιῶν ὁμοίως δύο ἢ τριῶν, τῆς δὲ ἐργασίας ἑκάστης ἴδιον ἐνθύμημα εὑρούσης πάλιν.*

*Ἰστέον δέ, ὅτι καὶ πολλάκις ἐργασία μία πολλὰ εὑρίσκει ἐνθυμήματα, καὶ εἰ ζητοίη τις οὕτω καθ' ἑκάστην ἐργασίαν τὸ ἐνθύμημα, ἀπὸ* [152] *τῶν αὐτῶν περιστά|σεων ζητήσει, ἀφ' ὧν ἐζήτησεν ἂν τὰ ἐπιχειρήματα τοῦ τεθέντος κεφαλαίου. ἔτι ὃ λέγω σαφέστερον ἐκθήσομαι, ὅτι καθ' ἑκάστην ἐργασίαν τὰ ἐνθυμήματα εὑρίσκεται σχῆμα μὲν ἔχοντα συγκριτικόν, εὕρεσιν δὲ ἐν τῇ συγκρίσει ἀπὸ τοῦ τόπου ἢ χρόνου ἢ τρόπου ἢ προσώπου ἢ αἰτίας ἢ πράγματος· συμβήσεται γὰρ οὕτως ἐν ἐργασίᾳ μιᾷ καὶ δύο καὶ πλείονα εὑρεθῆναι τὰ ἐνθυμήματα, ἅπερ εὑρεθέντα δόξαν ἐπενθυμημάτων παρέχει.*

*Ἐπενθύμημα γάρ ἐστι κυρίως ἐπὶ φθάνοντι ἐνθυμήματι ἕτερον ἐπεννοούμενον ἐνθύμημα· οἷον τὸ παράδειγμα «καὶ γὰρ βασιλεὺς διώρυξε τὸν Ἄθω», εἶτα τὸ ἐνθύμημα, ὃ ῥητέον ὅτι συγκριτικῶς πᾶν εὑρίσκεται συγκρινόμενον ἀπὸ τῆς ἐργασίας καὶ πρὸς αὐτὸ τεῖνον, οἷον*

1 χωρεῖν Vc Ba || 2 εἰ Ba; καὶ Ac; καὶ εἰ **P** Vc | schol. **P**: προσεπακουστέον τὸ μάλιστα ... καὶ στικτέον ἀπὸ τοῦ «εἰ καὶ ἡ λύσις» μέσας ἄχρι τοῦ «εὑρούσης πάλιν», ἐκεῖσε δὲ στικτέον τελέαν | εὐπορήσει Ac Ba | τε om. **V** || 4 et ἢ καὶ Pc || 5 ad πάλιν m. 2 Vc: λείπει et mg. κείμενον· εἰς ἄπειρον προχωρεῖ ὁ λόγος; schol. **P** (W VII 767 ann. 23): τινὲς ... φάσκουσιν ἐλλιπῶς ἔχειν τὸ χωρίον λείποντος τοῦ «πλείων ἡ δριμύτης γίνεται» ... ἀλλὰ μόνον προσυπακούειν δεῖ τῷ «εἰ καὶ ἡ λύσις» τὸ μάλιστα κτλ. || 7 καὶ om. **V** | καὶ πάλιν ante ἀπὸ add. Vc Ba, πάλιν καὶ Ac || 8 ζητήσοι **P** | τὸ ἐπιχείρημα **V**, v.l. **P** | alia v.l.: γρ´ εἴπερ ζητοίη τις οὕτω καθ' ἑκάστην ἐργασίαν τὸ ἐνθύμημα πάλιν ἀπὸ τῶν αὐτῶν περιστάσεων ἀφ' ὧν ἐζήτησε τὰ ἐπιχειρήματα· τοῦτο δέ (ος) ἐστι σαφέστερον Pc (om. γρ´) Pa || 13 τὰ om. Ald. || 14 ἐπενθυμημάτων **P** || 15 περὶ ἐπενθυμήματος supr. **P** Mr || 16-17 cf. 100, 22 || 17 πᾶν ex πάντα Pa || 18 καὶ om. **V**

then bring in the epikheireme for confirmation from the circum-
stances, then elaborate it in the way | that we said the ergasia of [151]
the epikheireme worked, then add the enthymeme to the ergasia.
For example, let a heading be proposed that it is difficult to dig a canal through the Chersonese; then the lysis from enstasis is that it is not difficult to dig through; then an epikheireme from the act: "for we shall dig earth, and the excavation will be child's play"; then an ergasia from example to the effect that "the king of the Persians once dug a canal through Athos when in need"; then an enthymeme for this, "yet he dug through a mountain while we shall dig earth." For just as the ergasia confirms the epikheireme, so the enthymeme confirms the ergasia, and again, just as we seek an ergasia for each epikheireme, so for each ergasia we seek an enthymeme. The result is that the striking effect can be limitless if the lysis is well supplied with enstasis and antiparastasis, and each of these in turn has the support of two or three epikheiremes, and each of the epikheiremes in the same way of two or three ergasiae, and if again there is a particular enthymeme for each invented ergasia.

You should know that often one ergasia acquires many enthymemes, and if someone thus were to seek the enthymeme for
each ergasia, he will seek it from the same circumstances | from [152]
which he sought the epikheiremes of the proposed heading. I shall explain what I am saying more clearly: the enthymemes invented for each ergasia take a comparative form,[140] and invention in comparison is derived from place or time or manner or person or cause or act; thus, the result will be that in one ergasia two or more enthymemes have been invented, which, when invented, have the appearance of epenthymemes.

## CHAPTER 9: <ON THE EPENTHYMEME>

An epenthymeme is, properly speaking, another enthymeme, thought up in addition to a preceding enthymeme; such as the example, "for the king dug through Athos," then the enthymeme, which, it must be said, is all invented comparatively, the com-

[140] Explained in the next paragraph. Note the comparison in "He dug through a mountain while we shall dig earth." The isthmus of the Chersonese is relatively flat.

*«καίτοι ἐκεῖνος μὲν ὄρος διῄρει, δυσκολώτερον πρᾶγμα, ἡμεῖς δὲ γῆν διασκάψομεν, πρᾶγμα οὐ δυσχερές», εἶτα ἀπὸ τῆς αἰτίας «καίτοι ἐκεῖνος μὲν ἵνα πλεονεκτήσῃ, ἡμεῖς δὲ ἵνα μὴ πάσχωμεν κακῶς πλεονεκτούμενοι»· τοῦτο ἐνθύμημα μέν ἐστιν ἀπὸ τῆς αἰτίας εὑρεθέν, ἐπιφερόμενον δὲ τῷ πρώτῳ ἐνθυμήματι τῷ ὅτι «ἐκείνῳ μὲν δυσχερέστερον, ἡμῖν δὲ ῥᾴδιον» ἐπενθυμήματος δόξαν ἤνεγκε.*

[153] *Καὶ μὴν ἔστι καὶ ἄλλο ἐνθύμημα εὑρεῖν εἰς τὴν αὐ|τὴν ἐργασίαν ἀπὸ τοῦ καιροῦ «καὶ ὃ μὲν ταῦτα ἐποίει ἐπείγοντος αὐτὸν τοῦ πολέμου παρέργῳ χρώμενος τῷ πράγματι, ἡμεῖς δὲ ἐν ἔργῳ τοῦτο θέσθαι δυνάμεθα». οὐκ ἀγνοητέον δέ, ὡς ἡ τοῦ λόγου μεταχείρισις τὸ ἐνθύμημα τὸ δεύτερον εὑρεθὲν ποιεῖ δοκεῖν ἐπενθύμημα εἶναι, εἴ τις τὸ πρῶτον εἰπὼν ἐνθύμημα καὶ παυσάμενος, εἶτα αὐτὸ ἐπαναλαβὼν πάλιν συνάψειε, καὶ τὸ δεύτερον προστιθεὶς τῷ πρώτῳ καθάπερ αὐτῷ λεῖπόν τι προσεξευρών, οὐκ ἄλλο εὑρών· οἷον «καὶ ὁ μὲν Περσῶν βασιλεὺς ἵνα πλεονεκτήσῃ διώρυξεν, ἡμεῖς δὲ ἵνα μὴ πλεονεκτώμεθα», εἶτα ἐπαναλαβόντες πάλιν φαμὲν ὥσπερ ἐπενθυμούμενοι «καὶ ὃ μὲν ἐπειγόντων αὐτὸν μειζόνων ὅμως τοῦ πλεονεκτεῖν ἕνεκεν ἐποίει τὰ χαλεπώτερα, ἡμεῖς δὲ οὐδενὸς ἄλλου καλοῦντος ἡμᾶς, ἢ ἵνα μὴ ζημιωθῶμεν, τὸ πρᾶγμα οὐχ ὑποστησόμεθα;»*

*Πολλάκις δὲ καὶ ἡ φύσις τῶν πραγμάτων ἐπενθυμήματος ἰδίαν εὕρεσιν κατασκευάζει, τοῦ ἐνθυμήματος καθ' ἑαυτὸ μὲν οὐκ ἀπαρτίσαντος, προσθήκης δέ τινος ἄλλης περιττοτέραν δριμύτητα χαριζομένης αὐτῷ τῷ ἐνθυμήματι· οἷον εἰ λέγοι τις «δεινὸν τὸ ἀδικεῖν πατρίδα», εἶτα ἐργάσαιτο ἐκ τοῦ ἐναντίου «χρὴ γὰρ ἀδικεῖν πολεμίους», εἶτα ἐνθύμημα θείη ὅτι «χαλεπώτερόν ἐστιν ὁ πολίτης ἀδικῶν τοῦ πολεμίου, ὅτι ὃ μὲν διὰ τὸ γένος συγγνώμην ἔχει, ὃ δὲ ἐπιτείνει διὰ τὸ πολίτης*
[154] *εἶναι τὸ μισεῖσθαι», τούτῳ εἰ προσγένοιτο τῷ ἐν|θυμήματι τὸ «καὶ*

1 διήιρει ὄρος Ac || 4 μέν om. Ac | εὑρεῖν **V** || 5 ἐκεῖνο Ac, m. po. Vc || 6 ἡμῖν **P** Ba, ?m. 1 Vc; τοῦτο Ac, m. po. Vc | post ῥᾴδιον add. εὑρεθὲν Vc, ὅπερ εὑρεθὲν Ba | δόξαν ἐπενθυμήματος Vc Ba || 7 καὶ μήν ἐστιν (om. alt. καὶ) Vc Ba; (pr. καὶ om.) ἔστι μὴν καὶ Ac || 9 τοῦτο ἔχειν θέσθαι Ac || 10 δὴ Ac || 12 εἶναι etiam post ἐνθύμημα add. **V** | αὐτῶ (ὁ supra) Pa || 13 αὐτ⌊ῶι ex ὁ, m. 1 ?] Vc; αὐτῶ ante 14 οὐκ Ac || 14 προσευρὼν Vc Ba | καὶ βασιλεὺς μὲν περσῶν Ac, (om. περσῶν) Vc Ba || 15 διώρυσσεν Ac || 18 ἢ om. **V** || 20 πολλάκι **P** | καὶ post πραγμάτων **V**, cf. schol. **P** (W VII 767, 14) || 21 κατασκευάσει Ac || 25 χαλεπώτερος Ac || 27 τοῦτο m. po. Pa

parison coming from the ergasia and applying to it; for example, "although he breached a mountain, a rather difficult thing, while we shall dig through earth, a thing not difficult"; then from the cause, "although he acted out of aggrandizement, but we in order not to suffer from being aggrandized." The latter is an enthymeme from cause, and when added to the first enthymeme—that is, "it is harder for him and easier for us"—is regarded as an epenthymeme.

And surely it is possible to find another enthymeme for the | ergasia from the occasion: "And he did these things incidentally [153] when war was oppressing him, while we are able to give full attention to doing this." One should not fail to recognize how the treatment of the speech makes the enthymeme that is invented second seem to be an epenthymeme if, after one has spoken the first enthymeme and paused, then returning to the subject, one should join on another, adding the second to the first as though filling in something left out, not as inventing something else; for example, "The king of the Persians dug a canal out of aggrandizement, while we do it in order that we may not be aggrandized," then taking it up again we say in the way of an epenthymeme, "and he did these more difficult things when great pressures were, nevertheless, on him to aggrandize, while we shall not undertake the action when anything is urging us other than that we not be harmed."

Often the nature of the subjects provides a particular epenthymeme, since the enthymeme in itself was not complete and the addition of something else contributes greater striking effect to the enthymeme; for example, if someone were to say, "It is a dreadful thing to wrong the fatherland," then added an ergasia from the opposite, "for it is necessary to wrong enemies," then put an enthymeme, saying, "The citizen who does wrong is a worse thing than the enemy, because the latter is excused because of his origin while the former increases hatred of himself because of being a citizen"; and if to this | enthymeme is [154]

*μάλιστα ἐὰν ὁ πολίτης φαίνηται τούτους ἀδικῶν, οὓς ἐδόκει πρότερον εὖ πεποιηκέναι», λοιπὸν τοῦτό ἐστι τὸ ἐκ τῆς φύσεως τοῦ αὐτοῦ πράγματος ἀληθινὸν ἐπενθύμημα μετὰ προσθήκης τινὸς περιττοτέραν δριμύτητα χαριζόμενον αὐτῷ τῷ ἐνθυμήματι· καὶ λοιπὸν οὕτω γίνεται καὶ καλεῖται ἐν ἑνὶ καὶ τῷ αὐτῷ προβλήματι διπλῆ συγκριτικὴ ἐπίτασις περιττοτέραν δριμύτητα χαριζομένη αὐτῷ τῷ ἐνθυμήματι.*

## *Περὶ τῶν ἀπ᾽ ἀρχῆς ἄχρι τέλους.*

*Τὰ ἀπ᾽ ἀρχῆς ἄχρι τέλους ἔστι μὲν τὸ συνεκτικώτατον πάντων τῶν κεφαλαίων ἔνθεν γὰρ καὶ τὰ ἄλλα γίνεται κεφάλαια, ἔχει δὲ οὐ τὴν αὐτὴν κατασκευὴν τῶν ἐπιχειρημάτων, οἷαν καὶ τὰ λοιπά· οὐ γὰρ ἡ περίστασις κατασκευάζει τὰ ἀπ᾽ ἀρχῆς ἄχρι τέλους, ἀλλ᾽ ὥσπερ ἴδιος ἐπιχειρημάτων τόπος ἔστι τῶν ἀπ᾽ ἀρχῆς ἄχρι τέλους, ἡ ὑποδιαίρεσις καλουμένη. ἔστι δὲ ἡ ὑποδιαίρεσις ἡ τοῦ ἀθρόου πράγματος εἰς λεπτὸν τομὴ εὑρισκομένη πολλή, καὶ γίνεται οὕτως, εἴ τις τὰ ἀπ᾽ ἀρχῆς ἄχρι τέλους ὁρίσας ἑαυτῷ ὁλοσχερῶς καὶ ἀπαραλείπτως καθ᾽ ἕκαστον ὄνομα τῶν λεγομένων ἐν αὐτοῖς δύναιτο ὑποδιαιρεῖν οὕτω πλάττων «εἰ γὰρ*
[155] *μὴ τόδε ἐποίησας ἀλλὰ μετριώτερον», «εἰ γὰρ μὴ τοσαῦτα | ἐποίησας ἀλλὰ ἐλάττονα». οἷον τρεῖς τις ἀπέκτεινε κατὰ τὸν τῶν ἀκρίτων νόμον υἱεῖς καὶ ἀξιοῖ δημοσίᾳ τρέφεσθαι νόμου κελεύοντος τὸν ἄπαιδα δημοσίᾳ τρέφεσθαι. γενόμενος ἐν τοῖς ἀπ᾽ ἀρχῆς ἄχρι τέλους οὕτω διασκοπήσεις· ὅπου τρεῖς ἀπέκτεινεν υἱεῖς, τὸ τρεῖς ὑποδιαιρήσεις «εἰ*

1 φαίνηται **P** Ac (ἀριστεὺς ἢ supr. m. po. Pa Ac); ἀριστεύοι (m. po. φαίνηται) Ba, (m. po. ἀποφαίνοι ?) Vc | δὲ ante τούτους supr. m. po. Ac | δοκεῖ Ac || 2 καὶ λοιπὸν Ba, ?m. 1 Vc || 2-3 γρ καὶ λοιπὸν τοῦτο τὸ ἐκ τῆς φύσεως τοῦ αὐτοῦ πράγματος Pa (om. γρ καὶ) Pc || 2 ἔστι om. m. 1 Ac, v.l. **P** || 4 χαριζόμενον (ης supra), m. 2 supr., Vc || 7 τοῦ Ac || 8 τὸ (pro τὰ) Ac || 10 οἷαν m. 2 ex οἷα Vc; ο⌊ῖο⌋ν Ba | γρ οὐ γὰρ ἡ προ(τ) κατασκευάζει **P** || 11 τὸ Vc Ba || 12 τῶν (οις supra) Pa; τοῖς Vc Ba || 17 ad ἐποιήσας (oportebat referri ad μετριώτερον) mg. **P**: οὐκ ἔδει εὐθύνας ὑποσχεῖν; cf. 110, 26 cet.

added "and especially if the citizen is shown to be wronging those whom he earlier seemed to have benefited," the result is a true epenthymeme from the nature of the subject that with some addition contributes greater striking effect to the enthymeme; and the result is created in this way and in one and the same problem it is called "a double comparative extension,"[141] contributing greater striking effect to the enthymeme.

*Chapters 10–15 are not listed in 3.1 as subjects to be discussed in this book. Possibly the editor has moved them from elsewhere. On grounds of style and technical terminology they seem to be the work of the same writer as chapters 1–9.*

## CHAPTER 10: ON AP' ARKHĒS AKHRI TELOUS

*Ap' arkhēs akhri telous*[142] is the most essential of all headings—for the other headings are derived from it[143]—but it does not have the same confirmation from epikheiremes as do the others, for the circumstances do not confirm headings from-beginning-to-end, but there is, as it were, a specific topic (*topos*) of epikheiremes belonging to from-beginning-to-end, which is called hypodiaeresis.[144] Hypodiaeresis is the invention of numerous cuttings (*tomē*) of the subject as a whole into small parts, and comes about if, after defining from-beginning-to-end in itself as a whole and without leaving anything out, one is able to make subdivisions (*hypodiairein*) in terms of each word of what has been said, forming them as follows: "for if he had not done this but acted with more restraint,"

[141] *Epitasis,* cf. 4.1 below, p. 140, 13; an emphasis or exaggeration; cf. *On Sublimity* 38.6.

[142] *Ap' arkhēs akhri telous*, hereafter "from-beginning-to-end," variously translated as "sequence of events" (Heath), "presentation of the case" (Lindberg), "examen des faits" (Patillon); in Latin *a summo ad imum* ("from top to bottom"), Fortunatianus 2.8–9, pp. 106–7 Halm; Sulpicius Victor (Zeno) §26, p. 326 Halm. In *On Stases* (47,9–48,2 Rabe) Hermogenes says that *ap' arkhēs akhri telous* is a heading generally belonging to the prosecutor and is used to exploit and amplify certain facts to his advantage; the defendant may sometimes use it to exploit and amplify certain other facts. See Heath's note, *On Issues,* 84.

[143] Rather than being a heading, it seems to be a technique in support of a heading.

[144] Cf. 1.2 above.

γὰρ ἕνα ἀπέκτεινε», τὸ υἱεῖς ὑποδιαιρήσεις «εἰ γὰρ μὴ αὐτοῦ παῖδα», τὸ ἀπέκτεινεν ὑποδιαιρήσεις «εἰ γὰρ ἀπεκήρυξεν». αὐτὰ δὲ ταῦτα νοεῖται μὲν οὕτως, ἰσχὺν δὲ λαμβάνει ἀπὸ τοῦ λόγου· ἐπεὶ δύναται καὶ ὡς πνεῦμα ἀποταθῆναι κατὰ τὸ τοῦ ἀντιθέτου σχῆμα, δύναται δὲ καὶ μετὰ τὸ πληρωθῆναι τὸ πνεῦμα ἕκαστον αὐτῶν, εἰ θέλοις, καὶ κατὰ περίοδον ἀπολαμβάνειν. καὶ δύναται ὡς πνεῦμα ἀποταθῆναι κατὰ τὸ τοῦ ἀντιθέτου σχῆμα οὕτως οἷον «εἰ γὰρ μηδὲν προσήκοντας ἀπέκτεινας, εἰ γὰρ ἀλλοτρίους, εἰ γὰρ ὀθνείους, εἰ γὰρ ξένους, οὐκ ἂν ἠγανάκτησα καὶ τότε; οὐκ ἂν ἐδυσχέρανα; οὐκ ἂν ἀπῄτησα τιμωρίαν; νυνὶ δὲ φιλτάτους, οὓς ἐγέννησας, οὓς ἔθρεψας, ὑπὲρ ὧν ἔδει μάχεσθαι, ὑπὲρ ὧν ἔδει δεδιέναι μή τις αὐτοὺς ἄλλος ἀποκτείνῃ, φθάσας τοῦτο ἐποίησας· ἆρα τὸ τοιοῦτον ἄγος καταδεξαίμην; οὐκ ἔστιν εἰπεῖν». εἰ δὲ βούλει, καὶ συνάγεται ὧδε «ἄλλος μὲν οὖν τις δικαίως ἂν ὑπόσχοι τιμωρίαν, εἰ καί τινα τῶν μὴ προσηκόντων ἀπέκτεινεν· οὗτος δὲ ἰδίους υἱεῖς τρεῖς ἀποκτείνας ἀφεθήσεται;» δύναται δὲ καὶ ἑκάστη ὑποδιαίρεσις ὁρισθεῖσα [156] χώραν προσωποποιίας ἀναδέξασθαι. ποίκιλλε δὲ | τοῖς σχήμασιν οἷον «εἰ γὰρ ἕνα ἀπέκτεινας, οὐκ ἂν εἶπον καὶ τότε, ὅτι φόνος ἀσεβής σοι τετόλμηται;»

Γίνεται δὲ ὑποδιαίρεσις ποτὲ μὲν αὐτοῦ τοῦ πράγματος εἰς λεπτὸν τεμνομένου, ποτὲ δὲ ἐκ τῶν ὁμοίων λαμβανομένη. καὶ ἀπ' αὐτοῦ μὲν τοῦ πράγματος οὕτως, οἷον προσῆλθε μάγος πατρὶ αἰτῶν θυγατέρα πρὸς

1 υἱεῖς m. 1 Ac; εἷς **P**, m. 1 Vc Ba | παῖδας Sc || 4 πνεύματα **V** || 5 εἰ θέλοις αὐτῶν Ac | κατὰ om. **V** || 6-7 καὶ — οὕτως om. m. 1 Vc Ba || 9 οὐκ — τιμωρίαν om. Pa || 11 ἄρ' ἂν Spengel || 12 καταδέξαιμι Ba, m. 1 Vc; κατεδεξαίμην (sic) Pa || 13 οὖν om. **V** | ὑπόσχοιτο Ac || 14 ἀποκτείνοιεν **P** | ἰδίους υἱεῖς τρεῖς Vc; τρεῖς ἰδίους υἱεῖς Ac | υἱοὺς Pc || 19 ἀπ' αὐτοῦ **V**, v.l. **P** | λεπτὰ **V**; cf. 18, 1. 106, 13. 110, 15 || 20 ποτὲ — λαμβανομένου suppl. m. po. Pc | λαμβανομένη scripsit Rabe (cf. 110, 11); λαμβανομένου **PV**

"for if he had not done so many things | but fewer."[145] For example, a man killed his three sons in accordance with the law about the untried[146] and demanded to be supported at public expense under the law requiring a man without a son to be supported at public expense. When approaching this with from-beginning-to-end you will examine it as follows: Where you mention that he killed *three* sons, you will subdivide the three: "for if he had killed one"; you will subdivide the *sons*: "for if it was not his own son"; you will subdivide the *killing*, "for if he had disinherited." These are thought of in this way, but they get their strength from how they are spoken, since it is possible to arrange them as a pneuma[147] in the figure of antitheton,[148] and also possible, after completing the pneuma, to take each of them up again, if you want, in a period. It is possible to draw them out in a pneuma in the figure of antitheton, thus: "For if you had killed people not connected to you, if strangers, if outsiders, if foreigners, would I not have been distressed even then? Would I not have refused to put up with it? Would I not have demanded punishment? But now against your nearest kin, whom you fathered, whom you reared, for whom you ought to fight, for whom you ought to fear that someone else might kill them, you took the initiative. Should I accept such pollution? That cannot be said." But if you want, it can be concluded as follows: "Now someone else might justly suffer punishment if he killed someone unrelated to him. Will this man be let go free who has killed his own three sons?" It is possible for each hypodiaeresis, when defined, to take the form of a *prosōpopoiia*.[149] Vary hypodiaereses | with figures;[150] for example, "For if you had killed only one person, would I not have said even then that you had dared an impious murder?" [155] [156]

Hypodiaeresis sometimes results from the action itself being cut into small bits and sometimes is derived from similarities. From the action itself as follows: for example, a wizard came to a

[145] As often, the author is here teaching a method of amplification.

[146] Cf. n. 8 above.

[147] On the pneuma, or extended period, see 4.4 below.

[148] On antitheton, see 4.2 below.

[149] I.e., a speech-in-character or personification.

[150] Probably regarding "would I not have said" as a prosopopoeia, even though the first person has been repeatedly used earlier and seems natural. Rhetorical question has also been used repeatedly.

*γάμον, οὐκ ἔδωκεν, ἐρᾷ εἰδώλου ἡ κόρη, καὶ κρίνεται ὁ μάγος φαρμάκων. ἐνταῦθα ὑποδιαιροῦντες τὸν τοῦ εἰδώλου ἔρωτα λέγομεν «ἐρᾷ εἰδώλου· εἰ γὰρ ἀνδρὸς ἤρα τινός, οὐκ ἂν ἐπὶ σὲ ἤγαγον τὴν αἰτίαν; εἰ γὰρ σοῦ αὐτοῦ ἤρα, οὐκ ἂν ἐπήγαγον ἐπὶ σὲ τὴν αἰτίαν;» ταῦτα ὑποδιαίρεσίς ἐστιν ἐκ τῶν μικροτέρων· τὸν γὰρ τοῦ εἰδώλου ἔρωτα ὑποδιαιροῦμεν ἀπὸ τῶν μικροτέρων εἰς ἄλλους. Ἀπὸ δὲ τῶν ὁμοίων οὕτως «εἰ γὰρ μὴ ἤρα, ἀλλ᾽ ἐνόσει νόσον ἄλλην τῷ σώματι, οὐκ ἂν καὶ τότε σε ἔκρινα;» Καθόλου δέ, ὡς ἔφαμεν, καὶ τῶν ὁμοίων καὶ τῶν ἰδίων αἱ λεπταὶ ὑποδιαιρέσεις ἀναδέξονται τὰς προσωποποιίας ἀναγκαίας οὔσας, ἅς, εἰ θέλοις, καὶ περιόδοις καὶ παντὶ τρόπῳ ἔξεστί σοι μηκύνειν.*

*Ἔστι δὲ ὑποδιαίρεσις καὶ ἐκ τοῦ μείζονος ἐνίοτε λαμβανομένη, ἵνα μὴ ἀεὶ τοῖς λεπτοῖς προσέχωμεν· συμβαίνει δὲ τοῦτο, ὅταν ἀξιώμεθά τι παρασχεῖν ἐπὶ μισθῷ φαινομένῳ ἢ χάριτι λέγοντες ὅτι «οὐδ᾽* [157] *εἰ μεί|ζονα ἐδίδου». οἷον πέπομφεν ἑκατὸν τάλαντα Φίλιππος πρίασθαι βουλόμενος τὸν Δημοσθένην· εἰς λεπτὸν ὑποτεμὼν ἐρεῖς «οὐδὲ ἄλλον τινὰ τῶν τυχόντων ἔδωκα ἄν, μή τί γε Δημοσθένην»· τὰ δὲ ἑκατὸν τάλαντα ἐκ τοῦ μείζονος «οὐδὲ εἰ μύρια διδοίη τάλαντα οὐδ᾽ ἂν πόλεις οὐδ᾽ ἂν ἔθνη, ἀντὶ Δημοσθένους λήψομαι».*

*Ἀλλ᾽ ἵνα μὴ προσκορὲς ᾖ τὸ ἐξ ὑποδιαιρέσεως ἀεὶ τῷ αὐτῷ σχήματι εἰσαγόμενον, ἀλλαττέσθω τὰ σχήματα ποτὲ μὲν οὕτω λεγόντων «εἰ γὰρ τόδε ἐποίησας, οὐκ ἔδει σε δοῦναι τιμωρίαν;» ποτὲ δὲ οὕτως «ἐγὼ μὲν γὰρ καὶ ἐπ᾽ ἐκείνῳ σε τιμωρίαν ἀπῄτησα ἄν, καίτοι μικρὸν ἦν καὶ μετριώτερον ἦν», ποτὲ δὲ οὕτως «ἄλλος μὲν οὖν τις ἐμίσησεν ἂν καὶ διὰ τόδε». ἔστι δὲ τούτων καλλίων ἡ μεταχείρισις, εἰ ἀναστρέφοι τις καὶ ὅλον τὸ πρᾶγμα, οὐκ ἀπὸ τοῦ πράγματος εἰς τιμωρίαν ἕλκων, ἀλλ᾽ ἀναστρέφων τὴν τιμωρίαν, οἷον «εἰ καί τι τούτου μετριώτερον*

1 ὁ μάγος m. po., ?m. 1, Pa || 2 ὑποδιαιροῦντες τὸ εἴδωλον λέγομεν (γρ τὸν τοῦ εἰδώλου ἔρωτα) Ac || 2-3 ἐρᾷ εἰδώλου suspect. || 4 ἐπηγάγομεν Vc Ba || 6 εἰς ἄλλους ἐκ τῶν μικροτέρων Vc Ba; suspect. || 8 p. 108, 15–16 || 10 ἃς om. **V** | δὲ post εἰ add. Ac, post θέλοις m. po. Vc || 11 δὲ om. Ac || 12 ὅταν **P** Ac; ἡνίκα Vc Ba || 14 ὁ φίλιππος **V** || 14-15 cf. 116, 22 || 15 ἐρεῖς om. Vc Ba || 16 γρ καὶ τῶν ἐπιτυχόντων ἢ παρατυχόντων **P** | ἔδωκα ἂν τῶν τυχόντων Vc Ba | τι (o supra) Pa || 22 σε ante καὶ Ac | ἐκεῖνο Vc Ba || 23 [καὶ μετριώτερον ἦν?] | alt. ἦν om. Vc Ba | ἄλλο⌊ν m. po.⌉ Vc || 24 διὰ om. Vc Ba | τούτου **V**, v.l. **P** | ἡ om. Vc Ba, v.l. **P** || 26 οἷον om. Vc Ba

father seeking his daughter in marriage; the father refuses, the girl falls in love with an *eidōlon*,[151] and the wizard is tried for poisoning.[152] Here, if we subdivide the love for the image, we say, "She is in love with an image. If she loved some man, would I not put the blame on you? If she loved you yourself, would I not put the blame on you?" This hypodiaeresis is from the smaller (*mikrotera*), for we apply hypodiaeresis to the love for the image by arguing from small things.[153] From similarities as follows: "For if she was not in love but had contracted some other disease in the body, would I not then too bring you to trial?" All in all, as I said, subtle hypodiaereses from similarities and from particulars will contribute to the speeches in character that are needed, and, if you want, you can extend them in periods and in every way.

Hypodiaeresis is also sometimes taken from the greater, so we should not always pay attention to the small elements. This happens whenever we are thought to be providing something for what seems to be pay or a favor and we say that "(*I would not have done this*) even if | you had given something greater." For example, [157]
Philip has sent a hundred talents, wanting to buy Demosthenes (*from the Athenians*). If you divide into small elements you will say, "I would not have given up any other of the ordinary people, to say nothing of Demosthenes," but speaking of the hundred talents from the greater: "Not even if someone gave ten thousand talents, nor even cities nor whole peoples, will I take them in exchange for Demosthenes."

But in order that the use of hypodiaeresis may not become tiresome because introduced always in the same form, let us change the figures from time to time, as when we say, "If you had done this, would it not have been necessary for you to be punished?" Or at another time, "I demanded your punishment for that, although it was a little and more moderate thing." Or sometimes, "Someone else, then, would have felt hatred even for this reason." The treatment of these is finer if one reverses the whole thing, not going from act to punishment, but putting the punishment first; for example, "Even if you had done something less

[151] Perhaps a phantom, possibly a picture of a man.

[152] *Pharmakon*, drug, probably intended as a love potion. For the theme, cf. *Anonymous Problemata* no. 48 (Walz 8:410).

[153] It is a "smaller" thing to love a man than to love a phantom; one might have expected *ellattona*, "lesser things."

*ἐποίησας», ἵνα ποτὲ μὲν ἀπὸ τοῦ πράγματος ἀρχόμενοι εἰς ἀξίωσιν καταβαίνωμεν, ποτὲ δὲ ἀπὸ τῆς ἀξιώσεως ἀρχόμενοι εἰς τὸ πρᾶγμα ἀνερχώμεθα.*

*Ὅταν δὲ αἱ ὑποδιαιρέσεις ἄλογοι γίγνωνται φασκόντων ἡμῶν «εἰ* [158] *γὰρ τόδε ἐποίησας, οὐκ ἂν ἔκρινόν σε;», | διὰ τὸ ἀλόγως ἂν κρῖναι δόξαι οὕτω σχηματίσεις «εἰ τόδε ἐποίεις, οὐκ ἂν ἔκρινον;» ὡς ὁ συνθάψας τὴν χλαμύδα τῷ ἐρωμένῳ καὶ μὴ κομίσας ἐκ τῆς ἀλλοδαπῆς ἐντειλαμένου ἐκείνου· ἐνταῦθα γάρ, ἐπεὶ μωρόν ἐστι τὸ λέγειν «ἔκρινα ἄν σε, εἰ καὶ ἐδάκρυες συνεχῶς», ἐρεῖς ὅτι «εἰ ἐδάκρυες, οὐκ ἂν ἐφρόντισα; εἰ παρεκαθέζου τῷ τάφῳ, οὐκ ἂν ἐμήνιον;» καίτοι καὶ τότε, εἰ δύνασαι, βίασαι ἀναιρεῖν, ὃ ἔδωκας. καὶ καθόλου πᾶσαν ὑποδιαίρεσιν ἂν πειραθείης συγχωρήσας ἀνελεῖν, εἶτα ἀνελὼν ἐπενέγκοις, πολλαπλασιάσεις τὸν λόγον δριμέως λέγων οὕτως «εἰ μὲν τόδε ἐποίησας, συγγνώμης ἄξιος· ἐπεὶ δὲ τόδε, οὐκέτι· καίτοι οὐδὲ τότε»· οὕτω γὰρ καὶ αἱ προσωποποιίαι χώραν ἕξουσι μυρίαν. ἵνα δὲ μὴ προσκορὴς εἶναι δόξῃς διὰ τῆς προσωποποιίας πληρῶν λόγους, θαυμαστὸς φανήσῃ ῥήτωρ τὸ γνώρισμα αὐτῆς ἀφαιρῶν καὶ χρώμενος αὐτῇ· εἰ γὰρ μὴ λέγοις «εἶπον ἄν», ἄλλο τι φαίνεται πρότερον ἢ προσωποποιία.*

1 ἔδει σε δοῦναι δίκην post ἐποίησας suppl. m. 2 Vc; mg. m. 1 **P**: ἐλλιπῶς τὸ (scr. τοῦ) «ἔδει σε δοῦναι δίκην»· ὃ δεῖ προτετάχθαι (προστετάχθαι?) ἐπὶ τοῦδε; cf. 106, 17 | τὴν ἀξίωσιν Vc Ba || 3 ἀνερχόμεθα Ba, (ώ m. 2 ex ό) Vc; ἐρχώμεθα Ac, v.l. **P**; ἐπανερχώμεθα **P** || 5 ἐποίεις[ησας] Pa; ἐποίησας[εις], m. 2 supr., Vc | μὴ post τὸ supr. m. po. Vc Ba | γρ´ μὴ ἂν ἀλόγως **P** | ἂν om. m. 1 Vc Ba || 6 ἐποίησας Ac | ἔκρινον ⌊I-II⌉ ὡς Pa; cf. m. 1 mg. **P**: παρήσεις τὴν σὲ ἀντωνυμίαν || 8 τὸ om. Ac || 9 συνεχὲς Ac | συνεχῶς etiam ante οὐκ m. 1 Vc || 10 ἐμηνίων **V** || 11 ἀναιρεῖν[ελ] **P**; ἀνελεῖν **V** (ρ m. 2 supr. Vc) | δέδωκας Pc || 12 εἰ post ἀνελὼν add. Ma, m. po. pro 9 ἂν Ba || 13 πολλαπλασιάσας[εις], εις m. 2, Vc; πολλαπλασιάσ⌊ε m. po. ex ο⌉ις Ba; πολυπλασιάσεις Ac | δριμέως πολλάκις τὸν λόγον Ac, (om. πολλάκις) Vc Ba || 16 δοκῇς **V** | τῶν προσωποποιιῶν **P**

serious than this (*I would have demanded punishment*)," so that sometimes beginning from the action we go on to the evaluation, and sometimes beginning from the evaluation we go back to the action.

Hypodiaereses may become unreasonable if we say, "For if you had done such-and-such, would I not be bringing you to judgment?" | Because of this seeming to be unreasonable, you will [158] change the figure and say, "If you were doing such-and-such, I would not be bringing you to judgment."[154] Thus, the case of the man who buried his own cloak with his beloved and did not take one from a stranger, although the boy had enjoined him to do so;[155] for here, since it is silly to say, "I would have brought you to trial even if you were crying continually," you will say, "If you were crying, would I not have cared? If you were stretched on top of the grave, would I not have been enraged?" And yet, then too, if you can, be forced to take back what you granted. And all in all, having tried to take back every hypodiaeresis that you granted, then, after taking it back you should bring it in again, multiplying the argument forcefully by speaking as follows: "If you had done this, you would have deserved forgiveness; but since you did this other thing, not so; at least, not at that time." For thus speeches in character will have many applications. But to avoid seeming tiresome by filling up the speech with too many of them, let the speaker be admired for removing the signs of it and still using it, for unless you say "I would have said," it seems to be something other than a speech in character.

154 Dropping the question mark of Rabe's text, as suggested by Patillon, *L'Art rhétorique*, 265 n. 2.

155 The theme is not otherwise known, and the situation is obscure. Apparently the speaker is prosecuting a man on the charge of murdering a lover, and the cloak is evidence. The boy may have been fatally injured in a hunting accident. The prosecutor probably was a relative of the boy, possibly also an enemy of the accused. The boy may have realized the danger to his friend.

*Πρόσκειται τοῖς ἀπ᾿ ἀρχῆς ἄχρι τέλους ὥσπερ ἴδιόν τι ἐπὶ τῷ τέλει καὶ τὸ πλαστὸν ἐπιχείρημα καλούμενον. τινὲς δὲ οὕτως αὐτὸ ἐκάλεσαν πλαστὸν οὐκ εἰδότες, ὅτι καὶ πᾶσα ὑποδιαίρεσις πλαστή ἐστι.*
[159] *τὸ γὰρ μὴ γε|νόμενον πλαττόμενον δὲ ὡς καὶ γενέσθαι δυνάμενον τῆς αὐτῆς ἂν εἴη δήπουθεν εὑρέσεως. καὶ τὸ μὲν κυρίως πλαττόμενον ἐπιφερόμενον δὲ πᾶσι τοῖς ἀπ᾿ ἀρχῆς ἄχρι τέλους οὕτως εὑρίσκεται καθολικῶς· εἰ μὲν ἐπ᾿ ἀγαθῷ τινι πραχθέντι δωρεὰν αἰτεῖς καὶ πλάττεις, οὕτως «εἶτα δὲ εἰ πρὶν ἢ ποιῆσαι τὸ ἀγαθὸν ᾔτουν δωρεάν, οὐκ ἄν μοι ἔδοτε; οὐκ ἂν ἐψηφίσασθε ἐπαγγελλομένῳ ποιήσειν;» καὶ ἐπὶ τούτῳ ἐρεῖς «δεινὸν δὲ ἐπαγγελλομένῳ μὲν ποιήσειν ψηφίσασθαι, μὴ δοῦναι δὲ πεποιηκότι»· εἰ δὲ ἐπὶ κακῷ τινι πραχθέντι πάλιν τιμωρίαν ἀπαιτεῖς καὶ πλάττεις, ὁμοίως «εἰ δὲ πρὶν ἢ γενέσθαι τὸ κακὸν ἔγνωμεν, ὅτι ἔσται, οὐκ ἂν ἐφιλοτιμησάμεθα κωλῦσαι; δεινὸν δὲ μέλλον μὲν γίνεσθαι κωλύειν, γενόμενον δὲ μὴ τιμωρεῖσθαι». καὶ ἐφεξῆς τούτῳ τῷ σχήματι τῆς ζητήσεως χρώμενος πολυτρόπως εὑρήσεις τὰ ἀπ᾿ ἀρχῆς ἄχρι τέλους καταστῆσαι.*

*Τὰ δὲ πλαστὰ χώραν ἔχει μετὰ τὴν ἀθρόαν εἰσβολὴν τῶν ἀπ᾿ ἀρχῆς ἄχρι τέλους, χώραν δὲ ἔχει καὶ ἐν ταῖς ἐργασίαις ταῖς ἀπὸ παραδείγματος, εἰ λέγοιμεν ἐπὶ τῷ πράγματι τῷ καλῶς πραχθέντι ἢ κακῶς τὸ πλαστὸν ἐπιφέροντες· οἷον «οὐ δεῖ ἐχθρῷ ἐπιτάττοντι πείθεσθαι»,*
[160] *τοῦτο τὸ ἐπιχείρημά ἐστιν· ἡ ἐργασία ἐκ | παραδείγματος «οὐδὲ γὰρ οἱ πατέρες ἡμῶν ἐπείσθησαν τῷ Ξέρξῃ γῆν αἰτοῦντι καὶ ὕδωρ, ἀλλ᾿ ἐξελθόντες πολλὰ καὶ καλὰ ἔπραξαν»· εἶτα πλαστὸν φέρε «εἰ δὲ τότε συνεβούλευέ τις δοῦναι γῆν καὶ ὕδωρ, οὐκ ἂν κατελεύσθη; ἐγὼ μὲν*

1 inter scholia tantum est titulus περὶ τοῦ καλουμένου πλαστοῦ Pc || 2-3 ἐκάλεσεν αὐτὸ Pc || 5 ἂν ᾖ Ac | καὶ τὸ μὲν **P**; τὸ μὲν γὰρ **V**, v. l. Pa, (γὰρ om.) v.l. Pc || 7 εἶτ᾿ ἐπ᾿ Ac | αἰτοίης Ac, m. 2 Vc, v.l. **P** | πλάττ$^{οις}$εις Pa, (m. 2 supr.) Vc || 8 εἶτα δὲ εἰ **P**; εἰ δὲ **V**; cf. Arist. Rhet. B 23 p. 1397b 28: Ἰφικράτης ἐν τῇ πρὸς Ἁρμόδιον ὅτι εἰ πρὶν ποιῆσαι ἠξίουν τῆς εἰκόνος τυχεῖν ἐὰν ποιήσω, ἔδοτε ἄν· ποιήσαντι δ᾿ ἄρ᾿ οὐ δώσετε; μὴ τοίνυν κτλ. | τὴν δωρεάν **V** || 9 π$^{ει}$οιήσειν Pa (πείσειν coniectum propter Π. στ. 59, 19) || 10 δὲ om. Ac || 11 πεπ$^{ει}$οιηκότι Pa || 12 γενέσθαι **P**; ποιῆσαι **V** || 13-14 γενέσθαι **P** || 15 χρώμενος Pa Ac, (ς m. 2 ex ν) Vc Ba; om. Pc || 16 m. po. κατασκευάσαι supr. Ba || 19 πράγματι Vδ; παραδείγματι **PV** || 20 τὸ om. **V** || 21 114, 20 ἐκ παραδείγματος om. **V**, v.l. **P** || 22 γρ ἀπαιτοῦντι **P** || 24 συνεβούλευσε (om. τις) Mr

## CHAPTER 11: <ON WHAT IS CALLED A PLASTON (FICTIVE) EPIKHEIREME>

What is called a *plaston*[156] epikheireme is added to argument from-beginning-to-end as a special point at the end. Some call it "plaston" without realizing that every hypodiaeresis is fictive (*plastē*), for what has not | happened but is imagined as able to [159]
happen would clearly belong to the same kind of invention. What is plaston in the proper sense of the word and applied to all arguments from-beginning-to-end is generally invented as follows. If you are demanding a gift (*from the city*) for some good deed and you use a plaston argument, you will say, "But then if, before doing the good deed, I asked for a gift, would you (*plural*) not have given it to me? Would you not have voted in favor of one who promised that he was going to do it?" And at this you will say, "But it is a strange thing to vote in favor of one who proclaimed he was going to do something but not to give it to one who has done it." If, on the other hand, you demand punishment for some bad deed and you use a plaston argument, you will say similarly, "But if before the evil deed was done we knew that it was possible, would we not have eagerly endeavored to prevent it? It is strange to hinder something that is going to happen and not to punish it when it has happened." And by using this form of the question in succession you will find how to employ from-beginning-to-end in many different ways.

These plasta have a place after the complete expression of arguments from-beginning-to-end and have a place also in ergasiae[157] from example, if in speaking we add the plaston to what has been done well or wrongly; for example, "One ought not to obey the orders of an enemy"; this is an epikheireme; the ergasia | [160]
from example is, "for our ancestors did not obey Xerxes when he demanded earth and water, but they marched out and did many fine things."[158] Then bring in a plaston: "If at that time someone had advised them to give earth and water, would he not have been stoned to death? For my part, I think so." In the case of some-

[156] I.e., fictive; literally, "molded, formed"; cf. Quintilian 5.10.95–99.

[157] On an ergasia as a supporting statement, see 3.7 above.

[158] Cf. Herodotus 7.32.

*οἶμαι». ἐπὶ δὲ τῷ κακῶς οἷον «οὐ δεῖ πιστεύειν Φιλίππῳ χαριζομένῳ· ἀπατεὼν γάρ ἐστιν»· εἶτα ἐργασία ἐκ παραδείγματος «οὐδὲ γὰρ τοῖς Ὀλυνθίοις συνήνεγκε πεισθεῖσιν αὐτῷ, ἀλλὰ Ποτίδαιαν λαβόντες ἅπαντα προσαπώλεσαν»· εἶτα πλαστὸν φέρε «εἰ δὲ τότε, ὅτε τὴν Ποτίδαιαν ἐλάμβανον, εἶπέ τις αὐτοῖς θεόθεν, ὅτι προσαπολοῦσι καὶ τὴν Ὄλυνθον, ἆρα ἂν ἐδέξαντο; οὐκ ἔστιν εἰπεῖν».*

*Ἔτι παραπειρᾶσθαι δεῖ τὰ πλαστὰ καὶ ἀπὸ τῶν ἐναντίων ζητεῖν πλάττειν, καὶ τοῦτο μυριάκις εὑρίσκεται· οἷον εἰ μὲν ἐπ᾽ ἀγαθῷ αἰτοίης γέρας, λέγε «εἰ δὲ κακόν τι ἐπεποιήκειν, οὐκ ἂν τιμωρίαν ἔδωκα;» ὡς ὁ Δημοσθένης ἐν τῷ Πρὸς Λεπτίνην· διεξελθὼν γὰρ τὰς πράξεις τοῦ Χαβρίου λέγει ἐκ τοῦ ἐναντίου πλάττων «ἀλλ᾽ εἰ μὲν μίαν ἀπώλεσε ναῦν, περὶ θανάτου ἂν ἐκινδύνευσε»· τοῦτο μέντοι καὶ διπλῆν ἔχει τὴν τῆς πλάσεως θεωρίαν, ἀπὸ γὰρ τοῦ ἐναντίου γενόμενον τῷ μικροτέρῳ συμπλέκεται. ἢ ἐάν τινα κελεύῃς δοῦναι τιμωρίαν ἐπ᾽ ἀδικήματι· ἔνεστι γὰρ λέγειν «εἰ ἃ ἔβλαψεν εὐηργέτησε, δωρεὰς ἂν ἔλαβε· δράσας* [161] *δὲ κακῶς | οὐ κολασθήσεται;» παντὸς δὲ τοῦ λεγομένου ζήτει τὸ ἐναντίον καὶ πολλάκις εὑρήσεις τοῦτο παρ᾽ ὅλον τοῦ πλαστοῦ τὸν λόγον, μεμνημένος ὅτι ὡς ἐπὶ τὸ πολὺ ἢ ἀθρόον τὸ πραχθὲν ὡς οὐ γενόμενον πλάττεται ἢ τὸ ἐναντίον αὐτοῦ· οἷον ἐπὶ τυραννοκτόνου «εἰ δὲ πρὶν ἢ ἀποκτεῖναι ἐπηγγελλόμην», τοῦτο τοῦ ἀθρόου πλάσμα ὡς μὴ γενομένου, καὶ ἄλλο ἐκ τοῦ ἐναντίου «εἰ δὲ μὴ κατώρθωσα ἀλλὰ ἐλήφθην, τί ἂν ἔπαθον;» καὶ εἰ Δημοσθένην αἰτοίη Φίλιππος ἤ τι τοιοῦτον, διάπλασον ἐκ τοῦ ἐναντίου «εἰ δὲ ὑμεῖς ἐβούλεσθε λαβεῖν τι τῶν Φιλίππου, πότε ἂν συνεχώρησεν ὑμῖν;*

*Εἰ δὲ καὶ εὐτελέστερόν τι συνεχώρει ἡ φύσις, οὐκ ἂν ὤκνησα διὰ τὸ σαφέστερον. σὺ δὲ παράπεμπε τῷ νῷ τὰς θεωρίας τῷ ῥητορικῷ σου*

**1** ἐπὶ δὲ **P**; ἢ ἐπὶ **V** | κακῶς πραχθέντι Ac; cf. schol. **P**: ἐπακουστέον τῶ (scr. τὸ) πραχθέντι || **2** ἐργασία post παραδείγματος Vc Ba; om. Ac || **4** τὴν om. Vc Ba Mr || **5** θεόθεν om. Vc Ba || **8** καὶ αἰτοίης **V** || **9** καὶ κακόν Vc || **11** cf. Dem. 20, 79 || **12** θάνατον **P** | ἂν om. Pc | ἐκινδύνευε Ac, (σ er.) Vc | μὲν (om. τοι) **V** || **13** γινόμενον Vc Ba || **14** ἢ respicit ad l. 11 εἰ μὲν | κελεύοις **P** || **14-15** ἔνεστι, ξ m. 2, Vc || **15** εὐεργέτησεν Vc || **18** τὸ om. Vc Ba || **19** οἷον οἱ τυραννοκτόνοι **V** | cf. 114, 8 | ἢ om. **V** || **20** ἐπηγγειλάμην Pc | πλάσις **V** || **21** ἐκ **P**; ἀπὸ **V** || **22** cf. 110, 14 || **22-23** δίπλασον Ac || **23** ἐβουλεύεσθε Ac || **24** συνεχώρησεν ἂν **V** | ὑμῖν om. Vc Ba || **25** τι om. **V** || **25-26** Sturm: *quodsi natura rei argumentum aliquod leve suppeditet, non vererer illo uti, ut res evaderet manifestior*

thing wrongly done, for example, "There is no need to believe Philip when he does a favor, for he is deceiving us"; then an ergasia from example, "for he has not benefited the Olynthians for obeying him, but after they received Potidea they lost everything."[159] Then bring in a plaston: "If at that time, when they were receiving Potidea, someone, inspired by a god, said to them that he would lose even Olynthus, would they have listened? That cannot be said."

Furthermore, one should try to form other kinds of plasta and seek to form them from opposites, and this takes countless forms; for example, if you are seeking a prize for some good deed, say, "If I had done something bad, would I not have been punished?" As Demosthenes ⟨*did*⟩ in *Against Leptines*, for going through the actions of Chabrias, he forms a plaston from the opposite, saying, "But if he had lost one ship, he would have been in danger of death."[160] This is, in fact, a double application of a plaston, for it combines something from the opposite with the smaller. Or if you demand that someone be punished for a crime, for it is possible to say, "If you had been benefited by the wrong he did, he would get gifts; since he has harmed you, | will he not be punished?" [161] Seek the opposite of everything said, and often you will find this to apply to the whole statement of the plaston, keeping in mind that for the most part either the whole action or its opposite is imagined as not having been done; for example, in the case of a tyrannicide, "If, before killing him, I had promised to do it, ⟨*would you have rewarded me*?⟩" This is a formation (*plasma*) of the whole action as not having happened. And another from the opposite: "But if I had not succeeded and had been captured, what would I have suffered?" And if Philip had demanded surrender of Demosthenes or some such thing, form a plaston from the opposite: "But if you wanted to take some of Philip's possession, would he ever let you?"

If the nature ⟨*of the subject*⟩ permits something rather easy, for the sake of greater clarity I did not avoid it.[161] For your part,

159 Cf. Demosthenes 23.107.

160 Cf. Demosthenes 20.79: "Had he lost a single city or as few as ten ships, these men would have indicted him for treason."

161 The author apologizes for the lack of elegant style in his examples; cf. the similar statement in 1.1 (p. 7) above. Strum's Latin version cited in Rabe's apparatus can be translated: "But if the nature of the subject supplies something

*κοσμῶν λόγῳ τὴν τέχνην. ἴσθι μέντοι, ὡς τοῖς ἀρχαίοις ἐντυγχάνοντες καὶ μάλιστα τῷ καθηγεμόνι μυρία καλὰ εὑρίσκομεν· ὅσα δὲ πρὸς τὸ κατεπεῖγον τῆς ὑπαγορεύσεως ἐπιτρέχει τῇ ψυχῇ, δίδωμι.*

*Δυσχερῆ λύσιν ἔχει τὰ ἀπ᾿ ἀρχῆς ἄχρι τέλους τῆς πραγματικῆς. εὕρηται οὖν καὶ μέθοδος πρὸς ταῦτα, ὥστε τῷ λύοντι τὰ ἀπ᾿ ἀρχῆς ἄχρι τέλους εὐπορίαν εἶναι, καὶ τοῦτο τὸ μάθημα σαφέστατα ἐκθήσο-* [162] *μαι. ἐὰν | μὲν τὸ πρᾶγμα παρ᾿ ἡμῶν ᾖ γεγονὸς καὶ ὑπὸ τῶν ἐχθρῶν εἰς τὴν ἡμετέραν βλάβην εἰσαγόμενον, οὕτως αὐτὸ λύσομεν· ζητοῦντες τῶν ἀντιθετικῶν στάσεων τὰ λυσιτελοῦντα ἡμῖν θήσομεν, ὥσπερ ποιοῦμεν καὶ ἐν τῇ ἀντιλήψει, πολλάκις δὲ θήσομεν καὶ τῶν ἄλλων στάσεων τὰ συντελοῦντα εἰς τὴν ἡμετέραν ὠφέλειαν. καὶ μεταληπτικὰ δὲ ἐὰν ἔχῃ τὸ κεφάλαιον τοῦ πλαττομένου, θήσομεν ἔσθ᾿ ὅτε καὶ οὕτω λύσομεν ὅτι «οὐδὲν πρὸς ἡμᾶς τὸ γενόμενον». καὶ μάλιστα ἐὰν ἐκ φύσεως ᾖ τι γενόμενον καὶ διὰ τοῦτο ἀξιῶμέν τι γενέσθαι, ὁ ἐνιστάμενος ἐρεῖ ὅτι «οὐ δι᾿ ἡμᾶς γίγνεται ἀλλὰ διὰ τὴν αὐτοῦ φύσιν». οἷον ῥεῖ ἀπὸ τῆς Αἴτνης ἐπὶ τὴν Κατάνην συνεχῶς τὸ πῦρ, καὶ συμβουλεύει τις αὐτοῖς μετοικίζεσθαι· τοῦτο τοίνυν λέξει ὁ φεύγειν συμβουλεύων ὅτι «κινδυνεύομεν ἐπιόντος ἡμῖν τοῦ πυρὸς καὶ ἀπαίρωμεν ἐνθένδε»· ἀπαντήσομεν οὖν*

1 λόγωι κοσμῶν **V** || 2 μάλιστά γε **V** | εὑρίσκομεν [ησ supra σκ], m. 2 supr., Vc || 4 titulum add. **P**: περὶ τῆς ἀπαρχῆς ἄχρι τέλους τῆς πραγματικῆς; om. **V** nec norat Anon. III 111, 5 Sp. | τὰ post τέλους add. Ac, v.l. **P** || 5 μέθοδος καὶ πρὸς ταῦτα Vc Ba; καὶ πρὸς ταῦτα μέθοδος Ac | τὸ λύον v.l. **P** || 7 ᾖ Ac, m. 2 Vc; εἴη **P** Vc Ba || 8 αὐτὰ Vc Ba || 9-10 καὶ ποιοῦμεν Vc Ba || 11 λυσιτελοῦντα Pc Ac || 12 δὲ καὶ Ba, ?m. 1 Vc || 13 γινόμενον Ac | τι **P** Ac; τὸ Vc Ba || 13-14 γιγνόμενον Vc, (γιν-) Ac || 14 ἀξιοῦμεν Pc Ba, (ῶ m. 2) Vc | οἷον ὅτι Ac || 15 cf. 36, 2 || 16 αὐτοὺς Pc || 17 τοίνυν **P**; εἰ Ac; om. Vc Ba | φεύγων [ειν supra ων] Ac || 18 ἀπαίρομεν Vc Ba, (ο ex ω) Pa, (ω ex ο) Pc | οὖν om. **V**

bring these theories to the thought of your speech while adorning your art with rhetorical language. Be continually aware that by studying the ancients, and especially their leader,[162] we discover countless fine things, but I am giving you (*only*) what contributes to impressing the teaching on the mind.[163]

## CHAPTER 12: <ON LYSIS OF FROM-BEGINNING-TO-END IN A PRAGMATIC QUESTION>

From-beginning-to-end is difficult to rebut in a pragmatic case.[164] A method has therefore been invented for this to provide facility to the one rebutting from-beginning-to-end, and I shall set out this teaching (*mathēma*) very clearly. If | the act is of our doing and has [162] been brought in by our enemies to our hurt, we shall rebut by seeking out and stating the antithetical stases that are most profitable to us, as we do in cases of antilepsis,[165] and often we shall state arguments from other kinds of stasis that contribute to our advantage. If the heading of the plaston epikheiremes include metalepsis,[166] we shall sometimes state this and refute it in the form, "What happened does not relate to us." And especially if it is natural for something to have happened and we think it did happen for that reason, the speaker who is resisting an action will say that "it is not happening because of us but because of its own nature." For example, fire continually runs down from Aetna on Catania, and someone urges the inhabitants to emigrate. The person advising them to flee will say, "We are in danger of the fire coming down on us and let us go away from here"; we shall then reply thus: "The

simple, I do not fear to use that so the subject may become clearer."

[162] I.e., Demosthenes.

[163] Rendered by Patillon as "mais je n'en donne que ce que m'impose la nécessité d'explique" (*L'Art rhétorique*, 268).

[164] Here meaning a case where the point at issue is the nature of an act; see n. 111 above.

[165] Cases in which the speaker claims the act was legitimate in the circumstances: cf. Hermogenes, *On Stases*, pp. 72–75 Rabe. The "antithetical stases" might include counteraccusation, shifting the blame, or some excuse for the act.

[166] Transference of the cause of an action to someone or something else; here, the opponent is imagined to have blamed the speaker for something.

*οὕτως «οὐ δι' ἡμᾶς ῥεῖ τὸ πῦρ ἀλλὰ διὰ τὴν αὑτοῦ φύσιν».*

## *Περὶ τάξεως ἐπιχειρημάτων.*

*Ἡ δὲ τάξις τῶν ἐπιχειρημάτων διπλῆ. εἰ γὰρ τύχοι τὰ μὲν αὐτῶν ἀποδεικτικὰ εἶναι πολιτικῆς ἑρμηνείας μόνης δεόμενα, τὰ δὲ πανηγυρικά, τηρήσεις τὰ πανηγυρικὰ τελευταῖα πρὸς τὸ δοκεῖν αὔξειν προχωροῦντα* [163] *| τὸν λόγον ἐπὶ τὸ ἀκμαιότερον, ἵνα τὰ τῆς τέχνης κατ' οἰκείαν τάξιν προχωροῦντα δόξαν ἀκμῆς τῷ λέγοντι παράσχῃ ὡς ὑπὸ τῆς ἐν τῷ λέγειν θερμότητος ἐπὶ τὸ ἀκμαιότερον προαγομένῳ· ἄλλως τε δὲ καὶ ἡδίων τοῖς ἀκούουσιν ὁ ἀπὸ τῶν ἀποδεικτικῶν ἐπὶ τὰ πανηγυρικώτερα χωρῶν, οὐχ ὁ ἀπὸ τῶν πανηγυρικῶν ἐπὶ τὰ ἀποδεικτικά.*

*Αὕτη μὲν ἰδέα πρώτη. δευτέρα δὲ ἐκείνης σοφωτέρα ἰδόντα τὰ ἐπιχειρήματα, ὁπόσα ἐστὶ καὶ οἷα, τὸ προκλητικώτερον τοῦ ἑξῆς κεφαλαίου τελευταῖον τιθέναι, ἵνα, ἐκ τῆς ἀνάγκης τοῦ ἐπιχειρήματος ἀνισταμένου τοῦ κεφαλαίου τοῦ ἐφεξῆς, ὕφος ἓν ὁ λόγος γένηται καὶ σῶμα, μὴ διασπώμενος ἐν ταῖς ὑποφοραῖς, ἀλλὰ αὐτὸς αὑτοῦ δοκῶν ἔχεσθαι καὶ ἀνίστασθαι δι' αὑτοῦ· ὥσπερ οὖν ἴσμεν καὶ ἐν ταῖς ἀντιλήψεσι τὸ ἀντιπαραστατικὸν μετὰ τὴν ἔνστασιν τελευταῖον τιθέμενον,*

2 cf. 122, 16 ann. || 3 δὲ **P** AC **Pπ**; om. Vc Ba | διάταξις Ac || 4 δεικτικὰ m. 1 Ba | μόνης om. **P** Ac Mr || 5 δοκοῦν Pc || 5-6 παραχωροῦντα Pc || 8 προσαγόμενωι Vc Ba | τε **P** Ac Mr; om. Vc Ba, v.l. **P** || 9 πανηγυρικώτατα Vc Ba, (τερα m. 1 supr.) Pa || 11 πρώτη **P**; μία **V**, v.l. **P** || 14 τοῦ v.l. Dox.; τὸ **V**; κατὰ τὸ **P** | ὕφος, ἓν **P**, m. 2 Vc, m. po. Ba; ὑφὲν Ac; ὑφ' ἑνὸς Ba, (ut.vid.) Vc; cf. Dox.: τριχῶς δὲ εὗρον τὴν γραφὴν ἐν τοῖς βιβλίοις· τὰ μὲν . . . 'κεφαλαίου, τὸ ἐφεξῆς, ἓν ὕφος ὁ λόγος' . . . τὰ δὲ . . . 'κεφαλαίου κατὰ τὸ ἐφεξῆς, ὕφος ἓν λόγος' . . . ἕτερα δὲ . . . 'κεφαλαίου τοῦ ἐφεξῆς, ἓν ὕφος ὁ λόγος' κτλ. | καὶ **V**, cf. v.l. Dox.; om. **P** || 15 διασπώμενον Ac, (σ m. 1 supr.) Vc || 16 cf. 78, 19 sq.

fire does not flow because of us but because of its own nature."[167]

## CHAPTER 13: ON THE ARRANGEMENT OF EPIKHEIREMES

There are two ways to arrange epikheiremes.[168] If some of them happen to be apodeictic, requiring a political style of expression alone,[169] and some are panegyrical, you will keep the panegyrical ones for last to seem to amplify | the speech as it advances to [163] a higher peak,[170] so that the progression of artistic skills in their proper places may enhance the speaker's reputation for achieving heightening, as he is led on by his warmth in speaking to a higher peak. Moreover, movement from apodeictic to panegyric epikheiremes is more pleasing to the audience than is movement from panegyric to apodeictic.

This is the first style (*idea*). The second and more clever than that is, after looking to see how many epikheiremes there are and of what sort, to put one provocative of the next heading last, so that, from the cogent connection of epikheiremes arising in each heading, the speech may have a single texture and body, not being borne off in separate directions (*hypophorai*) but seem to be held together by itself and to grow from itself. Thus also in cases of antilepsis[171] we see that the antiparastasis is put last after the

[167] The author has jumped from an example in a judicial to one in a deliberative theme: whether the inhabitants should emigrate because of the fire. Both fall under *pragmantikē*. Cf. 2.2 above, where the fact that this is a natural phenomenon is given as a reason against emigrating.

[168] The author offers a nuanced teaching differing from, though not necessarily conflicting with, standard doctrine, which recommended putting the strongest arguments first or last and weak ones in the middle, where they would be more easily overlooked; cf. *Rhetoric for Herennius* 3.18; Cicero, *On the Orator* 2.314; Quintilian 5.12.14; *Anonymous Seguerianus* §§192–193; Cassius Longinus, *Art of Rhetoric* 2.3. An emotional epikheireme might well prove effective as the last heading in an argument.

[169] The prose style used in political assemblies or in the law courts, relying, in the author's view, more on logical demonstrations (*apodeiktika*) than on emotional appeal.

[170] *Akmaioteron*; on *akmē*, see note 95 above.

[171] I.e., counterplea; cf. Hermogenes, *On Stases*, pp. 65–71 Rabe. The defendant pleads that an action is permitted, and the prosecutor admits that might be true in theory but not in a particular circumstance. On enstasis and antiparastasis, cf. 3.6 above.

*ἐπειδὴ ἐγερτικόν ἐστι τοῦ ὅρου, οἷον «ἐξῆν ἀποκτεῖναι τὸν υἱόν», ἡ ἔνστασις «οὐκ ἐξῆν· εἰ δὲ καὶ ἐξῆν, οὐκ ἐπὶ τῷ αἴτιον γενέσθαι σε τῇ μητρὶ θανάτου», ἵνα εὐθέως ὁ ὅρος ἀπαντήσῃ, τί τὸ αἴτιόν ἐστι θανάτου γενέσθαι. εἰ γὰρ καὶ ἀντιπαράστασίς ἐστιν ἡ ἀπαντήσασα οὐκ* [164] *ἐπιχείρημα, ὅμως εἰς παραδείγματος λόγον | ἐθήκαμεν, ὅτι χρὴ καὶ ἐπὶ τῶν ἐπιχειρημάτων οὕτω τιθέναι τελευταῖον τὸ τοῦ μέλλοντος κεφαλαίου προκλητικόν· ἐπεὶ καὶ ἡ ἔνστασις καὶ ἡ ἀντιπαράστασις τὸν αὐτὸν ἔχουσι λόγον, οὐκ ἀεὶ τῆς ἐνστάσεως ἢ τῆς ἀντιπαραστάσεως πρώτης τιθεμένης, ἀλλ' ἐναλλὰξ τοῦτο πασχούσης ἑκάστης, ὃν τρόπον φαμὲν δεῖν ἀνασκοπεῖν καὶ ἐπὶ τῶν ἐπιχειρημάτων· καὶ γὰρ τούτων ἑκάστη ἢ διὰ τὸ ἀκμαιότερον δευτέρα τεθήσεται ἢ διὰ τὴν τοῦ μέλλοντος κεφαλαίου προσδοκίαν.*

## *Περὶ ὅρου.*

*Ὅρος καὶ ἀνθορισμὸς καὶ συλλογισμὸς καὶ λύσις τοῦ συλλογισμοῦ τέσσαρα μέν ἐστιν ὀνόματα, τῇ δὲ δυνάμει δύο· ὅ τε γὰρ τὸν ὅρον ἔχων καὶ τὸν συλλογισμὸν τοῖς αὐτοῖς ἐπιχειρήμασι κατασκευάζειν ἑκάτερα δύναται, ὅ τε τὸν ἀνθορισμὸν καὶ τὴν λύσιν τοῦ συλλογισμοῦ τοῖς αὐ-*

1-2 ἡ ἔνστασις **P**; ἢ (om. ἔνστασις) Ac Ba, (ut vid.) Vc; εἶπα Sc || 2 ἐξῆν· εἶτα· εἰ Ac; fort. ἐξῆν'· <εἶτα ἡ ἀντιπαράστασις> 'εἰ δὲ . . .' || 8 alt. τῆς om. Vc Ba || 11 ἢ om. Vc Ba | cf. 80, 23 || 13 Dox.: τινὲς πρὸ τοῦ περὶ τάξεως ἐπιχειρημάτων (p. 120, 2) ἀνέγνων τὸ περὶ ὅρου κτλ. || 16 ὁ post καὶ supr. m. 2 Ba | Dox.: διάφορον . . . τὴν γραφὴν εὗρον . . . τὰ μὲν . . 'ὅ τε γὰρ τὸν ὅρον ἔχων καὶ τὸν συλλογισμὸν τοῖς αὐτοῖς ἐπιχειρήμασι κατασκευάζειν ἑκάτερα δύνανται'· τὰ δε οὕτως 'ὅ τε γὰρ τὸν ὅρον ἔχων καὶ τὸν ἀνθορισμὸν τοῖς αὐτοῖς ἐπιχειρήμασι κατασκευάζειν ἑκάτερα δύνανται' . . . τὰ δὲ . . . 'ὅ τε γὰρ τὸν ὅρον ἔχων καὶ ὁ τὸν ἀνθορισμὸν τοῖς αὐτοῖς ἐπιχειρήμασι κατασκευάζειν ἑκάτερα δύνανται· ὅ τε τὸν συλλογισμὸν καὶ ὁ τὴν λύσιν τοῦ συλλογισμοῦ τοῖς αὐτοῖς ἐπιχειρήμασι κατασκευάζειν ἑκάτερα δύνανται' . . . ὁ μέντοι ἐξηγητὴς οὕτως ἀνέγνω τὸ παρὸν ῥητὸν 'ὅ τε γὰρ τὸν ὅρον ἔχων καὶ τὸν συλλογισμὸν τοῖς αὐτοῖς ἐπιχειρήμασι κατασκευάζειν ἑκάτερα δύνανται ὅ τε τὸν ἀνθορισμὸν καὶ τὴν λύσιν τοῦ συλλογισμοῦ τοῖς αὐτοῖς ἐπιχειρήμασι κατασκευάζειν ἑκάτερα δύνανται' . . . μήπω γοῦν ἄμεινον οὕτως ἔχειν τὴν γραφὴν 'ὅ τε γὰρ τὸν ὅρον ἔχων καὶ τὴν λύσιν τοῦ συλλογισμοῦ τοῖς αὐτοῖς ἐπιχειρήμασιν ἑκάτερα κατασκευάζειν δύνανται' κτλ. | κατασκευάσαι **V** || 17 ὁ post καὶ add. Ac, m. 2 Ba

enstasis, since it prepares for the definition; for example, "It was permitted to kill my son,"[172] with the enstasis, "It was not permitted, and if it had been permitted, not so that you might be the cause of death to the mother," in order that the definition of what was the cause of her death might occur immediately. Even if this rejoinder is an antiparastasis and not an epikheireme,[173] nevertheless, | we have used it for an example because it is necessary also in [164] the case of epikheiremes to put last what is provocative of the next heading. Since enstasis and antiparastasis have the same function, neither the enstasis nor the antiparastasis always being put first but either in turn, we say that one should look at epikheiremes in the same way. For each of these will be put second either to heighten the intensity or in anticipation of the next heading.[174]

## CHAPTER 14: ON DEFINITION[175]

*Horos* and *anthorismos* and *syllogismos* and *lysis* of *syllogismos* are four different names[176] but in effect only two different things, for in the case of definition (*horos*) and syllogism (*syllogismos*) one can confirm either by the same epikheiremes, and in counterdefini-

[172] On the theme, cf. n. 8 above.

[173] There seems inconsistency here, since previously enstasis and antiparastasis have been referred to as epikheiremes; cf. esp. the first sentence of 3.7 above and more generally 3.5–6. Possibly the text should be emended to read "the rejoinder is an antiparatasis and not an *enstasis*."

[174] In the example given, the progression of epikheiremes (it is not permitted; even if permitted not in this case) leads to the heading of definition (What was the cause of the mother's death?), but it is hard to see how any other order of epikheiremes would be likely to occur. The chapter would have been clearer if the author had illustrated the possibilities of the arrangement of multiple epikheiremes in support of a single heading more extensively.

[175] Not definition in general, but stasis of definition; see Hermogenes, *On Stases*, pp. 59,10–65,8 Rabe. Rabe (app. crit. on 164,10) quotes John Doxapatres as reporting that "some" read this chapter before the chapter on the arrangement of epikheiremes.

[176] On these technical terms, see Hermogenes, *On Stasis,* pp. 60,6–8 and 81,6–18 Rabe, with Heath's commentary, *On Issues*, 104 and 139. The names can be translated as, respectively, definition, counterdefinition, syllogism (called "assimilation" by Heath and Patillon), and refutation of syllogism. In syllogism as understood here, an epikheireme is used to support the definition of an act; cf. the example of tyrannicide below.

[165] *τοῖς ἐπιχειρήμασι κατασκευάζειν ἑκάτερα | δύναται. τέχνη δὲ θαυμασία παρ᾽ ἡμῖν εὕρηται πρὸς τὸ μήτε πεφύρθαι τὸν λόγον μήτε ἄπορον εἶναι διῃρημένης τῆς διανοίας, ὥσπερ καὶ ἐπὶ τῶν ἐπιχειρημάτων, ἵνα ὅ τε τὸν ὅρον μελετῶν καὶ ὁ τὸν ἀνθορισμὸν ἀντιτιθεὶς τούτῳ τὰ πρὸ τοῦ πράγματος εἰωθότα συμβαίνειν λέγωσι, καὶ ὁ μὲν τὸν ὅρον κατασκευάζων οὕτω ζητῇ «τόδε πρὸ τοῦ πράγματος ἔδει γενέσθαι, οὐ γέγονεν», ὁ δὲ τὸν ἀνθορισμὸν κατασκευάζων ἵνα οὕτω λέγῃ «ἔδει τόδε γενέσθαι πρὸ τοῦ πράγματος, γέγονε». ταῦτα μὲν ἀπὸ τῶν πρὸ τοῦ πράγματος· οἷον μαινόμενος ἀπέκτεινε τύραννον, σωφρονήσας αἰτεῖ τὸ γέρας, ἐνίσταταί τις αὐτῷ «οὐ τοῦτό ἐστι τυραννοκτονία». ὃ δέ φησι «τοῦτό ἐστι τυραννοκτονία· ἔδει ἀνελθεῖν εἰς τὴν ἀκρόπολιν, ἀνῆλθον· ἔδει ἀποκτεῖναι, πεφόνευκα», ταῦτα πρὸ τοῦ πράγματος. ὁ δὲ τὸν ἀνθορισμὸν κατασκευάζων ἐρεῖ οὕτως «ἔδει βουλεύσασθαι πρῶτον τὸν μέλλοντα τυραννοκτονεῖν, σὺ μαινόμενος οὐκ ἐβουλεύσω· σωφρονούντων γὰρ ἔργον ἐστίν», ὥστε τῶν ὀφειλόντων τι πρὸ τοῦ πράγματος γενέσθαι παρὰ τοῦ τυραννοκτόνου λείπει· «ἔδει εἰδέναι τὸν τυραννοκτόνον, τί ποιεῖ, σὺ δὲ οὐκ ᾔδεις». ὁ δὲ συλλογισμὸς ἀπὸ τῶν ἐπισυμβαινόντων τῷ πράγματι ἐπικατασκευασθήσεται, οἷον «οὐδὲν διαφέρει, εἴτε ἐμαινόμην εἴτε*
[166] *ἐσωφρόνουν· | ἃ γὰρ ὡς σωφρονοῦντος ἀποκτείναντος ἐμοῦ ἐπισυνέβη ἂν ἀγαθά, ταῦτα καὶ νῦν γέγονεν· ἔδει τὸν τύραννον ἀνῃρῆσθαι, ἀνῄρηται· ἔδει ἐλευθερίαν γενέσθαι, γέγονεν· ἔδει μηδένα εἶναι ἐπὶ τῆς ἀκροπόλεως, οὐδείς ἐστιν». ὁμοίως καὶ ὁ τὴν λύσιν τοῦ συλλογισμοῦ ἔχων ἐκ τῶν μετὰ ταῦτα συμβαινόντων, εἴ τι μὴ ἐπιγέγονε, λαμβάνων ὡς ἐπιχείρημα φήσει ὅτι «πολὺ διαφέρει· ἃ γὰρ ἂν ἐπισυνέβη σωφρο-*

1 κατασκευάζειν **V**, v.l. **P**; om. **P** | δύνανται Ac | *a nobis* Laurentis, *apud nos* Sturm (at cf. Sturmii commentarium) || **3** τῆς om. **V** | καὶ om. **V** | τῶν **P**; om. **V**, v.l. **P** | ὁ om. Pc || **6** ζητεῖ **V**, (ῇ supr.) Pa | οὐ **P** Ac; om. Vc Ba; καὶ Sc; Dox.: ἔπταισται ... ἡ γραφή· προσθετέον γὰρ τῷ 'γέγονε' τὴν 'οὐ' ἄρνησιν κτλ.· cf. Π. στ. 59, 16 sq. || **8** οὐ γέγονε Pa Vc, (οὐ in ras.; m. po. ?) Ba; οὐ om. Pc Ac; Dox.: ἀφαιρετέον τοῦ «γέγονε» τὴν «οὔ» ἄρνησιν κτλ. | ἀπὸ τῶν om. Vc Ba | πρὸ om. Pc || **11** τὴν om. **V** || **12** ἀνθορισμὸν **V**; ὅρον **P**; Dox.: ἔπταισται ἡ γραφή· ἀντὶ τοῦ ἔχειν γὰρ «ὁ δὲ τὸν ὅρον κατασκευάζων ἐρεῖ οὕτως» ἔχει «ὁ δὲ τὸν ἀνθορισμὸν κατασκευάζων» κτλ. || **13** δεῖ Vc Ac, m. 1 Ba | βουλεύεσθαι Ac || **19** ἐμοῦ καὶ ἀπ. **P** || **24** ἐπισυνέβη ἂν **V**

tion (*anthorismos*) and rebuttal (*lysis*) one can confirm either by the same epikheiremes. | We have invented a wonderful technique to [165] avoid confusion and being at a loss in a speech, the thought being divided as it was also in the case of epikheiremes.[177] Using this technique, both one practicing definition and one replying to it with a counterdefinition speaks of things that usually have happened before the action. The one arguing for the definition claims that "this ought to have happened before the action, but it did not happen," while the one maintaining the counterdefinition says, "What ought to have happened before the action has happened." These statements refer to the time before the act under consideration; for example, in a fit of insanity someone killed a tyrant; when he came to his senses, he demands the prize; someone opposes him, saying, "This is not tyrannicide." He says it is: "This is tyrannicide: it was necessary to go up to the acropolis, and I did so; it was necessary to kill, and I have slaughtered him." These statements refer to the time before the act. One supporting the counterdefinition[178] will speak thus: "It was necessary for someone who was going to kill the tyrant to lay plans first, but you in your madness did not lay plans; for tyrannicide is a deed of those who are in their right minds," with the result that something that ought to happen before the act was omitted by the tyrant killer: "It was necessary for the tyrannicide to know what he was doing, but you did not know." A syllogism from what results from the act will provide additional confirmation; for example, "It makes no difference whether I was mad or sane; | the same good results [166] that would have happened if I had killed him when sane have happened now; it was necessary to eliminate the tyrant, and he has been eliminated; it was necessary for liberty to come to be, and it has come; it was necessary for no one to be in power on the acropolis, and no one is." Similarly, one furnishing lysis of the syllogism on the ground of what results from these things, if nothing more has happened, treating it like an epikheireme will assert, "It makes much difference; for what would have resulted if you killed him when sane has not occurred now that you have killed

[177] See 3.4 (p. 75), where the author also claims originality.

[178] Lindberg (2059 n. 424 *ad fin.*) wants to read "definition" with P and Doxapatres rather than "counterdefinition" with V and Rabe. But the original definition is that of the claimant, and this is the counterdefinition of the opponent.

*νοῦντός σου κτείναντος, ταῦτα οὐ γέγονε νῦν μαινομένου ἀποκτείναντος· οἷον ὁ σωφρονῶν ἀποκτείνας εὐθέως τιμᾶται, σὺ δὲ μετὰ τὸν φόνον ἐθεραπεύου ἰατροῖς ὑποκείμενος καὶ μάγοις», ὥστε τῇ μὲν δυνάμει τὰ αὐτὰ εἶναι κἀκεῖνα, οἷα τὰ ἐνθάδε, μόνῃ δὲ τῇ διαστάσει τῶν χρόνων* <*διαφέρειν. ἐξ οὗ συμβαίνει*> *μὴ διαμαρτεῖν τὰς δριμύτητας πρός τε εὐπορίαν τοῦ ἐπιχειροῦντος καὶ πρὸς διάκρισιν τῶν τε ἄνω κεφαλαίων καὶ τῶν ἐφεξῆς, ὡς ἂν μὴ τοῖς αὐτοῖς περιπίπτωμεν τῷ τὰς αὐτὰς δυνάμεις ἔχειν ἑκάτερα.*

## ***Περὶ διασκευῆς.***

1 σου suppl. m. po. Pc | ἀποκτείναντος Ac, m. 1 Pc || 2 σώφρων Vc Ba || 4 τοῦ χρόνου **V** || 5 add. m. po. **V**; schol. **P** (W VII 790 ann.): ... τῇ δὲ διαστάσει μόνον τῶν χρόνων διαφ[έ] et insequens scholion: «μόνῃ δὲ τῇ διαστάσει τοῦ χρόνου διαφ[έ]» ... ἐξ οὗτινος χρόνου συμβαίνει ἰσχυρὰς εἶναι τὰς ἐργασίας τῶν κεφαλαίων || 7 αὐτὰς om. Pc

him when insane; for example, the sane killer is immediately honored, but after the killing you underwent treatment by doctors and wizards." Thus, those things described here are effectively the same as what was described earlier but <differ> only in the contrast of time.[179] <The result is that> there is no lack of forceful expression (*drimytēs*) in an abundance of epikheiremes and in distinction of prior and subsequent headings, so we need not (*always*) use the same ones in that each has the same effects.[180]

*Patillon (*L'Art rhétorique*, 272–73) inserts here the chapter on comparative problems from the end of book 4 (4.14) on the ground that it deals with invention; but as will be shown in due course it is an addition to the text by an editor and the work of a different writer.*

## CHAPTER 15: ON DIASKEUĒ[181]

*Some Byzantine commentators regard diaskeuē as having its place mainly in the epilogue, and thus modern commentators suggest that this chapter should be regarded as taking the place of an account of the epilogue that would otherwise be expected in a handbook on invention (cf. Lindberg, 2060 n. 425; Patillon,* ANRW*, 2107–10). Omission of any reference to the traditional functions of an epilogue—to recapitulate the major point of a speech and to stir the emotions of the judges or audience to vote as the speaker demands—is not a fatal objection to this view, since the traditional functions of other parts of a speech have also gone unnoticed; however, the term "epilogue" never occurs in the chapter, and some of what is said clearly relates to the diegesis and kataskeuē (cf., e.g., paragraph 3 below).*

[179] The words in pointed brackets were added by Rabe from a scholion; see his apparatus here.

[180] Apparently a cumbersome way of summarizing what has just been said.

[181] As elsewhere, the chapter heading is a later addition. The chapter might better have been entitled "On Diatyposis."

*Διασκευὴ δὲ τοῦ προβλήματος ἡ διατύπωσίς ἐστι τοῦ πράγματος,*
[167] *ὥσπερ ἐν ποιητικῇ ἡ καθ᾽ ἕκαστον | τῶν γενομένων ἀφήγησίς τε καὶ*
*διατύπωσις, διὰ μὲν τῶν πεπραγμένων τοῦ διασκευάζοντος ὀφείλοντος πλατῦναι τὸ πρᾶγμα μόνον, οὐ μέντοι γε οὔτε αἰτίαις οὔτε λογισμοῖς τοσοῦτον οὔτε ἄλλῳ τινὶ ἐπιχειρήματι, ἀλλὰ μόνῳ τῷ τρόπῳ. διασκευάζεται μὲν γὰρ πάντως ἕν τι τῶν τῆς περιστάσεως, καὶ ὅ τι δᾶν ἐκείνων ᾖ, τῷ τρόπῳ πάντως πλατύνεται, καὶ μετὰ τοῦ τρόπου καὶ προσωποποιίαις καὶ οἷα εἰκὸς ἦν τελεῖσθαι ἐφ᾽ ἑκάστου τῶν πραττομένων καὶ λεχθῆναι δυναμένων παρὰ τῶν ἐμφαινομένων προσώπων ἐν τῇ διατυπώσει. ἔξεστι δὲ τὸν διασκευάζοντα πιθανῶς τολμᾶν καὶ λέγειν, ὅσα εἰκὸς ἐπισυμβαίνειν εἴωθε τοῖς πράγμασι παράδοξα ἢ θαυμαστά, καὶ ταῦτα λαμβάνοντα ἐκ τοῦ εἰκότος· ὃ γὰρ ἂν δυνηθῇ ποτε ἐπισυμβῆναι τοιούτῳ πράγματι, λέγειν ἔξεστιν, ὡς ἐπισυνέβη καὶ τότε, πᾶν δὲ τὸ παρὰ τὸ εἰκὸς ἢ λεχθῆναι ἢ πραχθῆναι λεγόμενον εἰς κακόζηλον ἐξάγει τὴν διασκευήν.*

*Γίνεται δὲ ἡ διατύπωσις τοῦ πράγματος ἢ ἐκ τῶν παρελθόντων ἢ ἐκ τῶν παρόντων ἢ ἀπὸ τῶν μελλόντων, ἢ οἷα πάλαι ἐγένετο ἢ ὁποῖα νυνὶ γίνεται ἢ ὁποῖα κατὰ τὸ μέλλον γενήσεται, ἡμῶν καὶ ταῦτα διατυ-*
[168] *πούντων. συνελόντι δὲ εἰπεῖν ἡ διασκευὴ ποιητικῆς ἔχει | φιλοτιμίαν·*
*οὐδὲν γὰρ ἕτερον ἡ ποιητικὴ ἔχει πλὴν ἑκάστου τῶν γενομένων ἀφήγησίν τινα καὶ διατύπωσιν.*

1 ἡ διασκευὴ Pa **P**π Ac | διασκευὴ δέ ἐστιν ἐν προβλήματι ἡ διατύπωσις τοῦ Vc Ba; γρ´ καὶ οὕτως· ἡ διασκευὴ τοῦ πράγματος ἡ διατύπωσίς ἐστι· καὶ οὕτω γρ´· ἡ διασκευή ἐστιν ἐν προβλήματι ἡ διατύπωσις τοῦ πράγματος mg. **P** | δὲ om. Ac || 2 καθάπερ Ac | γινομένων Pa | τε Pc Ac; τις Vc Ba, (τε supr.) Pa, cf. 128, 20–21 || 5 πλατύνεται post τρόπω add. Ac || 6 δ' om. Sc || 7 πάντως Ac, v.l. **P**; om. **P** Vc Ba || 8-9 γρ καὶ οἷα εἰκὸς ἦν ἐφ' ἑκάστω τῶν πραττομένων καὶ λεχθῆναι δυναμένων ἕξει παρὰ τῶν κτλ. **P**; eadem in lemmate (at δυναμένων ἐξ αἰτίας τῶν, om. παρὰ) Mr || 8 οἷα ⌊I⌉ Pc | τελεῖσθαι om. **V** || 9 ἕξει ante παρὰ add. **V**, cf. v.l. **P** || 10 τὸν om. **V** | καὶ post λέγειν Vc Ba || 11 εἰκὸς suspect. || 12 λαμβάνοντ⌊α m. 2 ex ο⌉ς, m. 2 ειν supr., Vc || 14 ἢ λεχθῆναι ἢ om. (ἢ λεχθὲν ἢ πραχθὲν m. 2 supr.) Vc | (ἢ om.; λεχθὲν ἢ πραχθὲν ἢ λεχθῆναι ἢ m. 2 supr.) πραχθ⌊ῆναι m. 2⌉ λεγόμενον Ba | πεπράχθαι Vc | cf. 182, 18 || 16-17 ἡ — πράγματος post 19 μελλόντων **V** || 17-18 ὁποῖα . . . ὁποῖα **P** Ac; ποῖα . . . ποῖα Vc Ba || 19 συνελόντι **V**, (τα m. 1 supr.) Pa; συνελόντα Pc || 20 cf. 128, 2

The *diatypōsis*[182] of the action constitutes a *diaskeuē*[183] of the problem, like a recounting (*aphēgēsis*) of events, one by one, and like vivid description in poetry; | the one making the elaboration by means of the various aspects of the action ought to enlarge upon the act alone, not so much, however, by stating causes or reasonings or some other epikheireme but only by the manner of treatment (*tropos*).[184] One of the attendant circumstances[185] is fully developed artistically, and whichever of them it is, is entirely amplified in the treatment, in connection with the treatment also by personifications and (*by saying*) what sort of things were probably accomplished in the case of each of the things that were done and what can be said on the part of the persons made to appear in the diatyposis. It is possible for one artistically developing an account in a persuasive way to venture also to say what unexpected or wondrous things are, with some probability, apt to result from the actions, deriving these from probability; for what could have resulted sometimes from such an action can be said actually to have resulted now, but everything alleged to have been said or to have happened contrary to probability will lead the account into bad taste (*kakozēlos*). [167]

Diatyposis of the action comes from describing things past, present, or future, either what sort of things happened long ago or what sort happen now or what sort will happen in the future, all of which we describe vividly. Briefly stated, diaskeuē rivals poetry, | [168]
for poetry contains nothing other than some recounting and some vivid description of each of the things that has happened.

[182] *Diatyposis* is vivid or emotional description of an action or the state of mind of someone; cf., e.g., the description of the Theban prisoners below (p. 133); Theon (vol. 2, pp. 106,25–107,1 and 109,3–10 Spengel); Quintilian on "ocular demonstration" (9.2.40): "when we do not restrict ourselves to mentioning that something was done but proceed to show *how* it was done and do so not merely in broad general lines but in full detail." In *Anonymous Seguerianus* (§233) diatyposis is associated with arousing emotion in an epilogue.

[183] *Diaskeuē* is the artistic development of a passage, "depiction" in Lindberg's account (2060), *représentation* in Patillon's translation (*L'Art rhétorique,* 274). The term *diaskeuē* does not occur in other Greek rhetorical treatises but is found in Latin in Fortunatianus (2.19, p. 112 Halm): Est et *diasceua*, quae res gestas non tam docet quam exaggerat.

[184] Cf. 2.7 above, p. 55.

[185] E.g., person, time, place.

*Χρὴ δὲ τὸν μέλλοντα μελετᾶν οἰκονομεῖν εἰδέναι. εἰ μὲν γὰρ εὑρίσκοιτο διήγησις καὶ ἐκ τῶν παρελθόντων καὶ ἐκ τῶν μελλόντων ἢ ἀπὸ τῶν παρόντων μόνων ἢ καὶ τῶν δύο καιρῶν ἢ καὶ τῶν τριῶν, ἔξεστι τὸν παρελθόντα ἀπολαβόντα ἐν τῇ διηγήσει ἐνδιασκεύως ἀποπληρῶσαι τὸ ἄνω μέρος, οὐ μέλλοντα ἐνοχλήσειν τοῖς κάτω μέρεσι τοῖς αὐτοῖς διὰ τὴν τῶν μελλόντων διατύπωσιν. εἰ δὲ εἴη τὸ πρᾶγμα ὀφεῖλον διασκευασθῆναι καὶ ἄνω καὶ κάτω ἐν ταῖς διηγήσεσι, μνήμην αὐτοῦ ποιησόμεθα κατασκευάζοντες ταῖς αἰτίας, αἷς ἔφαμεν τὴν διήγησιν κατασκευάζεσθαι, τοὺς δὲ τρόπους αὐτοὺς τῇ διασκευῇ φυλάξομεν. ἐὰν δὲ παντάπασιν ᾖ ἄπορον εἰς διατύπωσιν τὸ πρᾶγμα, τότε μεταχείρισίς ἐστιν οἰκονομίας ἀρίστη τὸ μηδὲ ἐν τοῖς ἀπ᾽ ἀρχῆς ἄχρι τέλους γενομένους ἀποχρήσασθαι ταῖς ὑποδιαιρέσεσιν, ἀλλ᾽ ἀθρόως εἰπόντες τὸ πρᾶγμα ἐκεῖ καὶ πλάσαντές τινα πλαστὰ καὶ ἐπὶ ἀθρόῳ τῷ πράγματι ἐπειπόντες τὰς καθ᾽ ἕκαστον ὑποδιαιρέσεις τοῖς ἐπιοῦσι φυλάξομεν τῇ κατασκευῇ χρώμενοι ἐνταῦθα ἀντὶ τῆς διασκευῆς, καὶ τοὺς ὑπομερισμούς, οὓς ἐμέλλομεν ἐν τοῖς ἀπ᾽ ἀρχῆς ἄχρι τέλους ποιεῖν ὡς*
[169] *κατασκευάζοντες, τού|τους φυλάξομεν τῇ διασκευῇ ὡς διατυποῦντες, μόνῃ τῇ τῶν κώλων ἁρμονίᾳ χρώμενοι διαφερούσῃ ἄλλα γάρ ἐστι κατασκευαζόντων κῶλα καὶ ἄλλα διασκευαζόντων, προσέτι δὲ καὶ τὰς περὶ τὴν κατασκευὴν περιόδους ἀφαιροῦντες· ἀλλότριον γὰρ περίοδος διασκευῆς. ὅθεν γίνεται καὶ ἡ τῶν προσωποποιιῶν εὐπορία· εἰ γὰρ καὶ ἀποροίη τὸ πρᾶγμα διασκευῆς ἀθρόως, ὁ ὑπομερισμὸς προσωποποιίας οὐκ ἀπορεῖ. Χρὴ δὲ εἰδέναι, ὅτι καὶ πᾶς ὑπομερισμὸς τὰ αὐτὰ λέγει τῇ*

2 καὶ — μελλόντων ante διήγησις **V**; ego potius post 6 καιρῶν transposuerim || 3 alt. τῶν om. Vc Ba | μόνων Pc, m. 2 Vc; μόνον **V**, (ων supr.) Pa | pr. καὶ **P** Ac; ἐκ Vc Ba | alt. καὶ om. **V** || 4 ἔν τισι διηγήμασιν Mr || 5 ἐνοχλεῖν Ba || 6 τὸ πρᾶγμα τὸ Ac || 7-8 αὐτοῦ μνήμην **V** || 8 τοῖς τρόποις οἷς Vc Ba | p. 54, 16 sqq. | ἔφαμεν (η supra α) **P** || 9 αὐτοὺς **P** Ac; τούτους Vc Ba || 10-11 Dox.: τινὲς . . . «οἰκονομία μεταχειρίσεως ἀρίστης τὸ . . .» || 12 γενομένους (ι supra ου) Pa || 13 ἐκεῖ τὸ πρᾶγμα **V** Mr | καὶ om. **V** || 14-15 et p. 169, 1 φυλάξωμεν Vc Ba || 16 ἐν om. Vc Ba || 17 τυποῦντες Pa || 18 χρησάμενοι Vc Ba || 19 κῶλα post διασκευαζόντων **V** || 21 schol. **P** (W VII 802, 3): δεῖ προσυπακούειν τὸ ἐπιφερόμνεον κτλ.; Dox.: λείπει, φησὶν ὁ ἐξηγητής, τὸ ἐπιφερόμενον κτλ.

One who is going to practice declamation needs to know how to arrange the material. Now if a diegesis is invented from an account of either past or future actions[186] or only from present ones, or from two or three of these, it is possible, by artistically developing a past happening in the diegesis to fill up the early part (*of the speech*) with these and not encumber the later parts with (*repetition of*) these same things on account of the diatyposis of future things.[187] But if the action should be one needing to be artistically described in diegeses both early and later (*in the speech*), we shall make mention of it (*in the earlier part of the speech*), supporting the account with the causes (*of the actions*), by which we said the diegesis was to be supported, and we shall keep stylistic treatments for the (*later*) diaskeuē. But if the action is wholly lacking in material for diatyposis, then the best way of handling the arrangement is not to use hypodiaereses[188] in from-beginning-to-end, but after describing the whole action all together here (*near the beginning*), and after imagining some plasta[189] and adding them to the whole account of the action, we shall keep the hypodiaereses for what is to come later, using confirmation (*kataskeuē*) here instead of diaskeuē, and as for the subordinate parts (*hypomerismoi*) that we were going to make when giving confirmations, | these we shall [169]
keep for later development in the diaskeuē, using a single different rhythm in the cola—for there are some cola appropriate for confirmations and others for diaskeuē—and also removing periodic sentences from the confirmation; for a period is foreign to diaskeuē.[190] The result of this is an ample opportunity for personifications, for if the action in itself lacks opportunity for diaskeuē, subordination creates no lack of opportunities for personifications.[191] One should know that every subordination expresses the

[186] Accepting Patillon's emendations of Rabe's *kai* (and) to *ē* (either . . . or). See *L'Art rhétorique*, 275 n. 5.

[187] By "later parts" the author seems to mean the epilogue, where future consequences of a judgment were often discussed. Instead of "on account of . . .," it would have been clearer if he had said "because that is the proper place for diatyposis of future things."

[188] I.e., "subdivisions," cf. 1.2 above.

[189] Fictional epikheiremes; cf. 3.11 above.

[190] On periods, see 4.3–4 below.

[191] By creating an opportunity for dialogue. *Hypomerismos* occurs only in this chapter; to judge from the next sentence, it is much the same as *hypodiaresis*.

*διασκευῇ ἀνεμποδίστως· δεῖ γὰρ πάντως ἐκ τῆς ὑποδιαιρέσεως εἰς τὸ πρᾶγμα αὐτὸ ἐπανελθεῖν, ἀλλὰ καὶ καθ' ἑκάστην ὑποδιαίρεσιν τοῦτο ποιεῖν ἀνεπαχθές ἐστιν ἀεί.*

*Ταυτολογεῖ δὲ διασκευῇ καὶ ἡ τῶν καλουμένων χωρίων ἀγωγή, καὶ ἐκείνη ἀνεπιλήπτως. ἀνάγκη γὰρ ἀπὸ τοῦ παραδείγματος ἢ τοῦ μυθικοῦ ἢ τοῦ ἱστορικοῦ μεταβαίνοντα εἰς τὸ ἴδιον πρᾶγμα τὸ αὐτὸ λέγειν πολλάκις· οἷον ὡς ἐπὶ παραδείγματος τοῦτο ἐπιδεῖν τινα σαφέστερον, ἐπίπρασκεν Ἀλέξανδρος τοὺς Θηβαίων αἰχμαλώτους, πριάμενοι Λακεδαιμόνιοι τριακοσίους κατέσφαξαν ἐπὶ τὸ ἐν Λεύκτροις τρόπαιον καὶ κρίνονται τῶν εἰς τοὺς Ἕλληνας ἀδικημάτων. ἐὰν γὰρ διασκευάζοντες λέγωμεν «τριακοσίους ἐθύσατε ὡς ἱερεῖα ὠμῶς καὶ ἀνηλεῶς τοῖς βωμοῖς ὡς σφάγια», ταῦτα πάλιν διασκευάσομεν, καὶ ἐν* [170] *ταῖς διατυπώσεσιν αὐταῖς ὡς | ἔφαμεν λέγοντες ὡς προσῆκον δεδακρυμένους, θρηνοῦντας, ἐστεφανωμένους, καὶ οἷα ἐποίουν περιπτυσσόμενοι ἀλλήλους καὶ οἷα ἔλεγον ἱκετεύοντες καὶ ὀδυρόμενοι· μέχρι τούτων ἡ διατύπωσις ἡ ἀπὸ τοῦ πράγματος. ἐὰν δὲ ἐπεισάγειν ἐθέλῃς χωρίον ἀπὸ ἑνὸς ὀνόματος, λήψῃ πρόφασιν ἱστοριῶν, ὡς ἐνταῦθα «τριακοσίους ἐθύσατε, διεφθείρατε τὸν ἀριθμὸν ὑμῶν τὸν ἐπαινούμενον τῶν τριακοσίων τῇ τούτων τελευτῇ»· μετὰ γὰρ τὸ εἰπεῖν ὡς «ἀνηλεῶς ἀπ-*

**4** διασκευὴ **V**; Dox.: ὁ μὲν οὖν ἐξηγητὴς «ταυτολογεῖ δὲ διασκευῇ καὶ ἡ . . . ἀγωγή» . . . τὰ δὲ ἀκριβέστερα τῶν βιβλίων «ταυτολογ⌊εῖ⌋ δὲ διασκευὴ τῇ . . . ἀγωγῇ» || **5** pr. ἢ om. Vc Ba || **6** ἐπαναβαίνοντα Vc Ba || **10** γὰρ om. Ac || **13** αὐταῖς om. Vc Ba | Dox.: ἔνια τῶν βιβλίων «ἃ προσῆκον» ἔχει κτλ. | προσῆκεν Ac || **14** περιπτύσσοντες Vc Ba || **16** θέλῃις Vc Ba; ἐθέλοις Ac || **19** τὸ **P** Vc; τοῦ Ac Ba | ὡς om. **V**

same things as a diaskeuē but in an unhindered way, for it is always necessary to go back from the subordination to the action itself, but to do this is always quite easy in the case of each subordination.[192]

The introduction of what are called "places" (*khōria*)[193] repeats the diaskeuē, and that in a way not open to objection. Going from an example, whether mythical or historical, to the specific action, it is often necessary to say the same thing; for example, to show this more clearly by an instance, Alexander sold the Theban prisoners; the Lacedaimonians bought three hundred of them and slaughtered them at the trophy in Leuctra and are charged with wrongs against Greeks. If, developing this artistically, we say, "You sacrificed three hundred men brutally as offerings and pitilessly as victims at the altars," we are artistically developing this again; and in these vivid descriptions, as | we said,[194] we speak [170]
in fitting terms of the men as having wept, having wailed, having crowned their brows, and we say what they did when embracing each other and what they said when beseeching pity and weeping. Up to this point this is diatyposis from the action. If you want to bring in a commonplace (*khōrion*) suggested by one word,[195] you will allude to an earlier report in histories, saying that "in sacrificing three hundred, you defamed the revered number of your three hundred by the death of these." After saying "You killed them

[192] This is a difficult passage, poorly expressed. The author's advice seems to be as follows: (1) If there are past or present actions that can be enumerated and developed, this should be done in the diegesis early in a speech, and the future consequences of the action should be treated artistically in the epilogue. (2) If there are actions needing to be mentioned in both the diegesis and the epilogue (probably because they are central to the case), the causes of the actions should be used to develop the account in the diegesis and stylistic elaboration postponed to the epilogue. (3) If there is a lack of any material suitable for stylistic elaboration, a brief description of the whole action can be given in the diegesis, together with fictive epikheiremes (as described earlier), but without hypodiaereses, which should be postponed to the epilogue, where confirmations of them can be supplied, using personifications and a distinctive rhythm but not a periodic style.

[193] I.e. *topoi,* in the sense of commonplaces; the usage is rare, but cf. 1.2 above and perhaps Lycurgus 31.

[194] At the beginning of this chapter.

[195] The word is apparently *triakosioi*, "three hundred," which suggests occurrences of that number in historical accounts, including the three hundred Spartans killed at Thermopylae.

*εκτείνατε» καὶ διασκευάσαι δύνασαι εἰπεῖν ὅτι «ἀπέθανον ὑμῶν καὶ ἐν Θυραίᾳ τριακόσιοι, ἀλλὰ πολέμου νόμῳ· ὑμεῖς δὲ ἱερείων νόμῳ τούτους κατεσφάξατε» καὶ πάλιν ἄλλο χωρίον «ἀπέκτεινεν ὑμῶν καὶ βασιλεὺς τριακοσίους ἐν Πύλαις, ἀλλ' οὐκ ἔθυσεν· ὑμεῖς δὲ παρεστήσασθε τριακοσίους ἱερεῖα τοῖς βωμοῖς» καὶ πάλιν ἐπὶ τὴν διασκευὴν χωρήσομεν, εἰ τύχοι παράδειγμα, κἂν Κλέωνος μνημονεύσῃς τὸ περὶ Πύλον καὶ Σφακτηρίαν χωρίον ἐπεισάγων, κἀκεῖθεν ἐπαναδραμεῖν εἰς τὴν διασκευὴν δύνασαι πάλιν ἀνεμποδίστως.*

1 ὅτι **P** ; πάλιν Vc Ba ; om. Ac | ἡμῶν m. 1 Ba || 1-2 cf. Herod. 1, 82 || 3 καὶ om. **V** || 4 πύλωι **P** || 5 βωμοῖς **P** ; θεοῖς **V** | χωρήσωμεν Vc Ba | cf. 100, 11 ann. || 8 γρ ἀνεπιλήπτως Pa | subscr.: τέλος τοῦ γ' λόγου Ac

pitilessly" you can develop this and say that "three hundred of you died in Thyria, but by the custom of war, while you slaughtered these men by the custom of sacrificers," and using another commonplace, "The king killed three hundred of you at Thermopylae, but he did not sacrifice you, while you made three hundred men stand as sacrifices at altars," and we shall go back to the diaskeuē, perhaps to an example, if you mention Cleon, introducing the commonplace about Pylos and Sphacteria, and from that you can return to the diaskeuē again without any problem.

## BOOK 4

*After finding, in succession, books devoted to prooemia, narrations, and proofs, a reader would expect discussion next of epilogues as the conclusion of a declamation. Instead, we are met with a book on some features of prose style, to which two chapters on declamation problems have been added. There is thus no discussion of epilogues in the work as we have it, except what may be implied in the last chapter of book 3. As will be noted below, book 4 has some similarities to chapter 10 of the rhetorical handbook falsely attributed to Dionysius of Halicarnassus and also to some handbooks of figures, though it differs from most treatments of figures in giving longer accounts of a few devices of style, with no distinction made between tropes, figures of diction, and figures of thought, and in using a distinctive terminology. The beginning of chapter 1 indicates that book 4 is probably by the same author as the previous books, doubtless depending heavily on the main source used therein, and this is confirmed by the prose style, except for chapters 13 and 14, which come from a different source (see introductory note to ch. 13 below).*

# Δ

## *Περὶ λόγου σχημάτων.*

*Ἐπειδὴ οὖν καὶ περὶ τῶν ἐπιχειρημάτων καὶ περὶ τῶν ἐργασιῶν* [171] *καὶ περὶ τῶν ἐνθυμημάτων τῆς εὑρέ|σεως πάντα εἰς τέλος πεπλήρωται, ἀναγκαῖον εἰπεῖν καὶ περὶ τῶν τοῦ λόγου σχημάτων, καθ᾽ ἃ προσήκει ἕκαστον αὐτῶν ἐκφέρεσθαι. ὅσα μὲν γὰρ τῶν ἐπιχειρημάτων ἢ τῶν ἐργασιῶν πολιτικά ἐστι τῷ νῷ καὶ ἀποδεικτικά, προσήκει ταῦτα στρογγύλως καὶ κατὰ ἀντίθετα καὶ κατὰ περιόδους ἐκφέρεσθαι, ὅσα δὲ πανηγυρικὰ τῷ νῷ, ἤτοι παραδειγματικὰ ἢ ἐκ παραβολῆς λαμβανόμενα, ταῦτα δεῖ πνευματικῶς ἀποτείνεσθαι καὶ ἀκμαίως· τὰ γὰρ ἐνθυμήματα πάντα στρογγύλως κατὰ τὴν σύγκρισιν ἐκφερόμενα δριμύτητος δόξαν πλείονα ἀποφέρεται, ἢ εἴ τις αὐτὰ ἁπλῶσαι θελήσειε τῷ λόγῳ. καίτοι καὶ τούτῳ τῷ σχήματι ὁ Δημοσθένης ἐκαλλωπίσατο πολλάκις, ὡς ἐν τοῖς βιβλίοις εὑρίσκομεν· ὡς ἐκεῖνο ἐν τῷ Περὶ τοῦ στεφάνου «ὑμεῖς τοίνυν, ὦ ἄνδρες Ἀθηναῖοι, Λακεδαιμονίων γῆς καὶ θαλάττης ἀρχόντων καὶ τὰ κύκλῳ τῆς Ἀττικῆς κατεχόντων ἁρμοσταῖς καὶ φρουραῖς, Εὔβοιαν, Τάναγραν, τὴν Βοιωτίαν ἅπασαν, Μέγαρα, Αἴγιναν, Κλεωνάς, τὰς ἄλλας νήσους, οὐ ναῦς, οὐ τείχη τῆς πόλεως τότε κεκτημένης, ἐξήλθετε εἰς Ἁλίαρτον καὶ πάλιν οὐ πολλαῖς ἡμέραις ὕστερον εἰς Κόρινθον, τῶν τότε Ἀθηναίων πολλὰ ἂν ἐχόντων μνησικακῆσαι* [172] *καὶ Κορινθίοις καὶ Θηβαίοις | τῶν περὶ τὸν Δεκελεικὸν πόλεμον πραχθέντων· ἀλλ᾽ οὐκ ἐποίουν ταῦτα, οὐδ᾽ ἐγγὺς τούτων. καίτοι τότε ταῦτα ἀμφότερα, Αἰσχίνη, οὔθ᾽ ὑπὲρ εὐεργετῶν ἐποίουν οὔτ᾽ ἀκίνδυνα ἑώρων· ἀλλ᾽ οὐ διὰ ταῦτα προΐεντο τοὺς καταφεύγοντας ἐπ᾽ αὐτούς, ἀλλ᾽*

**1-2** τόμος δ′· περὶ εὑρέσεως· περὶ λόγου σχημάτων **P**, (om. περὶ εὑρέσεως) Ac; περὶ τῶν τοῦ λόγου σχημάτων· τόμος δ′ (om. περὶ εὑρέσεως) Vc Ba || **3** ἐπεὶ (om. δὴ) Vc Ba | περὶ τῶν (ante ἐργασιῶν) om. Pc || **7** εἰσὶ Mr || **8** κατὰ τὰ ἀντίθετα **V** | κατὰ om. Pc | κατὰ τὰς περιόδους Ac || **9** ἤτοι **P**; ἢ **V** || **10** γρ ταῦτα δεῖ πνευματικῶς ἀποτείνειν καὶ ἀκμαίως ἐκφέρειν· γρ καὶ οὕτως· ταῦτα δεῖ πνευματικῶς ἀποτείνοντας καὶ ἀκμαίως ἐκφέρειν **P**; cf. schol. **P** (W VII 817, 6. 828 ann.); sed schol. sign. **P**: . . . ὅτι δεῖ ταῦτα ἑρμηνεύεσθαι καὶ ἀποτείνεσθαι πνευματικῶς καὶ ἀκμαίως | ἀποτείνοντας Vc Ba; ἀποτείν[ειν]οντας[ἐ] Ac | ἐκφέρειν post ἀκμαίως add. **V** || **11** τὴν om. Pc || **12** cf. 100, 12 | ἐθελήσειε Ac || **14** ταῖς βίβλοις αὐτοῦ Ac; τοῖς βιβλίοις αὐτοῦ Vδ | ὡς ἐν ἐκείνωι ἐν Vc Ba || **15** Dem. 18, 96. 97 || **17** τάναγραν καὶ τὴν Vc Ba | πᾶσαν Vc Ba || **21-22** πεπραγμένων Vc Ba || **22** τότε om. Pc || **24** ἐφ᾽ ἑαυτούς Sc

## CHAPTER I: ON FIGURES OF SPEECH

Since, now, the whole account of invention as concerned with epikheiremes and ergasiae and enthymemes | has been brought [171] to completion, it is necessary to speak about the figures of speech (*logou skhēmata*) by which each of these can be appropriately expressed.[196] Whatever epikheiremes or ergasiae are political in thought[197] and demonstrative should be expressed tersely in antitheses and periods, but whatever are panegyrical in thought, whether using examples or comparisons, should be stretched out in the form of a pneuma[198] and an akme,[199] for all enthymemes when expressed concisely have, because of the condensation, a greater appearance of striking effect (*drimytēs*) than if one were to leave them stated simply in the speech.[200] Moreover, Demosthenes often created beautiful effects by this figure,[201] as we find in his books; for example, this one in *On the Crown* (18.96–97): "Thus, you, men of Athens, at a time[202] when the Spartans were in control of land and sea and were retaining hold by means of governors and garrisons in the country encircling Attica—Euboea, Tanagra, all of Boeotia, Megara, Aegina, Cleonae, the other islands—when the city had no ships, no walls, you marched out to Haliartus and again, not many days later, to Corinth, although the Athenians at the time might have had a heavy grudge against both Corinthians and Thebans | for what had been done in the [172] Deceleian War; but they bore no grudge, far from it. Yet they did both of these actions at that time, Aeschines, neither for the sake of benefactors nor was the prospect without danger; but not for these reasons did they sacrifice those who fled to them for help, but they chose to expose themselves to dangers for glory and honor, rightly and nobly making their plans." The epikheireme[203] here

196 "Figures of speech" as used here includes period, pneuma, and other features of composition; see notes on ch. 3 below.

197 Judicial or deliberative; cf. 3.13 above.

198 On the pneuma, cf. 4.4 below.

199 On *akmē*, or "peak," see 2.7 above and 4.4 below.

200 Cf. 3.1 and 3.8 above.

201 I.e., pneuma.

202 In 396 B.C.E.

203 I.e., the underlying proposition.

*ὑπὲρ εὐδοξίας καὶ τιμῆς ἤθελον τοῖς δεινοῖς ἑαυτοὺς διδόναι, ὀρθῶς καὶ καλῶς βουλευόμενοι». καὶ γὰρ ἐνταῦθα τὸ μὲν ἐπιχείρημα ἦν «καλὸν τὸ μὴ μνησικακεῖν τοῖς ἀδικήσασιν, ἐὰν κινδυνεύωσιν», ἡ ἐργασία δὲ αὐτοῦ «οὐδὲ γὰρ Θηβαίοις οὐδὲ Κορινθίοις ἐμνησικακήσατε, ἀλλὰ κἀκείνοις ἐβοηθήσατε». τὸ δὲ ἐνθύμημα «καίτοι Λακεδαιμονίων γῆς καὶ θαλάττης ἀρχόντων καὶ φοβερῶν ὑμῖν ὄντων τῶν πραγμάτων», ἔλαθε δὲ ἁπλώσας αὐτὸ ἀπὸ τοῦ καὶ τὴν τάξιν ὑπαλλάξαι· δεινὸς γὰρ ἀεὶ σοφίσασθαι τὰς τέχνας καὶ ἀποκρύπτειν ὁ ῥήτωρ, καὶ ἄλλοτε μὲν ἄλλως ἐποίει, τῇ τάξει δὲ ἐνταῦθα· ὅθεν καὶ τολμήσας ἁπλῶσαι τὸν λόγον τοῦ ἐνθυμήματος, εἶτα προσελθὼν τῇ ἐργασίᾳ καὶ πάλιν ἀναγκασθεὶς ἐκ τῆς τέχνης μνησθῆναι τοῦ ἐνθυμήματος τῷ νῷ συνέστρεψεν αὐτὸ τῷ εἰπεῖν «καίτοι τότε ταῦτα ἀμφότερα οὔθ' ὑπὲρ εὐεργετῶν ἐποίουν οὔτ' ἀκίνδυνα ἑώρων» καὶ προσήγαγε τὴν ἐπίτασιν τῷ ἐπιχειρήματι· τὸ δὲ «οὐδὲ ἀκίνδυνα ἑώρων» τὸ ἐνθύμημά ἐστιν, ὃ φθάσας ἥπλωσεν ἤδη.*

[173] ## | *Περὶ ἀντιθέτου.*

*Ἀντίθετόν ἐστι σχῆμα λόγου διπλασιάζον πάντα τὸν ὑποκείμενον νοῦν τοῦτον τὸν τρόπον, εἴ τις τοῦ κατὰ φύσιν ζητουμένου τὸ ἐναντίον λαμβάνων καταβαίνοι εἰς τὸ ὑποκείμενον· οἷον «ἐπειδὴ ἡμέρα ἐστί, δεῖ ποιῆσαι τόδε», τοῦτο τὸ ζητούμενον, τὸ δὲ ἀντίθετον αὐτοῦ? «εἰ μὲν γὰρ μὴ ἦν ἡμέρα ἀλλὰ νύξ, ἴσως ἐχρῆν μὴ ποιεῖν», εἶτα καταβαίνει εἰς τὸ ἴδιον «ἐπειδὴ δὲ ἡμέρα ἐστί, ποιῆσαι προσήκει». οἷον καὶ ἐν τοῖς προβλήμασι «δεῖ καινοτομεῖν· πόλεμος γάρ ἐστι», τοῦτο τὸ κατὰ*

**1** τοῖς δεινοῖς om. Pc | ἐκδιδόναι Vc Ba || **3** μὴ suppl. m. po. Pa | κινδυνεύσωσιν Pa || **4** κορινθίοις οὐδὲ θηβαίοις Vc Ba cf. 138, 15 || **6** ὄντων ὑμῖν Vc | τῶν om. Ba || **7** ἁπλῶς m. 1 Pc || **10** προελθὼν Vc Ba || **11** αὐτὸ ἐν τῶι **V** || **12-13** οὔτ' ἀκίνδυνα ἑώρων om. V || **13** δὲ ⌊circ. VI⌋ Vc; δὲ εἰπεῖν Ba, (τὸ δὲ εἰπεῖν τὸ οὔτ') Ac || **16-17** ἀντίθετόν ἐστι σχῆμα τὸ διπλασιάζον πάντα τὸν ὑποκείμενον ὅρον κτλ. Anon. III 112, 4 Sp. || **16-142.1** (coll. 144, 8) cf. J. ab Arnim, Stoicorum vet. fragm. II p. 107 cet. A Rüstow, *Der Lügner*, 75 sq. | cf. Π. μεθ. δειν. p. 439 Sp. || **16** λόγου Vc Ba, m. po. Pa, v.l. **P**, schol. **P** (W VII 807, 11), Jo. Sard. (in Aphth. II 33, 10 Sp.); λόγος **P** Vδ, m. 2 Vc, m. po. Ba., Diac. f. 453r, (ου in ras. supr., m. 2 ?) Ac | διπλασιάζον m. 1 Ba, m. po. Pa Ac; διπλασιάζων **P** Vc δ Ac, m. po. Ba; Dox.: ὁ μὲν ἐξηγητὴς «ἀντίθετόν ἐστι σχῆμα λόγου», ἀναγνοὺς . . . τὰ δὲ πλειώ τῶν βιβλίων οὐκ ἔχει «σχῆμα λόγου», ἀλλὰ «ἀντίθετόν ἐστι σχῆμα, λόγος διπλασιάζων πάντα τὸν ὑποκείμενον νοῦν» κτλ., cf. Dox. (in Aphth. II 33, 10 Sp.) II 405, 1 W. || **20** μ⌊ὴ, m. po. ? tum II l. er.⌋ Vc | ποιῆσαι Vc Ba | καταβαίνεις Ac || **21** ἐπεὶ δέ ἐστιν ἡμέρα **V** | προσῆκεν **P** || **22** δεῖν **P** | cf. 72, 18 cet.

was "It was a noble thing not to hold a grudge against those who had wronged them if they were in danger"; its ergasia was "for you bore no grudge against Thebans and Corinthians but went to their aid"; the enthymeme was "although Lacedaimonians were in control of land and sea and your circumstances were frightening"; but it escapes notice that he has deployed this argument because of a change in the order. The Orator was always clever at contriving and concealing artistic effects, and sometimes he did so in one way, sometimes in another, and here by the arrangement. Thus, after venturing (*first*) to deploy the argument of the enthymeme and then continuing with the ergasia, and forced again from the rules of art to make mention of the enthymeme, he compressed it in the thought by saying, "Yet you did neither of these actions at that time for the sake of benefactors, nor was the prospect without danger," and he added an extension (*epitasis*)[204] to the epikheireme. "Nor was the prospect without danger" is the enthymeme that he had earlier deployed.

## | CHAPTER 2: ON ANTITHETON [173]

Antitheton[205] is a figure of speech, doubling all the underlying thought as follows: one posits the opposite of a question in natural form[206] and then comes to the subject; for example, "Since it is day,[207] it is necessary to do this"—this is what is in question, and its antitheton is "For if it were not day, but night, perhaps it would be necessary not to do it"; then one comes to the particular circumstance, "but since it *is* day, it is appropriate to do it." Similarly in problems (*about innovation*):[208] "It is necessary to innovate, for it is wartime." This is the natural form; what lies counter to it is "For if it were not wartime but (*a time of*) peace and quiet, it would

[204] Cf. 3.9 n. 141, above.

[205] For *antitheton* rather than *antithesis* as the name of this figure, cf. *Rhetoric for Alexander* 26; Tiberius (vol. 3, pp. 67 and 78 Spengel); Rutilius Lupus §16, p. 19 Halm; Aquilla Romanus §22, pp. 29–30 Halm; *Carmen de Figuris*, p. 64 Halm. In *Rhetoric* 3.9.9 Aristotle treats antithesis as a form of a period.

[206] *Kata physin*, i.e., statement of the proposition in positive form.

[207] A traditional example in ancient logic; Rabe (p. 173,2–11) cited the Stoic Chrysippus; see Hans F. A. von Arnim, ed., *Stoicorum Veterum Fragmenta* (4 vols.; Leipzig: Teubner, 1903–24), 2:107–8.

[208] Cf. 3.4 and 3.6 above.

*φύσιν· τὸ δὲ ἀντικείμενον αὐτοῦ «εἰ μὲν γὰρ μὴ ἦν πόλεμος ἀλλ᾽ εἰρήνη καὶ ἡσυχία, ἔδει μὴ καινοτομεῖν».*

*Ἀρετὴ δὲ τοῦ ἀντιθέτου, ὅτι καὶ ἁπλούμενον τῷ πλήθει τῶν κώλων πνεῦμα γίνεται καὶ συστρεφόμενον τῇ ἑρμηνείᾳ περιόδου τάξιν ἐπέχει, οἷον «εἰ μὲν γὰρ ἦν ἐν ἡσυχίᾳ τὰ καθεστηκότα καὶ ἀπραγμοσύνη κατεῖχεν ἡμᾶς καὶ μήτε ἄτοπον μήτε φοβερὸν ἐφειστήκει παρὰ τῶν* [174] *πολεμίων μηδέν, ἀδείας δὲ ἦμεν ἐπειλημμέ|νοι καὶ ἐξουσίας τοῦ πράττειν ὅσα βουλομένοις ἡμῖν ἐτύγχανεν, ἔδει φυλάττειν τὰ καθεστηκότα καὶ παρακινεῖν μηδὲ ἓν μηδὲ καινοτομεῖν, ἀλλὰ τοῖς ἀρχαίοις ἐμμένειν ἔθεσί τε καὶ ψηφίσμασι καὶ νόμοις· ἐπεὶ δὲ πόλεμος κεκίνηται καὶ πλησίον οἱ πολέμιοι καὶ ἐφέστηκε τὰ δεινὰ καὶ ταραχὴ τοσαύτη τῶν πραγμάτων, τίνος ἕνεκεν οὐ καινοτομήσομεν, αὐτοῦ τοῦ πολέμου ταύτην ἔχοντος τὴν φύσιν, ἀφ᾽ ἑαυτοῦ τεχνᾶσθαι τὰ πολλὰ καὶ τὸν τῶν ἀνθρώπων μεταποιεῖν ἐπὶ τὸ καινότερον βίον;» τοῦτο ἐκταθὲν τοῖς κώλοις ἐγένετο πνεῦμα, δύναται δὲ συστραφὲν εὐρύθμως γενέσθαι περίοδος, οἷον «ἃ γὰρ ἐφυλαξάμεθα ἂν ποιεῖν εἰκότως εἰρήνης ὑπαρχούσης, ταῦτα βέλτιον ἐργάσασθαι πολέμου καθεστηκότος». Καὶ οὔτε ἰσχυρότερον οὔτε ἀναγκαιότερον εὑρίσκεται σχῆμα τοῦ ἀντιθέτου παρὰ τοῖς ἀρχαίοις ῥᾳδίως οὐδέν. καίτοι γε παντὸς ἀντιθέτου τῆς μιᾶς προτάσεως περιττῆς οὔσης τῇ ἀληθείᾳ τοῖς ἀκούουσιν ὅμως τὸ λεγόμενον οὐκ ἔξω τοῦ εἰκότος δοκεῖ λέγεσθαι, ποιεῖ δὲ αὐτὸ δοκεῖν ἀναγκαῖον εἶναι ἡ τοῦ κατὰ φύσιν προσδοκία· ἐν ᾧ γὰρ τὴν πρότασιν ὁ ῥήτωρ λέγει τοῦ ἀντιθέτου, ἐν τούτῳ τὸ κατὰ φύσιν ἤδη τοῖς ἀκούουσι νοεῖται τῷ τῆς ἀποδόσεως νοήματι. Τὸ δὲ σχῆμα οὕτως ἐστὶν ἀξιέραστον, ὡς* [175] *μὴ πε|ρίοδον ποιεῖν μόνον καὶ πνεῦμα, ἀλλὰ καὶ καθάπαξ πάντα νοῦν κοσμεῖν. κοσμεῖ δὲ καὶ προοίμιον πολλάκις, εἴ τις τούτῳ τῷ σχήματι τὸ προοίμιον ἐξενέγκοι, ὡς ὁ Δημοσθένης «εἰ μὲν περὶ καινοῦ τινος*

1 mg. m. 1 γρ´ τὸ ἀντίθετον αὐτῶν Pc; mg. m. 1 τὸ δὲ ἀντίθετον αὐτῶ Pa | μὴ Pc Vc Ba; οὐκ Pa AC || **6** φοβερὸν **P** Ac, Anon. III 112, 14 Sp., schol. **P** (W VII 808, 10), πονηρὸν Vc Ba || **7** οὐδὲν, μη supr. (m. 1 ?) Vc | ἀδείας **P**, Anon. III 112, 14 Sp., schol. **P**; ἐπ᾽ ἀδείας **V** Vδ; Dox.: ἔνια τῶν βιβλίων οὐκ ἔχει «ἐπ᾽ ἀδείας»· ἀλλ᾽ «ἀδείας» χωρὶς τῆς ἐπὶ προθέσεως· ἐν οἷς δ᾽ ἂν «ἐπ᾽ ἀδείας» ἔχοι, μέσην στιγμὴν θετέον, εἰς τὸ «ἦμεν», καὶ τὸ ἑξῆς οὕτως ἀναγνωστέον «ἐπ᾽ ἀδείας δὲ ἦμεν, καὶ ἐξουσίας ἐπειλημμένοι». | ἐξουσία⌊Ι⌉ Vc || **9** μὴ post καὶ add. schol. **P** (W VII 808, 14) | μηδὲν **V** || **10** ἐπειδὴ δὲ Sc || **15** δὲ καὶ Sc || **16** καὶ περιόδος Ba | ποιεῖν ἂν Ac; ἂν om. Vc Ba, schol. **P** | εἰκότως om. Pc Ac || **19-20** γε τῆς προτάσεως πάντως τοῦ ἀντιθέτου περιττῆς m. 1 Vc Ba || **25** μόνον ποιεῖν Vc Ba | alt. καὶ om. Vc Ba || **26** τοιούτωι (om. τῷ) Vc Ba || **27** τὸ m. 2 suppl. Ac | Dem. 4, 1

be necessary not to innovate."

A virtue of an antitheton is that when it is deployed in a number of cola a pneuma is created and when the expression is inverted it takes on the arrangement of a period; for example, "If our accustomed ways prevailed in time of peace, and quietness held us and nothing troublesome or fearful threatened from our enemies, and if we had obtained security | and the opportunity to do whatever [174] we wanted, it would be necessary to keep to our established ways and to change not one thing and not to innovate but to remain with the ancient customs and decrees and laws; since, however, war has been set in motion and the enemy are near and have threatened dire things and there is great confusion, why shall we not innovate, since it is the nature of war to devise many things and to change the affairs of men into a more novel way of life?" Stated in cola, this became a pneuma, but when gracefully inverted it can become a period; for example, "For what we rightly kept from doing when peace prevailed, these things it is better to do when war is upon us."

A figure stronger or more compelling than antitheton is not easily found in the ancient writers. Indeed, although in every antitheton one protasis may, in truth, be superfluous, nevertheless, to the hearers what is said does not seem to be said beyond probability, and the expectation of the natural form of expression makes it seem to be compelling; for when the orator speaks the protasis of the antitheton, the natural form in the thought of the apodosis is suggested to the hearers.

This figure is thus deserving affection, since | it cannot [175] only create a period and a pneuma but in general can adorn every thought. Often it adorns a prooemion, if one expresses the prooemion in this form, as does Demosthenes (4.1): "If, O Athenians, it was proposed to speak about some new matter." Here the

*πράγματος προὐτίθετο, ὦ Ἀθηναῖοι, λέγειν»· καὶ γὰρ ἐνταῦθα τὸ κατὰ φύσιν ἐστὶν «ἐπειδὴ δὲ περὶ ὧν πολλάκις ἤδη πρότερον εἰρήκασιν οὗτοι, συμβαίνει καὶ νυνὶ σκοπεῖν, ἡγοῦμαι καὶ πρῶτος ἀναστὰς εἰκότως ἂν συγγνώμης τυγχάνειν», τὸ δὲ ἀντίθετον «εἰ μὲν περὶ καινοῦ τινος πράγματος προὐτίθετο λέγειν, ἐπισχεῖν ἔδει τοῖς πρεσβυτέροις παραχωροῦντα πρῶτον εἰπεῖν».*

*Ἰστέον δέ, ὅτι περὶ ῥητορικοῦ ἀντιθέτου διελέχθημεν· ἐπεὶ οἱ φιλόσοφοι ἐναντίον καὶ ἀντίθετον οὐ διαιροῦσι, παρ᾽ ἡμῖν δὲ τὸ ἀντίθετον σχῆμά ἐστι τοῦ λόγου, τὸ δὲ ἐναντίον δριμύτης νοήματος ἀπὸ τῆς ἐργασίας λαμβανομένη οἷον «οὐ δὴ θαυμαστόν ἐστιν, εἰ στρατευόμενος ἐκεῖνος καὶ παρὼν ἐφ᾽ ἅπασι καὶ μηδένα καιρὸν μηδ᾽ ὥραν παραλείπων ἡμῶν μελλόντων καὶ ψηφιζομένων περιγίνεται»· τοῦτο γάρ, εἰ μὲν ἀντίθετον ἐβούλετο ποιῆσαι, οὕτως ἂν μετεχειρίσατο «εἰ μὲν γὰρ μήτε*
[176] *πονῶν μήτε παρὼν τοῖς πράγμασι περι|εγένετο ἡμῶν, θαυμαστὸν ἦν». τὸ γὰρ ἀντίθετον ταύτην ἔχει τὴν δύναμιν τοῦ λέγειν «εἰ μὲν γὰρ μὴ ἐγίγνετο, ὃ ἐγίγνετο»· τὸ δὲ ἐναντίον ἀναστρέφει τὸ πρᾶγμα ἀπὸ τῶν δρώντων εἰς τοὺς πάσχοντας καὶ ἀπὸ τῶν πασχόντων εἰς τοὺς δρῶντας, ὃ πεποίηκεν ἐνταῦθα ὁ ῥήτωρ «τοὐναντίον γὰρ ἦν θαυμαστόν, εἰ μηδὲν ποιοῦντες ἡμεῖς, ὧν τοῖς πολεμοῦσι προσήκει, τοῦ πάντα ἃ δεῖ ποιοῦντος περιῆμεν»· πολὺ γὰρ διενήνοχε λέγειν ὅτι «θαυμαστὸν ἦν, εἰ Φίλιππος μὴ πονῶν ἡμῶν περιῆν», ὃ τοῦ ἀντιθέτου ἐστὶν ἰσχύς, ἢ λέγειν πάλιν «εἰ μηδὲν ποιοῦντες ἡμεῖς Φιλίππου περιῆμεν», ὅ ἐστιν ἐνάργεια τοῦ ἐναντίου. Καὶ περὶ μὲν ἀντιθέτου τοσαῦτα εἰρήσθω.*

1 προὔκειτο Sc, m. 2 Vc | λέγειν ὦ ἀθηναῖοι· ἐπισχεῖν ἔδει τοῖς πρεσβυτέροις παραχωροῦντα πρῶτον εἰπεῖν· καὶ γὰρ Vc Ba, cf. 144, 5 || **1-2** τὸ m. po. etiam post ἐστὶν Ac || **2** ἐπεὶ (om. δὴ) Vc Ba || **3** νῦν Vc Ba | πρῶτον Vc Ba || **5** προὔκειτο λέγειν ὦ ἄνδρες ἀθηναῖοι Sc || **5-6** προὐτίθετο — εἰπεῖν om. Vc Ba, cf. 144, 1 || **5** τοὺς πρεσβυτέρους m. 2 Ac || **7** διειλέχθημεν Ac, m. 2 Pa Vc || **7-8** οἱ φιλόσοφοι: cf. 140, 18 sq. || **10** Dem. 2, 23 | ἐστιν om. Vc || **11** ἐκεῖνος om. Pc | ἐκεῖνος καὶ πονῶν ἐκεῖνος αὐτὸς καὶ παρὼν Vc Ba; cf. 98, 27 | παραλείπών sic Pa; παραλιπὼν Vc || **12** ψηφιζομένων **P**; ῥαιθυμούντων Vc Ba; ψηφιζομένων καὶ πυνθανομένων Ac, v.l. **P**, Dem. || **12-13** ἐβούλετο ἀντίθετον Pc || **14** περιεγίγνετο Ba, (-γίν-) Ac, (-γ[ί]γν-) Vc | ἂν ἦν Ac || **15** λ$^{ο}$έγ$^{ου}$ειν **P** | γὰρ om. **V** || **16** ἀναστρέφεται Mr || **18** Dem. 2, 23; cf. 98, 27 sq. || **19** ὧν δεῖ post μηδὲν add. **V** | ὧν — προσήκει om. Vc Ba | δεῖ **P** Ac; προσῆκε Ba, (-ήκει cr. m. 2) Vc; γρ τοῦ πάντα ἃ δὴ προσῆκεν ποιοῦντος περιῆμεν **P** || **22** πονοῦντες Ac || **23** τοῦ ἀντιθέτου Ac

natural form of expression is "But since we happen now also to be considering what these men have said already on many previous occasions, I think that I will probably be excused even though the first to stand up," and the antitheton is "If it was proposed to speak about some new matter, it would have been necessary to hold back, allowing the elders to speak first."

You should know that we have been discussing rhetorical antitheton. Although philosophers do not distinguish between an opposite (*enantion*) and an antitheton, among us (*rhetoricians*) an antitheton is a figure of speech and an enantion is a forceful expression (*drimytēs*) of thought taken from the ergasia (*of an argument*); for example (Dem. 2.23), "It is no wonder if he (*Philip*) who goes on campaigns and appears everywhere and overlooks no opportunity and season in getting the better of us who are delaying and keep casting votes." If he had wanted to make this an antitheton, he would have treated it thus: "For if he were getting the best of us without toil and without appearing everywhere, | it would be [176]
a wonder," for the antitheton has the effect of saying, "For if what was happening was not happening." An opposite turns the subject from those acting to those affected and from those affected to those acting, which is what the orator has done next: "For the opposite would have been a wonder, if when we were doing none of the things that those engaged in war should do, we got the better of one doing everything that should be done." There is much difference between saying that "it would be a wonder if Philip were getting the better of us without toiling," which has the force of the antitheton, and saying, "if we were getting the better of Philip while doing nothing," which is an ergasia[209] of the opposite. Let this be enough said about antitheton.

[209] Rabe reads *enargeia* ("clarity") with the mss, but the author has above connected an *enantion* with *ergasia*.

## *Περὶ περιόδου.*

*Ἡ δὲ περίοδος οὐχ ἑνὶ ὑποπίπτει σχήματι, ὥστε αὐτὸ παραδοῦναι, ἀλλὰ πολλοῖς καὶ ποικίλοις, ἃ παρὰ τῶν ἀρχαίων λαμβάνοντες ἐν τηρήσει πεποιήκαμεν. ἔστι μὲν οὖν περίοδος κυρίως ἡ τοῦ ὅλου ἐπιχειρήματος ἀναγκαστικὴ σύνοδος καὶ κλεὶς τρόπον τινά, καὶ ἀληθινὴ περίοδος τοῦτό ἐστιν ἡ ἀπαρτίζουσα τὸ ἐπιχείρημα καὶ συνάγουσα, ὡς τό γε ἑτέρωθι λέγειν περιοδικῶς ἐστι λέγειν, οὐ περίοδον ποιεῖν, ἀλλὰ ἑρμηνεύειν περιοδικῶς καὶ σχῆμα περιόδου λαμβάνειν. ἡ δὲ ἀληθινὴ* [177] *περίοδος οὐ τῷ σχήματι μόνον ἀλλὰ καὶ τῷ νῷ συν|άγει τὸ ἐπιχείρημα, ὅ τινὲς καὶ ἐνθύμημα καλοῦσιν· οὐ πᾶσα δὲ δύναιτ' ἂν ἐνθυμηματικὴ περίοδος εἶναι, εἰ μὴ καὶ γνωμικὴ ἡ τὸ καθόλου εἰς τὸ ἴδιον κατάγουσα καὶ τὸ ἴδιον εἰς τὸ καθόλου ἀνάγουσα.*

*Τηρήσαντες οὖν εὕρομεν παρὰ τοῖς ἀρχαίοις τὰς μεταβολὰς τῶν πτώσεων ὀνομαστικῆς καὶ γενικῆς καὶ δοτικῆς καὶ αἰτιατικῆς ποιούσας περιόδους οἷον «ὁ γὰρ οἷς ἂν ἐγὼ ληφθείην ταῦτα πράττων καὶ κατασκευαζόμενος, οὗτος ἐμοὶ πολεμεῖ, κἂν μήπω βάλλῃ μηδὲ τοξεύῃ», τοῦτο κατὰ τὴν ὀνομαστικήν· κατὰ δὲ τὴν γενικὴν «ὧν οὖν ἐκεῖνος μὲν ὀφείλει τοῖς ὑπὲρ αὐτοῦ πεπολιτευμένοις χάριν, ὑμῖν δὲ δίκην προσήκει λαβεῖν, τούτων οὐχὶ νῦν ὁρῶ τὸν καιρὸν τοῦ λέγειν»· καὶ κατὰ τὴν δοτικὴν «οἷς γὰρ οὖσιν ἡμετέροις ἔχει χρῆσθαι, τούτοις πάντα τὰ ἄλλα ἀσφαλῶς κέκτηται»· κατὰ δὲ τὴν αἰτιατικὴν «εἶθ' ὃν ἡ τύχη καὶ τὸ δαιμόνιον φίλον μὲν ἀλυσιτελῆ, συμφέροντα δ' ἐχθρὸν ἐμφανίζει, τοῦτον ἡμεῖς φοβούμεθα;» τὸ γὰρ κλητικὸν σχῆμα πνεύματός ἐστι μέρος ἀποστροφὴν ἐργαζόμενον καὶ καταδρομὴν «εἶτα, ὦ τί ἂν εἰπών σέ τις ὀρθῶς προσείποι;» καὶ πάλιν «ἀπόκριναι γὰρ δεῦρο ἀναστάς μοι. οὐ γὰρ δὴ δι' ἀπειρίαν οὐ φήσεις ἔχειν, ὅ τι εἴπῃς.»*

**6-7** ὡς τό γε **P**; ὥστε τὸ Ac, (τῶι) Vc Ba || **7** ἑτέρωθι Pc, (ως supr.) Pa; ἑτέρωθί πως **V**, v.l. **P** | ἐστι etiam ante ποιεῖν Vc Ba || **8** περιοδικῶς ἑρμηνεύειν Ac || **10** ὅπέρ τινες Vc Ba | καὶ om. Mr | δύνανται ἂν Vc Ba || **11** ἡ om. **V** || **15** περιόδους ex περίοδον Vc | Dem. 9, 17 || **16** ἐμὲ Pa | μὴδὲ Pa **V**; καὶ Pc || **17** Dem. 2, 4 || **19** τοῦτον **V** | καὶ κατὰ **P** Ac; κατὰ δὲ Vc Ba || **20** Dem. 10, 12 | ὑμετέροις m. 1 Ba | τἆλλα πάντα Vc Ba || **21** Dem. 14, 36 | εἶτα ὃν οὖν ἡ Vc Ba || **22** ἐχθρὸν δὲ συμφέροντα Vc Ba || **24** καταδρομὴν **P**; καταφορὰν **V**, v.l. **P** | Dem. 18, 22 | εἶτα Pc, (οἷον supr.) Pa; οἷον **V** | Dem. 19, 120 || **25** ἀπόκριν[αι m. 2] Vc Ba | γὰρ m. 2 suppl. Vc || **26** ἀπειρίαν γε **V** | οὐ φήσεις **P** Ac; φήσεις οὐκ Vc Ba

## CHAPTER 3: ON PERIOD

*Periodos* does not fall under a single figure that we could describe simply but under many varied ones[210] of which we have made a study,[211] taking examples from ancient writers. Now in a proper sense a period is the compelling convergence and closure, in a certain way, of a whole epikheireme, and a true period is one that completes and unifies an epikheireme, since to speak in a periodic style otherwise is not to make a period but to express something in a periodic way and to adopt the form of a period.[212] A true period completes an epikheireme, which some call an enthymeme, not only in the figure but also in the thought; | but not every pe- [177]
riod can be enthymematic, only a didactic argument leading from the general to the particular or from the particular to the general.

In our study of the ancient writers we found different grammatical cases—nominative, genitive, dative, and accusative—used to make periods; for example, in the nominative (Dem. 9.17): "For *he* who does these things by which I might be captured and makes preparations against me, *this one* makes war against me even if he has not yet thrown a missile or shot an arrow"; in the genitive (Dem. 2.4): "*Of the services* for which he ought to thank those politicians working in his interest—services for which you ought to require punishment—*of these* I see it is not now the time to speak"; and in the dative (Dem. 10.12; cf. 6.17): "*By what* he is able to use that is ours, *by these* he has acquired everything else"; and in the accusative (Dem. 14.36): "*Him* whom Fortune and God have revealed to be an unprofitable friend and expedient enemy, *this man* do we fear?" The vocative is a part of a pneuma creat-

210 Another definition of a period is offered below (p. 151, para. 2). Aristotle discussed periodic style as one of the two forms of prose composition in *Rhetoric* 3.9; cf. Demetrius, *On Style* 10–11; Cicero *On the Orator* 3.173–186; Quintilian 9.4.121–128; Longinus in Spengel-Hammer, 193–94 (described as a kind of enthymeme); Lausberg §§923–47; but by the first century B.C.E. a period was sometimes regarded as one of the many figures of diction; cf. *Rhetoric for Herennius* 4.27; *Carmen de Figuris* 10–12; Alexander, *On Figures* 2.1.

211 The author thus claims originality for the following discussion.

212 I.e., a true period, in the author's somewhat unusual view, is found only at the end of an epikheireme, which here means a fully developed argument, but something resembling a period may be a general feature of style; cf. the example from Demosthenes 19.181 quoted below.

*Καὶ καθάπαξ εἴ τις ἐκλεξάμενος τὰ παρὰ τῶν ἀρχαίων σχήματα τῶν περιόδων μιμοῖτο, ἐν ταῖς μεταποιήσεσι πλῆθος ἂν εὕροι περιόδων. καὶ γὰρ τὸ ἐκ παραβολῆς σχῆμα ἄριστον «ὥσπερ γὰρ εἴ τις ἐκείνων προήλω, σὺ τάδε οὐκ ἔγραψας ἄν, οὕτως ἂν σὺ νῦν δίκην δῷς, ἄλλος οὐ γράψει». καὶ διαπορητικῶς ἔστι περιοδεῦσαι, ἂν ἄρξηταί τις, ὡς ὁ Δημοσθένης ἐν τῷ Κατὰ Τιμοκράτους· «διὰ τί ἄρα, νὴ Δία, διὰ τί τοῦτο οὐχὶ καλῶς ἔχειν δόξαι τισὶ τὸ ψήφισμα; πότερον, ὅτι παρὰ τοὺς νόμους; καὶ μὴν μόνον ἐστὶ κατὰ τοὺς νόμους. ἀλλ' ὅτι τάξεως λύσις; καὶ μὴν τοῦτο, ὡς οὐκ ἄλλο, θεμέλιος εὐταξίας. ἀλλ' ὅτι τόδε» καὶ ἀποδώσεις αὐτό. γίνεται δέ, ὅταν καὶ δύο καὶ τρία νοήματα ἔχῃς, οἷον εἴ τις ἐκείνην θελήσειε μεταποιῆσαι τὴν περίοδον, περιοδικὴν μᾶλλον οὖσαν ἢ περίοδον, «νῦν δέ, ἃ μὲν πλεύσασιν ἦν σῶσαι, βαδίζειν κελεύων ἀπολώλεκεν οὗτος, ἃ δ' εἰποῦσι τἀληθῆ, ψευδόμενος», καὶ πάλιν «διὰ τί γὰρ ἄν, νὴ Δία, διὰ τί φείσαιτό τις Αἰσχίνου; πότερον ὅτι τὴν ἔξοδον ἐπετάχυνε; καὶ μὴν πλεῖν ἔδει καὶ μὴ βαδίζειν. ἀλλ' ὅτι τἀληθῆ πρὸς ὑμᾶς ἔφησε; καὶ μὴν ψευσάμενος πάντα ἀπολώλεκεν». Ἡ δὲ*
[180] *τῆς μεταποιήσεως ἀρετὴ τοῦ ὑποτεθέντος | νοήματος πᾶν σχῆμα οὕτως ἐφαρμόσαι δύναται· ὃ μᾶλλον ἐκπλήττει γινόμενον ἐξ αὐτοσχεδίου ἢ γραφῇ παραδιδόμενον.*

[178] *Εἰσὶ δὲ καὶ ἀποδεικτικαὶ τοῖς σχήμασιν οἷον «ἐν | μὲν γὰρ τῷ γράψαι μηδένα εἶναι ἀτελῆ τοὺς ἔχοντας ἀφείλετο τὴν ἀτέλειαν, ἐν δὲ τῷ προσγράψαι μηδὲ τὸ λοιπὸν ἐξεῖναι δοῦναι ὑμᾶς τὸ δοῦναι ὑμῖν ἐξεῖναι.» ταύτης τὸ σχῆμα καλὸν μὲν ζηλοῦν καὶ ἀπὸ τῆς ἑρμηνείας, κρεῖττον δέ, εἰ τὸ ἐλλεῖπον ἀπὸ κοινοῦ ποιεῖ τις ἐν ταῖς μεταποιήσεσιν, ἵνα τὸ ἐν τῇ προτάσει εἰρημένον ἐν τῇ ἀποδόσει λείπῃ μὲν μὴ λεγόμενον, φαίνηται δὲ ὡς λεγόμενον, ὡς καὶ ἐνταῦθα τὸ «ἀφείλετο» ἐν τῇ προτάσει λέλεκται, ἐν δὲ τῇ ἀποδόσει συνυπακούεται.*

**1** τὰ om. Vc Ba || **2** τῶν om. Ac || **3** καὶ γὰρ καὶ Vc Ba || **4** ἂν ἔγραψας **V**, Dem. 22, 7 | δίκην δῶις νῦν Pc || **5** γρ ἐὰν ἀπαρχῆς ἄρξηταί τις διαπορεῖν **P** || **6** cf. Dem. 24, 81 | τί γε ἄρα **V** || **7** τὸ ψήφισμα ante δόξαι Vc Ba, post δόξαι Pc || **9** καὶ μὴν καὶ **P** || **11** ἐκείνων Pc | ἐθελήσειε **V** || **11-12** οὖσαν μᾶλλον Ac || **12** Dem. 19, 181 | μὲν om. Pc || **13** οὗτος om. Vc Ba | ⌊καὶ πάλιν⌉ Spengel || **14** γὰρ ἂν **P** Ac; γε ἄρα Vc Ba | διὰ τί om. Vc Ba || **15** ἐτάχυνε Ac || **18** δυνήσεται Pc | Dox.: ἔνιοι . . . «ὃ οὐ μᾶλλον» κτλ. || **20** Dem. 20, 2 || **22** προγράψαι Ac | ὑμῖν τὸ δοῦναι ὑμᾶς Ac, m. 2 Vc | τὸ⌊I⌉ Vc Ba | ἡμῖν Ba || **23** δὲ ante τὸ add. Vc Ba || **25** μὴ suppl. m. po. Pc || **26** φαίνεται Ba, (η supr.) Vc | l. 21 | ἐν μὲν Ma

ing an apostrophe and invective (Dem. 19.120): "Then, O you —; what name would anyone rightly use to address you?" Or again (Dem. 19.120): "Stand up and answer me, for you cannot say you do not have anything to say because of lack of experience." |[213] [179,3]

Briefly put, if after selecting examples of periods from the ancient writers one were to imitate them, one would find a good supply of periods by variations (*metapoiēseis*). The figure from comparison is best (Dem. 22.7): "For just as if any of them had been condemned, you would not have introduced this motion, so if you are now punished, another will not introduce it." And it is possible to compose periods as if in doubt, if one begins as does Demosthenes in *Against Timocrates*: "Why then, by Zeus, why does this decree not seem to be good to some? Is it because it is contrary to the laws? In fact, it is the only one that is in accord with the laws. But because it destroys the order? In fact, unlike everything else, it is the foundation of good order. But it is because of such and such," and you will give the apodosis.[214] This happens when you have two or three thoughts; for example, if you want to alter the following period, which is periodic rather than actually a period[215] (Dem. 19.181): "But now, all that could be saved by sailing he has lost by ordering us to come by land, and what (*could be saved*) by speaking the truth (*he has lost*) by lying"; and again, "For why, by Zeus, would anyone spare Aeschines? Because he hastened the departure? Surely it was necessary to sail and not to go by land. Or because he spoke the truth to you? Surely by lying he destroyed everything." It is the virtue of metapoiesis that
| it can harmonize every figure of the underlying thought in this [180]
way, a thing that amazes more when done extemporaneously than when transmitted in writing.

| There are also periods that are apodeictic because of their [177,23]
figures; for example (Dem. 20.2): "In [178] the provision that no one is to be exempt he took away exemption from those that have it and in the further provision that exemption is not to be granted

[213] The translation follows Patillon's insertion of 179,3–180,3 Rabe at this point.

[214] A very free adaptation of Demosthenes 24.81.

[215] Because it is not part of an epikheireme. The same applies to some of the examples that follow.

*Ἔστι καὶ ἐπιτιμητικὴ περίοδος τῷ σχήματι, ὅταν λέγωμεν «εἶθ', ἃ Φίλιππος ἂν εὔξαιτο τοῖς θεοῖς, ταῦθ' ὑμῶν τινες ἐνθάδε ποιοῦσιν;» κἀκεῖ πάλιν «εἶτα οὐκ αἰσχύνεσθε, εἰ μηδ' ἃ πάθοιτ' ἄν, εἰ δύναιτ' ἐκεῖνος, ταῦτα ποιῆσαι καιρὸν ἔχοντες οὐ τολμήσετε;» γίνεται δὲ καὶ ἐκ συμπλοκῆς δύο ἀδικημάτων οἷον «νῦν δέ, ἃ μὲν πλεύσασιν ἦν σῶσαι, βαδίζειν κελεύων ἀπολώλεκεν οὗτος, ἃ δ' εἰποῦσι τἀληθῆ, ψευδόμενος».*

*Καθόλου δὲ περὶ σχήματος περιόδου λεκτέον. περίοδός ἐστι σχῆμα αὐτοτελὲς ὅλου τοῦ ἐπιχειρήματος ἐν ἑρμηνείας ῥυθμῷ συντόμως ἀπηρτισμένον, τὰ δὲ ἐν αὐτῇ συντόμως ὑπερβατὰ καλῶς σχηματίζει τὰς περιόδους· «ὁ γὰρ οἷς ἂν ἐγὼ ληφθείην», ἔστι γὰρ τὸ ἑξῆς «ὁ γὰρ ταῦτα πράττων, οἷς ἂν ληφθείην ἐγώ».*

*Ἰστέον δέ, ὡς τὴν περίοδον ἤτοι ἰσοσκελῆ καὶ ἰσόπλευρον ἀπὸ τῶν*
[179] *κώλων εἶναι δεῖ κατὰ τὴν ἑρμηνείαν | ἢ συντομωτέραν ἐν τῇ ἀποδόσει· ἀτονία δὲ ῥήτορος τὴν ἀπόδοσιν τῆς περιόδου μακροτέραν ποιῆσαι τῆς προτάσεως.*

*Γίνεται δὲ καὶ μονόκωλος περίοδος, γίνεται δὲ καὶ δίκωλος καὶ τρίκωλος ἡ ἐκ τριῶν κώλων συνεστηκυῖα καὶ τετράκωλος ἡ ἐκ τεττάρων. κῶλον δέ ἐστιν ἡ ἀπηρτισμένη διάνοια. ἡ μὲν γὰρ μονόκωλος ἐκείνη, ἐπειδὴ κρέμαται ἡ διάνοια αὐτῆς μέχρι τοῦ τέλους τῷ ὑπερβατῷ οὕτω σχηματισθεῖσα σχοινοτενῶς διείληπται «εἶτα οὐκ αἰσχύνεσθε, εἰ μηδ' ἃ πάθοιτ' ἄν, εἰ δύναιτ' ἐκεῖνος, ταῦτα ποιῆσαι καιρὸν ἔχοντες οὐ τολμήσετε;» δίκωλος δὲ ἐκείνη ἡ προτάσεως μονοκώλου κειμένης ἀπόδοσιν ἀπαιτοῦσα μονόκωλον· μάλιστα δὲ αἱ γνωμικαὶ πάσχουσιν αὐτό· ἔστι δὲ γνωμικὴ περίοδος αὕτη «τὸ γὰρ εὖ πράττειν παρὰ τὴν ἀξίαν ἀφορμὴ τοῦ κακῶς φρονεῖν τοῖς ἀνοήτοις γίνεται». τρίκωλος δὲ ἐκείνη, ὅταν δύο κώλων διαφόρων προταθέντων ἀρκῇ μονόκωλος ἑκατέροις*

1 δὲ καὶ **V** | Dem. 8, 20 || **2** τῶι θεῶι Vc Ba | ἐνθάδε ποιοῦσί τινες Vc Ba || **3** Dem. 1, 24 || **4** τολμήσ[αι]ετε **P**; cf. l. 22 || **5** Dem. 19, 181 || **6** εἰποῦσιν ἀληθῆ Ac || **7** δέ ἐστι Ba || **10** Dem. 9, 17 | οἷον ante ὁ add. Ma || **16** cf. Demetr. De eloc. 16. 17 || **16-17** καὶ τρίκωλος δὲ **V** || **18** alt. ἡ om. **V** | μὲν om. Pc || **19** τοῦ om. Vc || **20** σχηματισθείσης **P** Ac | Dem. 1, 24 || **21** καιρὸν ἔχοντες ποιῆσαι Ac || **22** τολμήσ[αι]ετε Pc; cf. 150, 4 || **23** τοῦτο δὲ μάλιστα πάσχουσιν αἱ γνωμικαί Vc Ba || **24** Dem. 1, 23 || **24** τὴν ἑαυτοῦ post ἀξίαν add. Ba, (del.) Vc || **26** προτεθέντων **P** Ac

in the future (*he took away*) your right to confer it."[216] It is good to look for the figure here in the verbal construction, but better if one makes a departure from the usual in changes such that something said in the protasis is left unsaid in the apodosis but seems to be said, as here "he took away" has been stated in the protasis and implied in the apodosis.

There is also a period censorious (*epitimētikē*) in figure, as when we say (Dem. 8.20), "Then what Philip would pray for to the gods, this would some of you here do for him?" Or again (Dem. 1.24): "Are you not ashamed if what you would suffer if he had the power, these things you will not dare to do to him when you have the opportunity?" It also occurs from interweaving (*symplokē*)[217] of two wrongs; for example (Dem. 19.181): "But now, all that could have been saved by sailing, he has lost by ordering us to come by land, and by lying all that could be said by speaking the truth."

I should say something in general about the figure of a period. A period is a figure, complete in itself, belonging to a whole epikheireme, in rhythmical language, brought to a concise end, and the concise hyperbata[218] in it beautifully give periods their figure; (*for example*,) "For he, by what things I would be captured" (Dem. 9.17), where the normal order would be "for he doing the things by which I would be captured."

You should know that a period ought to be expressed with
cola of equal legs and sides[219] | or the apodosis should be shorter. [179]
It is a failing on the part of an orator to make the apodosis of a
period longer than the protasis. | There are monocolonic peri- [180,4]
ods, and there are dicolonic and tricolonic ones, consisting of three cola, and tetracolonic from four. A colon is a completed thought. A period is monocolonic when its thought is suspended until the very end by hyperbaton; thus figured by stretching it is divided as in this example (Dem. 1.24): "Then are you not ashamed, if what you would suffer if he had the power, these things when

[216] Patillon has suggested moving this and the next two paragraphs to follow the first sentence of p. 180 Rabe; cf. Patillon, *ANRW,* 2129.

[217] Cf. Alexander, *On Figures* 2.5.

[218] Changes in word order, as in the examples cited

[219] "Legs" in the case of monocolonic and dicolonic periods, "sides" in the case of the others.

*ἀπόδοσις, οἷον «ὧν οὖν ἐκεῖνος μὲν ὀφείλει τοῖς ὑπὲρ αὐτοῦ πεπολιτευμένοις χάριν, ὑμῖν δὲ δίκην προσήκει λαβεῖν», μέχρι τούτου ἡ πρότασις, εἶτα ἐπήρκεσεν ἑκατέροις τοῖς κώλοις ἡ ἀπόδοσις μονόκωλος «τούτων* [181] *οὐχὶ νῦν ὁρῶ τὸν καιρὸν τοῦ λέγειν». | τετράκωλος δὲ ἐκείνη ἡ ἐν τῇ πρώτῃ προτάσει ἀπόδοσιν ἰδίαν ἔχουσα καὶ ἐν τῇ δευτέρᾳ προτάσει ἀπόδοσιν ἰδίαν ἔχουσα, οἷον «ἐν μὲν γὰρ τῷ γράψαι μηδένα εἶναι ἀτελῆ τοὺς ἔχοντας ἀφείλετο τὴν ἀτέλειαν, ἐν δὲ τῷ προσγράψαι μηδὲ τὸ λοιπὸν ἐξεῖναι δοῦναι ὑμᾶς τὸ δοῦναι ὑμῖν ἐξεῖναι». τῆς τετρακώλου δὲ ταύτης καὶ ἡ χρεία καλλίστη ἐν ταῖς μεταποιήσεσιν, ὅτι καὶ δύναται στρέφεσθαι· τετράκις γὰρ μετασχηματιζομένη ἐκ τῶν προτάσεων καὶ τῶν ἀποδόσεων ἀλύπως δύναται λεχθῆναι τετράκις· εἰ δὲ δεῖ καὶ χιασθῆναι αὐτήν, τότε δὴ τότε δύναιτο ἄν τις αὐτὴν ἐκ τῆς τῶν νοημάτων ἀνάγκης καὶ πλεονάκις στρέφειν· οὐ πᾶσα δὲ χιασθῆναι δύναται τετράγωνος περίοδος. ἔστω δὲ πρῶτον αὕτη ἡ πολλάκις μὲν ἀναστρεφομένη, μηδὲ ἅπαξ δὲ χιαζομένη, οἷον «ἐν μὲν γὰρ τῷ γράψαι μηδένα εἶναι ἀτελῆ τοὺς ἔχοντας ἀφείλετο τὴν ἀτέλειαν, ἐν δὲ τῷ προσγράψαι μηδὲ τὸ λοιπὸν ἐ?ξεῖναι δοῦναι ὑμᾶς τὸ δοῦναι ὑμῖν ἐξεῖναι». δύναται δὲ αὕτη ἀθρόως ἀναστραφεῖσα καὶ ἄλλως γενέσθαι· ἡ γὰρ δευτέρα πρότασις καὶ ἀπόδοσις γίνονται πρῶται οἷον «ἐν μὲν γὰρ τῷ προσγράψαι μηδὲ τὸ λοιπὸν ἐξεῖναι δοῦναι ὑμᾶς τὸ δοῦναι ὑμῖν ἐξεῖναι ἀφείλετο, ἐν* [182] *δὲ τῷ γράψαι | μηδένα εἶναι ἀτελῆ τὴν ἀτέλειαν τοὺς ἔχοντας»· ἢ τὰς δύο προτάσεις ἐκλαβὼν συντίθημι «ἐν μὲν γὰρ τῷ γράψαι μηδένα εἶναι ἀτελῆ καὶ ἐν τῷ προσγράψαι μηδὲ τὸ λοιπὸν ἐξεῖναι δοῦναι καὶ τοὺς*

ἀ δο
1 ὑπόθεσις Pc | οἷον om. Pc | Dem. 2, 4 || 1-2 πολιτευμένοις Vc Ba || 2 τούτου, ων m. 2 supr., Vc || 3 εἶτα post κώλοις Vc Ba | ἀμφοτέροις Vc Ba | ἡ om. Vc Ba | τούτων **P**; τοῦτον Ac; τοῦτό ἐστιν Ba; τοῦτό ἐστι το⌊ύτω ex ῦτο, m. 2 ?⌋ν Vc || 4 ἐκείνη Ac, v.l. **P**; om. **P** Vc Ba || 4-5 τῆι πρώτηι **V**, v.l. **P**; ἑκατέρα **P** || 5 τῆι δευτέραι προτάσει **V**, v.l. **P**; τῆι ἀποδόσει **P** || 6 ἀπόδοσιν Vc Ba, v.l. **P**; πρότασιν **P** | ἀπόδοσιν ἰδίαν ἔχουσα om. Ac | Dem. 20, 2 || 8 ὑμᾶς **P** Vc Ba; ὑμῖν Ac | ὑμῖν **P**; ἡμῖν Vc Ba; ὑμᾶς Ac | τετραγώνου Vc Ba, v.l. **P** (cf. l. 14) || 9 καὶ om. Vc Ba || 11 γρ καὶ πολλάκις **P** (ad 12 πλεονάκις referendum?) || 12 τότε δὴ τότε: fort. ex loco p. 158, 21 laudato figuram petiit | ἂν om. **P** Ac || 13 καὶ om. Pc | γὰρ Ac || 14 τετράκωλος Ac | περίοδος τετράγωνος Pc | πρώτη Vc Ba || 14-15 ἡ — οἷον om. Vc Ba || 15 γράφειν Ac || 17 ἡμῖν Vc Ba || 18 δὲ **V**, v.l. **P**; γὰρ **P** | αὕτη **V**, v.l. Pc; αὕτη ἡ v.l. Pa; om. **P** | καὶ **V**, v.l. **P**; om. **P** | δευτέρα om. Pc || 20 δοῦναι om. Vc Ba | ἡμῖν Ba, ?m. 1 Vc | ἀφείλετο om. Pc || 20-21 προσγράψαι Pc || 21 ἔχοντας ἀφείλετο Sc || 22 ἐκβαλὼν Vc Ba | μὲν om. **V** | γράφειν Ac || 23 ἐν τῷ om. Vc Ba | προσγράφειν Ac | δοῦναι ὑμῖν Ac

you have the opportunity you do not dare to do?"[220] A dicolonic period is one in which a monocolonic protasis looks forward to a monocolonic apodosis. Maxims (*gnōmikai*) especially take this form. An example of a gnomic period is (Dem. 1.23): "To succeed beyond deserts becomes the beginning of perversity for the foolish."[221] A period is tricolonic when a monocolonic apodosis is sufficient response for two different colons; for example (Dem. 2.4): "Of the services for which he ought to thank those politicians working in his interest—services for which you ought to require punishment"—up to here is the protasis, then a monocolonic apodosis is sufficient for each of these cola—"of these I see it is not now the time to speak." | A tetracolonic period has [181] one apodosis specifically for the first protasis and another for the second protasis; for example (Dem. 20.2): "For in providing that no one is to be immune, (the law) took away immunity from those who have it, and in providing further that in the future it will not be permitted for you to give immunity, (*it took away from*) you the right to give it." The best use of this period with four cola is in metapoiesis,[222] because the order of the clauses can be interchanged. It is possible to change the order of protases and apodoses so as to be said in four different ways without harm to the thought, and if there is need to use chiasmus, then sometimes one might invert the period even more, depending on the thoughts, but it is not possible to arrange every four-clause period in chiastic order. Take this example first of something that can be rearranged in many ways without once using chiasmus: "For in providing that no one is to be immune, (*the law*) took away immunity from those who have it, and in providing further that in the future it will not be permitted for you to give immunity, (*it took away from*) you the right to give it." It can be inverted as a whole and varied in other ways, for the second protasis and apodosis come first if you say, "For in providing that in the future it is not

[220] The sentence contains several cola; the main clause, however, is "divided" and "stretched" by inserted clauses, and apparently this is the basis of calling the sentence monocolonic.

[221] "To succeed beyond deserts" is regarded as monocolonic; the infinitive could be replaced by a conditional clause: "If one succeeds beyond deserts. . ."

[222] I.e., in variations.

*ἔχοντας ἀφείλετο τὴν ἀτέλειαν καὶ ὑμᾶς τὸ δοῦναι ὑμῖν ἐξεῖναι»· ἢ τὰς ἀποδόσεις ποιῶ προτάσεις «καὶ τοὺς ἔχοντας ἀφείλετο τὴν ἀτέλειαν καὶ ὑμᾶς τὸ δοῦναι ὑμῖν ἐξεῖναι ἐν τῷ γράψαι μηδένα εἶναι ἀτελῆ καὶ ἐν τῷ προσγράψαι μηδὲ τὸ λοιπὸν ἐξεῖναι δοῦναι ὑμῖν». Καὶ αὕτη ἐστὶ καὶ οὕτως γίνεται ἡ πολλάκις μὲν ἀναστρεφομένη, μηδὲ ἅπαξ δὲ χιαζομένη. ἐκείνη δὲ ἡ παρὰ τῷ Δημοσθένει καὶ χιασθῆναι δύναται «ὁ μὲν γὰρ Φίλιππος ὅσῳ πλείονα ὑπὲρ τὴν ἀξίαν πεποίηκε τὴν ἑαυτοῦ, τοσούτῳ θαυμαστότερος παρὰ πᾶσι νομίζεται· ὑμεῖς δέ, ὦ Ἀθηναῖοι, ὅσῳ χεῖρον ἢ προσῆκε κέχρησθε τοῖς πράγμασι, τοσούτῳ πλείονα αἰσχύνην ὠφλήκατε», καὶ μυριάκις ἔστι μεταποιεῖν τὴν ἀναδεχομένην τοῦτο τὸ σχῆμα. πῶς δὲ ἀναδέχεται τὸν χιασμόν; ὅταν ἐν ἀμφοτέραις ταῖς προτάσεσιν ἀμφότεραι ἁρμόζωσιν αἱ ἀποδόσεις καὶ ἐναλλάξ, οἷον «ὁ μὲν γὰρ Φίλιππος ὅσῳ πλείονα ὑπὲρ τὴν ἀξίαν πεποίηκε τὴν ἑαυτοῦ», τοῦτο ἡ πρότασις, ἁρμόζει δὲ αὐτῇ ἑκατέρα ἀπόδοσις, εἴτε βούλοιτό τις* [183] *λέγειν «τοσούτῳ | θαυμαστότερος ἐκεῖνος παρὰ πᾶσι νομίζεται» εἴτε βούλοιτο λέγειν «τοσούτῳ πλείονα ὑμεῖς αἰσχύνην ὠφλήκατε»· καὶ πάλιν «ὑμεῖς δέ, ὦ Ἀθηναῖοι, ὅσῳ χεῖρον ἢ προσῆκε κέχρησθε τοῖς πράγμασιν» ἡ πρότασις ἡ δευτέρα πρὸς ἀμφότερα ἁρμόσει, εἴτε βούλοιτό τις λέγειν «τοσούτῳ πλείονα αἰσχύνην ὠφλήκατε» εἴτε βούλοιτο λέγειν «τοσούτῳ θαυμαστότερος ἐκεῖνος παρὰ πᾶσι νομίζεται». καὶ ὅλως ἄπειρος ὁ περὶ τούτου λόγος.*

## *Περὶ πνεύματος.*

*Δεῖ τοίνυν τὸν μέλλοντα λέγειν, τὰ ποῖα τῶν νοημάτων κατὰ πνεῦμα ἐξενεχθήσεται, πρῶτον εἰπεῖν, τί ἐστι πνεῦμα καὶ πόσα εἴδη αὐτοῦ καὶ πόθεν γίνεται καὶ πῶς συντίθεται. πνεῦμα μὲν οὖν ἐστι σύνθεσις λόγου διάνοιαν ἀπαρτίζον ἐν κώλοις καὶ κόμμασι, μετρούμενον*

1 τοῦ Pa Ba, m. 1 Vc | ἡμῖν Vc Ba || **1-2** ἢ τὰς ἀποδόσεις **P**; ἢ πάλιν τὰς δύο ἀποδόσεις **V**; γρ ἢ πάλιν τὰς ἀποδόσεις Pa, (καὶ pro ἢ) Pc || **3** τοῦ Pa Ba, m. 1 Vc | ἡμῖν Vc Ba | εἶναι m. 2, εἰδέναι m. 1 Vc || **4** δοῦναι ὑμῖν om. Vc Ba || **5** πολλάκι Ba, m. 1 Vc || **6** sic **P**, (ἡ et καὶ om.) Ac; ἐκείνη δὲ καὶ χιασθῆναι δύναται παρὰ τῶι δημοσθένει Vc Ba || **8** ὦ Ἀθηναῖοι om. Vc Ba, Dem. 2, 3 || **9** χρῆσθε **P** Ac || **11** τοῦτον τὸν Pc || **12** ἁρμόσωσιν Vc Ba || **13** Φίλιππος om. Vc Ba | πλείω Vc Ba || **14** ἁρμόσει Vc Ba || **15** τοσούτῳ — νομίζεται et l. 16 τοσούτῳ — ὠφλήκατε locum mutaverunt Ac || **16** ὑμεῖς post αἰσχύνην **V**; om. Sc || **17** ὦ ἀθηναῖοι om. Vc Ba | χρῆσθε **P** Ac || **21** ἄπορος m. 1 Pc | τούτ[ων m. 2 ex ου] Ba || **25** πόθεν **P**; πῶς **V**, v.l. **P** | οὖν om. Pc; μὲν οὖν om. Vc Ba || **26** ἀπαρτίζουσα Sturm; cf. Dox. II 253, 5 W.

permitted for you to give (*immunity*), (*the law*) took away your right to give it, and in providing | that no one is to be immune, (*it took away immunity from those*) who have it"; or taking out the two protases, I say, "For in providing that no one is to be immune and in further providing that for the future it is not permitted for you to give (*immunity*), it took immunity away from those who have it and from you the right to give it"; or I can make the apodoses become protases: "It took away immunity from those who have it and from you the right to give it, by providing that no one is to be immune and by further providing that for the future it is not permitted for you to give it." [182]

These are some of the many inversions, without once using chiasmus. The following is a period in Demosthenes (2.3) that can be made chiastic: "For the more Philip has done beyond his deserts, the more he is thought wonderful by all, while as for you, O Athenians, the more you have poorly used your opportunities, the greater disgrace you have incurred." It is possible to rearrange this in many ways. How does it take chiastic shape? When both apodoses harmonize with both protases, but crosswise; for example, "For the more Philip has done beyond his deserts"—this is a protasis and either of the apodoses accords with it, whether you were to say, "the more | he is thought wonderful by all," or if you [183] were to say, "the greater disgrace you have incurred"; and again, "But you, O Athenians, the more you have poorly used your opportunities." The second protasis will accord with either: if one wanted to say, "the greater disgrace you have incurred" or "the more he is thought wonderful by all." There is no limit to what can be said about this.

## CHAPTER 4: ON PNEUMA

Now it is necessary for one who is going to say what sort of thoughts are going to be expressed in a pneuma to say first what a pneuma is and how many kinds of it there are and from what it is derived and how composed.[223] Now a pneuma is a combination

[223] Pneuma was first mentioned in 3.10 above (p. 109), where an example using antitheton is supplied. As a technical rhetorical term, *pneuma* (literally "a blast of wind" or "a breath") is found only in *On Invention* and later commentaries on this text.

*πρὸς τὴν διάρκειαν τοῦ πνεύματος κατὰ τὴν φωνὴν τοῦ λέγοντος.*

*Ἐπεὶ δὲ καὶ περὶ κώλου καὶ κόμματος ἔφαμεν, ἰστέον ἐν συντόμῳ, ὅτι δεῖ καὶ κόμμα καὶ κῶλον ἀπαρτίζειν τὴν διάνοιαν· διαφέρουσι δὲ τοῖς μέτροις, ὅτι τὸ μὲν ἀπὸ τεττάρων καὶ πέντε συλλαβῶν μέχρι*
[184] *τῶν ἓξ κόμμα ἐστὶν [ἐπῳδῷ μετρούμενον], τὸ δὲ | ὑπὲρ τὰς ἑπτὰ καὶ*
*ὀκτὼ καὶ δέκα καὶ ἐγγίζον ἤδη τῷ τριμέτρῳ καὶ μέχρι τοῦ ἡρωικοῦ προχωροῦν κῶλον γίνεται ὀρθὸν καὶ τεταμένον. ὁ δὲ τῶν συλλαβῶν ἀριθμὸς περινενόηται ἤδη. τὸ δὲ ὑπὲρ τὸ ἡρωικὸν σχοινοτενὲς κέκληται, χρήσιμον προοιμίοις μάλιστα καὶ ταῖς τῶν προοιμίων περιβολαῖς. οἱ δέ φασι καὶ τὸν ἐπῳδὸν κῶλον εἶναι, τὸ δὲ ὑποκάτω κόμμα. ταῦτα μὲν οὖν κῶλά ἐστιν «ἀλλ' ὁ τὴν Εὔβοιαν ἐκεῖνος σφετεριζόμενος*

1 διάνοιαν Pc || 3 cf. W VII 931, 15 (schol. **P** in Herm. Π. ἰδ.; auctor est Lachares; cf. Studemund, *Pseudo-Castoris excerpta rhetorica*, p. 8): τὰ περὶ τοῦ κόμματος Ἀψίνου ... οὗτος γὰρ κατὰ μὲν τὴν διάνοιαν οὐδὲν διαφέρειν νομίζει τὸ κῶλον τοῦ κόμματος, μόνῳ δὲ διαχωρίζεσθαι τῷ μέτρῳ τῶν συλλαβῶν· ἀπὸ γὰρ τεσσάρων κτλ. || 4 δὲ suppl. m. po. Pc | δὲ ἀλλήλων τοῖς **V**, v.l. Pa | (ὅτι om.) τὸ μὲν γὰρ Vc Ba | μέχρι **P** Ac, W VII 931, 19; καὶ μέχρις Vc Ba || 5 ἐπῳδῷ μετρούμενον om. W VII | exsp. ὑπὲρ τὰς ἓξ || 6 ult. καὶ et τῷ om. W VII || 7-8 ὁ — περινενόηται suppl. m. 2 Ba; om. W VII 931, 31 || 8 ἤδη **P** Ac Mr, cf. shcol. **P** W VII 822, 2; om. Vc Ba || 8-9 κέκληται —περιβολαῖς om. W VII 931, 22 || 9 ὅπερ χρήσιμον ἐν Anon. III 113, 29 Sp. || 10 οἱ δὲ **P** Vc Ba; ἔνιοι δὲ W VII 931; οἷον Ac || 11 Dem. 18, 71

of words completing a thought in cola and commata, measured by the supply of breath in the voice of the speaker.[224]

Since we mentioned colon and comma, you should know, briefly put, that both comma and colon should complete a thought.[225] They differ in length, in that a comma consists of from four and five up to six syllables, while | anything beyond [184]
seven and eight and ten syllables, approaching the length of a trimeter and going up to that of a hexameter, becomes a straight extended colon.[226] [The number of syllables has already been considered.][227] What exceeds the heroic meter has been called *skhoinotenes*,[228] especially useful in prooemia and elaborated passages[229] in prooemia. Some say that the epode is a colon and anything shorter a comma. Now the following are cola[230] (Dem.

[224] I.e., a long periodic sentence, said in one breath. In 4.5 we are told that a pneuma becomes a tasis when it cannot be said in one breath, but the examples of pneuma given by the author would require brazen lungs if the requirement of delivery in one breath is taken literally. Quintilian 11.3.53–54 supplies some advice: "When about to deliver a lengthy period (*longiorem perihodon*) we should collect our breath but not take a long time over it, do it noisily, or make it in any way obvious; at other points, the best plan will be to recover breath at the natural breaks between phrases."

[225] Cf. Aristotle, *Rhetoric* 3.9.5–7; Demetrius, *On Style* §§1–11; Dionysius of Halicarnassus, *On Composition* chs. 7–9.

[226] The note in the apparatus (p. 156,3) may be understood as follows: cf. Walz 7:931,15 (scholia P to Hermogenes, *On Ideas;* the author is Lachares, according to Wilhelm Studemund, *Pseudo-Castoris excerpta rhetorica* [Vratislava: Typis officinae Universitatis, 1888], 9), citing Apsines' discussion of the comma, "for he thinks that in terms of the thought a colon does not differ from a comma, but is only distinguished by the number of the syllables; for <a comma consists of from four or five, up to six syllables, . . . elaborated passages in prooemia.>" Lachares lived in the fifth century. Apsines, in the third century, may have derived the passage, which is not found in his extant work, from the treatise used by the author of *On Invention*. On a possible second-century date for *On Invention* in its original form, see the introduction above. Rabe regarded Lachares' reference to Apsines as a conjecture; cf. above.

[227] This sentence is omitted in most mss and in Lachares' quotation.

[228] Elongated, stretched; cf. 1.5 above, p. 27. As a metrical term found only in these passages.

[229] *Peribolē*; cf. Hermogenes, *On Ideas* 1.11; translated as "abundance" by Wooten, 41–54.

[230] In the Greek there are two participial phrases of fifteen and seventeen syllables (fourteen and sixteen if the conjunctions are not counted), thus creating two cola on the basis of the definition above.

καὶ κατασκευάζων ἐπιτείχισμα ἐπὶ τὴν Ἀττικήν», εἶτα ἐπιφέρει κόμματα «καὶ καταλαμβάνων Ὠρεὸν καὶ κατασκάπτων Πορθμόν», εἶτα διαδέχεται καὶ κῶλον πάλιν «καὶ καθιστὰς ἐν μὲν Ὠρεῷ Φιλιστίδην τύραννον», εἶτα κόμμα πάλιν «ἐν δ' Ἐρετρίᾳ Κλείταρχον» ἢ κῶλον ἐπῳδῷ ἴσον. καὶ διόλου τὸ πνεῦμα τούτοις συνέχεται οὔτε γὰρ ἀριθμῷ οὔτε ἕξει ὑποπίπτει, ἀλλὰ τὸ παρατυχὸν λέγεται, δι' ἄλλων μέντοι οὐ γίνεται. Ἰστέον δέ, ὅτι καὶ ἀπὸ τῶν πέντε συλλαβῶν, ὡς ἔφαμεν, καὶ τεττάρων δέ γε καὶ ἥττόνων συνίσταται τὸ κόμμα· εἰ γὰρ ἀπαρτίζοιτο διάνοια, καὶ ἐν δύο συλλαβαῖς κόμμα ἔστι κόμμα δέ ἐστι σύνθεσις [185] διανοίας μικροτέρα κώλου· ἐπεὶ τὸ πνεῦμα αὐτὸ μετ' ὀλίγον καὶ | εἰς τοιαῦτα καταλήξει κόμματα, ὅταν λέγῃ «πότερον ταῦτα ποιῶν ἠδίκει καὶ παρεσπόνδει καὶ τὴν εἰρήνην ἔλυεν ἢ οὔ;» καὶ γὰρ αἱ ἐπὶ τέλει δύο συλλαβαὶ «ἢ οὔ» κόμμα ἐστίν, ἐρωτῶντος ὁλοκλήρως ἀνθρώπου τὴν διάνοιαν.

Εἴδη δὲ πνευμάτων δύο· ἤτοι γὰρ ἓν νόημα λαβόντες καὶ τοῦτο ἐργαζόμενοι τῇ ἑρμηνείᾳ πλείοσι κώλοις, ὡς ἔφην, διαρκοῦμεν τὸ ἓν ἐπεκτείνοντες, οἷον «ὅτε γὰρ περιὼν ὁ Φίλιππος Ἰλλυριοὺς καὶ Τριβαλλούς, τινὰς δὲ καὶ τῶν Ἑλλήνων κατεστρέφετο καὶ δυνάμεις πολλὰς καὶ μεγάλας ἐποιεῖτο ὑφ' ἑαυτόν, καί τινες τῶν ἐκ τῶν πόλεων ἐπὶ τῇ τῆς εἰρήνης ἐξουσίᾳ βαδίζοντες ἐκεῖσε διεφθείροντο, ὧν εἷς οὗτος ἦν, τότε δὴ τότε πάντες, ἐφ' οὓς ταῦτα παρεσκεύαζεν ἐκεῖνος, ἐπολεμοῦντο. εἰ δὲ μὴ ᾐσθάνοντο, ἕτερος οὗτος λόγος, οὐ πρὸς ἐμέ», τοῦτο γὰρ σύμπαν ἑνός ἐστι νοήματος ἑρμηνεία τοῦ ὅτι πάλαι Φίλιππος τοῖς Ἕλλησιν ἐπεβούλευεν· ἢ ὅταν πολλὰ πράγματα ἀθρόως ἔχοντες εἰπεῖν καθ'

1 ἐπιτειχίσματα Pa || 3 καὶ om. Ac Mr | κῶλα Vc || 5 καθόλου Vc Ba || 6 ἕξει Ac; λέξει Pc Vc Ba, (λ er.) Pa, schol. **P** W VII 822: τῇ δυνάμει τοῦ λέγοντος | ὑποπίπτει τὸ πνεῦμα Vc Ba | λέγεται Vc Ba; γίνεται **P** Ac || 7 ὡς om. Vc Ba | p. 156, 4 || 8 συνίσταται Pc, (post κόμμα transp.) Ac; συνίστασθαι (post κόμμα transp.) Vc Ba; om. Pa | συνίστατει τὸ κῶλον συλλαβῶν W VII 931, 25 || 9 ἔσται W VII | κόμμα δέ ἐστι om. Pa; κόμμα γάρ ἐστι? || 10 ὀλίγα[ον] **P** || 11 sc. p. 156, 11 sq.: Dem. 18, 71 || 13-14 ἐρωτῶντος τοῦ ῥήτορος ὁλοκλήρως μετὰ τῶν δύο συλλαβῶν τούτων τὴν προκειμένην πᾶσαν διάνοιαν W VII 931, 29 || 13 τὴν om. Vc Ba || 16 ἐργασάμενοι Vc Ba || 16-17 p. 154, 26–156, 1 || 17 Dem. 18, 44 | περιϊὼν **P** Mr | ὁ om. Vc || 18 δὲ suppl. m. 2 Vc || 19 ἐκ τῶν **V**; om. (mg. γρ τῶν πολεμίων) **P** || 20 αἰσχίνης post ἦν add. Vc Ba || 21 δὴ τότε hic om. Dem.; v. p. 152, 12 ann., 164, 25 || 22 λόγος οὗτος Vc Ba | ὁ λόγος Pc || 23 ὅτι εἰ πάλαι Vc Ba

18.71): "But he who was appropriating Euboea / and preparing it as a stronghold against Attica"; then he brings in commata: "and seizing Oreus / and raising the walls of Porthmus";[231] then he uses a colon again, "and setting up Philistides as tyrant in Oreus"; then a comma again, "and Cleitarchus in Eretria," or a colon equal to an epode.[232] And altogether, a pneuma consists of these parts, for it is not a matter of a number or rule of art but of what happens to be said, and it does not result from other things.

You should know that, as we said, a comma consists of five syllables, or indeed, four and less, for if the thought is completed, there is a comma even in two syllables—a comma being a expression of thought shorter than a colon—; this very pneuma (Dem. 18.71) a little later | will end in a comma of that sort, when he says, [185]
"In doing these things was he guilty of wrong and did he violate the truce and break the peace, or not?" Here the two syllables at the end, "or not," are a comma, since the man's question contains the whole thought.

There are two kinds of pneuma. In one kind, after taking a single thought and elaborating it in expression with numerous cola, as I said, we continue to stretch out that one thought; for example (Dem. 18.44), "For when Philip was going around and subduing the Illyrians and Triballi and some of the Greeks as well, and was bringing under his control many large forces, and when some men from the cities, taking advantage of the peace to go to Macedon, were being corrupted there, of whom this man was one, at that very time all those against whom he was making preparations were really being attacked. If they did not realize it, that is another subject, not my concern." All this is the expression of the one thought, that Philip was plotting against the Greeks long ago. Or (*in the other kind*) when we have many actions to mention

[231] Two participial phrases of nine and seven syllables (eight and seven if the connectives are not counted).

[232] I.e., eight syllables, as in the epodes of Archilochus.

*ἕκαστον κῶλον πρᾶγμα ἀπαρτίζωμεν, ὡς ἐν ἐκείνῳ «ἀλλ' ὁ τὴν Εὔβοιαν ἐκεῖνος σφετεριζόμενος καὶ κατασκευάζων ἐπιτείχισμα ἐπὶ τὴν Ἀττικὴν καὶ καταλαμβάνων Ὠρεὸν καὶ κατασκάπτων Πορθμόν», καὶ* [186] *διόλου τοῦτο τὸ πνεῦμα συναπαρτίζει τῷ πράγματι | καὶ κῶλον. καὶ παρὰ ταῦτα οὐκ ἔστιν ἄλλο εἶδος πνεύματος.*

*Ἐλέγχεται δὲ τὸ πνεῦμα καὶ γίνεται τῇ ἐπιμονῇ τοῦ σχήματος· δεῖ γὰρ ἐπιμείναντα τῷ σχήματι τῇ ὁμοιότητι τοῦ σχήματος δεῖξαι τὴν τέχνην. συνδεῖται δὲ τὸ πνεῦμα καὶ συντίθεται μάλιστα καὶ εὔτονον γίνεται τοῖς συνεχέσι συνδέσμοις τοῖς συμπλεκτικοῖς, καὶ πάσχει δέ γε κοσμούμενον ἀπ' ἀρχῆς ἄχρι τέλους. καὶ παράδειγμα οὐκ ἔθηκα· οὐδὲν γὰρ ἔστιν, ὅ τι μὴ οὕτως ἔχει.*

*Σχήματα δὲ πνευμάτων, ὅσα καὶ λόγων· ἔξεστι γὰρ ὅθεν βούλει σοι τὸ πνεῦμα λαβόντι καὶ λέγοντι μόνον ἐπιμεῖναι, ὅτῳ δ' ἂν ἐπιμείνῃς, πνεῦμα ποιεῖς. μετρίως δὲ ἀπὸ τῶν παραδειγμάτων τὰς τηρήσεις ἀναγκαῖον ἐκθεῖναι. ἔστι γὰρ αὐτῶν τὸ μὲν ἀποφαντικὸν κατὰ τὴν ὀρθὴν πτῶσιν οἷον «ἀλλ' ὁ τὴν Εὔβοιαν ἐκεῖνος σφετεριζόμενος»· ἀπὸ γὰρ τοῦ «σφετεριζόμενος» ἡ ἐπιμονὴ γενομένη τὸ σχῆμα προήγαγεν. Ἔστι καὶ κατ' ἐρώτησιν, ἐάν τις λέγῃ «τίς γὰρ ὁ τὴν Εὔβοιαν ἐκεῖνος σφετεριζόμενος; τίς ὁ καταλαμβάνων Ὠρεόν; τίς ὁ κατασκάπτων Πορθμόν; τίς ὁ κατασκευάζων ἐπιτείχισμα ἐπὶ τὴν Ἀττικήν;» καὶ διόλου ἀλλάξας τὸ σχῆμα σῷον ἐποίησας τὸ πνεῦμα, κἂν αὐτὰ λέγῃς τὰ ῥήματα, μόνον ἀντὶ τοῦ ἄρθρου τοῦ ὁ τὸ τίς παραλαβὼν διὰ τὸ σχῆμα μόριον.* [187] *Ἔστι καὶ ἐλεγκτικόν, ἐάν τις λέγῃ | «οὐχ οὗτός ἐστιν ὁ τὴν Εὔβοιαν σφετεριζόμενος; οὐχ οὗτός ἐστιν ὁ κατασκευάζων ἐπιτείχισμα ἐπὶ τὴν Ἀττικήν;» καὶ τὰ ἑξῆς ὁμοίως. Καὶ δεικτικὸν γίνεται πάλιν τοῦ οὐχὶ ἀφαιρεθέντος οἷον «οὗτος ὁ τὴν Εὔβοιαν σφετεριζόμενος, οὗτος ὁ*

1 <ἓν> πρᾶγμα? | ἀπαρτίζομεν Vc Ba | ὡς ἐκεῖνο Ac, m. 2 Vc | p. 156, 11 || 3 καὶ μεγάροις ἐπιχειρῶν post ἀττικὴν add. Ac, post ὠρεὸν Sc || 4 τούτου Vc Ba | τὸ om. Ac | συναπαρτίζεται Vc Ba; συναρτίζει Ac | κῶλον **P** Ac, Anon. III 114, 26 Sp.; τοῖς κώλοις Vc Ba; τὸ κῶλον m. 2 Vc || 5 ταῦτα v.l. **P**, τοῦτο **PV** || 6 καὶ γίνεται om. Ac || 7 ἐπιμείναντι Ac | τοῦ σχήματος om. Vc Ba || 11 ὃ (om. τι) **V** | ἔχει οὕτως Ac || 13 ἐπιμεῖναι καὶ **P** || 14 δὲ καὶ ἀπὸ Ac || 15 ἀποφατικὸν **V** || 16 οἷον om. **V** | p. 156, 11 || 17 παρήγαγεν Ac; πεποίηκεν Vc Ba | δὲ ante καὶ add. **V** || 18 τις om. **V** | λέγῃς Vc Ba || 19 κατακόπτων (pro κατασκάπτων) Ba || 22 μόνα ἀντὶ τοῦ ō ἄρθρου τὸ τίς μόριον παραλαμβάνων διὰ τὸ σχῆμα Vc Ba | διὰ τὸ om. Ac | σχῆμα καὶ μόριον Ac, v.l. **P** (at recte hic scholiasta **P** interpretatur: τὸ τίς παραλαβὼν μόριον, διὰ τὸ σχῆμα) || 23 δὲ καὶ Vc Ba | ἐὰν λέγῃς **V** || 25 καὶ — ὁμοίως om. Vc | ἑξῆς ὡσαύτως· ὁμοίως καὶ Ac || 26 οὗτός ἐστιν ὁ **V**

together in each colon we complete a subject, as in this example (Dem. 18.71): "But he was appropriating Euboea / and preparing it as a stronghold against Attica / and seizing Oreus / and razing the walls of Porthmus," and throughout this pneuma he fits one colon to one thought. | There is no other kind of pneuma. [186]

The existence of a pneuma is proved by the continuation of the figure,[233] for by dwelling on the figure one necessarily shows his art by the sameness of the figure. A pneuma is held together and to the greatest extent composed and made vigorous by repeated conjunctions connecting the parts, and it receives ornamentation by use of from-beginning-to-end. I have not offered an example, for there is no pneuma that is not like this.

There are as many figures of pneumas as there are figures of language, for it is possible to derive the pneuma from anything you want and in speaking to linger on it, and whatever you continue you make into a pneuma. It is necessary, however, for us to give some moderate attention to the examples, for some of them are declarative in the nominative case, as is "but he who was appropriating Euboea," for the continuation from "was appropriating" carried on the figure.[234] There are also interrogative pneumas, as if someone said, "Who is he that is appropriating Euboea? Who is capturing Oreus? Who is razing Porthmus? Who preparing a fortification against Attica?" Although changing the figure throughout, you preserve the pneuma, even if you say the same words, only substituting the particle "who?" for the article "he who" for the sake of the figure. It is elenctic[235] if one says, | [187]
"Is not this man the one who is appropriating Euboea? Is he not the one who is preparing a fortification against Attica?" And the rest similarly. A deictic pneuma, on the other hand, is one in which the "not" is dropped; for example, "This is the man who is appropriating Euboea, this the one preparing a fortification against

233 I.e., by the grammatical inflexion; cf. the examples below.

234 Patillon (*L'Art rhétorique*, 295 n. 5) reads *to skhēma pepoiēken,* "a produit le pneuma."

235 I.e., incriminating.

*κατασκευάζων ἐπιτείχισμα ἐπὶ τὴν Ἀττικήν.» Καὶ ἡ ἔνστασις μέντοι τοῦ πνεύματος ποιεῖ σχῆμα κάλλιστον, ἐὰν λέγωμεν «οὐ τὴν Εὔβοιαν ἐσφετερίζου; οὐ κατεσκεύαζες ἐπιτείχισμα ἐπὶ τὴν Ἀττικήν;» Καὶ καθόλου ἀποστροφὴ πᾶσα εἰς πρόσωπον ἐπιμείνασα πνεῦμα ἐγένετο, κἂν εἰς ἐμαυτὸν ἐπιστρέψας λέγω «ἐγὼ μὲν ἤμην ὁ τὴν Εὔβοιαν σφετεριζόμενος, ἐγὼ δὲ ὁ κατασκευάζων ἐπιτείχισμα ἐπὶ τὴν Ἀττικήν, ἐγὼ δὲ ὁ καταλαμβάνων Ὠρεόν, ἐγὼ δὲ ὁ κατασκάπτων Πορθμόν»· δύναται γάρ που ἐν προβλήματι καὶ Φίλιππος λέγειν ταῦτα. Ἢ ἀρνητικὸν πάλιν πνεῦμα, ἐάν τις λέγῃ «οὐκ ἐγὼ τὴν Εὔβοιαν ἐσφετεριζόμην, οὐκ ἐγὼ κατεσκεύασα ἐπιτείχισμα ἐπὶ τὴν Ἀττικήν». Ἔστι καὶ ἀποτρεπτικὸν σχῆμα, ὃ ἐπιμεῖναν πνεῦμα γίνεται, ὅταν λέγῃ «μή μοι μυρίους μηδὲ δισμυρίους λόγους μηδὲ τὰς ἐπιστολιμαίους ταύτας δυνάμεις πρόφερε».*

*Ἰστέον δέ, ὅτι ἐπὶ πάντων τούτων αἵ τε τῶν ἀριθμῶν ἀλλαγαὶ ἑνικῶν καὶ πληθυντικῶν ἀλλάσσουσι καὶ μετασχηματίζουσιν αἵ τε τῶν* [188] *γενῶν καὶ τῶν πτώσεων καὶ | αἱ τῶν ἐγκλίσεων. ἀριθμῶν μέν, ὁπόταν τις λέγῃ «οὗτός ἐστιν ὁ τόδε ποιῶν», ποτὲ δὲ λέγῃ «οὗτοί εἰσιν οἱ καταλαμβάνοντες Ὠρεόν, οὗτοί εἰσιν οἱ κατασκάψαντες Πορθμόν». γενῶν δέ, ἂν ποτὲ μὲν ἀρσενικὸν ὄνομα προθῇς, ποτὲ δὲ θηλυκόν, ποτὲ δὲ οὐδέτερον, εἶτα ἐπιμείνῃς· γένους γὰρ ἀλλαγὴ σχήματός ἐστιν ἐναλλαγή. πτώσεων δέ, ἐὰν ποτὲ μὲν ὀνομαστικῶς, ποτὲ δὲ γενικῶς, ποτὲ δὲ κατὰ τὴν δοτικήν, ποτὲ δὲ κατὰ τὴν αἰτιατικὴν ἐξενέγκῃς τὸ σχῆμα· καὶ τὰς πτώσεις ἑνικῶς μὲν ἐκφέρων ἄλλο πνεῦμα ποιεῖς, πληθυντικῶς δὲ ἄλλο. καὶ κατὰ τὰς ἐγκλίσεις ὁμοίως. Ταῦτα μὲν οὖν φύσιν ἔχει τοιαύτην καὶ πάντα, ἵνα μὴ καθ᾽ ἕκαστον λέγωμεν· πᾶσα γὰρ πτῶσις, πᾶσα ἔγκλισις, πᾶς ἀριθμός, πᾶν γένος, πᾶσα μετοχή, πᾶσα ἀντωνυμία μεταποιούμεναι καὶ μεταλλαττόμεναι τὰ σχήματα ἀλλάττουσιν.*

1 ἐπὶ om. Pa || 4 ἐπιστροφὴ Pc || 5 ἀποστρέψω λέγων **V** || 7 ἐγὼ — Πορθμόν om. Vc Ba || 8-9 πνεῦμα πάλιν Ac; [πνεῦμα]? || 10 κατεσκεύαζον Vc Ba | ἀπαγορευτικὸν Vc Ba || 11 ἐγένετο Vc || 12 Dem. 4, 19 (ξένους pro λόγους) | ἐπιστολιμαίας Vc Ba || 13 sq. cf. Alex. III 33, 15 sq. Sp. Π. ὕψ. 23 | τούτων πάντων **V** | αἵ τε αἱ Pc || 14 σχηματίζουσιν Vc Ba | καὶ αἱ τῶν Ac, m. 2 Vc || 15 alt. τῶν om. Vc | αἱ om. Ba; αἱ τῶν om. m. 1 Vc || 16 λέγῃ τις Ac; λέγωμεν Ba, (ῃς m. 2) Vc | τὸ οὗτός Vc Ba | καὶ ὅτε (om. δὲ) Ac | λέγει Ac; λέγεις Vc Ba || 17 κατασκάπτοντες Ac, (ψαν m. 1 supr.) Pc | ⌊II-III⌉ πορθμόν Vc || 18 ἀρσενικὸν ὄνομα Vc Ba; θηλυκὸν (om. ὄνομα) **P** Ac | θηλυκὸν Vc Ba; ἀρσενικόν **P** Ac || 19-20 ἐναλλαγή **P**; ἀλλαγή **V** || 20-21 ποτὲ δὲ γενικῶς — δοτικήν om. Pc || 21 τὸ σχῆμα καὶ Ac, (m. 1 cr. τὰ σχήματα) Pc; τὰ σχήματα καὶ Pa; om. Vc Ba || 22 καὶ τὰς πτώσεις· **P** Ac; τὰς πτώσεις· καὶ Vc Ba || 23 ταῦτα (ι supr.) Pa | ἔχει φύσιν Vc Ba || 26 τὰ om. Ac

Attica." Enstasis of a pneuma makes a fine figure, if (*for example*) we say, "You were not appropriating Euboea. You were not preparing a fortification against Attica."[236] And in general every apostrophe repeatedly addressing a person becomes a pneuma, and also if turning to myself I say, "I was the one appropriating Euboea, and I the one preparing a fortification against Attica, and I the one capturing Oreus, and I the one razing Porthmus."[237] Philip might say these things somewhere in a declamation. Or a pneuma, again, can be negative, if one says, "I was not the one appropriating Euboea, not the one preparing a fortification against Attica." And the figure is apotreptic, which becomes a pneuma by continuing, when he says (Dem. 4.19), "Do not speak to me of ten and twenty thousand mercenaries[238] nor of any of these paper armies."

You should know that in all of these pneumas there are alternations of number between singular and plural, and changes of gender and case and inflection provide different figures. | Of [188]
number when one says, "This is the man doing this thing," but then says, "These are the ones capturing Oreus, these are the ones razing Porthmus." Of gender when at one time you offer a masculine name, then a feminine, then a neuter, and then continue. Change of gender is alteration (*enallagē*)[239] of figure. There are changes of case when sometimes you express the figure in the nominative, sometimes in the genitive, sometimes in the dative, and sometimes in the accusative, and by expressing the cases in the singular you make one pneuma and in the plural another, and similarly in changes of declensions. These things all have the same nature, so we need not discuss each separately: every case, every declension, every number, every gender, every participle, every pronoun, when changed and exchanged, alters the figure.

[236] As Patillon notes (*L'Art rhétorique,* 296 n.1), Rabe's punctuation of the text as questions is wrong.

[237] If this is also an apostrophe, these cola should be regarded as questions: "Was I the one. . .?"

[238] Read *xenous* with the text of Demosthenes.

[239] Cf. Phoebammon, *On Figures* 1.5, where this term applies to a variety of alterations.

*Ἐκεῖνο δὲ ἄξιον εἰδέναι, ὅτι προχωροῦν τὸ πνεῦμα ἐν τῷ σχήματι εἰς συχνὰ κῶλα ὀφείλει καὶ μεταπεσεῖν εἰς ἄλλο σχῆμα λόγου προχωροῦν καὶ τῷ δευτέρῳ πάλιν ἐπιπίπτειν εἰ τύχοι τὸ τρίτον· ἡ γὰρ κοινωνία ἡ τοιαύτη καὶ ἡ διαδοχὴ ὡραῖον ποιεῖ τὸν λόγον ἐν τῷ πνεύματι, οἷον ἐὰν ἀπὸ τῆς ἀποφάνσεως εἰς τὴν* [189] | *πεῦσιν καταστῇς, ὡς ὁ Δημοσθένης τὰ πρῶτα κῶλα ἀπεφήνατο «ἀλλ᾽ ὁ τὴν Εὔβοιαν ἐκεῖνος σφετεριζόμενος», εἶτα κατέβη εἰς τὴν πεῦσιν «πότερον ταῦτα ποιῶν ἠδίκει καὶ παρεσπόνδει;» ἢ τὸ ἔμπαλιν, ἂν ἐρωτήσας εἰς τὸ δεικτικὸν μεταβάλῃς ἢ εἰς ἄλλο τι. πλὴν ἰστέον, ὅτι καλὸν ἐπιμείναντα τῷ πνεύματι ἐν τῷ ἑνὶ σχήματι καὶ εἰς διαδοχὴν ἄλλου προχωρῆσαι· πολλάκις γὰρ τοῦτο οὕτω περικαλλῆ τὸν λόγον ἐποίησεν, ὥστε καὶ εἰς τρίτον σχῆμα μεταβαίνοντας ἀναστῆσαι τοὺς ἀκούοντας, ὥσπερ ἀκμαζούσης τῆς τοῦ λέγοντος φορᾶς, ἣν παρίστησι τοῖς ἀκούουσιν ἡ τοῦ σχήματος μεταβολή. τοὺς πολλοὺς δὲ καὶ ἠπάτησεν ἡ θεωρία ὡς ἀκμὴ οὖσα. ὁ δὲ ἀκμαῖος λόγος οὐχ ὁ αὐτός ἐστιν ἐν λόγῳ καὶ νοήματι, ἀκμὴ δὲ ἄλλο τι διανοίας ἐστὶ καὶ ἄλλο λόγου· ἀκμὴ γάρ ἐστι λόγου τῶν κατὰ πνεῦμα σχημάτων μεταβολή, νοημάτων δέ, ὅταν πληρώσας τις ἓν νόημα ἐν πνεύματι εἰς ἄλλο νόημα λαθὼν μεταβῇ κἀκεῖνο ποιῇ πνεῦμα, εἶτα ἀπ᾽ ἐκείνου εἰς ἄλλο πνεῦμα· καὶ οὕτως ἐκ τῶν ἀδήλως ἄλληλα διαδεχομένων ἡ ἀκμὴ γίνεται. ὡς δ᾽ ἐπὶ παραδείγματος τὸ Δημοσθενικὸν ῥητέον, ὅπως εἰδείημεν, ὅτι ἡ τῶν πνευμάτων συνθήκη ἀκμή ἐστιν· «ὅτε γὰρ περιὼν ὁ Φίλιππος Ἰλλυριοὺς καὶ Τριβαλλούς, τινὰς δὲ καὶ τῶν Ἑλλήνων κατεστρέφετο καὶ δυνάμεις πολλὰς καὶ μεγάλας ἐποιεῖτο ὑφ᾽ ἑαυτόν, καί τινες τῶν ἐκ τῶν πόλεων ἐπὶ τῇ τῆς* [190] | *εἰρήνης ἐξουσίᾳ βαδίζοντες ἐκεῖσε διεφθείροντο, ὧν εἷς οὗτος ἦν, τότε δὴ τότε πάντες, ἐφ᾽ οὓς ταῦτα παρεσκευάζετο ἐκεῖνος, ἐπολεμοῦντο. εἰ δὲ μὴ ᾐσθάνοντο, ἕτερος λόγος οὗτος, οὐ πρὸς ἐμέ», μέχρι τούτου τὸ πνεῦμα· εἶτα τὸ «οὐ πρὸς ἐμέ» θελήσας ἐργάσασθαι ἄλλο πνεῦμα ἐποίησεν «ἐγὼ μὲν γὰρ*

**1** ἐν om. Vc Ba || **2** καὶ μεταπεσεῖν καὶ εἰς Vc Ba | λόγου πάλιν Vc Ba || **3** προχωρεῖν Ba, m. 1 Vc; om. Ac | εἰ τύχοι ἐπιπίπτειν Vc Ba, (ἐμπ-) Ac || **4-5** τὸν ἐν πνεύματι λόγον Ac || **5** ἀποφάσεως **V** | cf. Demetr. De eloc. 279 | μεταστῇς? || **6** Dem. 18, 71 | ἐκείνην Vc || **7** μετέβη? || **9** κάλλιον Vc Ba || **11** ὡς (om. τε) Vc Ba || **12** ὥσπερ Pa **V**; ὥστε Pc || **15** λόγος ἐν λόγωι καὶ ἐν πράγματι οὐχ ὁ αὐτός (om. ἐστιν) Vc Ba || **16** pr. τοῦ λόγου **V** | μὲν γάρ **V** || **18** ποιεῖ **P** Ac Ba || **19** ἀδήλως ἀλλήλων Ba, m. 1 Vc; ἀδήλων (m. po.: ἀλλήλων) εἰς ἄλληλα Pc; ἀδήλως εἰς ἄλληλα Pa Ac || **20** ἡ om. Vc Ba | ὡς ἐπὶ παραδείγματος δὲ Ac || **22** Dem. 18, 44-49 (cf. 158, 17) | περιϊὼν **P** | ὁ om. Pc | pr. καὶ Pa **V**; ἢ Pc || **24** ἑαυτῷ Ac, m. 2 Vc | τῆς πόλεως Ac || **26** παρεσκεύαζεν Vc Ba || **27** οὗτος λόγος Ac | τὸ ἓν πνεῦμα schol. **P** (W VII 828, 20)

It is worth knowing that a pneuma continuing in (*the same*) figure for many cola ought then to change and fall into a different figure, and perhaps a third might follow the second in turn, for such continuity and succession makes the language in the pneuma rich; for example, if you change from the declarative to | the in- [189]
terrogative, as Demosthenes began with declarative clauses, "But he who was appropriating Euboea," and then ended with a question, "whether in doing these things he was doing harm and was breaking the truce?" Or, conversely, if you change to the deictic or to something else after having asked a question. But you should know that after remaining in one figure it is good to change to another, for often this has made the language in the pneuma so beautiful that when speakers changed into a third figure the hearers leaped to their feet, as though the course of the speaker's eloquence was reaching its peak (*akmē*), which the change of figure has conveyed to the hearers.

Speculation about what an *akmē*[240] is has misled many. The akme of a speech is not the same in language and in thought, and the akme of a thought is something different from that in language. An akme in language is a change of the figures in a pneuma; an akme in thoughts occurs when, after completing one thought in a pneuma, one changes to another thought without being noticed and makes that a pneuma, then goes from that to another pneuma. In this way an akme comes into being from things succeeding each other unnoticed. As an example, this Demosthenic passage should be cited, that we may know that the combination of the pneumas is an akme (Dem. 18.44): "For when Philip was going around and subduing the Illyrians and Triballi, and some of the Greeks as well, and was bringing many large forces under his control, and some men from the cities, under the | opportunity [190]
offered by the peace, going there were being corrupted, of whom this man was one, then, then it was, that all against whom he was making these preparations were at war. But if they did not realize it, that is another question, not my concern." The pneuma continues up to this point; then wanting to elaborate "not my concern" he composed another pneuma (18.45): "For I was con-

[240] Cf. note 95 on 2.7 above, p. 59. In 4.9, p. 177 below, the author cites what he regards as a wrong definition of akme.

*καὶ προὔλεγον καὶ διεμαρτυρόμην καὶ παρ᾽ ὑμῖν ἀεὶ καὶ ὅποι πεμφθείην· αἱ δὲ πόλεις ἐνόσουν»*, *καὶ τοῦτο μέχρι τῶν προδοτῶν προχωροῦν ἓν πνεῦμά ἐστιν· εἶτα λέγει «καὶ τὰ ἄλλα πλὴν ἐκείνους ὅμως ἄλλους οἰομένους πωλεῖν πρώτους ἑαυτοὺς πεπρακότας ᾐσθῆσθαι», ἀπὸ γὰρ τούτου καταλιπὼν πάλιν τὸ «ἐγὼ οὐκ αἴτιος» ἐργάζεται πνεῦμά τι ἄλλο, ὅτι οἱ προδόται πρὸ τῶν ἄλλων ἑαυτοὺς πιπράσκουσιν «ἀντὶ γὰρ φίλων καὶ ξένων, ἃ τότε ὠνομάζοντο, νῦν κόλακες καὶ θεοῖς ἐχθροὶ καὶ πάντα ἃ προσῆκεν ἀκούουσι», καὶ τὰ παραδείγματα ληφθέντα εἰς κατασκευήν ἐστι τούτου, καὶ ἔστη ἐνταῦθα «ἐπεὶ διά γε ὑμᾶς καὶ πάλαι ἂν ἀπωλώλειτε»· ὥστε ἡ τῶν τριῶν πνευμάτων σύνθεσις ἀκμὴ γέγονεν ἐντελὴς ἐκ νοημάτων οὖσα. Ἐπὶ τούτῳ προσθετέον ἐκεῖνο, ὅπερ ἐστὶ λαμπρὸν πάνυ καὶ ποιεῖν καὶ εἰδέναι, ὅτι* | [191] *ἀκμῆς γινομένης ἀπὸ τῶν νοημάτων δεῖ τελευταῖον τηρεῖν τὸ ποριμώτερον δεῖ γὰρ ἀεὶ τὸν λόγον αὔξειν, πορικώτερον δέ ἐστι τὸ ἐκ παραδειγμάτων τὴν σύστασιν λαβεῖν δυνάμενον ἢ παραβολῶν. οὕτω γὰρ τῆς τέχνης τὴν τάξιν σε διδασκούσης καὶ ἐπὶ τὸ κρεῖττον κατ᾽ ὀλίγον προαγομένης καὶ ἀναγούσης εὐδοκιμεῖν ἡ ψυχὴ δοκεῖ, τῆς τέχνης δι᾽ ὧν προσῆκεν ὁδευούσης· καὶ γὰρ ὁ Δημοσθένης τὰ περὶ τοὺς προδότας παραδείγματα τελευταῖα ἐφύλαξε, καὶ Ὅμηρος τὸ κατὰ κῶλον πνεῦμα ἐν πράγμασι πληρώσας ἐπὶ τὴν παραβολὴν ἦλθεν*

*«ἀσπὶς ἄρ᾽ ἀσπίδ᾽ ἔρειδε, κόρυς κόρυν, ἀνέρα δ᾽ ἀνήρ·*
*ψαῦον δ᾽ ἱππόκομοι κόρυθες λαμπροῖσι φάλοισι*
*νευόντων· ὡς πυκνοὶ ἐφέστασαν ἀλλήλοισιν»,*

*εἶθ᾽ ἡ παραβολὴ*

1 καὶ **P**; om. **V**, schol. **P**, Dem. 18, 45 | διεμαρτυράμην **V**, schol. **P** || 3 Dem. 18, 46 | γρ τοῖς δὲ προεστηκόσι (προεκστηκόσι Pa) καὶ τἆλλα· πλὴν ἑαυτοὺς οἰομένοις πωλεῖν **P** | ἐκείνους om. Vc Ba | ὅμως om. **V** || 4 οἰόμενοι Vc Ba | πεπρακότες ᾔσθεσθε Vc Ba || 5 οὐκ ἐγὼ **V** | τι om. Ac || 7 καὶ τοῦ θεοῦ ἐ. Vc Ba || 9 ἐνταῦθα πληρώσας Vc Ba | γρ καὶ οὕτως· καὶ ἔστη ἐνταῦθα πληρώσας· γρ καὶ οὕτως καὶ τὰ παραδείγματα ληφθέντα εἰς κατασκευήν ἐστι τοῦ ἀλλ᾽ οὐκ ἔστι ταῦτα οὐκ ἔστι mg. **P**; γρ΄ τοῦ ἀλλ᾽ οὐκ ἔστι ταῦτα οὐκ ἔστιν· ἐπεὶ διά γε ὑμᾶς καὶ πάλαι ἂν ἀπωλωλε⌊evan.⌉ m. 2 Vc | καὶ **P**; om. **V**, Dem. 18, 49 || 10 ἀπολώληται Ba; ἀπολώλ⌊ει; m. 2 ?⌉τε Vc || 11 τούτοις Pa || 12 πάνυ καὶ τὸ εἰδέναι καὶ τὸ ποιεῖν Ba, (⌊I⌉ καὶ et καὶ τὸ ποιεῖν er.) Vc | γενομένης Vc Ba || 14 ἐκ **PV**; ἀπὸ schol. **P** || 16-17 ἀναγούσης Pa Ac; ἐναγούσης Pc; προαγούσης Ba; ?m. 1 (ἀν m. po.) Vc || 17 εὐοδουμένης Ac; εὐοδούσης schol. Pa, (mg. ad scholion γρ΄ ὁδευούσης) Pc || 18 καὶ γὰρ καὶ Vc Ba | Dem. 18, 48 || 19 ἐδίδαξε Pc || 19-20 versuum ordo cum his pugnat || 21 Hom. Π 215 | δ᾽ ἄρ᾽ Pa

tinually warning and protesting, both among you and wherever I was sent, but the cities were diseased," and this continues as one pneuma up to the reference to the traitors. Then he says (18.46), "those others who were thinking that they were selling everything except themselves have come to realize that they had sold themselves first"; for departing from the I-am-not-the-cause argument he elaborates another pneuma, to the effect that the traitors had sold themselves before selling others: "for instead of friends and guest-friends, as they were called then, now they hear themselves called flatterers and god-forsaken and all the things that they deserve," and examples are cited in support of this, and he stopped here (18.49), saying, "since left to yourselves you would have perished long ago." And so the combination of the three pneumas becomes an akme, being complete from the thoughts.

We should add to this something that is very splendid to do and to know: that | when an akme occurs from the thoughts, it is [191]
necessary to keep the finer point to the last—for it is always necessary to amplify the speech—and it is finer to be able to derive the composition from examples or comparisons. For thus, while the art is teaching you arrangement and little by little leads you forward and upward to the better, your mind seems to gain distinction, the art pointing the way to go. Demosthenes kept the examples of the traitors to the end, and Homer, after completing a pneuma describing things colon by colon, came to a comparison (*Iliad* 16.215–217:

> Shield pressed on shield, helm on helm, and man on man;
> The horse-hair crests on the bright helmet-ridges touched each other, As the men nodded, so close they stood to each other.

Then the comparison (16.212–214):[241]

[241] The comparison actually precedes the description in the Homeric text.

*«ὡς δ' ὅτε τοῖχον ἀνὴρ ἀράρῃ πυκινοῖσι λίθοισι*
*δώματος ὑψηλοῖο, βίας ἀνέμων ἀλεείνων,*
*ὣς ἄραρον κόρυθές τε καὶ ἀσπίδες ὀμφαλόεσσαι.»*

## *Περὶ τάσεως.*

*Τάσις δέ ἐστι λόγου, ὅταν ὑπεραίρῃ τῷ μέτρῳ τὸ πνεῦμα μακρότερον γινόμενον ὑπὲρ τὸ δύνασθαι ἐν ἰδίῳ ληφθῆναι τοῦ λέγοντος πνεύματι. τοῦτο γάρ ἐστιν* | [192] *ἡ τάσις τὸ ἀποτετάσθαι ἐπὶ μήκιστον ἢ χρὴ τὸ πνεῦμα. καταφορὰ δέ ἐστιν ἡ ἐν τῇ κατηγορίᾳ τάσις. τίνι δὲ διαλλάττει; ὅτι ἡ τάσις καὶ ἐν ἀπολογίαις εἶναι δύναται, ἡ καταφορὰ δὲ οὐκ ἂν γένοιτο ἐν ἀπολογίᾳ.*

## *Περὶ διλημμάτου.*

*Τὸ δὲ διλήμματόν ἐστι σχῆμα μὲν λόγου, δριμύτητος δὲ δόξαν ἔχον καὶ ἀληθείας. ἔστι δὲ τοιοῦτον, ὅταν δύο ἐρωτήσεις ἐρωτῶντες τὸν ἀντίδικον πρὸς ἑκατέραν ὦμεν εἰς λύσιν παρεσκευασμένοι. δεῖ δὲ τὰς ἐρωτήσεις ἐναντίας ἀλλήλαις εἶναι ὡς πάντως ἢ ταύτην ἢ ἐκείνην ἀποκριθησομένου τοῦ ἐχθροῦ· εἰ μὲν οὖν ἔχοιμεν ἀμφοτέρας λῦσαι, δεῖ ἐρωτᾶν κατὰ διλήμματον, εἰ δὲ μή, μὴ προτείνειν τὸ σχῆμα. ἐὰν γὰρ τῶν ἐρωτήσεων ἡ ἑτέρα ῥᾳδία ᾖ τῷ ἐχθρῷ πρὸς ἀπόκρισιν, σοὶ δὲ δύςλυτος, πάντως ἡττήσῃ· ἐρωτᾷς γὰρ ἢ ὡς οὐκ ἀποκριθησομένου ἢ ὡς, εἰ καὶ ἀποκρίναιτο, λῦσαι· εἰ δὲ ἀποκρινόμενός σε νικήσειεν, ἑαυτῷ αἴτιος ἐγένου τῆς ἥττης. οὐδὲ γὰρ ἐν ταῖς ἁπλαῖς ἐρωτήσεσι, μή τί*

1 Hom. Π 212 || **2-3** **V**; om. **P** || **4** περὶ τασεως λόγου **V** || **5** δὲ **P Pπ**; om. **V** | μέτρωι τοῦ λόγου τὸ Pc || **6** γενόμενον τοῦ δύνασθαι Ba, (τοῦ ex cr.; m. 2 ?) Vc || **7** μακρότερον Portus || **8** τῇ **P**; om. **V**, W VII 903, 24, Anon. III 115, 15 Sp. || **9** ἀπολογίαι Pc || **12** τὸ δὲ **P Pπ**, m. 2 Vc; om. **V** | σχῆμα μὲν Pa **Pπ**, m. 2 Vc; μὲν[β] σχῆμα[α] Pc; μὲν om. **V**, cf. schol. **P**; γρ τὸ δὲ διλήματτον ἔστι μὲν σχῆμα λόγου Pa, (om. γρ; om. μὲν) Pc | δὲ om. **V**, schol. **P** (W VII 834, 7) || **13** ἀληθείας Ac; mg. ἐχρῆν ἀληθείας εἰπεῖν οὐχὶ ἀλή[θ] κτλ. schol. **P**; ἀλήθειαν **P** Vc Ba | cf. Aps. I 2 p. 285, 12 Sp.-H. || **14** ἑκατέραν Pa Ac, (σ m. 1 supr.) Pc; ἑκατέρας Vc Ba || **15** ἀλλήλ[αις, ex ων ?] Pa || **16** ἀποκρινομένου **P** | εἰ μὲν οὖν **P**; καὶ εἰ μὲν **V** || **17** διλήμματον[τα] **P**; διλήμματα Vc Ba; ?Ac || **18** ῥαιδία μὲν τῶ Ac | ἧι post γὰρ **V** || **19** ἡττήσει **P**; ἡττηθήσῃ Ac, v.l. **P**; ἥττησαι Vc Ba | ἀποκριθησομένου τοῦ ἐχθροῦ ἢ **V** (cf. l. 16) || **20** καὶ om. Vc Ba | ἀποκρίνοιτο **V** | τοῦ ante λῦσαι add. Vc Ba; λύσων ? | σε om. Pc | νικήσει σεαυτῶ Sc

As when a man builds a wall with close-set stones,
The wall of a lofty house, to avoid the force of winds,
Even so close were arrayed their helms and bossed shields.

## CHAPTER 5: ON TASIS

It is a *tasis*[242] in speech whenever a pneuma exceeds the mean, becoming longer than can be taken in any one breath of the speaker, for | tasis is stretching out a pneuma to a longer extent than neces- [192]
sary. Tasis in prosecution is *kataphora.*[243] In what does it differ? In that there can be tasis in defenses, but there would not be kataphora in a defense.

## CHAPTER 6: ON DILEMMATON

*Dilēmmaton* is a figure of speech[244] with a reputation for startling effect (*drimytēs*) and truth. It occurs whenever we ask our opponent two questions and are prepared to refute either answer. The questions must be opposites of each other, stated so our enemy (*ekthros*) will accept one or the other completely as his answer. If then we can refute both, we should pose the questions as a dilemmaton, but if not, we should not employ the figure; for if one of the questions is easy for the enemy to answer and his answer difficult for you to refute, you will be quite defeated, for you are asking either on the assumption that he will not answer or if he were to answer, so that you may refute him. But if he answers and prevails, you have yourself become the cause of your own defeat. Even in

242 I.e., "extension.," not used as a rhetorical term in any earlier text.

243 I.e., "tirade, verbal diarrhea," attacking the defendant; kataphora is not used as a rhetorical term in any earlier text.

244 *Dilēmmaton* rather than *dilēmma* is the usual name of the figure (cf. *antitheton* for *antithesis*); Apsines 8.1; anonymous, *On Figures* (in vol. 3, p. 115 Spengel); Latin *complexio* (Cicero, *On Invention* 1.45), *conclusio* (*Rhetoric for Herennius* 2.38), or *divisio* (4.52); described by Aristotle as a topos in *Rhetoric* 2.23.15 but without being given a name.

[193] *γε κατὰ διλήμ|ματα ἐρωτᾶν δεῖ, εἰ μὴ τότε, ὅταν ἢ μὴ ἔχῃ, τί ἀποκρίνηται, ἢ ὅταν μέλλῃ τοῦτο ἀποκρίνεσθαι, ὃ σοὶ συμφέρει· καθόλου γὰρ ὁ ἐρωτῶν ὡς εἰς νίκην τῇ ἐρωτήσει θαρρῶν ἐρωτᾷ.*

*Τὸ δὲ διλήμματόν ἐστι τοιοῦτον οἷον «πότερον παρῆς τούτοις γινομένοις καὶ συνευφραίνου ἢ οὐ παρῆς;» ἐάν τε γὰρ εἴπῃ «παρήμην καὶ συνευφραινόμην», παρεσκεύασται ὁ ῥήτωρ εἰπεῖν «πῶς οὖν κατηγορεῖς τούτων, οἷς συνευφραίνου;» ἐὰν δὲ λέγῃ «οὐ παρήμην», ἀπαντήσεται αὐτῷ ὅτι «δίκης ἄξιος τοῖς ἀγαθοῖς τοῖς τῆς πόλεως μὴ συμπαρών». καὶ πάλιν «ᾔδεις τὰ μέλλοντα ἢ οὐκ ᾔδεις;» ἐάν τε γὰρ εἴπῃ «ᾔδειν», ἀπαντᾷ «τί οὖν οὐ προέλεγες;» ἐάν τε εἴπῃ «οὐκ ᾔδειν», «τί οὖν ἡμῶν ὡς μὴ εἰδότων κατηγορεῖς; εἰ μὲν γὰρ ᾔδεις, προειπεῖν ὤφειλες· εἰ δὲ οὐκ ᾔδεις, τί τῶν ἄλλων ὡς μὴ εἰδότων κατηγορεῖς, τῆς ἀγνοίας τῶν μελλόντων κοινῆς οὔσης πρὸς πάντας ἀνθρώπους;»*

*Γίνεται δὲ τὰ διλήμματα ἤτοι τῶν δύο ἐρωτήσεων δι᾽ ἓν πέρας ἐρωτωμένων οἷον «εἴτε καλὴν ἔγημας εἴτε αἰσχράν, οὐκ ἔδει γῆμαι»· ἓν γὰρ πέρας συνάγεται ἐξ ἀμφοτέρων, τὸ μὴ δεῖν γῆμαι, διὰ μὲν τὸ καλὴν κοινήν, διὰ δὲ τὸ αἰσχρὰν ποινήν· καὶ τὰ μὲν κοινὰ διλήμματα*
[194] *ταῦτά ἐστιν· ἢ ὅταν τῶν ἐρωτήσεων ἑκάστη | ἰδίας ἀποδόσεως δέηται, τοῦτο δὲ τὸ διλήμματον σεσόφισται καὶ Δημοσθενικόν ἐστι σχῆμα.*

1 γε ταῖς κατὰ Ac | p. 170, 1 διλήμματον (α supra ον) Pc || 1-2 ἀποκρίνοιτο Ac || 2 ὅταν om. **V** | μέλλ⌊ηι m. 2⌉ Vc; μέλλει Ba; μέλλοι Ac | σοὶ om. Pa || 3 ὡς om. Pa | εἰς om. m. 1 Pc || 4 οἷον om. Ac | cf. Dem. 18, 217 || 7 συνηυφραίνου Vc Ba | δὲ **P**; τε **V** | εἴπηι **V** || 8 ἄξιος εἶ Sc | τοῖς om. Vc Ba || 9 cf. Dem. 18, 196; Π. στ. p. 69, 15 | μέλλοντα ἔσεσθαι **V** || 10 ἐρεῖ ante alt. τί suppl. m. 2 Vc (ἐρεῖ ὅτι τί Sc) || 10-11 ὡς ἡμῶν (om. μὴ) **V** || 11 γρ ὡς εἰδότων Pa || 12 μὴ om. **V** || 14 ⌊δὲ τὰ⌉ Pa; τὰ om. Pc || 15 cf. Antisthenes, Diog. Laert. VI 3. Bion, D. L. **IV** 48 || 16 mg. ἐν ἄλλοις οὐκ ἔστι τὸ πέρας **P** || 16-17 διὰ μὲν — ποινήν suspecta || 17 τοῦ καλὴν . . . τοῦ αἰσχρὰν **P** || 17-18 καὶ — ταῦτα post. p. 170, 18 δέηται Vc Ba || 18 ἐστιν om. Vc Ba || 19 Δημοσθενικόν: cf. Π. στ. 69, 11 ann.; W **IV** 632, 18. 633, 1 | σχῆμά ἐστιν **V** | ὅπερ καὶ παρ᾽ ἡμῶν ἐν τῆι τέχνηι <cf. Herm. Π. στ. 68, 19 sq.> ὡς παραγραφικὸν μεμελέτηται post σχῆμα add. **P** (παρημῶν — μεμελέτηται lemma) Mr, (τῆ διαιρετικῆι τέχνηι ὡς παραγραφικὸν ἀντιληπτικῶς μ.) Ac; mg. m. 1 γρ καὶ παρ᾽ ἡμῶν ἐν τῆι διαιρετικῆ τέχνη ὡς παραγραφικὸν ἀντιληπτικῶς μεμελέτηται **P**; interpolationem om. m. 1 Vc Ba (m. 2 add.: ὅπερ . . . τῆ <διαιρετικῆ m. po. add. Vc> τέχνηι ὡς παραγραφικὸν ἀντιληπτικῶς μ.)

single questions one should not ask something | in the manner of [193]
dilemmata,[245] unless (*your opponent*) has nothing that he can say in answer or when he is going to give an answer that is to your advantage. Generally speaking, he who asks a question asks with confidence in winning a point by means of the question.

A dilemmaton is something such as, "Were you present at these happenings and did you share the joy or were you not present?"[246] If he says, "I was present and shared the joy," the orator has laid the basis for saying, "How, then, do you bring an action against those with whom you shared the joy?" But if he says, "I was not present," you will confront him with the statement that "a person deserves to be punished who did not share in the city's good fortunes." Or again, "Did you know what was going to happen or did you not?"[247] If he says he did know, meet him with, "Why then did you not give warning?" If he says he did not know, (*ask*,) "Why then do you prosecute us because we did not know? For if you had known, you ought to have given warning, and if you did not know, why prosecute others as not knowing, since ignorance of what is going to happen is common to all men?"

Dilemmata result either from two questions asked for one conclusion—for example, "Whether you marry a beautiful woman or an ugly one, there is no necessity to marry";[248] one conclusion is drawn from both, that there is no need to marry, because a beautiful woman is promiscuous and an ugly one is a pain (*to look at*); these are common forms of dilemmata—or when each of the ques-
tions | requires its own reply; this kind of dilemmaton is clever [194]
and is a Demosthenic figure [which has been studied by us in our *Art* as an example of counterplea in stasis of exception.[249]]

[245] I.e., as a rhetorical question.

[246] The dilemma is derived from Demosthenes 18.217, which, however, is not in the form of a question: "If he (Aeschines) was present (and joined in rejoicing with others)..., surely his present action is atrocious... If he was not present, surely he deserves to die for grieving at the sight of things that brought rejoicing to others."

[247] Based on Demosthenes 18.196, which is, however, not in the form of a question.

[248] Cf. Diogenes Laertius 4.48 (Bion) and 6.3 (Antisthenes).

[249] Cf. Hermogenes, *On Stases,* pp. 68–69 Rabe, but in editing *On Invention* Rabe deleted the clause as a later addition.

## *Περὶ παρηχήσεως.*

*Παρήχησις δέ ἐστι κάλλος ὁμοίων ὀνομάτων ἐν διαφόρῳ γνώσει ταὐτὸν ἠχούντων. γίνεται δέ, ὅταν δύο ἢ τρεῖς ἢ τέσσαρας λέξεις ἢ ὀνόματα εἴπῃ τις ὅμοια μὲν ἠχοῦντα, διάφορον δὲ τὴν δήλωσιν ἔχοντα, ὡς παρὰ τῷ Ξενοφῶντι «πείθει τὸν Πειθίαν» καὶ παρὰ τῷ Ὁμήρῳ «ἀλλ᾽ Εὐπείθει πείθοντο», κἀκεῖ μάλιστα ἐναργῶς*

*«ἤτοι ὅ γ᾽ ἐς πεδίον τὸ Ἀλήιον οἶος ἀλᾶτο*
*ὃν θυμὸν κατέδων, πάτον ἀνθρώπων ἀλεείνων».*

*ἐνταῦθα γὰρ ὅμοια μὲν ἀλλήλοις ἠχεῖ τὸ «Ἀλήιον» καὶ τὸ «ἀλᾶτο» καὶ τὸ «ἀλεείνων», ἀλλὰ τὸ μέν ἐστι τόπου ὄνομα, τὸ «Ἀλήιον», τὸ δὲ «ἀλᾶτο» πρᾶγμα, τὸ δὲ «ἀλεείνων» πρᾶγμα μὲν καὶ αὐτό, ἄλλο δὲ παρὰ τὸ σεσημασμένον. καὶ ὁ Θουκυδίδης «καὶ μὴν τότε Αἴγυπτος ὑπὸ* [195] *βασιλεῖ ἐγένετο πλὴν Ἀμυρταίου τοῦ | ἐν τοῖς ἕλεσι βασιλέως· τοῦτον δὲ διὰ μέγεθος τοῦ ἕλους οὐκ ἠδύναντο ἑλεῖν καὶ ἅμα μαχιμώτατοί εἰσι τῶν Αἰγυπτίων οἱ Ἕλειοι»· ἕλος μὲν γὰρ ὁ τόπος, ἑλεῖν δὲ τὸ πρᾶγμα, Ἕλειοι δὲ οἱ ἐνοικοῦντες.*

## *Περὶ κύκλου.*

*Κύκλος ἐστὶ σχῆμα λόγου καὶ αὐτὸ ἑρμηνείας ἴδιον κάλλος ἐμπεριέχον. γίνεται δέ, ὅταν, ἀφ᾽ οὗ ἄρξηταί τις ὀνόματος ἢ ῥήματος, εἰς τὸ αὐτὸ καταλήξῃ πάλιν μήτε πτῶσιν ἀλλάξας μήτε σχῆμα μήτε χρόνον μήτε ἀριθμὸν μήτε ἄλλο τι· οἷον «σοὶ μὲν γὰρ ἦν κλέπτης ὁ πατήρ, εἴπερ ἦν ὅμοιος σοί»· ἀπὸ γὰρ οὗ ἤρξατο μορίου, τῆς ἀντωνυμίας, εἰς <τὸ> αὐτὸ κατέληξεν. ἐγχωρεῖ δὲ καὶ περιοδικῶς αὐτὸ*

**2** δὲ **P**; om. **V** **P**π || **3** γίνεται δὲ **V**, schol. **P** (W VII 837, 1); οἷον **P** | δύο ἢ **V**, schol. **P**; om. **P** | ἢ καὶ τέσσαρας **V** || **4** εἴποι **P** || **5** Xen. Hell. VII 1, 41 (Πεισίαν . . . πείθει) | π⌊ει m. 2; ex υ ?⌉θίαν Vc; πιθίαν Ac Ba | τῷ om. **V** | Hom. ω 465 || **6** ἀλλ᾽ οὐκ **P** | πεπίθοντο Vc Ba, schol. **P** | κάλλιστα (κ m. 1 ex μ) Pa, (μ m. po.) Pc || **7** ὁ καππεδιον schol. **P**, Hom. Z 201 || **9** ἀλήϊον πεδίον Vc Ba || **12** τὸ suppl. m. 2 Vc | ⌊προ supr. m. po.⌉σεσημασμένον Pc | Thuc. 1, 110 || **13** ἀμυνταίου Ba, (ρ ex ν) Vc | τοῦτο Ba || **14** μέγεθός τε Ac, Thuc. | ἠδύνατο Pc Vc Ba | εἰσὶν post 15 ἔλιοι Vc Ba || **18** λόγου post ἐμπεριέχον **P** Ac || **18-19** ἐμπεριέχ⌊ο ex ω⌉ν Vc || **19** ἄρξεται Pc Ac || **20** ἐναλλάξας Ac || **20-21** μήτε σχῆμα μήτε χρόνον om. schol. **P** (W VII 838, 8) || **21** Dem. 10, 73 || **23** τὸ Spengel | κατέληξεν Ac; ἔληξεν **P**; καὶ κατέληξεν Vc Ba

## CHAPTER 7: ON PAREKHESIS

*Parēkhēsis*[250] is an ornament consisting of similar words with different meanings echoing the same sound. It occurs when someone says two or three or four expressions or words having similar sounds but a different denotation, as in Xenophon (*Hellenica* 7.1.41), "He persuades (*peithei*) the Pithian," and in Homer (*Odyssey* 24.465), "They were persuaded (*peithonto*) by Eupeithes," and most clearly (*Iliad* 6.201–202), "Then indeed he wandered (*alato*) alone over the Aleian Plain, / devouring his spirit, shunning (*aleeinōn*) the path of men." Here, *Alēion* and *alato* and *aleeinōn* are similar to each other in sound, but the first is the name of a place, the Aleian Plain, and *alato* is an action, and *aleeinōn* is also an action but with a different signification. Also Thucydides (1.110): "Now at that time Egypt was under the king (*of Persia*), except for Amyrtaeus, the | king in the marshes, but [195]
they were unable to capture (*helein*) him because of the extent of the marsh (*helous*) and also because the marshmen (*Heleioi*) are the most warlike of the Egyptians." A *helos* is a place, and *helein* is an action, and *Heleioi* are the inhabitants.

## CHAPTER 8: ON KYKLOS

*Kyklos*[251] is a figure of speech with its own special beauty of expression. It occurs whenever one ends (*a sentence, clause, or phrase*) with the same noun[252] or verb with which one began, changing neither case nor figure[253] nor tense nor number nor anything else; for example (Dem. 10.73), "You had a thief for a father if he was like you," for he ended with the same part of speech, the pronoun, with which he began. Kyklos can be said in a periodic way

[250] I.e., resemblance in sound, paronomasia, including alliteration; cf. anonymous, *On Figures* (in vol. 3, p. 115 Spengel).

[251] Cf. what Alexander (*On Figures* 2.5) calls *symplokē* and the figure Quintilian (9.3.31) describes without naming it. The term *kyklos* is not used in this sense elsewhere; cf. Martin, 302.

[252] *Onoma*, "name, noun," includes pronouns and adjectives.

[253] Here meaning grammatical mood.

*λεχθῆναι δύνασθαι, καὶ μὴν καὶ διηγηματικῶς, ὡς ὁ Δημοσθένης ἐν τῷ Πρὸς Λεπτίνην «λέγεται τοίνυν τειχίζειν ἐκεῖνος εἰπὼν οἴχεσθαι πρεσβεύων εἰς Λακεδαίμονα», καὶ διελθὼν τὰ κατὰ τὸν Θεμιστοκλέα πάλιν ὁμοίως ἐπαύσατο «καὶ πάντες ἴστε, ὃν τρόπον ἐξαπατῆσαι λέγεται»· τὸν γάρτοι κύκλον οὐχ ὁ ῥυθμὸς ἐλέγχει ἀλλὰ ἡ ἀρχὴ καὶ ἡ τελευτή.*

*Εἴρηται δὲ κύκλος ἀπὸ τῶν ἐν τῇ γῇ γραφομένων κύκλων· ὥσπερ*
[196] *γὰρ ἐκείνων διὰ τὸ ἐξ ἴσου πανταχόθεν | περιφερὲς ἡ ἀρχὴ ἄδηλος, ὅθεν ἂν ἐθελήσωμεν τεκμήρασθαι οὐ δυναμένων τὴν ἀρχήν, οὕτω δὴ καὶ τούτων, ἐκ τῆς ὁμοιότητος τῶν ὀνομάτων ἀμφιβόλου τῆς ἀρχῆς καθισταμένης, ὅθεν εἶναι δύναται. διόπερ εἰ θέλοιμεν, αὐτὸ τοῦτο ἀφοριζόμενοι τὸ τί ἐστι κύκλος, ποιῆσαι τὸ σχῆμα τοῦ λόγου ἐν τῷ περὶ αὐτοῦ λέγειν τοῦ κύκλου, ἔσται δὴ οὕτω· κύκλος ἐστὶ τὸ ἀφ᾽ ὧν ἂν ἄρξηταί τις ὀνομάτων ἢ ῥημάτων εἰς τὰ αὐτὰ καταλήγειν δύνασθαι πάλιν· τοῦτο γάρ ἐστιν ὁ κύκλος.*

## *Περὶ ἐπιφωνήματος.*

*Τὸ ἐπιφώνημα λόγος ἐστὶν ἔξωθεν ἐπὶ τῷ πράγματι παρ᾽ ἡμῶν λεγόμενος. δεῖ δὲ αὐτὸν καὶ προσέχεσθαι τῷ ὑποκειμένῳ ὡς ἐκείνου μέρος ὄντα, ἵνα μὴ ἀπᾴδῃ, δεῖ δὲ αὐτὸν καὶ ἔξωθέν τι προσειληφέναι, ἵνα ᾖ καὶ ἡ τοῦ ἐπιφωνήματος φύσις φανερά. τὸ δὲ προσλαμβανόμενον ἔξωθεν τετολμῆσθαι δεῖ ἀσφαλῶς· διὰ τοῦτο γάρτοι καὶ ἐπιφώνημα λέγεται, οὐχ ὅτι αὐτὸ τὸ πεπραγμένον λέγεται, ἀλλ᾽ ὅτι τῷ γιγνομένῳ ἐπιφωνεῖται· μέχρι γὰρ ἄν τις κατὰ κῶλον μεμετρημένως διατυποῦν*
[197] *ἐθέλῃ τὸ γινόμενον, τὸ πρᾶγμα λέγει, ἐὰν δὲ πανσά|μενος ἐπενέγκῃ τι τῷ παντὶ ὡς παρ᾽ αὐτοῦ ἔξωθεν, τοῦτο ἐπιφώνημα λοιπόν ἐστιν, οἷον*

**2** ἐκεῖνος τειχίζειν **V**, Dem. 20, 73 || **3** πρεσβεύσων Pa | τὰ Pa Ac, (ὁ m. 1 supr.) Pc; τὸ Vc Ba | τὸν om. Pc || **4** καὶ ante πάλιν add. Pa **V** | ἐπαύσατο ὁμοίως Pc || **5** τοι om. Pc || **5-6** καὶ τὸ τέλος **V** || **8** ἐπ᾽ ἐκείνων Vc Ba | πανταχόθεν λαμβάνεσθαι· ὅθεν (om. cet.) Vc Ba || **9** θελήσωμεν Pc | δυναμέν⌊ων m. po.⌉ Ba | εὑρεῖν post ἀρχὴν add. **V** || **9-10** οὕτω (δὴ om.) καὶ ἐπὶ τούτου Vc Ba; γρ οὕτωσι δὲ καὶ τούτων m. 2 Vc || **10** νοημάτων Pa || **11** δύναται (αι ο), m. 1 supr., Pc; δύναιτο Ac | διόπερ **P** Ac; διὸ καὶ Vc Ba || **12** ὁ κύκλος **V** || **13** ἔσται δὴ **P**; λελέχθω **V**, v.l. **P** || **14** ἢ ῥημάτων **V**, v.l. **P**, schol. **P** (W VII 840, 3 sq.), cf. p. 172, 19; om. **P** || **15** ἐστι ⌊II⌉ κύκλος Pc || **16** ἐπιφωνημάτων Pa **P**π Ac || **17** τὸ **P P**π; om. **V**, Dox. II 253, 9 W. | ἐστι λόγος **V**, Dox. || **19** δὲ om. **P** || **20** ἧι post φύσις **V** || **21** τοι om. Vc Ba || **22** τὸ om. Pa | τῶ πεπραγμένω ἐπ. Ac || **23** μὲν γὰρ vulg. | ἂν m. 2 suppl. Vc | τις ante διατυποῦν **V** || **24** ἐθέλει Ba, (η m. 2) Vc | γένόμενον (ι supr.) Pa || **25** λοιπόν om. Vc Ba

and in narrative as well, as Demosthenes does in *Against Leptines* (20.73): "It is said (*legetai*), then, that after telling them to build the wall, he[254] went off as an ambassador to Lacedaimon." After going through an account of Themistocles' doings, he ended in the same way: "And you all know in what way he deceived them it is said (*legetai*)." It is not the rhythm that is evidence of the kyklos but the beginning and the ending.

*Kyklos* has its name from circles drawn in the ground, for just as | it is unclear where the line begins because their circum- [196] ference is everywhere equidistant (*from the center*), and thus from wherever we want to start the beginning cannot be determined, so here the similarity of the words makes it doubtful where the beginning can be. Thus, in making the very definition of what a kyklos is, if we want to create that figure of speech in speaking about the kyklos, it will be this: Kyklos is the ability to end with the same nouns or verbs from which one began, for this is a kyklos.[255]

## CHAPTER 9: ON EPIPHONEMA

An *epiphōnēma* is a comment from outside the subject said by us.[256] It should be applied to the subject as being a part of it, in order not to be irrelevant, but it also should be something introduced from outside in order that its nature as an epiphoneme may be clear. Introducing something from outside must be ventured cautiously. An epiphoneme is called this because it does not state what has been done but makes an additional comment (*epiphōneitai*) about what has happened. So long as one tries to give a vivid description of something, measured colon by colon, he is stating the subject, but if at the end | he adds to the whole some- [197] thing, as it were, of his own from outside the subject, what results

254 Themistocles in 480 B.C.E.

255 An example of the figure being defined.

256 It is a sententia or comment at the end of a description implying the speaker's opinion on a situation; cf. Theon, vol. 2, p. 103 Spengel, where an epiphoneme is a comment "appropriately and briefly approving what is said . . . to the effect that it is true or noble or beneficial, or that other famous men have thought the same"; cf. also Quintilian 8.5.11 and n. 46 above for additional references. In this chapter the author, turgid at best, expresses himself in a particularly awkward way, and the example offered seems singularly poorly chosen.

*«σὺν δ᾽ Εὖρός τε Νότος τ᾽ ἔπεσε Ζέφυρός τε δυσαὴς*
*καὶ Βορέης αἰθρηγενέτης μέγα κῦμα κυλίνδων»*

*καὶ «σὺν δὲ νεφέεσσι κάλυψε γαῖαν ὁμοῦ καὶ πόντον», μέχρι τούτων ἡ διατύπωσις, τὸ δὲ «ὀρώρει δ᾽ οὐρανόθεν νύξ» ἐπιφώνημα λοιπόν ἐστιν· ᾗ μὲν γὰρ ἐκ τῶν νεφῶν σκότος γίνεται, προσέχεται τῇ ἀληθείᾳ καὶ ἴδιον τοῦ πράγματος ἐγένετο, ᾗ δὲ ἐξ οὐρανοῦ λέγει τὴν νύκτα γεγονέναι, δὶς ἐτόλμησε, καὶ νύκτα εἰπὼν τὸ ἄλλο σκότος καὶ ἐξ οὐρανοῦ γεγονέναι, ὅθεν οὐδέποτε γίνεται σκότος οὐδὲ νύξ. Καὶ τὸ μὲν ἀληθινὸν ἐπιφώνημα τοῦτό ἐστιν.*

[198] *|῎Εστι δὲ καὶ ἄλλο ἐπιφωνήματος εἶδος τρόπον τινὰ γινόμενον, ὃ καὶ ἀκμὴν ἐκάλεσαν τινές, οὐκ ὀρθῶς ὁρίζοντες ἐν ἑνὶ κώλῳ ἀκμήν, ἐπεὶ μηδέ, ὅθεν γίνεται, δύναταί τις εἰδέναι. ἔστι δὲ τοῦτο τοιοῦτον, ὅταν πνεύματος κατὰ μέρος ἀποταθέντος ἐν πολλοῖς κώλοις ἐπὶ τέλει πάλιν ἓν κῶλον τεθῇ, συλλήβδην ὡς εἰπεῖν πᾶν τὸ πνεῦμα δυνάμενον ἀφορίσασθαι καὶ ἔχειν ἐν ἑαυτῷ· οἷον*

*«Αἴας δ᾽ οὐκέτ᾽ ἔμιμνε, βιάζετο γὰρ βελέεσσι»*

*καὶ ὅλον τὸ παρ᾽ Ὁμήρῳ πνεῦμα· κατὰ μέρος γὰρ εἰπὼν τὰ συμβάντα τῷ Αἴαντι καὶ ἐπισυμβαίνοντα ἐπὶ τέλει πάλιν ὥσπερ ἐν ἑνὶ κώλῳ*

1 Hom. ε 295 | ἔπεσε Vc Ba; ἔπεσον Ac, m. 2 Vc; ὄρωρ᾽ ἐπαΐξας **P**; om. schol. **P** (W VII 841, 8) || **3** Hom. ε 293 | νεφέεσι Pa, (alt. σ supr.) Pc; νέφεσσι Vc || **5** εἰ μὲν Vc Ba || **ad 5-8** m. 1 Pa ascripta sunt: <v.l. I> ἣ δὲ ἐξ οὐρανοῦ λέγοιτο τὴν νύκτα γεγονέναι. δὶς ἐτόλμησεν· καὶ νύκτα εἰπὼν τὸ ἄλλο σκότος· καὶ τῶ ἐξ οὐρανοῦ γεγονέναι εἰπεῖν· ὅθεν οὐδέποτε γίνεται σκότος οὐδὲ νύξ· <v.l. II> γρ καὶ οὕτως· ἧι μὲν γὰρ ἐκ τῶν νεφῶν σκότος γίνεται. προσέχεται τῆι ἀληθεία· καὶ ἴδιον τοῦ πράγματος ἐγένετο· ἣ δὲ ἐξ οὐρανοῦ λέγοιτο τὴν νύκτα γεγονέναι. δὶς ἐτόλμησεν· καὶ νύκτα εἰπὼν τὸ ἄλλο σκότος· καὶ ἐξ οὐρανοῦ γεγονέναι εἰπών, ὅθεν οὐδέποτε γίνεται σκότος οὐδὲ νύξ: <v.l. III> γρ καὶ οὕτως· ἣ δὲ ἐξ οὐρανοῦ λ<sup>έ</sup> τὴν νύκτα γεγονέναι. δεῖ σε τολμήσαντα καὶ νύκτα εἰπόντα τὸ σκότος· τὸ καὶ ἀλλὰ καὶ ἐξ οὐρανοῦ γεγονέναι εἰπεῖν· ὅθεν οὐ γίνεται σκότος οὐδὲ νύξ: —sic Pa; in Pc legitur v.l. I (add. γρ). sed lectionis II finis (inde a δὶς ἐτόλμησεν) et lectionis III initium (usque ad νύκτα γεγονέναι) interciderunt et in v.l. III γέγονεν εἰπεῖν legitur || **6** γίνεται **V** | εἰ (ᾗ m. po.) δὲ Ba, (εἰ in ras.) Vc || **ad 6-8** m. 2 Vc: γρ ἧι δὲ ἐξ οὐρανοῦ λέγει τὴν νύκτα γεγονέναι δὶς ἐτόλμησε· καὶ νύκτα εἰπὼν τὸ ἄλλο σκότος καὶ τὸ ἐξ οὐρανοῦ γεγονέναι — τοῦτό ἐστιν || **6** λέγεις Vc Ba || **7** δεῖ σε τολμήσαντα καὶ νύχτα εἰπόντα τὸ σκότος Vc Ba, (τὸ ἄλλο σκότος) schol. **P** | καὶ τὸ ἐξ **V** || **8** εἰπεῖν post γεγονέναι add. **V**, schol. **P** | σκότος ἐπιγίνεται Ac | καὶ et μὲν om. Vc Ba || **11** cf. 164, 14 sq. || **13** ἐν om. Vc Ba || **14** τὸ αὐτὸ Ac || **16** Hom. Π 102 || **17** ὅλον τὸ . . πνεῦμα Vδ, m. 2 Vc, (τὸ ὅλον τὸ) Ac; ὅλον τῶι . . πνεύματι **P** Vc Ba | λέγεται post πνεύματι add. Vc Ba || **18** καὶ ἐπισυμβαίνοντα om. Vc Ba | πάλιν ἐπὶ τέλει Ac | ἐν om. Ac

is an epiphoneme; for example (*Odyssey* 5.295), "Euros and Notos and ill-blowing Zephyros fell upon him together, and Boreas, begetter of clear sky, rolling a great wave," and "hid the earth and sea together with clouds." Up to this point there is diatyposis, but the rest, "night rose from the heavens," is an epiphoneme. In so far as darkness comes from clouds, the statement keeps to the truth and was a property of the subject, but in that he says night has come from heaven, he ventured two thoughts, calling this other darkness "night" and saying it came from heaven, which is never the source of darkness or night. And this is a true epiphoneme.

| There is another species of epiphoneme occurring in a certain way that some have called an *akmē*, wrongly defining an akme as something occurring in one colon, since then it is impossible for anyone to know where it came from.[257] This occurs whenever a pneuma has been divided, part by part, into many cola and one colon has again been put at the end, being able, as it were, to sum up the whole pneuma in one clause and include it in itself; for example (*Iliad* 16.102): "Ajax no longer remained, for he was forced by the spears," and the whole pneuma as it continues in Homer. [198]

[257] For the author's definition of *akmē,* see 4.4 above, pp. 165–67.

*πάντα ἐπαλιλλόγησεν εἰπὼν «πάντῃ δὲ κακὸν κακῷ ἐστήρικτο».*

*Ἔστιν ἐπιφωνηματικὰ καὶ τὰ ἀπὸ τῶν τροπῶν ὀνόματα ἑλκόμενα λοιπὸν εἰς τὸ πρᾶγμα, τολμηρῶς ἡμῶν βιαζομένων τὰ ἐκ τοῦ ἀλλοτρίου πράγματος εἰς τὸ ἡμέτερον μεταφέρειν ὡς τὸ ἀσφαλὲς ἐχόντων διὰ τὸ καὶ εἰς τὴν παραβολὴν αὐτὰ προειρηκέναι· οἷον ἐάν τις ναυάγιον ἐκ παραβολῆς εἰπὼν ἐν λόγῳ, εἶτα μεταβαίνων εἰς τὰ πράγματα ἐθελήσῃ λέγειν κατ᾽ ὄνομα ἕκαστον τῶν ἐκ τῆς ναυαγίας σημαίνων τὸ ὑποκείμενον, οἷον «ἐν χειμῶνι καὶ νῦν ἐστι τὰ τῆς πόλεως πράγματα καὶ κλύδωνι, καὶ σαλεύεται τὰ καθεστηκότα καὶ δεῖται τοῦ κυβερνήσον|*[199]*τος αὐτά». καὶ πάλιν αὐτοῦ μεμνησόμεθα τούτου ἑξῆς ἐν τῷ περὶ τροπῆς λόγῳ.*

## *Περὶ τροπῆς.*

*Τροπὴ δέ ἐστι τὸ μὴ ἐξ ὑποκειμένου πράγματος ἀλλοτρίου δὲ σημαντικὸν ὄνομα θεῖναι κοινὸν εἶναι δυνάμενον καὶ τοῦ ὑποκειμένου καὶ τοῦ ἔξωθεν ἐμφαινομένου, ὃ καλεῖται καὶ μεταφορὰ παρὰ τοῖς γραμματικοῖς, οὐχ ὡς ἐκεῖνοι λέγουσι τὸ ἀπὸ τῶν ἀψύχων ἐπὶ τὰ ἔμψυχα καὶ τὸ ἀνάπαλιν· ἀλλὰ καθόλου ἡ ῥητορικὴ πολυπραγμονοῦσα μηδὲν μήτε ἐμψύχων μήτε ἀψύχων, οὕτω χρῆται τοῖς ἀλλοτρίοις ὀνόμασιν, οἷον «προπέποται τὰ τῆς πόλεως πράγματα», ἀντὶ τοῦ προδέδοται, καὶ «τιθασεύουσιν»· ἐμφαίνεται γὰρ ἐκείνῳ τε τῷ ὀνόματι τὸ συμπόσιον μὴ ὑποκείμενον καὶ τούτῳ τὰ θηρία τιθασευόμενα τῷ λόγῳ μὴ ὑποκείμενα. τούτου δὲ τοῦ εἴδους εἴ τις ἐφαψάμενος πληρώσειε καὶ τὸ ἐφεξῆς τῆς τροπῆς ὄνομα, ὡς πᾶσαν ἐνθεῖναι τὴν παραβολήν, ἀρετὴν*

1 Hom. Π 111 || **2** ἔστι δὲ Ac | ἔστι δὲ καὶ ἐπιφωνηματικὰ τὰ Vc Ba | ἑλκόμενα Ac, v.l. Pc, v.l. m. 2 Vc; ἐκλαμβανόμενα **P** Vc Ba; mg. ἑλκομένων Pa || **3** τὰ **P** Ac; αὐτὰ Vc Ba || **4** πράγματα **P**, ?m. 1 Ac | ὡς τὸ **P** Vc Ba; τὸ δὲ Ac, cf. schol. **P** (W VII 845, 19) || **7** ἐθελήσειεν **V** | τῆς om. Ac | σημαῖνον Ac || **10** τούτου μεμνησόμεθα **V** | l. 22 || **13** δὲ **P**; om. **VPπ** || **15** παρὰ om. Pa || **16** ἐμψύχων ἐπὶ τα ἄψυχα Vc Ba || **17** ἀνάπαλιν· καθόλου γὰρ **V**, v.l. **P** || **19** Dem. 3, 22 || **20** Dem. 3, 31 | τιθασεύουσιν ἀντὶ τοῦ κολακεύουσιν Sc | τε om. Ba || **21** μὴ suppl. m. 2 Vc Ba | μὴ ὑποκείμενον om. Ac, v.l. **P** | τιθασευόμεθα om. Ac

After saying, part by part, what happened to Ajax, he added the following again at the end, as though repeating everything in one colon, saying (*Iliad* 16.111): "And everywhere evil was heaped on evil."

Furthermore, words brought into the account from tropes[258] are also epiphonematic when, in a daring way, we are forcefully transferring a meaning from another subject to ours, thinking ourselves to be safe because of having said this earlier in a comparison; for example, if someone uses a comparison to a shipwreck in a speech, then going back to the subject he wants to say how each word in the comparison applies to the original subject; thus, "The affairs of the city are now in a storm and sea of troubles, and the established order is being shaken and needs some one to steer | it." [199]
We shall mention this again below in the discussion of trope.

## CHAPTER 10: ON TROPE

*Tropē* is a matter of using a word whose signification is not derived from the subject matter at hand but from something else, but which can be applied in common to the subject and a subject brought to light from elsewhere.[259] Among the grammarians it is called metaphor, but it is not, as they say, something transferred from the lifeless to the living or the reverse.[260] Generally, rhetoric uses transferred words without making much of whether something is living or lifeless; for example (Dem. 3.22), "The interests of the city have been poured out (*like wine*)," instead of "betrayed," and (Dem. 3.31), "They are taming you." By the former word a drinking party, which is not under discussion, is implied, and by the latter wild animals being tamed, which is not the subject under discussion. If after using this kind (*of transference*) one supplied the word for which the trope stands,[261] so as to com-

[258] I.e., metaphors, which imply a judgment on the part of the speaker.

[259] For an enthusiastic discussion of this chapter, which differs significantly from accounts of metaphor by Aristotle and other ancient writers, see Patillon, *Théorie du discours*, 314–19; more briefly in *L'Art rhétorique*, 306–8.

[260] Generally four kinds of metaphor were identified: animate for animate; inanimate for inanimate; inanimate for animate; animate for inanimate; cf., e.g., Quintilian 8.6.9–10.

[261] I.e., explained the metaphor.

ἐποίησεν, εἰ δὲ ἐλλείψειε, κακοζηλότερόν ἐστιν· οἷον «ἐχθρὸν ἐφ᾽ ἡμᾶς
αὐτοὺς τηλικοῦτον ἠσκήσαμεν», εἰπὼν ὄνομα καὶ λαβὼν ἀπὸ τοῦ ἀγῶνος εὐθέως ἀπέδωκεν «ἢ φρασάτω τις ἐμοί, πόθεν ἄλλοθεν ἰσχυρὸς ἢ
παρ᾽ ἡμῶν αὐτῶν γέγονε Φίλιππος» καὶ τὰ ἑξῆς ὁμοίως. Δεῖ μέντοι
εἰδέναι, ὅτι, ὅσα μέν ἐστι συντελικὰ τῆς τροπῆς, εὐθὺς ἀποδοθήσεται,
[200] ὅσα δὲ | γελοιότερα, διὰ πολλοῦ, τῷ χρόνῳ λανθάνοντα καὶ τῷ μὲν
τεχνίτῃ κατάδηλα ὄντα, τοῖς ἀτέχνοις δὲ μὴ φαινόμενα. τοῦτο μὲν οὖν
σεμνὸν ὂν εὐθέως ἀπεδόθη· τὸ δὲ «προπέποται τὰ τῆς πόλεως πράγματα» εἰ μὲν εἶχεν ἐγγὺς παρακειμένην τὴν ἀπόδοσιν, γελοιότερον ἂν
ἦν, διὰ πολλοῦ δὲ λανθάνον οὐ φαίνεται· ὑποβαίνων γὰρ ἐρεῖ ὧδέ που
«μεθύει τῷ μεγέθει τῶν πεπραγμένων Φίλιππος», ὥρμητο δὲ τὸ τοῦ
μεθύειν ὄνομα ἀπ᾽ ἀρχῆς τοῦ «προπέποται», ἐδόκει δὲ εἶναι γελοιότερον εὐθὺς παρακείμενον τῷ «προπέποται» τὸ «μεθύει». τῷ μέντοι
«μεθύει» παρακείμενον τὸ «ὀνειροπολεῖ» σεμνὸν ὂν ἐκόσμησε τὸν λό-
γον· κοινὸν γάρ ἐστι τῶν μεθυόντων τὸ ὀνειροπολεῖν.

## Περὶ σεμνοῦ λόγου.

Σεμνὸν δέ, εἴ τί πού ἐστιν ἐν τοῖς οὖσι, τί ἄλλο μᾶλλόν ἐστιν ἢ
λόγος; καὶ τὸ μὲν σεμνὸν τοῦ νοῦ σεμνῶς οὐχ ἑρμηνεύεται ὑπὸ τῆς τοῦ
ῥήτορος δυνάμεως ἀλλ᾽ ὑπὸ τῆς ἀνάγκης αὐτοῦ τοῦ πράγματος, οἷον
«ὁ μὲν δὴ μέγας ἐν οὐρανῷ Ζεὺς πτηνὸν ἅρμα ἐλαύνων» καὶ ὅσα ἄλλα
[201] τοιαῦτα· ὅπου δ᾽ ἂν ὁ νοῦς αἰσχρὸς ᾖ, | ἐκεῖ χρεία τῆς σεμνότητος τοῦ
λόγου, ἵνα τὸ νοούμενον αἰσχρῶς οὕτως ἐξενέγκῃ τις τῷ λόγῳ εὐφυῶς,
ὄνομα ἀντ᾽ ὀνόματος ἀμείβων, ὡς μὴ δόξαι τισὶν αἰσχρὸν εἶναι τὸ πρᾶγμα διὰ τὴν τοῦ λόγου σεμνότητα, ὡς παρὰ τῷ Μενάνδρῳ· πυθομένου

1 Dem. 3, 28 | ἐφ᾽ ἡμᾶς ἐχθρὸν **P** || **2** τοιοῦτον, m. 1 τηλικοῦτον supr., Vc | ἠσκήκαμεν Ac | εἰπὼν γὰρ Ac || **3-4** γέγονε φίλιππος ἢ παρ᾽ ἡμῶν αὐτῶν **V** || **5** εὐθέως **V** || **6** λανθάνεται Pc | τῶι μὲν τῶι Vc || **7** δὲ μηδὲ Pa Ba || **8** ὂν om. Vc Ba | Dem. 3, 22 || **9** εὐθὺς **V** (cf. 10) || **9-10** ἦν ἄν **P** || **10** διὰ om. Ba | δὲ τεθὲν λανθάνον **V**, v.l. **P** | οὐ Pc, (δὲ m. 1 supr.) Pa; οὐδὲ **V**, v.l. Pa | ὑποβαίνων: at in alia oratione leguntur! | ὧδέ om. **V** || **11** Dem. 4, 49 (ἐκεῖνον μεθύειν κτλ.) | ὥρμηται Vc Ba, m. 1 Pa | τοίνυν (pro δὲ) Ac | τοῦ om. Ac || **12** δὲ Ac; γὰρ **P** Vc Ba || **13** τ⌊ῷ m. 1 ex ὁ] Vc Ba | pr. μεθύειν Ac | τ⌊ῷ m. 2 ex ὁ] Vc; τὸ Ba || **14** alt. μεθύειν Pc | ὂν **P** Ac; ἂν Vc Ba || **15** τῶν μεθυόντων Ac, v.l. Pa; τῆς μέθης **P** Vc Ba || **17** εἴ Vδ; ἦν Pc Vc Ba; ἣν Pa | τί ἂν ἄλλο Vc Ba || **17-18** σεμνὸν δέ τι. ἢ νοῦ ἐστιν ἢ λόγου· καὶ τὸ Ac, v.l. **P**; alia v.l. **P**: γρ καὶ οὕτως· σεμνὸν δὲ ἢ νοῦ ἐστιν ἢ λ^ό || **20** Plat. Phaedr. 246 E || **21** δὲ (om. ἂν) Vc Ba | εἶ Ba; εἴη Sc; ?m. 1 Vc | ἐκεῖ **V**; τότε **P** || **22** ἐξενέγκοι Pc, (η supr.) Pa | τῷ λόγῳ om. Ac || **23** ὄνομα ὀνόματι **V** || **24** Men. fr. 558, III p. 170 Kock

plete the comparison, it would be a good thing, but if one left it out it is rather bad style (*kakozēloteron*); for example (Dem.3.28), "we have provided a *training ground* for this formidable rival," using a word taken from athletics; then he continued immediately, "or let someone tell me the source of Philip's strength if it is not from us," and similarly in what follows. It is, however, necessary to know that whatever completes the meaning of the trope will be
added immediately, and whatever | is rather laughable (*geloiotera*) [200]
will be added after an interval, (*thus*) escaping notice by the passage of time and being clear to the artist but not evident to the untrained. In the passage just cited, being serious, the explanation is offered immediately, but "the interests of the city have been poured out" would be rather laughable if the apodosis were near at hand, but after many words it escapes notice of seeming so. Further on[262] he will say somewhere (4.49), "Philip *is drunk* with the greatness of what has been done <and has visions in his mind>," and the expression "is drunk" was inspired by the earlier "poured out," but being drunk seemed rather laughable if placed next to "poured out." "To have visions (*oneiropolei*)," however, being serious, when put next to "is drunk" adorned the speech, for having visions is associated with being drunk.

## CHAPTER 11: ON SOLEMN LANGUAGE

If anything in the world is solemn (*semnon*), what else is more so than speech?[263] Now solemnity in thought is not given solemn expression from the orator's ability but derives from the needs of the subject itself; for example (Plato, *Phaedrus* 246e4–5), "Zeus, the great one in heaven, driving a winged chariot," and every-
thing else like that; but wherever the thought is shameful | there is [201]
need of solemnity of speech in order that one may express what is shameful in thought in speech that is discreet, changing one word for another so that the thing may not seem shameful to someone because of the solemnity of the language, as in Menander;[264] for

[262] The author is thinking of a scroll containing several speeches by Demosthenes, but he may not have remembered that two different speeches are here in question.

[263] Cf. Hermogenes, *On Ideas* 1.6.

[264] Frg. 382 Koerte.

*γάρ τινος κόρης, πῶς εἴη διεφθαρμένη, σεμνῶς ἀφηγήσατο πρᾶγμα αἰσχρὸν ὀνόμασι βελτίστοις «Διονυσίων ἦν πομπή, ὃ δέ μοι ἠκολούθησε μέχρι [τὰ] πρὸς τὴν θύραν, ἔπειτα φοιτῶν καὶ κολακεύων τὴν μητέρα ἔγνω με»· τὸ γὰρ ἐφθάρθαι καὶ ὑβρίσθαι σεμνῶς «ἔγνω με» εἰπὼν ἐκόσμησε πρᾶγμα αἰσχρὸν σεμνοτέρᾳ λόγου συνθέσει. γίνεται μὲν οὖν ἢ ὀνόματι ἡμῶν ἀντ' ὀνόματος χρωμένων, ἢ πολλάκις οὐδὲ λέγεται τὸ πρᾶγμα, ἐὰν αἰσχρὸν ᾖ πάνυ, ἀλλὰ τὰ πρὸ τοῦ πράγματος εἰωθότα γίνεσθαι λέγονται καὶ τὰ ἐπισυμβαίνοντα τῷ αἰσχρῷ πράγματι, ἅπερ ἐξ ἀνάγκης ἐναργῶς καὶ σεμνῶς δηλοῖ καὶ αὐτὰ τὰ σιγώμενα, σεμνῶς μὲν ὅτι μὴ λέγεται, ἐναργῶς δὲ ὅτι τοῖς ἑκατέρωθεν νοεῖται· ὡς παὶ παρ' Ὁμήρῳ*

*«λῦσε δὲ παρθενικὴν ζώνην, ἐπὶ δ' ὕπνον ἔχευεν.*
*ἡ δ' ὑποκυσσαμένη»*

*τέκετο, ὃν ἔφη τεκεῖν· ἐνταῦθα γὰρ τὴν συνουσίαν ἐδήλωσε τῷ καὶ τὰ* [202] *γενόμενα πρὸ τῆς συνουσίας εἰπεῖν | «λῦσε δὲ παρθενικὴν ζώνην» καὶ ἐπενεγκεῖν, ἃ μετὰ τὴν συνουσίαν γίνεται, «ἡ δ' ὑποκυσσαμένη».*

## *Περὶ κακοζήλου.*

*Τὸ δὲ κακόζηλον γίνεται ἢ κατὰ τὸ ἀδύνατον ἢ κατὰ τὸ ἀνακόλουθον, ὃ καὶ ἐναντίωμά ἐστιν, ἢ κατὰ τὸ αἰσχρὸν ἢ κατὰ τὸ ἀσεβὲς ἢ κατὰ τὸ ἄδικον ἢ κατὰ τὸ τῇ φύσει πολέμιον, καθ' οὓς τρόπους καὶ ἀνασκευάζομεν μάλιστα τὰ διηγήματα ἐκβάλλοντες ὡς ἄπιστα. διά τοι τοῦτό φαμεν καὶ τὰς διασκευὰς μέχρι τοῦ εἰκότος προχωρεῖν, ὡς, εἰ παρὰ τὸ εἰκὸς εὑρεθείη τι, πάντως καὶ κακόζηλον ἐσόμενον καὶ ἐμπεσούμενον τῇ ἀνασκευῇ· καὶ γὰρ ἐκεῖ λέγομεν «οὐκ εἰκὸς τόδε πραχθῆναι», ἢ ὅτι ἀδύνατον ἢ ὅτι αἰσχρὸν καὶ τὰ ἑξῆς. γίνεται δὲ τὸ κακόζηλον ὅμως καὶ*

1 ⌊I-II⌉πρᾶγμα Ac || **2** με Vc Ba || **3** τὰ **PV**, Anon. III 118, 1 Sp.; τοῦ Sc; del. m. 2 Vc || **4** διεφθάρθαι Pc; ἐσχίσθαι Ba; ἐ⌊φθ (ἀρ supra) m. 2⌉θαι Vc || **5** συνθήκηι **V** | μὲν οὖν **P**; οὖν οὕτως **V**, v.l. **P** || **6** ἢ om. Vc Ba | χρωμένων ante ἀντ' Pc || **7-8** γίνεσθαι καὶ λέγεσθαι Pa; λέγεσθαι καὶ γίνεσθαι (β α supr. m. 1) Pc || **9** δηλοῖ **P**; μηνύει **V** || **12** Hom. λ 245. 254 | παρθενίην Ba, ex cr. Vc | κατὰ (pro ἐπὶ) Ac || **14** γὰρ καὶ Vc Ba || **15** παρθενίην Vc Ba | τῶι add. ante καὶ **P** Ac, post καὶ Sc || **16** τέκετο add. Ac; τέκετο ὃν ἔφη τεκεῖν add. Vc Ba, cf. p. 182, 14 || **20** τῇ om. Pc Ac || **21** τοῦτό τοι Ac; τοῦτο γὰρ (om. τοι) Vc Ba || **22** p. 128, 14 | προχωρεῖν **V**, v.l. **P**; om. **P** || **23** pr. καὶ om. **V** || **23-24** τῆι ἀνασκευῆι ἐμπεσούμενον **V**

when a maiden was asked how she had been sexually violated, she narrated a shameful act solemnly in well-chosen words, saying, "It was at the procession of the worshipers of Dionysus, and the man followed me to the gate; then he kept coming back and flattering my mother and 'knew' me." By referring to the harm and insult done her in the solemn phrase "he knew me," she adorned a shameful action by a more solemn turn of phrase. Now this happens when we use one word for another, or often the action is not even stated, if it is quite shameful, but things that usually happen before the action are stated and things that ensue the shameful deed, all of which necessarily also makes what is left unspoken evident in a clear and solemn way: solemn because not stated but clear because it is suggested by the attendant circumstances; as indeed in Homer (*Odyssey* 11.245 and 254), "He loosed her maiden girdle,[265] and shed sleep upon her /. . . And she, having conceived," gave birth to those he said that (*Poseidon*) had begotten. He indicated their coming together by saying what happened before their coming together, | "He loosed her maiden girdle," and by [202]
adding what resulted from their intercourse, "And she, having conceived."

## CHAPTER 12: ON KAKOZELON

*Kakozēlon*[266] originates by (*stating*) what is impossible or inconsistent, which is also incompatible, or what is shameful or irreverent or unjust, or what is hostile to nature. These are the main ways we most refute narratives, rejecting them as incredible.[267] For this reason we say that artistic developments (*diaskeuai*) should only proceed up to the limit of probability, since if something is invented beyond what is probable it will be quite inept and subject to refutation; for then we say, "It is not probable that this was done," or that it is impossible or shameful, and so on. Kakozelon also occurs when we use one metaphorical term

[265] Poseidon is described as impregnating Tyro, who gives birth to Pelias and Neleus.

[266] Literally, "striving for what is bad"; affectation, bad taste, a faulty style; cf. Demetrius, *On Style* 186–189.

[267] Cf. Theon, vol. 2, p. 93 Spengel; Pseudo-Hermogenes, *Progymnasmata*, ch. 5.

*τροπικῇ λέξει μιᾷ χρησαμένων, εἶτα τὸ πλῆρες τῆς τροπῆς ἀποδοῦναι μὴ δυναμένων.*

*Ἰστέον μέντοι, ὅτι τὰ κακόζηλα ἔστι πολλάκις ἰᾶσθαι τῇ προκατασκευῇ καὶ προθεραπείᾳ· τὰ γὰρ προμαλαχθέντα τῇ ἑρμηνείᾳ νοῦν εἰσάγει, ὅθεν καὶ τὸ τόλμημα προσδοκᾶται τοῖς ἀκούουσιν, ὃ καὶ πρὶν λεχθῆναι ἀσφαλὲς εἶναι δοκεῖ, γυμνὸν δ' ἂν τεθῇ πρὸ τῆς κατασκευῆς*
[203] *τοῦ λόγου, κακόζηλον ἔδοξεν ἢ τῷ νῷ | ἢ τῷ λόγῳ. καὶ σκόπει, πῶς καὶ Ὅμηρος ἐποίησεν· ὡς γὰρ λέξειν ἔμελλεν*

*«ἧκε δ' ἀπορρήξας κορυφὴν ὄρεος μεγάλοιο»,*

*φοβούμενος τούτου τὸ ἀδύνατον προκατασκευάζει τοιοῦτον ἄνδρα τῷ λοιπῷ διηγήματι, ὡς μηδὲ τὸν περὶ τούτου λόγον ἄπιστον καταστῆναι λεχθέντα, τῷ τε τροφὰς αὐτῷ παραθεῖναι μείζονας ἢ κατὰ ἄνθρωπον τῷ τε ἀποδοῦναι αὐτῷ ῥόπαλον βαστάζειν, οἷον οὐκ ἄνθρωπος, καὶ λίθον καὶ τῷ τὴν ἰδέαν αὐτοῦ διελθεῖν ὡς μεγάλην καὶ φοβερὰν καὶ τῷ εἰπεῖν*

*«οὐδὲ ἐῴκει*
*ἀνδρί γε σιτοφάγῳ, ἀλλὰ ῥίῳ ὑλήεντι»·*

*πάντες γὰρ οἱ περὶ τούτου προγυμνασθέντες λόγοι πιστὸν ἐποίησαν εἶναι δοκεῖν τὸ παράδοξον τὸ περὶ τοῦ Κύκλωπος ῥηθὲν τὸ*

*«ἧκε δ' ἀπορρήξας κορυφὴν ὄρεος μεγάλοιο»·*

*εἰ γὰρ καὶ τοιοῦτος ἦν, οἷον αὐτὸν προκατεσκεύαζεν, οὐδὲν ἦν τὸ καὶ τοιοῦτον αὐτὸν ποιῆσαι δυνηθῆναι.*

*Γίνεται δὲ τὸ κακόζηλον καὶ κατὰ τὸ εὐτελὲς πολλάκις, ὡς ἐκεῖνο*

*«οἴμοι, δράκων μου γίνεται τὸ ἥμισυ».*

1 μιᾷ om. Pc | χρωμένων Vc Ba; χρησαμένων ἡμῶν Ma || 3 cf. Π. ὕψ. 32, 3 || 4 τῆι add. ante καὶ Vc, (m. 1 supr.) Ac; post καὶ Ba | mg. ἐν ἄλλοις τῇ προθεραπεία καλουμένη **P** | καλουμένηι post προθεραπείαι add. **V** || 5 ὅθεν et τὸ om. Ac | ὃ **P**; διότι Vc Ba; ὅτι v.l. **P**; om. Ac || 6 προκατασκευῆς Ac || 7 καὶ σκόπει om., ὡς pro πῶς Vc Ba || 9 Hom. ι 481 || 10 sq. cf. schol. Odyss. ι 187 || 11-12 λεχθέντα καταστῆναι Ac || 13 ῥόπαλον αὐτῶι δοῦναι **V** | ἀ̅ν̅ο̅ς̅ (ν supr.) **P**; ἄ̅ν̅ο̅ς̅ Vc, m. 1 Ba; ἀ̅ν̅ο̅ν̅ Ac || 16 Hom. ι 190 || 19 τὸ ῥηθὲν παράδοξον περὶ τοῦ (τοῦ om. Ac) κύκλωπος τὸ **V** || 22 <τι> τοιοῦτον? || 23 γὰρ (pro δὲ) Ac || 24 Eurip. fr. 930 N.[2]

and then cannot continue with what completes the trope.[268]

You should know, however, that kakozelon is often remedied by preparation (*prokataskeuē*) and preventive treatment (*prothera-peia*), for what is softened in expression ahead of time introduces a thought from which the hearers expect something daring; it seems to be safe even before it is said, but if baldly stated before given support by the language, it would seem kakozelon either in thought | or in word. Consider how Homer managed it (*Odyssey* [203]
9.481). When he was about to say (*of the Cyclops*), "He broke off and hurled the peak of a mighty mountain," fearing the impossibility of this, he prepared for such a man in the rest of the narrative, so that the remark would not be incredible when spoken about him, by attributing to him food greater than a human eats and by giving him a club to hold that a human could not, and a stone, and by describing his appearance as large and fearsome, and by saying (9.190), "nor was he like / a man who eats grain but like a wooded peak"; for all the preparatory words (*progym-nasthentes logoi*) about him made the paradoxical statement about the Cyclops, that "he broke off and hurled the peak of a mighty mountain," seem credible, for if he was such as Homer had earlier described, it was nothing for him to be able to do something like this.

Kakozelon also occurs often by cheapening something, as in "Alas, the half of me is becoming a snake."[269] These kakozela

[268] Cf. 4.10 above, p. 180,1.

[269] Euripides, frg. 930 Nauck², of Cadmus; cf. Hermogenes, *On Ideas* 2.10, p. 391 Rabe.

*θεραπεύεται δὲ τὰ κακόζηλα οὐ τῇ προδιορθώσει μόνῃ ἢ τῇ? προκα-*
[204] *τασκευῇ, ὡς ἐδείξαμεν, ἀλλὰ καὶ τῇ ἐπιδιορ|θώσει καλουμένῃ. δεῖ δὲ εἰδέναι, ὅτι τὰ εὐτελῶς εἰρημένα ἡ σεμνότης διορθοῦται, ὡς παρὰ τῷ Εὐριπίδῃ*

*«οἴμοι, δράκων μου γίνεται τὸ ἥμισυ»,*

*τοῦτο γὰρ κοινῶς καὶ εὐτελῶς εἰπὼν ἐθεράπευσε τῇ ἐπιφορᾷ*

*«τέκνον, περιπλάκηθι τῷ λοιπῷ πατρί»·*

*τοῦτο δὲ οὐ μόνον σεμνῶς εἴρηται, ἀλλὰ καὶ ἐπιφωνηματικῶς διὰ τὸ τετολμῆσθαι. οὗ τὸ ἐναντίον, ἐὰν συμβῇ τινι μετὰ σεμνότητα εἰς αἰσχρὸν κατενεχθῆναι, κακόζηλον ἐγένετο, ὡς ἑτέρωθι ὁ αὐτὸς*

*«ἣ δὲ καὶ θνήσκουσ᾽ ὅμως*
*πολλὴν πρόνοιαν εἶχεν εὐσχήμως πεσεῖν»,*

*τοῦτο σεμνῶς εἰπὼν ἐπήνεγκεν εὐτελὲς καὶ κοινὸν καὶ κακόζηλον*

*«κρύπτουσ᾽, ἃ κρύπτειν ὄμματ᾽ ἀρσένων χρεών».*

## ***Περὶ ἐσχηματισμένων προβλημάτων.***

1 τὸ^α κακόζηλον^α Pc | καὶ (pro ἢ) Ac || 2 p. 184, 3 || 8 τοῦτο δὲ **P**; καὶ τοῦτο **V** | εἴρηκεν Vc; εἴρ^η Ba || 11 θνήσκουσ᾽ Pc, Eurip. Hec. 568; πίπτουσ᾽ Pa **V** Mr || 12 εὐσχημόνως Pa Ba, m. 1 Vc || 13 cf. Elsperger, Philologi suppl. XI 87 || 14 ὄμμασιν Ba; ?m. 1 Vc || 15 περὶ τῶν Sc || 15-190.5 cf. Π. ἰδ. p. 286, 5-8. 386, 26 sq. Sp.; [Dion.] II 1 p. 295 sq. Us.; Fuhr, Nov. Symb. Joachim. 1907 p. 112

are remedied not only by preventive treatments and preparations, as we have shown, but also by what is called *epidiorthōsis* (*subsequent correction*),[270] | and you should know that solemnity corrects [204]
whatever is meanly said, as (*here*) in Euripides, "Alas, the half of me is becoming a snake," for after saying this in a common and mean way he remedied it by this addition: "Child, embrace what remains of your father." This is not only said in a solemn way but resembles an epiphoneme[271] in its daring. The opposite of this, if someone happens to descend to what is shameful after a solemnity, becomes a kakozelon, as elsewhere (*Hecuba* 568) the same poet says, "And as she was dying, nonetheless she kept much care to fall modestly." This is solemnly spoken, but he added what is cheap and common and affected, "hiding what it is right to hide from male eyes."

## CHAPTER 13: ON FIGURED PROBLEMS

*The final two chapters probably derive from a source or sources other than that on which the rest of* On Invention *is based and may have been added to the text by the creator of the Hermogenic corpus in the fifth century or by some subsequent editor. One kind of evidence for this conclusion is the use of terminology common in other rhetorical texts but either unknown to or deliberately rejected by the author of* On Invention*: forms of the verb* meletaō, *meaning "to practice declamation," and the adjective* meletikos, *for example, or the term* ephodoi, *meaning "approaches." Other differences include the phrase* ta auta noēmata, *used here to mean "and so on," but not found in that sense earlier in the work, and of course the special terminology describing "figured problems."*

*The original author of chapter 13 may be Apsines of Gadara. Syrianus attributes to Apsines a declamation that the author of this chapter claims to have invented and published.*[272] *Furthermore, ex-*

[270] Cf. Alexander, *On Figures* 1.3–4.

[271] Cf. 4.9 above, p. 175.

[272] See 4.13 below, p. 193.

*Τῶν ἐσχηματισμένων προβλημάτων τὰ μέν ἐστι κατὰ τὸ ἐναντίον, τὰ δὲ πλάγια, τὰ δὲ κατὰ ἔμφασιν.*

[205] | *Ἐναντία μὲν οὖν ἐστιν, ὅταν τὸ ἐναντίον κατασκευάζωμεν, οὗ λέγομεν· οἷον ᾔτησαν Ἀθηναῖοι παρὰ Λακεδαιμονίων εἰρήνην, οἳ δὲ ἀντῄτησαν Περικλέα, βουλευομένων τῶν Ἀθηναίων αὐτὸς ὁ Περικλῆς ὑβριοπαθῶν ἐπὶ τῇ βουλῇ ἀξιοῖ ἀπέρχεσθαι· ὁμολογουμένως γὰρ ὁ Περικλῆς, εἰ καὶ λέγει «πέμψατέ με», σχήματι μόνον λόγου λέγει, ἐπεὶ καὶ μεταχειρίσεσι χρῆται ταῖς κατασκευαζούσαις, ὅτι οὐ χρὴ πεμφθῆναι αὐτόν.*

*Πλάγιον δέ ἐστιν, ὅταν μετὰ τοῦ κατασκευάζειν τὸ ἐναντίον καὶ ἄλλο τι περαίνῃ ὁ λόγος· οἷον πλούσιος ἐν λιμῷ ὑπέσχετο θρέψειν τὴν πόλιν, εἰ λάβοι τὸν πένητα πρὸς σφαγήν, οὐκ ἔδωκεν ὁ δῆμος, ὁ πένης ἑαυτὸν προσαγγέλλει. ἐνταῦθα γὰρ τὸ ἐναντίον βούλεται ὁ πένης, οὗπερ λέγει· ἀποθανεῖν γὰρ οὐ βούλεται, κατασκευάζει δὲ ἐκ πλαγίου καὶ τὸ μὴ εἶναι τὸν σῖτον καὶ τὸ εἰ ἔστιν ἁπλῶς λαβεῖν.*

[206] | *Κατὰ ἔμφασιν δέ ἐστιν, ὅταν λέγειν μὴ δυνάμενοι διὰ τὸ κεκωλῦσθαι καὶ παρρησίαν μὴ ἔχειν ἐπὶ σχήματι ἄλλης ἀξιώσεως ἐμφαίνωμεν κατὰ τὴν σύνθεσιν τοῦ λόγου καὶ τὸ οὐκ ἐξὸν εἰρῆσθαι, ὡς εἶναί τε*

1-2 κατὰ τὸ ἐνάντιον **P**, Aps.; ἐναντία (om. κατὰ τὸ) **V** || 2 πλάγια **V**, Aps.; κατὰ τὸ πλάγιον **P** | ἔμφασιν **V**, Aps.; τὴν ἔμφασιν **P** || 3 ἐναντία **V**, Aps.; ἐναντίον Pc; ἐναντίον Pa (α m. 1 supr. !) | τὸ ἐναντίον post 1. 2 κατασκευάζωμεν Pc || 4 λέγωμεν Pa, Apsinis B | ἀθηναῖοι **V**, Aps.; οἱ ἀθηναῖοι **P** | cf. 190, 14 || 6 ὁμολογουμένως **P** Ac, Aps.; ὡμολογημένως Vc Ba | γὰρ om. Ac || 8 χρήσεται **V** || 11 περαίνει Pa Ba, ?m. 1 Vc || 12 cf. 10, 15 | πένητα m. 2 suppl. Vc || 13 γὰρ **P**, Aps.; γὰρ καὶ **V** | cf. [Dion.] II 1 p. 329, 15 Us. || 14 schol. **P**: παρὰ τῷ πλουσίῳ δηλονότι μὴ εἶναι σῖτον || 15 τὸν Pa **V**; om. Pc, Aps., cf. schol. **P** || 16 λέγειν **V**, Aps.; τι λέγειν **P**; ad λέγειν suppl. ἀντι m. 2 Vc || 17-18 ἐμφαίνωμεν **P**, Aps.; ἐμφαίνωμέν τι **V**, v.l. **P** || 18 τὸ **P** Vc Ba; ὃ Ac, (om. καὶ) v.l. Pc

*cerpts from the first four paragraphs of the chapter are preserved elsewhere and attributed to Apsines (Spengel-Hammer, 330–31; see Heath, "Apsines"). These excerpts appear in small print above the apparatus criticus in Rabe's Greek text but are not reprinted here.*

*The earliest reference to figured problems is found in Demetrius,* On Style *§294, dating from the first century* B.C.E.*; the fullest discussions are found in Pseudo-Dionysius,* Art of Rhetoric *2, chapters 8–9; Quintilian 9.2.65–92; and Apsines in Spengel-Hammer, 330–39 (= Patillon,* Apsinès, *112–21).*

Some problems are figured (*eskhēmatismena*) by saying the
opposite (*of what is meant*), some are deflected, and some contain
an implied meaning. | Problems are "opposed" (*enantia*) when- [205]
ever we are arguing for the opposite of what we actually say; for example, the Athenians sought peace from Lacedaimonians, but the latter demanded the surrender of Pericles in return. While the Athenians are debating, Pericles himself, indignant at the Council (*for not rejecting the proposal immediately*), proposes giving himself over. Even if he says, "Send me," Pericles is admittedly only using a figure of speech, since his treatment of the case demonstrates that it is not right for him to be sent.

It is a "deflected" (*plagion*) problem whenever, while arguing for the opposite side, the speech also accomplishes something else; for example, in time of famine a rich man promised to feed the city if he could take a poor man and slaughter him; the people refused, and the poor man denounces himself. Here the poor man wants the opposite of what he says, for he does not want to die, but he argues by deflection both that there is no grain and if there is it
can be simply got.[273] | [206]

It is "by implication" (*emphasis*) whenever we are not able to speak (*openly*) because hindered and lacking freedom of speech, but in the figure of giving a different opinion we also imply what cannot be spoken by the way the speech is composed, so that the hearers understand and it is not a subject of reproach to the speaker; for example, the law has ordered persons suffering from madness to go into exile. There being a rumor that a father has had intercourse with his son's wife, the son claims he (*himself*) should

[273] If grain cannot be obtained otherwise, he should be put to death so the rich man will supply it; but if there is grain somewhere (as there clearly is), there are other ways to get it (by taking it from the rich man).

*νοῆσαι τοῖς ἀκούουσι καὶ μὴ ἐπιλήψιμον εἶναι τῷ λέγοντι· οἷον τὸν μαινόμενον φεύγειν ὁ νόμος ἐκέλευε, φήμης οὔσης, ὅτι σύνεστιν ὁ πατὴρ τῇ τοῦ υἱοῦ γυναικί, ἀξιοῖ ὁ παῖς ὡς μαινόμενος φεύγειν· ἐνταῦθα γὰρ τῷ μὲν δοκεῖν περὶ τῆς φυγῆς διαλέγεται καὶ τούτῳ τῷ λόγῳ ἐπερείδεται, διόλου δὲ ἐμφαίνει τὴν μοιχείαν τοῦ πατρὸς κατὰ τῆς γυναικός.*

*Τὰ μὲν οὖν πλάγια καὶ τὰ ἐναντία ἐν τούτῳ διαλλάττει μόνον, ὅτι τὰ μὲν ἐναντία ἓν μελετᾶ, τὰ δὲ πλάγια καὶ διπλοῦν ἐκφέρει τὸν νοῦν, πολλάκις δὲ καὶ πλείονα. ἡ μέντοι μεταχείρισις ἡ αὐτή, ἀφ' ἧς τὸ μελετᾶν εἰδέναι γίγνεται. μελετῶνται γὰρ τῶν τοιούτων προβλημάτων αἱ ὑποφοραὶ ἀπὸ τῆς κατασκευῆς ἐκφερόμεναι κἀκεῖθεν πάλιν ἐκ τῶν ἐπιχειρημάτων, ὅσα ἂν εὑρίσκηται. ὁ γὰρ παρὰ τῶν ἐχθρῶν λόγος ἰσχυροποιούμενος, ἀσθενεστέρας ἀναγκάζων εἶναι τὰς λύσεις, ἐκεῖ* [207] *| δείκνυσι βούλεσθαι πλέον τὸν σοφιστὴν ἢ κατὰ τὸ δοκοῦν εἰσάγεσθαι, οἷον ὁ Περικλῆς ἐν τῷ αὐτὸς ἀξιοῦν ἀπελθεῖν εἰς Λακεδαίμονα. ὁ γὰρ ὑπὲρ αὐτοῦ λέγων ταῦτα ἐκ τῆς ὑποφορᾶς κατασκευασθῆναι ποιήσει, ἃ Περικλῆς εἶπεν ἂν αὐτὸς ὑπὲρ αὐτοῦ πάντως ἢ εἴ τις αὐτὸν ἄλλος μὴ διδόναι Λακεδαιμονίοις ἠξίου· «φήσει τοίνυν ἴσως παρελθών, ὡς οὐ δεῖ τοῖς ἐχθροῖς ἐπιτάττουσι πείθεσθαι· δεινόν τε γὰρ εἶναι τὸ πρᾶγμα καὶ ἠλίθιον, εἴ τις χαριεῖται κελεύουσιν ἐχθροῖς· φίλοις γὰρ ἐπιτάττουσι δεῖ πείθεσθαι καὶ οὐ πολεμίοις», καὶ ὅτι «οὐδὲ οἱ πατέρες ὑμῶν ὑπήκουσαν μηδενί, μήτε Ξέρξῃ μήτε Μαρδονίῳ μήτε Δαρείῳ μήτε ἄλλῳ τινί», καὶ ὅτι «μηδὲ ὑμεῖς μήτε Λακεδαιμονίοις πολλὰ ἐπιτάττουσι περὶ Ποτιδαίας καὶ περὶ Αἰγινητῶν καὶ περὶ Μεγαρέων». καὶ καθάπαξ μία μεταχείρισις ἐν τοῖς ἐσχηματισμένοις ἡ τῶν ὑποφορῶν κατασκευή.*

**2** ὁ **P**, Aps.; om. **V** | cf. W VII 24, 15 sq. || **6** ἐν om. Vc Ba || **8** δὲ Pc; om. Pa **V** || **9** γὰρ **P** Ac; δὲ Vc Ba || **10-11** κἀκεῖθεν — ἐπιχειρημάτων **P**, (ἐκ om.) **V**; κακῶν ἐπιχειρημάτων (om. cet.) Sc; γρ κἀκ τῶν ἐπιχειρημάτων m. 2 Vc || **13** τῶι βούλεσθαι Vc Ba Mr | γρ δείκνυσι τὸ ἐκεῖ βούλεσθαι πλέον εἶναι τὸν σοφιστὴν κτλ. **P** | πλέον εἶναι **P**; εἶναι om. **V** Mr || **14** cf. 188, 5 | αὐτὸν **P** Ac | ἀξιῶν Vc Ba || **15** ἀνθυποφορᾶς Vc Ba || **16** ἃ — αὐτὸς Pa, (om. ἂν) Pc; ἅπερ ἂν αὐτὸς ὁ περικλῆς εἶπεν **V** | ἢ om. Ac Ba, (er. ?) Vc | μὴ om. **V** || **18** ἐπιτάττουσι τοῖς ἐχθροῖς Ac (om. τοῖς) Vc Ba | similia Diodorus XII 39, 5 || **18** τε **V**; om. **P**, Anon. III 118, 26 Sp. || **18-20** εἶναι . . . δεῖ: vix utrumque sanum || **19** ἐπιτάσσουσι (ττ supra σσ) Pc || **20** οὐδὲ **P** Ac, Anon.; μηδὲ Vc Ba | ἡμῶν **V**, Anon. || **22** ἡμεῖς **V**, Anon. || **23** ποτιδαίας (non ποτιδαιατῶν) etiam Anon. | cf. Thuc. 2, 139 || **24** ἀνθυποφορῶν Vc Ba; cf. l. 15

go into exile because he is insane. Here he seems to be talking about exile, and he puts stress on that argument, but throughout he is hinting at the adultery of his father with his wife.[274]

Deflected and opposed problems differ only in that opposed problems practice (*meleta*) only one thing and deflected ones convey a double meaning and often more. The treatment by which one learns to practice this is the same. The treatment of hypophoras[275] in such problems is to present them with their supporting arguments and whatever epikheiremes have been invented. The argument taken from the opponents, being strongly made and requiring the refutations to be weaker, shows in this case | that the sophist means more than what he seems to be proposing; for example, the case of Pericles claiming that he should go off to Lacedaimon. Someone speaking for him will cause argument to be confirmed from a hypophora, (*citing*) everything that Pericles himself would have said if arguing in his own defense, or everything someone else (*might have said*) who thought he ought not to be given up to the Lacedaimonians: "Now perhaps he[276] will say as he goes on that there is no need to obey the orders of the enemy; for it would be a terrible and stupid thing for anyone to favor the enemy's orders, for one should obey the injunctions of friends, not of enemies, and (*he will say*) that our ancestors hearkened to no one, neither to Xerxes nor Mardonius nor Dareius nor anyone else, and that you did not obey the Lacedaimonians when they gave orders about Potidea or about the Aeginetans or about the Megareans."[277] And supporting the argument of the opponents is generally one treatment in figured problems. [207]

There is also another treatment, which is to introduce the thoughts by attributing the speech to someone else; for example, "Now some other person might speak and demand that he not be

[274] See the treatment of this theme by Libanius in *Declamations* 39. The speaker assumes that the hearers are familiar with the rumor about his father's actions; the son can then say, for example, "I can no longer bear my embarrassment before my fellow citizens"; see Rabe, *Prolegomenon Sylloge*, 211.

[275] I.e., the opponent's arguments as taken up by the speaker; cf. 3.4 above, p. 75.

[276] I.e., the opponent. This is the hypophora, taken up by the speaker.

[277] These are strong arguments against surrendering Pericles; the speaker attributes them to his opponent and pretends to be rejecting them, but they are being "figured" and thus validated by his dwelling on them.

*Ἔστι καὶ ἄλλη μεταχείρισις, τὸ περιτιθέντα ἑτέρῳ τὸν λόγον εἰσ-
άγειν τὰ νοήματα, οἷον «ἄλλος μὲν οὖν ἂν εἶπέ τις μὴ πέμπεσθαι κελεύων αὐτὸν Λακεδαιμονίοις, ὡς οὐ χρὴ πολεμίοις ἐπιτάττουσι πείθε-
σθαι· δεινόν τε γὰρ εἶναι τὸ πρᾶγμα καὶ ἠλίθιον καὶ μήτε τοὺς πατέρας*
[208] *μήτε | ὑμᾶς ποτε τοιοῦτόν τι πεπραχέναι», καὶ τὰ αὐτὰ νοήματα, «ἐγὼ
δὲ οὔ φημι ταῦτα». ἔστι δὲ καὶ ἐν ἄλλῳ μεταβαλεῖν σχήματι, ἐάν τις
λέγῃ «ἐγὼ δέ, εἰ μὲν ἄκοντά μέ τις ἠξίου βιαζόμενος ἀπελθεῖν πρὸς
Λακεδαιμονίους, εἶπον ἂν τάδε καὶ τάδε», καὶ τὰ αὐτὰ νοήματα, ἅπερ,
εἰ καὶ μὴ ἐσχηματισμένως ἐμελετῶμεν, ἐλέγομεν ἄν· διὰ τοῦτο γὰρ
καὶ ἐσχηματισμένα καλεῖται τὰ τοιαῦτα προβλήματα, ἐπειδὴ τὰ αὐτὰ
δεῖ λέγεσθαι νοήματα, ἅπερ, εἰ καὶ μὴ ἐσχηματισμένως ἐμελετῶμεν,
εἴπομεν ἄν. δεῖ δὲ μεταχειρίσεως καὶ τοιούτου σχήματος ἀσφαλοῦς εὐ-
πορῆσαι, ἵνα μὴ λύοντες τὰς ἐμφάσεις γυμνοὺς εἰσάγωμεν τοὺς λόγους
ὡς ἄντικρυς μὴ θέλοντες. Καὶ ταυτὶ μὲν περὶ πλαγίων καὶ ἐναντίων.*

*Τὸ δὲ κατὰ ἔμφασιν σχῆμα τοιοῦτόν ἐστιν, οἷον καὶ προειρήκα-
μεν. μελετᾶται δὲ ἐνίοτε μὲν σχήματος εὑρέσει κἀκεῖνο τοιούτου, ἵνα
τις ἄντικρυς λέγων τὸ πρᾶγμα μὴ δοκῇ λέγειν, ὃ δὴ καὶ εὕρημά ἐστιν
ἐμὸν ἐν μελέτῃ γενόμενον ἐμῇ καὶ ἐκδέδοται· οἷον φήμη ἦν, ὅτι σύνεστιν
ὁ πατὴρ τοῦ υἱοῦ τῇ γυναικί, ἔγκυος ἐγένετο ἡ γυνή, ἔχρησεν ὁ θεὸς*
[209] *τὸ γεννηθησόμενον φονέα ἔσεσθαι | τοῦ πατρός, οὐ βούλεται ἐκτιθέναι
τὸ γεννηθὲν ὁ παῖς καὶ ὑπὸ τοῦ πατρὸς ἀποκηρύσσεται. ἐνταῦθα γὰρ ὁ*

1 τὸ **P** AC; τῶ Vc Ba || 2 εἶπεν ἄν **V** | μήτε **V** || 4 εἶναι καὶ τὸ πρᾶγμα ἠλίθιον **V** || 5 ὑμᾶς Ld, (ἡ m. 1 ex ὑ) Pa; ἡμᾶς Pc **V** | τὰ αὐτὰ **V** (αὐτῶν m. 2 Vc); τοιαῦτα Pc; τ$^{οι}$αῦτά Pa; schol. **P** solam lectionem τάυτά novit || 6 τὰ αὐτά **V** | μεταβάλ$^{λ}$λειν (sic) Pa; μεταβά$^{λ}$λεῖν Pc || 9 ult. καὶ om. Ac | εἴπομεν Vc Ba || 10 τὰ μὲν αὐτὰ **V** || 11 ἐμελετῶμεν om. Vc Ba || 12 ἐλέγομεν ἄν Vc Ba | καὶ om. Vc Ba || 13 γυμνοὺς post λόγους Ac || 15 p. 188, 16 | καὶ om. Vc Ba || 16 καὶ αὐτὸ post μὲν add. **V** | κἀκεῖνο om. **V** || 17 δόξηι Vc Ba || 18 ἐμὸν om. Vc Ba Ld | γεγενημένον Ac; λεγόμενον (m. 2 γέγονεν supr.), m. 1 mg. γρ γενόμενον, Vc | ἐμοὶ Ld | οἷον om. Vc Ba || 18-194.7 sq. cf. Syr. 1 p. 36, 22: ἐσχηματισθέντα δὲ ζητήματά εἰσιν ὡς <τὰ S> παρὰ Ἀψίνῃ τῷ Γαδαρεῖ ἐν ἐκείνῳ <τε S> τῷ ζητήματι· φήμη ἦν, ὅτι σύνεστιν ὁ πατὴρ τῇ τοῦ παιδὸς (**V**; υἱοῦ S) γυναικί, «καὶ τοῦ μοιχοῦ λαβόμενος ἐβόων «πάτερ», σὺ δὲ ἦς οὐδαμοῦ»· καὶ πάλιν ἐν τῇ περὶ τῆς ἐκθέσεως τοῦ παιδίου φιλονεικίᾳ, ὅπερ ὁ θεὸς ἀνεῖλε τὸν πατέρα φονεύσειν «σὸν εἶναι νόμισον, ὦ πάτερ, τὸ παιδίον, οὐκ ἐμόν. [ἐκτιθεῖς ὃν ἔσπειρας ῥίπτεις] ἐκτίθης (ἐκτιθεὶς **V**), ὃ ἐγέννησας, ῥίπτεις τὸ παιδίον (οὐκ ἐμὸν — παιδίον **V**, om. S), οὗ γέγονας πατήρ» || 19 τῆι ante τοῦ **V**, Anon. III 119, 16 Sp., Diac. f. 431 v || 20 ἔσεσθαι φονέα **V**

sent to the Lacedaimonians on the ground that it is not right to obey the enemy's orders, for it would be a dreadful and stupid thing and neither your ancestors nor | you ever did anything of [208] the sort," and the same thoughts (*ta auta noēmata*), "but I for my part do not aver these things." And it is possible to cast it into still another figure if one says, "But if someone, being forced, demands that I go to the Lacedaimonians unwillingly, I would for my part say this and that," with the same thoughts that we would say even if we were not practicing in a figured way.[278] It is for this reason that such problems are called "figured," since it is necessary for the same thoughts to be said that we would speak even if we were not practicing in a figured way. There is need to exercise careful control of such treatment and figure, lest we refute the implications and introduce the arguments in a bare form, as if openly opposing them. So much about deflected and opposed problems.

The figure by implication is such as we stated earlier. It is sometimes practiced (*meletatai*) by invention of a figure of such a sort that when saying the thing outright one does not seem to say it, which is my own discovery in a declamation that has been published;[279] for example, there was a rumor that a father is having intercourse with his son's wife. The woman becomes pregnant, and there is an oracle from the god that the child to be born will be the murderer | of the father.[280] The son does not want the child [209] to be exposed, and (*as a result*) he is disowned by the father. Here, when defending himself against being disowned, the son ought to reveal the current rumor of adultery by implication, so as to defeat his father in an unexceptional and seemly way without openly

[278] The same thoughts, but said in such a way that a different meaning is conveyed.

[279] This is the passage attributed to Apsines by Syrianus (1:36).

[280] Cf. Quintilian 9.2.69–70.

*παῖς πρὸς τὴν ἀποκήρυξιν ἀπολογούμενος ὀφείλει τὴν ἐντρέχουσαν φήμην τῆς μοιχείας κατὰ ἔμφασιν δηλοῦν, ὡς ἀνεπιλήπτως ἐλέγχειν τὸν πατέρα καὶ εὐσχημόνως, φανερῶς δὲ μὴ λέγειν ὅτι «μοιχεύει τὴν γυναῖκα τὴν ἐμήν» καὶ δηλοῦν, ὅτι τοῦτο γίνεται. οὕτως οὖν εὐπορήσαμεν σχήματος τοιούτου καὶ ἄντικρυς εἰπόντες αὐτὸ λέγειν οὐκ ἐδόξαμεν· ἔστι δὲ τόδε «σὸν εἶναι λόγισαι, πάτερ, τὸ παιδίον, οὐκ ἐμόν· ἐκτίθης, ὃ ἐγέννησας, ῥίπτεις παιδίον, οὗ γέγονας πατήρ». Δεῖ δὲ ἐν τοῖς τοιούτοις, τοῖς κατ᾽ ἔμφασιν λέγω, καὶ ὀνομάτων εὐπορῆσαι διττὰ δηλῶσαι δυναμένων, καὶ τὸ ἀνεύθυνον καὶ τὸ σεσημασμένον· οἷον φήμη ἦν, ὅτι σύνεστι τῇ ἰδίᾳ θυγατρὶ ὁ πατήρ, ἀπόρρητόν τι ἡ μήτηρ εἰποῦσα τῷ υἱῷ ἀπήγξατο, πυνθάνεται ὁ πατὴρ τὸ ἀπόρρητον καὶ οὐ λέγοντα τὸν υἱὸν ἀποκηρύσσει, οἷον ἡμῖν ἐξενήνεκται καὶ περὶ τοῦδε προοίμιον δεύτερον τόδε «τῆς μὲν οὖν ἀποκηρύξεως ταύτης ἔλαττον ἐμοὶ μέλει·* [210] *λυποῦμαι δὲ ὑπὲρ τοῦ πατρός, εἰ μετὰ τοσαύτην εὐθηνίαν γένους μόνῃ | συνέσται τῇ θυγατρὶ καὶ συζήσεται»· κοινὰ μὲν γάρ ἐστι καὶ τοῦ ἄλλου βίου τὰ τοιαῦτα ὀνόματα τοῖς ἀνθρώποις, δοκεῖ δὲ μάλιστα ἴδια εἶναι τῇ ὑποκειμένῃ ἐμφάσει ὡς δηλῶσαι δυνάμενα καὶ τὸ ἀνεύθυνον καὶ τὸ σεσημασμένον, τό τε «συνέσται» φημὶ καὶ τὸ «συζήσεται». Ἀλλὰ καὶ ἡ τῆς συνθέσεως πάλιν ἀκολουθία συγκειμένη μὲν ἄλλο δηλοῖ, διαιρουμένη δὲ ἄλλο ἐμφαίνει· οἷον φήμη ἦν, ὅτι σύνεστιν ὁ πατὴρ τῇ τοῦ υἱοῦ γυναικί, μοιχὸν καταλαβὼν ἐγκεκαλυμμένον ὁ υἱὸς ἀφῆκε καὶ ἀποκηρύσσεται ὑπὸ τοῦ πατρός· ἐρεῖ γὰρ «ὅπου καὶ τοῦ μοιχοῦ λαβόμενος ἐβόων «πάτερ»· τὸ γὰρ ὄνομα τοῦ πατρὸς εὐθέως τῷ μοιχῷ παρακείμενον ἐν τῇ συνθέσει ἐποίησε τὴν ἔμφασιν. καὶ τὸ ἐπενηνεγμένον δὲ ὁμοίως ἔχει «καὶ τοῦ μοιχοῦ λαβόμενος ἐβόων «πάτερ»· σὺ δὲ ἦς οὐδαμοῦ«· τῷ γὰρ μοιχῷ καὶ τῷ πατρὶ προστεθὲν εὐθέως τὸ «σὺ δὲ ἦς»*

1 ὀφείλει καὶ **V** || 2 καὶ ante ἐλέγχειν **V** || 3 δὲ **P**; τε **V** | μοιχεύεις? | pr. τὴν om. Ac || 4 οὖν om. Ac | εὐπορήσαμεν **P** (sc. ἐν τῇ μελέτῃ, cf. 192, 16); εὐπορήσομεν Vc Ba; εὐπορήσοιμεν Ac || **6-7** ἐκτιθεῖς m. 1 Vc Ba || **7** τὸ παιδίον Pa, Syr. || **9** pr. τὸ om. **P** || **10** εἰποῦσα ἡ μήτηρ Vc || **12** ἀποκηρύ$^{σσ}$ττει Pc || **13** τόδε **P**; τοῦτο Ac; om. Vc Ba; ἔστι δὲ τόδε Sc, m. 2 Vc; τοῦτο καὶ πρόβλημα ἕτερον Ma || **16** τοῖς ἀνθρώποις τὰ τοιαῦτα ὀνόματα **V** || **17** καὶ τὸ Pc **V**; τό τε Pa || **18** ult. τὸ om. **V** || **20** οἷον ⌊ὅτι er.⌋ φ. Vc | cf. 192, 19 ann. || **21** schol. **P** (W VII 951, 24; in Π. ἰδ. 286, 7 Sp.): «καὶ τὰ ἐσχηματισθέντα τῶν ζητημάτων οὐ σαφῶς λέγει τὰ πράγματα»· ὧν τὴν ὑπόθεσιν ὁ Ἀσπάσιος ἐμφαντικῶς λίαν διηγήσατο· λέγει γὰρ οὕτως «κατείληπτο (Pc; κατείληπται Pa) γὰρ συγκεκαλυμμένος ὁ μοιχός· ἐγὼ δὲ ἐβόων πάτερ, σὺ δὲ ἦσθα οὐδαμοῦ». Vide ad 192, 18 || **22** ἐρεῖ γὰρ v.l. **P**; εἴρηται **PV** (schol. **P**: εἴρηται, φησί, παρ᾽ ἐμοῦ ἐν τῇ μελέτῃ οὕτως) || **25** ὦ πάτερ Pc, Eustath. in Iliad. K 330 || **25-26** οὐδαμ$^{οῦ}$ῶς Pc || **26** τὸ δὲ σὺ εἶς Ba

saying that "he is committing adultery with my wife" and yet making it clear that this is so. Thus we made use of such a figure, and when speaking openly we seemed not to say it. This is the statement: "Reckon, father, that the child is yours, not mine. You are discarding what you begat; you are throwing away a child of which you have been the father."

In such cases, those by implication I mean, there is need for a facility with words that can have two meanings, both what is unexceptionable and what is significant; for example, there was a rumor that a father is having intercourse (*synesti*) with his own daughter. The mother, after telling her son some unspeakable thing, hanged herself. The father asks what the unspeakable thing was and when the son does not say, he disowns him. An example of this sort has been published by us and has the following as a second prooemion: "Now this disinheritance is of little concern to me, but I am distressed for my father if after such abundance of family he is left with (*synesti*) only | a daughter and will live with (*synēzetai*) her [210]
alone." Such words—*synesti*, I mean, and *synzēsetai*—are common of other aspects of human life and seem most suited for the underlying implication as being able to indicate both what is unexceptionable and what has been implied.

But again the sequence of composition indicates one thing when the words are closely joined and implies something else when they are separated; for example, there is a rumor that a father is having intercourse with his son's wife. The son had taken him in adultery when disguised but let him go[281] and is disowned by the father. (*Here the son*) will say,[282] "When seizing the adulterer, I was calling 'Father'"; the word "father" when put right close to "adulterer" in the sentence created an implication. Similarly, what is added: "And seizing the adulterer I was calling 'Father,' but you were nowhere." By adding "you were" right next to "adulterer" and "father" in the sentence he revealed the implication, but in each case "nowhere" preserves the ostensible meaning.

[281] I.e., the son does not recognize the father because of the disguise.

[282] See Rabe's apparatus, citing scholia in Paris manuscripts (Walz 7:951) that add, "Aspasius narrated this hypothesis very allusively, for he speaks in this way: 'The adulterer was taken in disguise. I cried Father, but you were nowhere.'"

*τῇ συνθέσει τὴν ἔμφασιν ἐδήλωσε, τὴν ἀσφάλειαν δὲ ἔχει ἑκάτερον ἀπὸ τοῦ «οὐδαμοῦ».*

## *Περὶ τῶν συγκριτικῶν προβλημάτων.*

*Τὰ συγκριτικὰ προβλήματα εἰ μὲν στοχασμῷ περιπέσοι ἢ ὅρῳ,* [211] *ῥᾳδίαν ἔχει τὴν διαίρεσιν· διπλοῖς γὰρ | τοῖς κεφαλαίοις καθ᾽ ἕκαστον χρώμεθα, ἐν μὲν τοῖς στοχασμοῖς ταῖς βουλήσεσι καὶ ταῖς δυνάμεσι, λέγοντες «ἐμὲ μὲν οὐκ εἰκὸς βουληθῆναι τόδε ποιῆσαι διὰ τόδε, σὲ δὲ εἰκὸς βουληθῆναι τόδε ποιῆσαι διὰ τόδε», καὶ πάντα ἐκφέρειν εἰς δέον τὰ ἐπιχειρήματα· εἶτα πάλιν «ἐμὲ μὲν οὐκ εἰκὸς δυνηθῆναι τόδε ποιῆσαι διὰ τόδε, σὲ δὲ εἰκὸς τόδε ποιῆσαι διὰ τόδε», καὶ τοῦτο κατασκευάζοντες καὶ τὸ χρῶμα τὸ μὲν ἡμέτερον τιθέντες καὶ κατασκευάζοντες, τὸ δὲ παρὰ τοῦ ἐχθροῦ τεθὲν λύοντες τοῖς ἐπιχειρήμασι, καὶ τὴν πιθανὴν ἀπολογίαν τὴν ἐκείνου μὲν λύοντες, κρατύνοντες δὲ τὴν ἡμετέραν.*

*Καὶ μὴν καὶ τὰ ἐν τοῖς ὅροις ὁμοίως διπλῶς μελετῶντες λέγομεν, οἷον «τοῦτό ἐστι τὸ ἐργάσασθαί τι, ὃ πεποίηκα ἐγώ», εἶτα ἐνεγκεῖν, ἅπερ εἰργάσω, εἶτα ἐπενεγκεῖν «σὺ δὲ τούτων ἐποίησας οὐδέν», εἶτα ἀνθυπενεγκεῖν ἐκεῖθεν τὰ ἐκείνῳ πεπραγμένα καὶ λέγειν, ὡς ταῦτα οὐδέν ἐστι.*

*Χρησόμεθα δὲ τοῖς ἐπιχειρήμασι καὶ ταῖς ἐφόδοις ταῖς μελετητικαῖς καὶ ἐν τοῖς διπλοῖς ὅροις, αἷς ἐδιδάξαμεν δεῖν χρῆσθαι, καὶ ἐν τοῖς* [212] *ἁπλοῖς ἀπό τε τῶν πρὸ τοῦ | πράγματος καὶ ἀπὸ τῶν μετὰ τὸ πρᾶγμα συμβαινόντων· ἐκεῖθεν γὰρ ἡ ἁπλῆ εὐπορία ἐνταῦθα διπλῆ γίνεται.*

1 ἐν τῆι **V** || 3 τῶν om. Ac **P**π || 4 τὰ **P** **P**π; τὰ δὲ **V** || 5 καὶ ante τὴν add. **P** Ac || 6 alt. τοῖς om. Ac || 7-8 σὲ — alt. τόδε om. Pc || 8 βουληθῆναι τόδε **P**; om. Vc Ba; βουληθῆναι om. Ac | ἐκφέροντες? | τὰ ante εἰς Ba; om. Vc || 9 γρ εἶτα ἀνάπαλιν **P** | ⌊δυν m. 1⌉ηθῆναι Ac; βουληθῆναι Sc || 10 τόδε ποιῆσαι Pc; ποιῆσαι τόδε **V**; τόδε ποιῆσαι δυνυθῆναι Pa || 12 παρὰ τοῦ ἐχθροῦ **PV**, mg. ἐν ἄλλοις παρ᾽ ἐκείνου **P** || 13 μὲν ἐκείνου Ac || 15 διπλῶς om. Ac || 16-17 ὃ — alt. εἶτα sic Pc; ὃ πεποίηκα ἐγώ· ⌊circ. XX**V**; m. po.: καὶ εἰπεῖν ἅπερ εἰργάσατο⌉· εἶτα Pa; ὅπερ ἐποίησα ἐγώ (καὶ εἶπεν mg. m. 1 Ba)· εἶτα ἐνεγκεῖν ἅπερ εἰργάσατο (καὶ εἰπεῖν ἃ εἰργάσατο εἶτα ἐπ m. 2 supr. Vc)· εἶτα Vc Ba; ὅπερ ἐποίησα ἐγώ· καὶ εἰπεῖν ἃ εἰργάσατο· εἶτα Ac || 18 ἐκείνωι Pa **V**; αὐτῶι Pc || 20 δὲ καὶ τοῖς Ac | καὶ ταῖς μελετητικαῖς ἐφόδοις Ac || 20-22 καὶ ταῖς μεθόδοις ταῖς μελετητικαῖς αἷς ἐδιδάξαμεν δεῖν χρῆσθαι ἐν τοῖς διπλοῖς ὅροις καὶ ἐν τοῖς ἁπλοῖς ἀπό Vc Ba || 21 τοῖς om. Pc

## CHAPTER 14: ON COMPARATIVE PROBLEMS

Comparative problems, whether falling under stasis of conjecture or of definition, have an easy basis for division, for | we use double [211] headings in each.[283] In conjecture[284] (*we use*) intentions and abilities, saying "It is not probable that I wanted to do this for such and such a reason, but it is probable that *you* wanted to do this for such and such a reason," and expand all the epikheiremes as needed; then again, "It is not probable that I could have done this for such and such a reason, but it is probable that *you* did this for such and such a reason," and confirming this and adding our explanation (*khrōma*) and confirming that, and refuting the proposition of the enemy with epikheiremes and refuting persuasive features of his defense while strengthening our case.

Similarly, when practicing (*meletōntes*) cases of definition[285] we also use double headings; for example, "This is doing what I have done,"[286] then adding what you did, then further adding, "but *you* did none of these things," then in contrast bringing in next what was done by him and saying how those things amount to nothing.

We shall use epikheiremes and approaches (*ephodoi*)[287] practiced in declamation (*meletētikai*) both in double definitions, as we have taught it should be done, and in cases of single definitions from both | what happened before the action and what happened [212] after the action, for from that source the simple argument becomes double.

[283] See Hermogenes, *On Stasis*, pp. 56,5–59,3 and 61,21–65,9 Rabe.

[284] Cases in which the issue is whether or not something was actually done.

[285] Cases in which the issue is the legal definition of an acknowledged action; e.g., murder or homicide.

[286] I.e., is defined in a way that we state. The speaker is probably competing with someone else for a reward for performing some deed; his action is not in question, but whether the action satisfies the definition is disputed.

[287] *Ephodoi* appears only here in the Hermogenic corpus; otherwise, see *Rhetoric for Herennius* 1.6; Apsines 2.1; Aphthonius 13 (*Aphthonii progymnasmata* [ed. Hugo Rabe; Bibliotheca scriptorum Graecorum et Romanorum Teubneriana; Rhetores Graeci 10; Leipzig: Teubner, 1926], 42) and John of Sardis's note thereon.

*Εἰ δὲ πραγματικὴ ἀμφισβήτησις παρεμπέσοι, τότε δεῖ ζητεῖν, τίνα ἐστὶ τὰ συγκρινόμενα, δύο ἢ καὶ πλείονα, καὶ οὕτως ἐκ τῶν παρακολουθούντων ἑκάστῳ τὰς συγκρίσεις ποιήσεις. μάλιστα δέ, εἰ πρόσωπον συγκρίνοιτο, τότε ἔχειν δεῖ τὴν ἀπὸ τῶν ἐγκωμίων καὶ ψόγων σύγκρισιν, καὶ γένη καὶ ἐπιτηδεύματα καὶ πράξεις καὶ τύχας καὶ ἅπαντα τὰ συγκρινόμενα. ὁμοίως δὲ ἔχει καὶ τὰ ἐκ τῆς ἄλλης περιστάσεως· ὅ τι ἂν εἰς σύγκρισιν ἐμπέσῃ, τὰ παρακολουθοῦντα ἑκάστοις συγκρίνομεν· παρακολουθεῖ δὲ ἄλλα μὲν τόποις, ἄλλα δὲ χρόνοις, ἄλλα δὲ ἑκάσταις τῶν ἄλλων περιστάσεων.*

1 ζήτησις Ac | παρεμπέσῃ Pc; περιπέσοι Vc Ba; cf. 196, 4 || 3 ποιεῖσθαι **V** || 3-4 γρ εἰ πρόσωπον συγκρίνοιτο ἔχον τὴν ἀπὸ τῶν κτλ. **P** || 3 πρόσωπα? || 5 pr. καὶ et τὰ om. Vc Ba || 6 γρ καὶ συγκρίνομεν Pa, (om. καὶ) Pc | ἔχει om. Sc | τὰ om. Ba, ?m. 1 Vc | ἄλλης om. Ac | περιστάσεως Pc, m. 1 Pa; περιουσίας **V**; schol. **P** praefert περιστάσεως; aliud schol. **P**: ἐκ τῶν ἄλλων περιστατικῶν || 6-7 ὅ,τι γὰρ ἂν Ac, (om. ἂν) v.l. **P** || 7 ἐμπέσῃ (οι supra) Pa; ἐμπέσοι Pc Ac; ἐμπέσοι· ἢ Vc Ba | καὶ τὰ Vc Ba || 9 subscr. τέλος τῶν εὑρέσεων **P**; τέλος τοῦ τετάρτου τόμου Vc Ba; om. AC

If the question at issue falls under the category of *pragmatikē*,[288] then it is necessary to ask what are the things being compared, whether two or even more, and in this way you will make comparisons from the consequences of each. Especially if a person is being compared, then there is need to make the comparison by praises and blames, speaking about origins and habits and actions and fortunes and all the things that can be compared. Similarly, in the case of another circumstance; whatever comes into the comparison, we compare what results to each. Different results follow from the places (of an action), different from the times, different from each of the other circumstances.

End of the Treatise *On Invention*

[288] I.e., referring to a future action; see p. 71 n. 111 above.

# ON METHOD OF FORCEFUL SPEAKING [414]

## As Found in the Hermogenic Corpus

*At the end of his discussion of forcefulness* (deinotēs) *in the treatise* On Ideas *(2.9), the author we know as Hermogenes gives a perceptive account of all the many things that should be discussed in a general treatise on style, which he hopes to complete and to which he proposes the title* On Method of Forcefulness (p. 380,2 Rabe). *The treatise preserved under this title, however, has little resemblance to his description and is certainly not by Hermogenes.*[1] *One telling difference is that the term "forcefulness" occurs only in the title, which was probably given to the treatise by an editor who assembled the Hermogenic corpus and knew of Hermogenes' reference to such a work. The term* methodos *does occur in the treatise (e.g., chs. 2, 22, 26, 28), where it usually refers to prose style and means ways, sources, or verbal techniques of saying something, including especially use of figures of thought, a meaning found also in* On Ideas.

*The name of the author is unknown. Not only is the treatise not the work of Hermogenes, but it is clearly not by the same author as* On Invention, *for each work has its own distinctive terminology; compare, for example, the difference between the account of antitheton in* On Invention *4.2 and that in* On Method *15. Some similarities to Pseudo-Dionysius's* Art of Rhetoric *(2.10–11), identified in the notes and apparatus criticus, suggest that the author of that work may have used the same source as did the author of* On Method. *Just as*

[1] The evidence was carefully examined, with this conclusion, by E. Bürgi, "Ist die dem Hermogenes zugeschriebene Schrift *Peri methodou deinotētos* echt?" *Wiener Studien* 48 (1930): 187–97; 49 (1931): 40–69. See also Barbara P. Wallach, "Pseudo-Hermogenes and the Characterizing Oath," *Greek, Roman, and Byzantine Studies* 22 (1981): 257–67.

*the author of the treatise* On Invention *shows no awareness of traditional discussions of that subject, the author of* On Method *shows no knowledge of discussions of style by Aristotle, Demetrius, Dionysius of Halicarnassus in his genuine works, Longinus, or other writers on the subject, nor does the author make any use of the common division of style into diction and composition or the division of the ornaments of style into tropes, figures of speech, and figures of thought, though these concepts would have been useful to him. The treatise was already attributed to Hermogenes in the fifth century, when it was cited by Syrianus (1:96; 2:2,) and there is a collection of scholia by Gregory of Corinth printed in Walz 7.2:1090–1352.*

*Although at first glance the treatise seems a miscellaneous collection of chapters dealing with figures and some other features of prose composition, the sequence of chapters indicates some intent to organize the subject systematically. The first four chapters deal with word choice; chapters 5 to 16 with figures, mostly figures of thought, though chapter 11 on asyndeton and chapter 16 on parison deal with verbal figures; and chapter 12 on preliminary headings and recapitulation is unexpectedly inserted in the middle of the series. Beginning with chapter 17 and continuing, more or less, to chapter 32, the author seems to be discussing matters of invention, though with some attention to stylistic features of the thought. Of the remaining chapters, 33, 34, and 36 deal with kinds of style; into this is inserted chapter 35, in which the author tries to answer critics who have found ambiguities in classical authors, and chapter 37, on negation (litotes), is tacked on at the end. It is possible, of course, that a later editor is responsible for some of the confusion, and it is also possible that some of the later chapters were added by an editor from other sources. Note, for example, that* parōidia *as described in chapter 36 is quite a different thing from* parōidia *in chapter 30.*

*In making this translation I have consulted, though not always followed, the French version by Marcel Patillon,* L'Art rhétorique, *511–50.*

[414] # ΠΕΡΙ ΜΕΘΟΔΟΥ ΔΕΙΝΟΤΗΤΟΣ

*Πᾶν μέρος λόγου εὕρηται μὲν ἐπὶ μηνύσει πράγματος, καιροῦ δὲ ἰδίου τυχόν, ὁ δὲ καιρὸς κατὰ ἤθους προσθήκην γινόμενος ἰδίαν διάνοιαν ἀπεργάζεται, οὐ μόνον ἰδίαν, ἀλλὰ καὶ διάφορον, οὐ μόνον διάφορον, ἀλλὰ καὶ διαφόρους, οὐ μόνον διαφόρους, ἀλλὰ καὶ ἐναντίας. οἷον κακοῦργος πᾶς ὁ κακόν τι ἐργαζόμενος, ἰδίως δ' ὁ κλέπτης. διάφορον δέ, οἷον δημηγορεῖν τὸ ἐν δήμῳ ἀγορεύειν, ἰδίως δὲ τὸ κεχαρισμένα λέγειν καὶ τὸ ἀπαίδευτα λέγειν. διαφόρους δέ, οἷον ἄνθρωπος γένους ὄνομα καὶ ἤθους ἡμέρου καὶ τύχης ὄνομα καὶ πανουργίας. ἐναντίας δέ, ὡς τὸ «μεῖνατ' ἐπὶ χρόνον», τὸν πολύν, τὸν ὀλίγον, καὶ παρὰ Πλάτωνι*
[415] *«χρόνον» δὴ τὸν πολὺν δηλοῖ· καὶ τὸ «αὐτός, ὦ Φαίδων, παρε|γένου; αὐτός, ὦ Ἐχέκρατες»· ὃ μὲν γὰρ ἤρετο ὡς θαυμάζων καὶ μακαρίζων τὸν παραγενόμενον, ὃ δὲ ἀποκρίνεται σεμνυνόμενος καὶ μεγαφρονῶν.*

## *Περὶ πάσης λέξεως.*

*Πάσης λέξεως τῆς ἀγνοουμένης ἐν πεζῷ λόγῳ τρεῖς μέθοδοι τῆς εὑρέσεως· ἢ γὰρ ἐθνική ἐστιν ἡ λέξις ἢ τεχνικὴ ἢ νομική. ὁ γοῦν παρασάγγης οὐκ οἶδα τίς ἐστιν· ἐθνικὸν γάρ ἐστι καὶ Περσικὸν ὁδοῦ μέτρον,*

1 sic **P** Vc Sf Ph; Ἑρμογένους om. Ac Lb Md Og Vil, m. 1 Nc; ἑρμογένους τέχνης ῥητορικῆς τὸ περὶ μεθόδου δεινότητος Of || **3** pr. δὲ om. Vf | vix san. | ὁ — γινόμενος post 5 ἀπεργάζεται Sc || **4** ἐργάζεται Vc Sf Ph, v.l. **P** | καὶ οὐ Ld | καὶ add. ante οὐ **P** || **5** καὶ add. ante οὐ Od | <ἰδίαν μὲν> οἷον? || **6** δ' om. m. 1 Sf || **7** δὲ om. Ph | cf. Plat. Gorg. 502 CD || **8** ἢ καὶ Vt | καὶ — λέγειν om. Va || **10** Hom. B 299 | [τὸν πολύν] Spengel; schol. Ven. A: ὅτι Ζηνόδοτος γράφει «ἔτι χρόνον», ἀπιθάνως· ἔμφασις γὰρ γίνεται πολλοῦ χρόνου διὰ τοῦ «ἔτι» || **11** Plat. Phaedr. 278 D (ἐν χρόνῳ), Tim. 21 D (διὰ χρόνον)? fortasse l. 10 παρὰ Θουκυδίδῃ [2, 18] vel tale quid submotum est, cum glossema παρὰ Πλάτωνι ad l. 11 ascriptum eo irreperet | Plat. Phaedon. 57 A || **12** εἴρετο Vc || **13** ἀποκρίνεται (supra ε α ο) Pa || **14** mg. **P** Pπ; om. Vc Sf; περὶ πάσης λέξεως ἀγνοουμένης ἐν πεζῶι λόγωι Lc Pe; πόσαι μέθοδοι τῆς ἀγνοουμένης λέξεως ἐν πεζῶι λόγωι mg. (m. 1?) Ac; πόσαι καὶ ποῖαι μέθοδοι τῆς εὑρέσεως ἀγνοουμένης λέξεως ἐν πεζῶι λόγωι mg. Ph | mg. ᾱ **P** Ac || **15** aliter [Dion.] Art. II 1 p. 366, 18. 386, 13 Us. || **17** τί Ald. | καὶ om. Nc Ov Viq

## | CHAPTER 1: (ON DIFFERENT POSSIBLE MEANINGS OF A WORD) [Rabe 414]

Every piece of language is applied to designating something in a particular context, and the context, by addition of moral character,[2] creates a particular meaning, not only a particular meaning, but also a different one (*in different contexts*), and not only a different meaning but several, and not only several but even opposite meanings; for example, everyone who does something evil (*kakon*) is an "evildoer" (*kakourgos*), but in a particular context *kakourgos* means a thief. As an example of a different meaning, to address the people (*dēmēgorein*) is to speak in public but has the particular meaning of saying things that flatter and things that are vulgar.[3] As an example of multiple meanings, *anthrōpos* is the name of a genus and of a civilized character and the name of a lot in life[4] and of roguery.[5] Opposite meanings are, for example, things like "Abide for a time" (*Iliad* 2.299), which can mean much or little time, as in Plato (e.g., *Phaedrus* 278d9) "time" indicates much time. And (*there are different meanings reflected in Phaedo* 57a), "Were you present yourself, Phaedo? | I was myself, O Echecrates." One per- [415]
son asked the question in admiration and thinking him happy at having been there, but the other answers gravely and seriously.

## CHAPTER 2: ON ALL (UNFAMILIAR) DICTION

There are three sources[6] of all unfamiliar vocabulary in prose, for either the term is foreign (*ethnikē*) or technical (*tekhnikē*) or legal (*nomikē*).[7] I may not know what a parasang is,[8] for it is a foreign

[2] Seen in what is said just below about positive and negative meanings of *dēmēgorein* and *anthrōpos*; cf. "sophist," a teacher of rhetoric or a deceitful speaker, depending on the context.

[3] Cf. Plato, *Gorgias* 502c-e.

[4] I.e., the human condition.

[5] *Anthrōpos* was sometimes used contemptuously in Greek to mean a bad fellow or slave, especially in the phrase "O, Man"; cf., e.g., Herodotus 3.3.

[6] Literally, "three methods of invention."

[7] The author seems unfamiliar with the term *glōssa* or *glōtta*, used by Aristotle (e.g., *Rhetoric* 3.3.2 and 3.10.2) and many others to refer to a strange or foreign word.

[8] The term would be familiar to readers of Xenophon's *Anabasis*.

*οἱ τριάκοντα στάδιοι· σχοῖνος δὲ Αἰγύπτιον, οἱ ἑξήκοντα στάδιοι. νομικὸν δὲ ὄνομα τὸ τοιοῦτον «πομπεύειν ἀντὶ τοῦ κατηγορεῖν εἵλετο»· ἐν Ἀθήναις τοῖς Διονυσίοις ἐπόμπευον καὶ ἀλλήλοις διελοιδοροῦντο καὶ τοῦτο ἐκαλεῖτο πομπεύειν· καὶ ἡ εἰσαγγελία καὶ ἡ φάσις καὶ ἄλλα τοιαῦτα ὀνόματα νομικά ἐστι. τεχνικὰ δὲ ἐκεῖνα· «ζεύξαντες τὰς παλαιὰς ναῦς» ναυπηγικὸν ὄνομα, καὶ δὶς διὰ τεσσάρων μουσικόν, καὶ μοσχεύειν γεωργικόν, καὶ ὅσα τοιαῦτα.*

## *Περὶ τῶν κατὰ τὴν λέξιν ἁμαρτημάτων.*

*Τὰ ἁμαρτήματα κατὰ τὴν λέξιν κατὰ δύο τρόπους γίνεται, ἀκυρίαν καὶ παραφθοράν· ἀκυρίαν μέν, οἷον,* [416] | *ἐὰν εἴπῃ τις «ἐρωτῶ καὶ παρακαλῶ» ἀντὶ τοῦ δέομαι, ἀκύρως εἴρηκε· τὸ μὲν γὰρ παρακαλεῖν ἢ καλεῖν ἐστιν ἢ προτρέπεσθαι, τὸ δὲ ἐρωτᾶν πυνθάνεσθαι. παραφθορὰν δέ, οἷον, ὃ καλοῦσι διάζωμα, ἐάν τις εἴπῃ διαζώστραν ἢ τὸ αἱμωδεῖν ἀμμωδεῖν καὶ τὰ τοιαῦτα.*

## *Πότε ταυτότητι ὀνομάτων χρησόμεθα καὶ πότε ποικιλίᾳ.*

*Πότε ταυτότητι ὀνομάτων χρησόμεθα καὶ πότε ποικιλίᾳ; ταυτότητι μέν, ὅταν τοῦ πράγματος ἓν ὄνομα ᾖ τὸ ἐναργέστατον· τότε γὰρ οὐ ζητεῖν δεῖ χορηγίαν ἀφανίζουσαν τὴν ἐνάργειαν τοῦ πράγματος, ἐὰν δέ τις παραλάβῃ, ἐπίδειξιν μὲν ἄκαιρον ἐποιήσατο, τὴν χρείαν δὲ*

1-2 σχοῖνος — τοιοῦτον om. Pc; cf. Herod. 2, 6; Athen. III 121 f sq. || 1 αἰγύπτιος Ac | οἱ om. Vb, cf. Herod. || 1-2 νομικὸν δὲ om. Ph || 2 Dem. 18, 124 || 3 τιμᾶν εν αλλοις (vel αλλω?) mg. Ph | γὰρ τοῖς Ac || 4 εἰσαγγελία δὲ καὶ Ald. || 4-5 τὰ ἄλλα La || 5 Thuc. 1, 29 || 6 τὸ ὄνομα Sc Vt | διὰ πασῶν Md Oh Vs, v.l. Lb || 8 supr. **P Pπ**; om. Vc Ac Sf Ph | mg. β̅ **P** Ac || 9 τὰ περὶ τὴν λέξιν ἁμαρτήματα Sc Vt, cf. [Dion.] II 1 p. 365, 3 Us. || 10 καὶ om. Ph || 11 cf. Suid. s. v. παρακαλεῖν | ἀκυρίως Ph | γὰρ om. Ph || 13 διαζώστραν εἴπηι Pc | ἢ (pro καὶ) Ph || 14 de eodem verbo: [Dion.] II 1 p. 366, 2 sq (cf. 365, 3) Us. || 15 **Pπ**, mg. **P**; om. Vc Ac Ph; περὶ ταυτότητος ὀνόματος καὶ ποικιλίας mg. Sf, (ὀνομάτων) Vt | mg. γ̅ **P** Ac || 16 πηκιλία (οι supra) (sic) Ph || 17 ἧι ὄνομα Ac Sf Ph || 17-18 τότε γὰρ om. Vc Ph || 19 μὲν om. Sf Ph | cf. [Dion.] II 1 p. 366, 16. 17 Us.

word, a Persian measure of a road, equal to thirty stades, while a schoinos is an Egyptian measure, equal to sixty stades.[9] A legal usage is something like, "He chose to abuse with jests (*pompeuein*) rather than prosecute" (Dem. 18.124). At Athens at the Dionysia they made processions (*pompai*) and verbally abused each other, and this was called *pompeuein*. *Eisangelia* and *phasis* and other such words are legal terms.[10] Technical terms include "having undergirded (*zeuxantes*) their ancient ships" (Thucydides 1.29), a word used in naval architecture, and *dis dia tessarōn* ("twice every four") is a musical expression, and *moskheuein* ("plant a sucker") is agricultural, and everything of that sort.

## CHAPTER 3: ON MISTAKES IN WORD USAGE[11]

Mistakes (*harmatēmata*) in word choice occur in two ways: failure to use the proper word (*akyria*) and corruption (*paraphthora*). It is failure to use the proper word; for example, | if someone says *erōtō* [416]
*kai parakalō* ("I ask and call for") in place of *deomai* ("I need"), he has spoken improperly, for *parakalein* is either "to call (someone to come)" or "to urge," and *erōtan* is "to make an inquiry." It is an example of corruption if one says *diazōstra* for what they call a *diazōma* ("girdle") and says *ammōdein* for *haimōdein* ("to set teeth on edge"), and the like.

## CHAPTER 4: WHEN TO USE THE SAME AND WHEN TO USE VARIED WORDS

When shall we repeat the same word and when use a variety of words? Use the same word whenever one name for the thing is the clearest, for then there is no need to seek a supply of words obscuring the clarity of the subject, and if one does, he has, on the one hand, made the demonstration unsuitable and, on the other, de-

[9] Cf., e.g., Herodotus 2.6.

[10] These are terms of Athenian law meaning indictment and denunciation.

[11] For another account of this subject, see Pseudo-Dionysius, *Ars Rhetorica* 10.7 (vol. 2, pp. 365–67 Usener-Radermacher). Neither author seems aware of Aristotle's discussion in *Rhetoric* 3.3, nor of the grammatical categories of solecism (= *akyria*?) and barbarism (= *paraphthora*?).

*ἀπολώλεκε τῆς συγγραφῆς. Ὅμηρος*

*«ὡς δὲ χιὼν κατατήκετ᾽ ἐν ἀκροπόλοισιν ὄρεσσιν,*
*ἥν τ᾽ Εὖρος κατέτηξεν, ἐπὴν Ζέφυρος καταχεύῃ,*
*τηκομένης δ᾽ ἄρα τῆς ποταμοὶ πλήθουσι ῥέοντες·*
*ὣς τῆς τήκετο καλὰ παρήια δακρυχεούσης.»*

*οὔτε τὸ λείβεται οὔτε τὸ χεῖται οὔτε τὸ λύεται οὕτως ἁρμόζει ὡς τὸ «τήκεται»· ὄψις γάρ ἐστι χιόνος ἀναλισκομένης ἡ τηκεδών.*

*Ὅταν δὲ πολλὰ ὀνόματα ἔχῃ τις ἰσότιμα καὶ ὁμοίως ἔχοντα ἐνάργειαν χρήσιμον, ἡ ποικιλία ἁρμόζει, οἷον Ὅμηρος*

[417] | *«ὡς δ᾽ ὅταν ὠδίνουσαν ἔχῃ βέλος ὀξὺ γυναῖκα,*
*δριμύ, τό τε προϊεῖσι μογοστόκοι Εἰλείθυιαι,*
*Ἥρης θυγατέρες πικρὰς ὠδῖνας ἔχουσαι»·*

*ἔχομεν ὀξύ, δριμύ, πικρόν, ἐπεὶ δ᾽ οὐκ ἔχει ἄλλο ἰσότιμον, ἐπὶ τὸ πρῶτον ἐπανέρχεται*

*«ὣς ὀξεῖ᾽ ὀδύναι δῦνον μένος Ἀτρείδαο».*

*καὶ ὁ Θουκυδίδης ἐν τῷ προοιμίῳ τεκμήριον, σημεῖον, παράδειγμα, μαρτύριον, καὶ ἀεὶ κύκλον ποιεῖται τῶν ὀνομάτων· «ἐκ δὲ τεκμηρίων, ὧν ἐπὶ μακρότατον σκοποῦντί μοι πιστεῦσαι ξυμβαίνει», καὶ «μαρτύριον δέ· Δήλου γὰρ καθαιρομένης ὑπὸ Ἀθηναίων», καὶ «σημεῖον δ᾽ ἐστὶ ταῦτα τῆς Ἑλλάδος ἔτι οὕτω νεμόμενα περί τε Λοκροὺς τοὺς Ὀζόλας καὶ Αἰτωλοὺς καὶ Ἀκαρνᾶνας», καὶ «παράδειγμα τόδε τοῦ λόγου οὐκ ἐλάχιστόν ἐστι διὰ τὰς μετοικίας ἐς τὰ ἄλλα μὴ ὁμοίως αὐξηθῆναι».*

**1** γραφῆς Sf || **2** Hom. τ 205 | δὲ om. Ph || **5** δάκρυα χεούσης Pa || **7** ἀναλισκομένη ἡ Ph, m. 1 Vc || **8** τις μὴ ἰσότιμα μηδὲ ὁμοίως Ac || **10-12** Hom. Λ 269 || **10-23** cf. [Dion.] II 1 p. 385, 15-386, 8 Us. (loci Thucydidei simili modo turbati) || **11** τό om. Ph || **13** ἔχει μὲν Ac | πικρόν· ὀξύ· δριμύ Vc | ἐπειδὴ δ᾽ Vc Sf Ph || **15** Hom. Λ 272 | ὀξεῖαι **P** Vc | ὀξεῖεσο· δῦναι Ph || **17** Thuc. 1, 1 | Thuc. 1, 8 || **18-19** καὶ μαρτύριον δέ om. Vc || **19** καθαιρουμένης **P** Ac Ph | Thuc. 1, 6: σημεῖον — νεμόμενα; ea laudat etiam [Dion.] l. l. 386, 7 | δ᾽ om. Sf || **20** νεμόμενα Sc Vt, Thuc. 1, 5; γενόμενα Vc Ac Ph, (γρά καὶ νεμόμενα ἤγουν κατοικούμενα m. 2) Sf; γινόμενα **P** || **20-21** περί τε — Ἀκαρνᾶνας leguntur Thuc. 1, 5 (καὶ μέχρι τοῦδε πολλὰ τῆς Ἑλλάδος τῷ παλαιῷ τρόπῳ ν έ μ ε τ α ι περί τε Λ. κτλ.); om. [Dion.] || **21** Thuc. 1, 2: κ α ὶ παράδειγμα κτλ.

stroyed the usefulness of the composition. Homer (says, *Odyssey* 19.205–208):

> And as snow melts in the high mountains, snow that Eurus has melted, when Zephyrus has blown upon it, and as it melts the rivers run full; so were her beautiful cheeks melted as the tears ran down.

Neither "is shed" nor "is poured" nor "is dissolved" fits so well as "is melted" (*tēketai*), for "melting" gives a vision of snow disappearing.

But when one has many words of equal weight and similar clarity, variation is suitable; for example, Homer (says, *Iliad* 11.269–271):[12]

> | As when a sharp shaft strikes a woman in pain, piercing, [417]
> which the Eileithyai, goddesses of childbirth, send, daughters of Hera keeping charge of bitter pains.

We have "sharp," "piercing," and "bitter," but when he does not have another word of equal weight, he goes back (272) to the first: "Thus sharp pains came upon the mighty son of Atreus." And Thucydides in his prooemion speaks of evidence, sign, example, witness, and makes a circuit of these words: "from evidences (*tekmēria*) that an enquiry carried as far back as possible leads me to trust"(1.1); and "there is a witness (*martyrion*); for when Delos was being purged by Athenians" (1.8), and "a sign (*sēmeion*) is that these customs are still maintained among the Ozolian Locri and the Aetolians and Acarnanians" (1.6), and "not the least example (*paradeigma*) of what I am saying is that migrations were the cause of there not being similar growth elsewhere" (1.6).

[12] With what follows, cf. Pseudo-Dionysius, *Ars Rhetorica* 11.9 (vol. 2, pp. 385–86 Usener-Radermacher).

## *Περὶ περιττότητος.*

*Ἡ περιττότης ἐστὶ διπλῆ, καὶ κατὰ λέξιν καὶ κατὰ γνώμην· ἑκατέρα δὲ διπλῆ, καὶ ἡ κατὰ λέξιν καὶ ἡ κατὰ γνώμην, καὶ ἡ μὲν κατὰ λέξιν γίνεται διατριβῇ καὶ |* [418] *πλήθει, ἡ δὲ κατὰ γνώμην κατὰ ἐπενθυμήσεις καὶ λόγων καθολικῶν τοῖς ἰδίοις συμπλοκήν.*

*Διατριβή ἐστι βραχέος διανοήματος ἠθικοῦ ἔκτασις, ἵνα ἐμμείνῃ τὸ ἦθος τοῦ λέγοντος ἐν τῇ γνώμῃ τοῦ ἀκούοντος, οἷον «τὴν μὲν ὕβριν Μειδίου πάντες ἴστε», ἐξέτεινε δ᾽ αὐτὸ οὕτως «τὴν μὲν ἀσέλγειαν καὶ τὴν ὕβριν, ᾗ πρὸς ἅπαντας ἀεὶ χρῆται Μειδίας, οὐδένα οὔθ᾽ ὑμῶν οὔτε τῶν ἄλλων πολιτῶν ἀγνοεῖν οἴομαι»· καὶ τὸ Περὶ τοῦ στεφάνου προοίμιον ὁμοίως ἔχει.*

*Πλῆθος δέ ἐστι ποικίλων ὀνομάτων ἰσοτίμων ἐπίχυσις εἰς κίνησιν ἤθους, οἷον «τοῦ δὲ παρόντος ἀγῶνος ἡ προαίρεσις αὐτὴ ἐχθροῦ μὲν ἐπήρειαν ἔχει καὶ ὕβριν καὶ λοιδορίαν καὶ προπηλακισμὸν ὁμοῦ καὶ πάντα τὰ τοιαῦτα», ὅπου καὶ τὸ πλῆθος ἔδειξεν εἰπὼν «ὁμοῦ».*

*Ἡ δὲ ἐπενθύμησίς ἐστιν ἐνθύμημα ἐπιφερόμενον, ὃ μὴ προστεθὲν μὲν οὐ ποθεῖται, προστεθὲν δὲ τὸ πᾶν ὠφελεῖ. οἱ δὲ καθολικοὶ λόγοι δῆλον ὅ τί ποτέ εἰσι. παραδείγματα καὶ τῶν ἐπενθυμήσεων καὶ τῶν καθολικῶν λόγων παραλλάξ εἰσιν, ὡς ἐν τῷ Θουκυδίδου ἐπιταφίῳ· ὧν ὁ καιρὸς οὗτος· πρὸς μὲν τὰ σκληρὰ καὶ αὐθάδη διανοήματα ἐπενθυμήσεις παραλαμβάνονται, ἵνα μαλάξωσι τὰ ἤθη, πρὸς δὲ τὴν πίστιν τῶν ἰδίων λόγων οἱ κοινοὶ λόγοι καὶ καθολικοί. ἀμφοτέρων δ᾽ ἦν ἐν τῷ ἐπιταφίῳ χρεία· καὶ γὰρ αὔθαδές ἐστι καὶ ἄπιστον τὸ λέγειν «οὐκ ἔδει λέγεσθαι ἐπιτάφιον», τῶν |* [419] *πάλαι οὕτω δοκιμασάντων. πρὸς μὲν οὖν τὸ αὔθαδες αἱ ἐπενθυμήσεις, πρὸς δὲ τὸ ἄπιστον οἱ καθολικοὶ λόγοι.*

1 supr. **P** **P**π, mg. Sf; om. Vc Ac Ph | mg. δ̅ **P** Ac || 2 pr. καὶ om. Sf || 3 pr. καὶ — γνώμην om. Sf | utrumque ἡ om. Ph || 3-4 καὶ ἡ μὲν κατὰ λέξιν om. Ph || 6 διατριβή δε ἐστὶ Vδ | ἔκστασις Vc Ph || 8 αὐτὸ Vc Sf Ph; αὐτὴν **P** Ac | Dem. 21, 1 || 9 πάντας Ph | χρῆται μειδίας ἀεὶ Pc | οὔθ' Vc Sf; om. **P** Ac Ph || 10 τὸ τοῦ περὶ στεφάνου Ph || 13 Dem. 18, 12 | αὕτη codd. || 18 δὲ (pro καὶ) Sf | ἐνθυμήσεων Ph || 19 παραλλὰξ εἰσίν Sf, m. po. **P**, v.l. **P**; παραλλάξεις Ph, m. 1 **P** Vc; παραλλάξεις εἰσίν Ac | ὡς om. v.l. **P** || 20 νοήματα Ac || 24 γενέσθαι Pa | p. 210, 24 τοῖς πάλαι οὕτως ἐδοκιμάσθη Thuc. 2, 35 | οὖν Ac Sf; γὰρ Vk Nc; om. **P** Vc Ph || 25 Vc: τὸ ⌊Ι⌉ἄυ⌊θαδες m. po.⌉ Vc; Ph: τὸ θαυμᾶσαι | αἱ Ac Sf; om. **P** Vc | λόγοι om. Pa

## CHAPTER 5: ON ABUNDANCE

There are two kinds of abundance (*perittotēs*),[13] in word choice
and in thought, and each of these, that in word choice and that
in thought, is double also; abundance in words comes about from
dwelling (*diatribē*) on something and | by fullness (*plēthos*), in [418]
thought by inserting extra arguments (*epenthymēseis*) and by mix-
ing in general statements (*katholikoi logoi*) with particulars.

*Diatribē* is an extension of a short ethical thought in order for the character of the speaker to remain fixed in the mind of the listener; for example (Dem. 21.1), "You all know the hybris of Meidias," which he extended by saying, "None of you, nor any of the other citizens, is, I think, unaware of the brutality and insolence that Meidias always uses toward everyone." The prooemion of *On the Crown* is similar.[14]

*Plēthos* is a pouring on of a variety of words of equal value to give liveliness to character; for example (Dem. 18.12): "The motivation for the present suit is the malice of a personal enemy and his insolence and abuse and slander together and all such things," where he pointed to the fullness of expression by saying "together."

*Epenthymēsis* is bringing in an enthymeme that would not be
missed if it were omitted but when added helps the case. What
general statements are is self-evident. Examples of epenthymeses
and general statements alternate, as in Thucydides' Funeral Oration, where they are occasioned as follows: epenthymeses are
added to difficult and presumptuous thoughts in order to soften
their character, and common and general statements are introduced for proof of particular statements. There is use of both
in the Funeral Oration, for it is presumptuous and unpersuasive to say (2.35) that "there was no need for a funeral oration
to be spoken," | (*but he will speak*) since the ancients approved. [419]
Epenthymeses are thus directed toward presumptuous remarks
and general statements to those that are unpersuasive.

[13] Cf. Phoebammon 1.3. Hermogenes' term for abundance is *peribolē*, cf. *On Ideas* 1.11.

[14] Demosthenes dwells in 18.1–8 on the need for fairness and his disadvantage in the trial.

*Τῶν δὲ αὐθαδῶν καὶ τολμηρῶν διανοημάτων θεραπεῖαι καὶ παραμυθίαι δύο, ἢ βραχεῖα προσθήκη ἢ ὁμολογία τοῦ τολμήματος. βραχεῖα μὲν οὖν προσθήκη οὕτως «ὁ μὲν οὖν παρὼν καιρός, ὦ Ἀθηναῖοι, μονονουχὶ λέγει φωνὴν ἀφιείς, ὅτι τῶν πραγμάτων ὑμῖν ἐκείνων αὐτοῖς ἀντιληπτέον ἐστί» καὶ πάλιν ἀλλαχοῦ «ὥσπερ ἑωλοκρασίαν τινά μου τῆς ἑαυτοῦ πονηρίας κατασκεδάσας»· καὶ Πλάτων «ἁλμυρὰν ἀκοὴν ἀποκλύσασθαι ποτίμῳ λόγῳ», αὔθαδες τοῦτο· τίς οὖν ἡ βραχεῖα προσθήκη; «οἷον ἁλμυρὰν ἀκοήν». Ὁμολογία δὲ τοῦ τολμήματος, ὡς ἐν τῷ Κατὰ Τιμοκράτους «καὶ γὰρ εἰ φορτικὸς ὁ λόγος εἶναι δοκεῖ, ὅμως ἐρῶ· ἀποκτείνατε αὐτόν, ἵνα τοῖς ἀσεβέσιν ἐν Ἅιδου θῇ τοῦτον τὸν νόμον».*

## *Περὶ παραλείψεως καὶ ἀποσιωπήσεως.*

*Πότε παράλειψις καὶ ἀποσιώπησις γίνεται; ὅταν βουληθῶμεν* [420] *τὴν ὑπόνοιαν μείζονα καταστῆσαι τοῦ πράγ|ματος ἐν τῇ γνώμῃ τῶν ἀκουόντων, ἢ λέγομεν· οἷον λάβωμεν πρῶτον ἐκ τοῦ λόγου παράδειγμα «πῶς οὗτος κέχρηται τῷ πατρί»· λέγω ἴσως ἢ ἀντεῖπεν ἢ οὐκ ἐπείσθη, ἡ δὲ ἀποσιώπησις μείζονα τὴν ὑπόνοιαν πεποίηκεν, ὡς «ἐπιβουλεύων τῷ πατρί». Δημοσθένης δὲ τῇ ἀποσιωπήσει τῇ τελείᾳ οὕτως κέχρηται ἐν τῷ Περὶ τοῦ στεφάνου «ἀλλ' ἐμοὶ μὲν οὐ βούλομαι δὲ δυσχερὲς οὐδὲν εἰπεῖν ἀρχόμενος τοῦ λόγου».*

*Ἐν προσποιήσει δὲ παραλείψεως μνήμη τῶν πραγμάτων κατὰ τρεῖς τρόπους γίνεται, ἤτοι ὅταν μικρὰ μὲν ᾖ τὰ πράγματα, χρήσιμα δὲ τῷ λέγοντι· ἢ ὅταν ᾖ γνώριμα, διὰ μὲν τὸ γνώριμα εἶναι φησὶ*

1 non incipit novum caput Vc Ac Sf Ph; caput ε̄ **P** (mg. πόσαι καὶ ποῖαι παραμυθίαι τῶν αὐθαδῶν καὶ τολμηρῶν διανοημάτων **P**); ε̄ περὶ αὐθαδῶν ἐπινοημάτων **P**π, mg. int. Pa | δὲ om. Ph | ἐπινοημάτων **P**π || 2 ⌊ἡ m. 2 ex ἢ⌉ βραχεία προσθήκη. ⌊καὶ add. m. 2; ἡ m. 2 ex ἢ⌉ Sf | cf. 256, 2; de metaphoris (τὸ ὡσπερεὶ φάναι καὶ οἱονεί κτλ.) cf. Aristotelem et Theophrastum Π. ὕψ. 32, 3. 4; cf. Arist. Rhet. Γ 7 p. 1408b2. Π. εὑρ. p. 184, 3 || 3 Dem. 1, 2 | ὦ ἀθηναῖοι om. Vc Sf Ph || 4 ἐκείνων om. Ac || 4-5 αὐτοῖς om. Sf | αὐτοῖς ἀντιληπτέον ἐστί om. Ph || 5 ἐστί om., ἢ ἐκείνων εἴπερ σωτηρίας αὐτῶν φροντίζετε add. Ac, cf. Dem. | Dem. 18, 50 || 5-6 τινὰ ἀλλ' οὐ τῆς Ph || 6 κατεσκέδασεν Ph Sf; κατεσκεδάσας Vc | Plat. Phaedr. 243 D | οἷον ἁλμυρὰν **P** || 7 δὲ ante τοῦτο add. Sf, (er.) Vc || 9 cf. Dem. 24, 104 || 10 τοιοῦτον (om. τὸν) Ph || 12 supr. Ac, mg. **P** Sf; om. Vc Ph | mg. ε̄ Ac Sf, ϛ̄ **P** || 13 τότε Ac || 15 ᾗι λέγομεν Ac; ἢ εἰ λέγοιμεν Vδ; ἢ λεγομένων Ph | exsp. ἐκ τοῦ βίου, cf. 258, 24 || 16 ad problema p. 192, 18 refert Diac. | πρί̄⌊Ι⌉ Ac Sf || 18 τελ⌊εί ex ευταί⌉αι Ph || 19 τοῦ om. Ph | Dem. 18, 3 | cf. Π. ἰδ. 361, 13 | δὲ m. 1, γὰρ m. po., Vc || 20 εἰπεῖν οὐδὲν Ac Sf Ph, Dem.; οὐδὲν om. Vc

### CHAPTER 6: <ON REMEDYING PRESUMPTUOUS AND RASH THOUGHTS>

There are two remedies and excuses of presumptuous and rash thoughts, either by a short addition or by an acknowledgement of the rashness;[15] a short addition as in the following (Dem. 1.2): "The present crisis, Athenians, calls on you, almost with an audible voice, that you take into your own hands control of those events." And again, elsewhere (Dem. 18.50): "as it were, having drenched me with some dregs of his villainy." And Plato (*Phaedrus* 243d): "to wash away the brackish sound with potable water"; this is presumptuous. What, then, is the brief addition? "Brackish sound, as it were." There is an example of acknowledgement of rashness in *Against Timocrates* (Dem. 24.104): "For even if the statement seems to be strong language, I shall say it: put him to death so he can pass this law for the wicked in Hades."

### CHAPTER 7: ON PARALEIPSIS AND APOSIOPESIS

When do *paraleipsis* and *aposiōpēsis* occur?[16] Whenever we want to implant greater suspicion about the subject | in the mind of the [420]
hearers than we actually state. Let us take the first example from the remark, "How this man has treated his father—" I am perhaps saying that he contradicted him or did not obey him, but the aposiopesis has increased suspicion that he was plotting against his father. Demosthenes uses a complete aposiopesis in *On the Crown* (Dem. 18.3) as follows: "But for me—I do not want to say anything harsh at the beginning of my speech."

In affecting paraleipsis, mention of things is made in three ways, either when the things (*passed over*) are minor but useful to the speaker, or when they are known and he claims he is

[15] Cf. Aristotle, *Rhetoric* 3.7.9; Longinus, *On Sublimity* 32.3–4.

[16] In paraleipsis (*praeteritio* in Latin) the speaker claims to pass over some matters without discussion but itemizes briefly what is to be omitted; in aposiopesis (*reticentia* in Latin), the speaker starts to say something and then breaks off suddenly, leaving some impression on the audience of what was about to be said. The terminology was in common use; cf., Alexander, *On Figures* 1.16 and 19; Lausberg, §§882–89.

*παραλιπεῖν, διὰ δὲ τὸ χρήσιμα εἶναι λέγει αὐτά· ἢ ὅταν ἐπαχθῆ ᾖ, χρήσιμα δὲ τῷ λέγοντι, διὰ μὲν τὸ ἐπαχθῆ εἶναι φησὶ παραλιπεῖν, διὰ δὲ τὸ χρήσιμα εἶναι λέγει αὐτά.*

*Παραδείγματα τούτων, τῶν μὲν μικρῶν ἐν τῷ Κατὰ Μειδίου «ὅσα μὲν οὖν ἢ τοὺς χορευτὰς κωλύων ἀφεθῆναι τῆς στρατείας ἠνώχληκεν, ἢ προβαλλόμενος καὶ κελεύων ἑαυτὸν εἰς Διονύσια χειροτονεῖν ἐπιμελητήν, ἢ τἄλλα ὅσα τοιαῦτα, ἐάσω», εἶτα τὴν αἰτίαν ἐπιφέρει τοῦ προσποιεῖσθαι παραλιπεῖν «οὐ γὰρ ἀγνοῶ τοῦθ', ὅτι τῷ μὲν ἐπηρεαζομένῳ τὴν αὐτὴν τούτων ἕκαστον ὀργὴν ἥνπερ ἄλλ' ὁτιοῦν τῶν*
[421] *δεινοτάτων παρίστη, | ὑμῖν δὲ τοῖς ἔξω τοῦ πράγματος οὖσιν οὐκ ἂν ἴσως ἄξια αὐτὰ καθ' ἑαυτὰ ἀγῶνος φανείη». Τῶν δὲ γνωρίμων ἐν τῷ Περὶ τῆς ἀτελείας «ἐγὼ δ' ὅτι μὲν τινῶν κατηγοροῦντα πάντας ἀφαιρεῖσθαι τὴν δωρεὰν τῶν ἀδίκων ἐστίν, ἐάσω», εἶτα τὴν αἰτίαν ἐπιφέρει τοῦ προσποιεῖσθαι παραλιπεῖν «καὶ γὰρ εἴρηται τρόπον τινὰ καὶ ὑφ' ὑμῶν ἴσως γινώσκεται». Τῶν δὲ ἐπαχθῶν παράδειγμα ἐν τῷ Περὶ τοῦ στεφάνου «ἐν μὲν δὴ τοῖς ἰδίοις εἰ μὴ πάντες ἴστε ὅτι κοινὸς καὶ φιλάνθρωπος καὶ πᾶσι τοῖς δεομένοις ἐπαρκῶν, σιωπῶ καὶ οὐδὲν ἂν εἴποιμι περὶ αὐτῶν, οὔτε εἴ τινας ἐκ τῶν πολεμίων ἐλυσάμην, οὔτε εἴ τισι θυγατέρας ἀποροῦσι συνεξέδωκα», εἶτα τὴν αἰτίαν τοῦ παραλιπεῖν ἐπιφέρει «ἐγὼ νομίζω τὸν μὲν εὖ παθόντα δεῖν μεμνῆσθαι παρὰ πάντα τὸν χρόνον, τὸν δ' εὖ ποιήσαντα εὐθὺς ἐπιλελῆσθαι, εἰ δεῖ τὸν μὲν χρηστοῦ, τὸν δὲ μὴ μικροψύχου ποιεῖν ἔργον ἀνθρώπου. τὸ δὲ τὰς ἰδίας εὐεργεσίας ἀναμιμνήσκειν μικροῦ δεῖν ὅμοιόν ἐστι τῷ ὀνειδίζειν».*

## *Περὶ περιπλοκῆς.*

*Τὸ περιπλέκειν διαβάλλεται μὲν ὡς κακία τοῦ λέγειν, εἰ δὲ ἐν καιρῷ γίγνοιτο, ζηλωτὸν ἂν σχῆμα εὑρεθείη. καιρὸς οὖν τῆς περιπλοκῆς*

**1** λέγη (ει supr.) Pa || **2** μὲν τὸ Pa Vc Ac Sf; δὲ τὸ Pc; ⌊τὸ del.⌋ μὲν τὸ Ph | παραλείπει Ph || **3** λέγηι (ει supr.) Pa || **5** Dem. 21, 15 | τὰς Pa | στρατιᾶς Ph || **8** προσποιεῖσθαι hic et p. 214, 14 suspect. | παραλείπειν Ac; παραλειπεῖν Ph || **9** ⌊ἥν m. po.⌋περ Vc; ὥσπερ Sf || **10** παρίστη Ac Ph, (σι add. m. po.) Pc Vc Sf; παρίστησι Pa || **12** τῆς om. **P** Ac | Dem. 20, 2 | τινῶν m. po. suppl. Sf || **13-14** εἶτα — παραλιπεῖν om. Sf Ph, (m. 2 suppl.) Vc; utique προσποιεῖσθαι suspect., cf. p. 214, 8 || **15** διαγιγνώσκεται Pa | τοῦ om. Ac || **16** ἐν δὲ τοῖς Dem. 18, 268 | δὴ om. Vδ || **16-17** κοινῶς καὶ φιλανθρώπως Ph || **18** τούτων Vc Ac Sf Ph | τισιν Ph || **20** δεῖν **P**, Dem.; om. Vc Ac Sf Ph || **23** μικροῦ δεῖν om. Pc || **24** supr. Vc Sf, mg. **P**; περὶ τοῦ περιπλέκειν **P**π; περιπεριπλοκῆς πότε περιπλέκειν εὔκαιρον καὶ ποσαχῶς γίνεται mg. Ph, (om. περὶ περιπλοκῆς) mg. Ac | mg. ϛ̄ Ac, ζ̄ **P**

leaving them out because they are known but he mentions them because they are useful, or when they are invidious but useful to the speaker and he claims to leave them out because they are invidious but speaks them because they are useful. Now examples of these:

— of claiming to pass over small things, in *Against Meidias* (Dem. 21.15): "The trouble he caused by hindering the exemption of the chorus members from military service, or by putting himself forward and demanding to be elected overseer at the Dionysia, or other such things, I omit." Then he adds the reason for affecting to omit these facts: "for I am not unaware that each of these things has caused the same anger to the one insolently treated as any more serious action, but | to you who are not directly concerned, these [421] things in themselves would probably not seem to be worthy of litigation."

—of claiming to pass over things that are known, in *On Immunity* (Dem. 20.2): "For my part, I shall omit the fact that it is unjust to take away this gift from all because you are attacking some." Then he brings in the reason for affecting to pass it over: "for it has in a way been stated and is probably known to you."

— an example of passing over invidious things in *On the Crown* (Dem. 18.268): "If you do not all know that in private life I was openhearted and generous and available to all who had need of me, I am silent and say nothing about it, nor whether I ransomed some from the enemy or helped some others to give their daughters in marriage." Then he brings in the reason for the omission: "I think that one who has received a kindness ought to remember it for all time, but the doer of the benefit should forget it straightaway, if the former is to behave like a good man and the latter like one free from meanness. To be remembering private benefactions is almost the same as to reproach (*the recipients*)."

## CHAPTER 8: ON CIRCUMLOCUTION

To speak in a roundabout way (*periplokein*) is criticized as a fault of style,[17] but if done on the right occasion an admirable figure would be created. There are three occasions for circumlocution

[17] As a fault, periphrasis is sometimes called *perissologia*; cf. Quintilian 8.6.61.

[422] *τῶν λόγων τριπλοῦς. | περιπλέκομεν γάρ, ἤτοι ὅταν αἰσχρὰ ᾖ τὰ λεγόμενα· φυλαττόμενοι γὰρ τὴν ἀπρέπειαν τοῦ λόγου αὐτῷ τῷ περιπλέκειν δηλοῦμεν ἃ θέλομεν εὐπρεπῶς καὶ πικρότερον τὸν λόγον ποιούμεθα· ἢ ὅταν λυπηρὰ ᾖ τοῖς ἀκούουσιν, ἢ ὅταν ἐπαχθῆ τοῖς λέγουσι.*

*Παραδείγματα τῶν μὲν αἰσχρῶν ἐν τῷ Κατὰ Τιμάρχου φησὶν Αἰσχίνης «εἰδὼς δ᾽ αὐτὸν ἔνοχον ὄντα», θέλει μὲν εἰπεῖν «τῇ πορνείᾳ», φυλαττόμενος δὲ τὸ αἰσχρὸν περιπλέκει λέγων «οἷς ὀλίγῳ πρότερον ἠκούσατ᾽ ἀναγινώσκοντος τοῦ γραμματέως». Τῶν δὲ λυπηρῶν ὁ Δημοσθένης, ὡς ἐν τοῖς Φιλιππικοῖς φησιν «ὁ μὲν οὖν παρὼν καιρὸς μονονουχὶ λέγει φωνὴν ἀφιείς, ὅτι τῶν πραγμάτων ὑμῖν ἐκείνων αὐτοῖς ἀντιληπτέον ἐστί», καὶ ἐπειδὴ λυπηρόν ἐστι τὸ λέγειν «εἰ δὲ μή, ἀπολεῖται τὰ πράγματα», περιέπλεξεν «εἴπερ ὑπὲρ σωτηρίας ὑμῶν αὐτῶν φροντίζετε»· καὶ πάλιν παρὰ πόδας ἔνεστί γε περιπλοκὴ μετὰ συλλήψεως «ἡμεῖς δέ», ὑπακούεται «ἀμελοῦμεν», ἀλλὰ τοῦτο λυπηρόν ἐστι τοῖς Ἀθηναίοις· πῶς οὖν περιέπλεξεν; «οὐκ οἶδ᾽ ὅντινά μοι δοκοῦμεν ἔχειν τρόπον πρὸς αὐτά». Τῶν δὲ ἐπαχθῶν τὸ παράδειγμα ἐν τῷ Κατὰ Μειδίου· φησὶ γὰρ ὁ Δημοσθένης πρῶτον μὲν ὅτι «ἐθελοντὴς χορηγεῖν* [423] *ὑπέστην», ὅπερ ἐστὶ φιλοτιμίας, εἶτα δὲ «κληρουμένων | πάντων πρῶτος αἱρεῖσθαι τὸν αὐλητὴν ἔλαχον», ὅπερ ἐστὶν εὐτυχίας· ἐπάγει γοῦν λέγων «ὑμεῖς μὲν οὖν, ὡς εἰκός, ἀμφότερα ἀπεδέξασθε, τήν τε φιλοτιμίαν τὴν ἐμήν», καὶ ἐπειδὴ ἐπαχθές ἐστι τὸ λέγειν «τὴν εὐτυχίαν», περιέπλεξε «καὶ τὸ συμβὰν ἀπὸ τῆς τύχης».*

*Ὅτι δὲ τὸ ὄνομα τοῦ σχήματος τοῦτό ἐστιν ἡ περιπλοκή, Αἰσχίνης φησὶν ἐν τῷ Κατὰ Τιμάρχου «οὗτος φανήσεται οὐ μόνον ἡταιρηκώς, ἀλλὰ μὰ τὸν Διόνυσον, οὐκ οἶδ᾽ ὅπως δεῖ περιπλέκειν ὅλην τὴν ἡμέραν*

**2** γὰρ om. Ph, (suppl. m. po.) Vc | αὐτῶ⌊ι⌉ τ⌊ῶ m. po. ex ὸ⌉ Vc || **5** παράδειγμα Vc Ac Sf Ph; cf. 214, 4 || **5-6** Aesch. 1, 2 || **9** ὡς ante ὁ Pe; suspect., cf. l. 23 | φησιν **P** Ac; om. Vδ; ἐστιν Vc Ph; ⌊ἐστὶ, del. m. 1⌉φησίν Sf | Dem. 1, 2 || **9-10** cf. 212, 3 || **11** καὶ ἐπειδὴ **P** Sf; καὶ om. Vc Ph; ἐπειδὴ δὲ Ac || **11-12** ἀπολεῖτ⌊ε m. po. ex αι⌉ Sf || **12** ὑμῶν om. Vc Ac Sf Ph, Dem. || **13** ἐφροντίζετε Ph || **14** ὑμεῖς Ac Ph, (ὑ ex cr.) Vc | ὑπακούεται **P**, (γρ[ά] καὶ ὑπόκειται m. 2) Sf; ὑπακούετε Ac Ph; ⌊ὑ m. po.⌉πακούετ⌊αι er.; οντ ?ες supr. m. po.⌉ Vc || **16** τρόπον ἔχειν Vc Ac Sf Ph | δέ γ' Ph | τὸ om. Ma || **18** ὑπέστη Ald.; ὕπεστιν Vc; ὑπεσχόμην mg. **P**; Dem. 21, 13: ὑπεσχόμην ἐγὼ χορηγήσειν ἐθελοντής | πάντων om. Vc Sf Ph || **18-19** πρῶτον m. 1 Pa || **19** τῆς εὐτυχίας Vc Ac Sf Ph || **20** ὁῦν Ph || **21** καὶ τὴν εὐτυχίαν Ma || **22** τῆς om. Vc || **23** τοῦ σχήματος ante τὸ Vc Ac Sf Ph || **24** οὗτος Ph; οὕτως· **P** Vc Ac Sf; Aesch. 1, 52: οὐκέτι δήπου φάινεται μόνον ἡταιρηκὼς κτλ. | δὲ οὐ Vc || **25** δεῖ om. Vc, (add. m. 2) Sf; δυνήσομαι Aesch.

(*periplokē*)[18] in speech. | We speak in a roundabout way either [422] when what is being said is shameful—for to avoid the impropriety of a word by circumlocution we indicate what we want in an appropriate way and make the speech more pointed—or when the subject is distressing to the hearers or when it is invidious for the speakers.

Aeschines provides examples of circumlocution of shameful matters in *Against Timarchus* (1.2) when he says, "knowing him to be liable..."; he means to say, "on a charge of prostitution," but avoiding the shameful word he speaks of it in a circumlocution: "for what you heard the clerk read out a little earlier." In the case of something distressing, Demosthenes in his speeches against Philip (*First Olynthiac* 2) says, "The present occasion calls on you, almost with an audible voice, to take control of your affairs," and since it is distressing to say "if not, those affairs are ruined," he spoke in a circumlocution: "if you care for your own safety." And again, in the next line there is a circumlocution along with the resumption of the thought: "But as for us," where "we are indifferent" is implied, but this is grievous to the Athenians. How then did he say it indirectly? "I do not quite know what attitude we seem to have toward these things." There is an example of circumlocution of invidious matters in *Against Meidias* (21.13). Demosthenes first says, "I volunteered to act as choregus," which reveals ambition, but then, | "when all the lots were drawn I had [423] the good fortune to get first choice of a flute player," which is a matter of luck. He continues (21.14) by saying, "You then, as was right, welcomed both these things, my ambition,"[19] and since it is invidious to say "my good luck," he paraphrased it with "and what resulted from chance."

As to the fact that the name of the figure is *periplokē*, Aeschines says in *Against Timarchus* (1.52), "He will not only be shown to have been a kept lover—by Dionysus, I do not know why it is necessary to beat about the bush (*periplokein*) all day—but to

[18] Elsewhere usually called *periphrasis*; cf., e.g., Dionysius of Halicarnassus, *Epistle to Pompeius* 2.5 and *On Thucydides* 29; Lausberg §§589–98.

[19] In the text of *Against Meidias* 14 Demosthenes says "my offer."

*καὶ πεπορνευμένος», ὡς δι᾽ ὅλου τοῦ λόγου περιπλέξας διὰ τὸ αἰσχρὰ εἶναι τὰ ῥήματα, ἐπὶ τέλει δὲ νικηθεὶς ὑπὸ τῆς χολῆς εἶπε «καὶ πεπορνευμένος».*

## *Περὶ ἐπαναλήψεως.*

*Ἐπανάληψις γίνεται κατὰ τρόπους τρεῖς, ἐπὶ πράγματος διδασκαλίᾳ, ἐπὶ προσώπου συστάσει ἢ διαβολῇ, ἐπὶ ἤθους βεβαιώσει.*

*Ἐπὶ πράγματος διδασκαλίᾳ, ὡς παρ᾽ Ὁμήρῳ*

*«ἀλλ᾽ ὃ μὲν Αἰθίοπας μετεκίαθε τηλόθ᾽ ἐόντας,*
*Αἰθίοπας, τοὶ διχθὰ δεδαίαται, ἔσχατοι ἀνδρῶν»·*

[424] | *ἐπανέλαβε τὸ ὄνομα, ἵνα δείξῃ, ὅτι δύο γένη Αἰθιόπων. Ἐπὶ προσώπου συστάσει*

*«Νιρεὺς δ᾽ Αἰσύμηθεν ἄγε τρεῖς νῆας ἐίσας,*
*Νιρεύς, Ἀγλαΐης υἱὸς Χαρόποιό τ᾽ ἄνακτος,*
*Νιρεύς, ὃς κάλλιστος ἀνὴρ ὑπὸ Ἴλιον ἦλθεν»·*

*ἐπανέλαβεν, ἵνα κοσμήσῃ τὸ πρόσωπον. ἐπὶ διαβολῇ δὲ «Ἆρες, Ἄρες βροτολοιγέ»· ἐπανέλαβεν, ἵνα τὸ πρόσωπον διαβάλῃ. Ἐπὶ ἤθους βεβαιώσει*

*«τοῦ δ᾽ ἐγὼ ἀντίος εἶμι, καὶ εἰ πυρὶ χεῖρας ἔοικεν,*
*εἰ πυρὶ χεῖρας ἔοικεν»·*

*ἐπανέλαβεν, ἵνα τὸ ἀνδρεῖον βεβαιώσῃ.*

*Παρὰ δὲ τοῖς πεζοῖς ἐπὶ μὲν πράγματος διδασκαλίᾳ Ξενοφῶν ἐν Ἀπομνημονεύμασιν «ἀδικεῖ Σωκράτης οὓς μὲν ἡ πόλις νομίζει θεοὺς*

1 γρ καὶ ὅς· ἀντὶ τοῦ ὅστις αἰσχίνης **P** || 2 ῥήματα **P**; εἰρημένα Vc Ac Sf Ph, v.l. **P** | εἶπεν ὑπὸ τῆς χολῆς Pa || 2-3 καὶ πεπορνευμένος **P**; om. Vc Ph, (suppl., m. 2 ?) Sf; καὶ περιπλέκειν (sic) Ac || 4 supr. Vc Sf, mg. **P**; ἐπανάληψις mg. Ac; περὶ ἐπαναλήψεως ἐπὶ πόσοις καὶ ποίοις ἐπαναλήψεις (sic) γίνεται mg. Ph | mg. ζ̄ Ac, η̄ **P** || 5 τρεῖς m. po. suppl. Pc || 7 καὶ ante ἐπὶ add. m. po. Pc || 8-9 Hom. α 22 || 8-19 eadem fere exempla [Plut.] De vita et poesi Homeri 32-34 || 10 ὅτι om. Vc || 12 Hom. B 671 | δ᾽ om. Ph Sf, (m. 2 suppl.) Vc | αἰσύμηθεν **P** Ac, (ἰ ex ὐ) Vc; αὖ σύμηθεν Ph, (αἰ post αὖ postea add.; m. 1 ?) Sf || 13 om. **P** || 15 γρ συστήσῃ **P** | Hom. E 31: μιαιφόνε add. Vc; μιαιφόνε τειχεσιβλῆτα add. Pc || 16 διαβάλλῃ Vc, m. 1 Pc Sf | ἤθους δὲ Vc || 18-19 Hom. Υ 371 || 18 cf. Π. ἰδ. 304, 10 | ἐγὼν **P** | αἴτιός εἰμι m. 1 Vc || 19 μένος δ᾽ αἴθωνι σιδήρῳ add. vulg.; δέμας δ᾽ αἴθωνι σιδήρῳ (om. altero εἰ — ἔοικεν) Vδ || 22 Xen. Mem. I 1, 1

have prostituted himself." As though throughout the speech he had avoided saying it because the words are shameful, but finally overcome by anger he said "prostituted himself."[20]

## CHAPTER 9: ON EPANALEPSIS

*Epanalēpsis*[21] occurs in three ways: as an explanation of something; as a recommendation of a person or a prejudicial attack; as strengthening characterization. As explanation of something as in Homer (*Odyssey* 1.22):

> But he (*Poseidon*) had gone to visit the Ethiopians who live far off, the Ethiopians who are split into two groups, the remotest of men. | [424]

He repeated the name to show that there are two races of Ethiopians. As a recommendation of a person (*Iliad* 2.671–673):

> Nireus led three shapely ships from Aesyme, Nireus, son of Aglaïa and lord Charops, Nireus, who was the handsomest man who came to Ilium.

He repeated the name to honor the person.[22] As a prejudicial attack, "Ares, Ares, bane of mortals" (*Iliad* 5.31). He repeated the name to attack him. As strengthening characterization (*Iliad* 20.371–372):

> I (*Hector*) shall go against him (*Achilles*), though his hands be like fire, though his hands be like fire.

He used repetition to stress his bravery.

Among prose writers, Xenophon in the *Memorabilia* (1.1.1) used epanalepsis in explanation of something, *(quoting the indictment of Socrates)*: "Socrates does wrong by not believing in the

[20] Cf. also Euripides, *Phoenician Women* 494–95: *periplokas logōn*.

[21] Resumption or repetition; cf., e.g., Demetrius, *On Style* §196; Alexander, *On Figures* 1.13.

[22] Cf. Aristotle, *Rhetoric* 3.12.4; Demetrius, *On Style* §§61–62.

*οὐ νομίζων, ἕτερα δὲ καινὰ δαιμόνια εἰσφέρων· ἀδικεῖ δὲ καὶ τοὺς νέους διαφθείρων». καὶ Δημοσθένης ἐν Φιλιππικοῖς «πάντες ὅσοι πώποτε ἐκπεπλεύκασι στρατηγοὶ παρ' ἡμῶν, ἢ ἐγὼ πάσχειν ὁτιοῦν ἕτοιμός εἰμι, παρὰ τούτων τῶν τὰς νήσους οἰκούντων χρήματα λαμβάνουσι. λαμβάνουσι δὲ οἱ μὲν πλείονας ἔχοντες ναῦς πλείονα». Ἐπὶ δὲ προσώπου συστάσει, ὡς Ξενοφῶν πολλάκις Κῦρον ἐπαναλαμβάνων. ἐπὶ δὲ διαβο-*
[425] *λῇ, ὡς ὁ Δημοσθένης | «ἀλλ' Ἀνδροτίων ἡμῖν πομπείων ἐπισκευαστής, Ἀνδροτίων, ὦ γῆ καὶ θεοί», καὶ ἀλλαχοῦ «ὑμεῖς δὲ Χαρίδημον εἰ χρὴ φρουρεῖν βουλεύεσθε; Χαρίδημον; οἴμοι.» Ἐπὶ ἤθους βεβαιώσει «ἔστιν ὑμῖν, ὦ Ἀθηναῖοι, χρήματα, ἔστιν ὅσα οὐδενὶ τῶν ἄλλων ἀνθρώπων στρατιωτικά», καὶ πάλιν ἐν τῷ Κατὰ Μειδίου «ἀλλ' ἵππον, ἵππον μὲν οὐκ ἐτόλμησεν ὁ κατάρατος οὑτοσὶ πρίασθαι». καὶ Ἡρόδοτος «φονεὺς μὲν τοῦ ἑωυτοῦ ἀδελφεοῦ, φονεὺς δὲ τοῦ καθήραντος».*

## *Περὶ τοῦ κατὰ πεῦσιν σχήματος.*

*Τὸ κατὰ πεῦσιν σχῆμα ἀναντίρρητόν ἐστι· γίνεται γὰρ ἢ περὶ τῶν φύσει ὁμολογουμένων, οἷον «ἆρ' οὐκ ἔστι νῦν ἡμέρα;» ἢ περὶ τῶν τῷ λόγῳ προαποδεδειγμένων, οἷον «εὑρέθης ἐπὶ τῆς οἰκίας διορωρυγμένου τοῦ τοίχου ὑφαιρούμενος τὸ ἱμάτιον· ἆρ' οὐκ εἶ κλέπτης;» καὶ γὰρ τὰ τῷ λόγῳ προαποδεδειγμένα ἴσα τοῖς φύσει ὁμολογουμένοις τῇ δυνάμει ἐστίν.*

*Ἀναντίρρητον δὲ ὂν τὸ σχῆμα τρεῖς ἔχει μορφάς, ἢ πρὸς τοὺς ἀκούοντας ἢ πρὸς τοὺς ἀντιλέγοντας ἢ αὐτοῦ πρὸς ἑαυτὸν τοῦ ῥήτορος.*

[426] *Ἡ πρὸς τοὺς ἀκούοντας πεῦσις ἐλεγκτική, οἷον «πότε | οὖν, ὦ Ἀθηναῖοι, πότε ἃ δεῖ πράξετε; ἐπειδὰν τί γένηται;» Ἡ πρὸς τοὺς ἀντιλέγοντας ἀνατρεπτική, οἷον «τὸ λαβεῖν οὖν τὰ διδόμενα ὁμολογῶν*

**3** ὑμῶν Pc, Dem. 8, 24 || **5** πλείους Pc || **6** ὡς **P** Vc Ac; ὁ Sf; om. Ph | e.g. ad Cyrop. III 2, 14sq. relegat Diac. || **7** ὁ **P**; om. Vc Ac Sf Ph | cf. Π. ἰδ. 353, 3 et 11; 356, 15 | Dem. 22, 78 | ὑμῖν Ac Sf Dem.; cf. Π. ἰδ. 220, 8 || **8** Dem. 23, 210 || **8-9** εἰ χρὴ φρουρεῖν χαρίδημον Vc Ph || **9** χαρίδημον; ὦ γῆ καὶ θεοί· οἴμοι Pc || **9-10** Dem. 1, 19 || **10** ὑμῶν **P** | ὠ (om. Ἀθηναῖοι) Ph || **11** Dem. 21, 174 | μὲν om. Sf Ph || **12** οὗτος Pch Vc | Her. 1, 45 || **13** ἀδελφοῦ Sf, m. 1 Vc || **14** supr. Vc Sf mg. **P**; om. Ac; περι τοῦ κατὰ πεῦσιν· περι τίνων γίνεται τὸ κατὰ πεῦσιν σχῆμα καὶ πόσας καὶ ποίας ἔχει μορφάς· καὶ οἷα ἑκάστη· πόσας δ' ἐπιστροφὰς ἔχει ἡ πρὸς ἑαυτόν Ph | mg. $\bar{\eta}$ Ac Ph, $\bar{\theta}$ **P** || **15** δὲ (pro γὰρ) **P** || **16** cf. Π. ἰδ. 362, 17 || **17** εὑρέθης (ει supra) Vc || **17-18** τοῦ τοίχου διορωρυγμένου Vc Sf Ph || **19** τοῦ λόγου m. 1 Vc Sf || **23** p. 220, 25: Π. ἰδ. 277, 5. 6. 360, 17 | Dem. 4, 10 | ω (om. Ἀθηναῖοι) Ph || **24** πράξατε Ph || **25** Dem. 18, 119

gods in whom the city believes and by introducing other new divinities, and he does wrong by corrupting the young." And by Demosthenes in his speeches against Philip (*On the Chersonese* 24): "All the generals that have ever set sail from your land—I am ready to suffer any punishment (*if I am wrong*)—raise money from those inhabiting these islands. And they raise more who have more ships." Out of respect for his person, Xenophon often repeats the name of Cyrus. And for prejudicial attack as in Demosthenes (22.78): | "But Androtion is the repairer of your [425] processional plate. Androtion! by Heaven and Earth!" And elsewhere (cf. Dem. 23.210): "And you are deliberating whether Charidemus should have protection! Charidemus! Heaven help us." For strengthening characterization (Dem. 1.19): "You have money, Athenians, you have more than any other peoples for military purposes." And again in *Against Meidias* (21.174): "But this accursed creature did not even dare to buy a horse, not a horse!" And in Herodotus (1.45, of Adrastus): "destroyer of his own brother, destroyer of his purifier."

## CHAPTER 10: ON THE FIGURE OF INTERROGATION

The figure of interrogation (*peusis*)[23] involves a supposition that cannot be denied, for it concerns either things naturally agreed upon—for example, "Is it not now day?"—or things previously shown in the speech; for example, "You were discovered stealing a cloak at the house after having dug a hole in the wall. Are you not a thief?" What has been previously shown in the speech is equal in effect to things naturally agreed upon.

This figure, although a supposition that cannot be denied, takes three forms (*morphai*): addressed either to the listeners or the opponents or by the orator to himself.

A question to the listeners is a reproof; for example (Dem. 4.10), "When, | then, Athenians, when will you do what is [426] needed? When what occurs?" One to the opponents is refutative; for example (Dem. 18.119), "Having agreed, then, that it was legal to accept what is given, do you indict as illegal the return of

[23] I.e., rhetorical question; cf. Longinus, *On Sublimity* 18.1; Apsines 10.13.

*ἔννομον εἶναι, τὸ χάριν τούτων ἀποδοῦναι παρανόμων γράφῃ;» Ἡ αὐτοῦ πρὸς ἑαυτὸν τοῦ ῥήτορος πεῦσις διπλῆ· ἀκοῆς ἐπιστροφὴν ἔχει καὶ πίστωσιν κατὰ πρόληψιν ὑπονοίας καὶ λύσιν. ὅταν γὰρ αὐτὸς ἑαυτοῦ πυνθάνηται ὁ ῥήτωρ, ἅμα καὶ ἐπέστρεψε τοὺς ἀκούοντας καὶ τὴν πίστιν προκατέλαβε· πιστεύει γὰρ ἕκαστος τῶν ἀκουόντων ἐννοῶν, ὅτι οὐκ ἂν ἠρώτησεν ἑαυτὸν ὁ ῥήτωρ, εἰ μὴ ἐπίστευεν ἀποδείξειν, καὶ εἴ τινα ἔχει ὑπόνοιαν ὁ ἀκροατής, θεραπεύεται· ὥσπερ ἐπὶ ταύτης τῆς ἐρωτήσεως «ἔστιν ὑμῖν πόρος, ὃν ἂν μὲν ἤδη ζητῆτε οὐχ εὑρήσετε, ἐὰν δὲ περιμένητε, εὑρήσετε», εἶτ᾽ ἐπιφέρει «τίς οὖν ἔσθ᾽ οὗτος ὁ νῦν μὲν οὐκ ὤν, αὖθις δὲ γενησόμενος; αἰνίγματι γὰρ ὅμοιον τοῦτο· ἐγὼ φράσω.»*

## *Περὶ ἀσυνδέτου.*

*Τὸ ἀσύνδετον σχῆμα καὶ τὸ μετὰ τῶν συνδέσμων λεγόμενον δοκεῖ τὸ μὲν δεδέσθαι, τὸ δὲ λελύσθαι. ταὐτὸ* | [427] *δὲ ἀμφότερα δηλοῖ, καὶ ἐργάζεται καὶ μέγεθος ὁμοίως καὶ ἦθος, ὅταν ἑκατέρου καιρὸς ᾖ. ταὐτὸν δ᾽ ἐργαζόμενα οὐχ ὁμοίως ἐργάζεται, ἀλλὰ τὸ μὲν μετὰ συνδέσμων πραγματικὸν πλῆθος ἢ μέγεθος, οἷον «Ὄλυνθον μὲν δὴ καὶ Μεθώνην καὶ Ἀπολλωνίαν καὶ δύο καὶ τριάκοντα πόλεις ἐπὶ Θρᾴκης ἐῶ», τὸ δὲ ἄνευ συνδέσμων λεγόμενον ἠθικόν ἐστι «καὶ πάλιν ἡνίκα Πύδνα, Ποτίδαια, Μεθώνη, Παγασαί, τἆλλα, ἵνα μὴ καθ᾽ ἕκαστον λέγων διατρίβω, πολιορκούμενα ἀπηγγέλλετο».*

**2** διπλῆ· **P**; διπλῆν Ac Ph, (ν er.) Sf, (ν m. po. in ras.) Vc; Diac.: διότι γράφεται διπλῆ, διὰ τοῦτο ἀσαφὲς ἔδοξέ τισι τὸ ῥητὸν κατὰ τὸ ἐλλειπτικόν· ὤφειλε γὰρ εἰπεῖν οὕτως «ἡ ... διπλῆν ἔχει τὴν ἐνέργειαν, ἀκοῆς ..» .. ἐμοὶ δὲ μηδὲν ἐλλείπειν δοκεῖ· χρὴ γὰρ στίξαι τελείαν εἰς τὸ «διπλῆν ἀκοῆς ἐπιστροφὴν ἔχει» κτλ. | ἀκοῆς (β) ἐπιστροφὴν ἔχει (α) καί (γ), numeri m. po., Sf | καὶ om. Ph || **3** καὶ ante ὑπονοίας Ma | ἑαυτὸν Ph || **5** ἐννο⌊ι er.⌉ῶν Pc || **6** ἐπίστευσεν Ac Ph || **7** ὑπόνοιαν ἔχει Ac, (εἶχεν) Pc || **8** Dem. 14, 24 | ζητεῖτε Ph || **8-9** περιμείνητε Vc || **10** γενησόμενος (α), αἰνίγματι (γ) γὰρ ὅμοιον, τοῦτο ἐγώ (β), numeri m. po., Sf | ὅμοιον. τὸ τοῦτο (ν) Pa; ὅμοιον· ⌊I-II⌉ τοῦτο⌊I⌉ Pc | τοῦτο m. 1 (m. po. γρ τοῦτον) Vc || **11** supr. Pa Sf, (καὶ συνδεδεμένου add. m. 2) Vc; mg. Pc Ac Ph | mg. θ̄ Ac Ph, ῑ **P** || **12** cf. Π. ἰδ. 316, 2. 319, 4. 357, 1-20 | alt. τὸ om. Ph **P**π || **14** ἦθος **P** Ac; πλῆθος Vc Sf Ph v.l. **P** || **16** ἦθος Ac | Dem. 9, 26 || **16-17** καὶ ἀπολλωνίαν καὶ μεθώνην Ac || **18** συνδέσμου Vc | Dem. 1, 9 || **19** παγασαὶ μεθώνη Vc | ἕκαστα Ac | ἅμα λέγων Ph | λέγω pa || **20** ἀπήγγελτο Ph

gratitude for them?" A question of the speaker to himself has two functions: it attracts the attention of the audience and includes a proof and refutation of suspicion by anticipation. For whenever the orator asks himself a question, at the same time he has attracted the attention of the hearers and has attained their agreement in advance. For each of the listeners trusts him, knowing that the orator would not address a question to himself if he did not believe he could provide the answer, and if the listener had any suspicion of him, it is remedied. As in this question (Dem. 14.24): "You have a resource, which you will not find if you look for it now, but if you wait, you will find it"; then he adds, "What then is this resource that is not now but will be hereafter? That sounds like a puzzle. I shall explain."

## CHAPTER 11: ON ASYNDETON

The figure asyndeton and what is said with connectives (*syndesmoi*)[24] seem in the latter case to be tied together, in the other to be disconnected. Both convey the same thought, | and magnitude and character are respectively conveyed whenever there is occasion for either. Though conveying the same thought, they do not do it in the same way, but what is stated with connectives conveys quantity or importance; for example (Dem. 9.26), "I pass over Olynthus and Methone and Apollonia and thirty-two cities in Thrace"; while what is said without connectives conveys character[25] (Dem. 1.9): "And again when it was reported that Pydna, Potidea, Methone, Pagasae, and other places were besieged, not to waste time enumerating each." [427]

[24] Polysyndeton; cf. Aristotle, *Rhetoric*.

[25] I.e., contributes to the characterization of the speaker; in the example cited, Demosthenes' impatience is revealed.

## *Περὶ προεκθέσεως καὶ ἀνακεφαλαιώσεως.*

*Τὸ ἐν ἀρχῇ τι λέγειν ἐπὶ κεφαλαίων, περὶ ὧν τις μέλλει κατασκευάζειν ἢ διδάσκειν, οἱ τεχνικοὶ καλοῦσι προέκθεσιν, τὸ δ' ἐπὶ τέλους ἀναμιμνήσκειν τὰ ἀποδεδειγμένα ἢ λελεγμένα οἱ τεχνικοὶ καλοῦσιν ἀνακεφαλαίωσιν. οἱ δὲ παλαιοὶ τὴν μὲν προέκθεσιν καλοῦσιν ὑπόσχεσιν, τὴν δὲ ἀνακεφαλαίωσιν ἐπάνοδον, ὡς Δημοσθένης δηλοῖ λέγων οὕτως «δίκαιόν ἐστιν ἐμὲ τρία ὑμῖν ὑπεσχημένον ἀποδείξειν, ἓν μὲν ὡς παρὰ τοὺς νόμους», καὶ τὸ ἕτερον οὕτως «ἐπάνειμι δὴ πάλιν ἐπὶ τὰς ἀποδείξεις, ὡς τὰ τούτων ἀδικήματα καὶ δωροδοκήματα τῶν νῦν πραγ-*
[428] *μάτων»· καὶ Πλάτων ἐν ἀρχῇ | φησι προοίμια καὶ διηγήσεις, εἶτα πίστεις, «τὸ δὲ δὴ τέλος τῶν λόγων ἔοικε πᾶσιν εἶναι κοινῇ συνδεδογμένον, οὗ τινὲς μὲν ἐπάνοδον ὄνομα τίθενται, τινὲς δὲ ἄλλο τι», καὶ ἄξιον ζητῆσαι, τί ἐστι τὸ «ἄλλο τι». «συλλογίσασθαι δὴ βούλομαι», <φησὶν ὁ> Δημοσθένης, «τὰ κατηγορημένα».*

## *Περὶ τῶν ἴσων σχημάτων.*

*Τὰ ἴσα σχήματα ταὐτὰ ὄντα ποτὲ μέν ἐστιν ἀγωνιστικά, ποτὲ δὲ ἐπιδεικτικά, ποτὲ δὲ σοφιστικά.*

*Ἀγωνιστικὰ μέν ἐστιν, ὅταν τῇ φύσει τῶν πραγμάτων συνδράμῃ ἔξωθεν πάρεργον, ὃ καὶ χωρὶς τῶν ὀνομάτων ἕκαστον αὐτὸ καθ' ἑαυ-*

1 supr. Pa Vc Sf; mg. Pch (add. ἢ ὡς οἱ παλαιοὶ ὑποσχέσεως καὶ ἐπανόδου) Ac | mg. ι̅ Ac Ph, ι̅α̅ **P** || 4 τὰ ἀποδεδ⌊ει ex ιδα, m. 2 ?⌉γμένα Sf | λελεγμένα **P** Ac, m. 2 v.l. Vc; δεδειγμένα Vc Ph, (ειγ ex ιδαγ, m. 2 ? po. ?) Sf; δεδιδαγμένα mg. **P** || 6 cf. Π. ἰδ. 236, 22 || 7 Dem. 23, 18 || 8 Dem. 18, 42 || 10 ὁ πλάτων Ac | Plat. Phaedr. 266 DE || 12 ᾧ Plat. Phaedr. 267 D | ὄνομα ἐπάνοδον Sf Ph || 12-13 καὶ — ἄλλο τι om. Ac || 13 ἐστι etiam post ἄξιόν Vc | Dem. 19, 177 | cf. Π. στ. 52, 11. 12 | συλλογεῖσθαι Ph | δὴ om. Pa || 14 φησὶν ὁ Vδ; φησὶ ante 6 τὰ add. Portus | τὰ εἰρημένα Ph || 15 supr. Vc Sf; (om τῶν) **P**π, mg. Pa Ac; om. Pc Ph | mg. ι̅α̅ Ac, ι̅β̅ **P** || 19 πάρεργ⌊α ex ον⌉ Sf | ὃ Ph, (τε add. m. 2) Vc; ὅτε **P**; ἃ Ac, (ex ὃ) Sf; γρ ὃ καὶ χωρὶς τῶν ὀνομάτων ἑκάστου mg. **P** || 19-226.1 αὐτῶν καθ' αὑτὸ Vc Ac Sf Ph

## CHAPTER 12: ON PRELIMINARY HEADINGS AND RECAPITULATION

To state at the beginning headings for what one is going to prove or teach is called by technical writers *proekthesis*, and to give at the end a reminder of what has been demonstrated the technical writers call *anakephalaiōsis*.[26] The ancients, however, call proekthesis *hyposkesis*[27] and anakephailosis *epanodos*, as Demosthenes reveals when he says (23.18), "It is right for me, having promised (*hypeskhēmenon*) three things, to demonstrate first, that it is contrary to the laws," and in the other case (18.42), "I go back[28] to the proofs that the crimes and corruption of these men is the cause of the present problems." And Plato (*Phaedrus* 266d-e) | says [428] that at the beginning (*of a speech*) there are prooemia and narrations, followed by proofs, "but as to the end of speeches it seems to be agreed to by all in common; some use the name *epanodos* and some something else." It is worthwhile asking what "something else" is. "I want, says Demosthenes (19.177), "to reckon up (*syllogisthasthai*) the charges."

## CHAPTER 13: ON EQUAL FIGURES

Equal figures (*ta isa skhēmata*),[29] although much the same, are sometimes agonistic, sometimes epideictic, and sometimes sophistic.

They are agonistic[30] whenever, by the nature of the subjects, an addition of something from outside the subject runs parallel to

[26] "Preliminary exposition (of headings)" = "partition," and "recapitulation," respectively; for *proekthesis*, see Dionysius of Halicarnassus, *On Composition* 23 (vol. 2, p. 117,11 Usener-Radermacher); Quintilian 9.2.106, citing Rutilius; Anonymous Seguerianus §10; Fortunatianus 2.12 and 15; for *anakephalaiōsis*, see Anonymous Seguerianus §§203, 206, and 236; Apsines 10.54.

[27] Cf. Isocrates 4.14, but not a technical rhetorical term.

[28] *Epaneimi*, using a verb related to *epanodos*.

[29] I.e., amplification, adding detail parallel to the original thought, sometimes playing on words. See Patillon, *Théorie du discours*, 321–24. The term "equals" probably derives from the use of the word by Plato in *Symposium* 185c but is not found in other rhetorical treatises.

[30] I.e., "contentious," used in argument.

*τὸ πρᾶγμα μηνύει καὶ λεχθὲν λανθάνει, πολλάκις δὲ ἀναγινωσκόμενον εὑρίσκεται· οἷον*

*«νῦν δ' ἄγε νῆα μέλαιναν ἐρύσσομεν εἰς ἅλα δῖαν,*
*ἐς δ' ἐρέτας ἐπιτηδὲς ἀγείρομεν, ἐς δ' ἑκατόμβην*
*θείομεν, ἂν δ' αὐτὴν Χρυσηίδα καλλιπάρῃον*
*βήσομεν»·*

*τέσσαρα ἴσα, «ἐρύσσομεν», «ἀγείρομεν», «θείομεν», «βήσομεν». καὶ Θουκυδίδης «αἴτιον δ' ἦν οὐχ ἡ ὀλιγανθρωπία, ὅσον ἡ ἀχρηματία· τῆς*
[429] *γὰρ τροφῆς ἀπορίᾳ | τόν τε στρατὸν ἐλάσσω ἤγαγον». καὶ Δημοσθένης «ἂν τοίνυν ἐξελέγξω σαφῶς Αἰσχίνην τουτονὶ καὶ μηδὲν ἀληθὲς ἀπηγγελκότα καὶ κεκωλυκότα ἐμοῦ τὸν δῆμον ἀκοῦσαι τἀληθῆ καὶ ἀνηλωκότα τοὺς χρόνους καὶ πάντων τούτων δῶρα καὶ μισθοὺς εἰληφότα».*

*Ἐπιδεικτικὰ δέ ἐστιν, ὅταν τὰ ἀγωνιστικὰ πολλὰ γένηται καὶ ἐπιτηδευθῇ εἰδημόνως εἰς ἡδονὴν ἀκοῆς σώφρονα, ὥσπερ τὰ παρὰ Ἰσοκράτει ἴσα τὰ ἐν ταῖς παραινέσεσι μάλιστα.*

*Σοφιστικὰ δέ ἐστιν, ἃ νῦν μὲν ἐπαινεῖται, ὑπὸ δὲ τῶν παλαιῶν κωμῳδεῖται, ὅσα αἰσχρῶς καὶ κενῶς κολακεύει τὴν ἀκοήν· ἃ Πλάτων διαβάλλει «ὦ λῷστε Πῶλε, ἵνα προσείπω σε κατὰ σέ» καὶ «Παυσανίου δὲ παυσαμένου· διδάσκουσι γάρ με ἴσα λέγειν οὑτωσὶ οἱ σοφοί». Δημοσθένης δὲ καὶ Ὅμηρος καὶ τὰ τοιαῦτα ἐποίησαν ἀγωνιστικά, «Πρόθοος θοὸς ἡγεμόνευεν», ὄνομα καὶ ἀρετή, καὶ «ἐρρῶσθαι πολλὰ φράσας τῷ σοφῷ Σοφοκλεῖ».*

## *Περὶ ὑπερβατοῦ.*

*Οἱ νῦν οἴονται τὸ ὑπερβατὸν πλοκὴν εἶναι ἑρμηνείας καὶ περίοδον κεκαλλωπισμένην· οὐκ ἴσασι δέ, τί ἐστιν ὑπερβατόν. τὸ γὰρ ὑπερβατὸν*

**1-2** μηνύηι . . . λανθάνηι . . . εὑρίσκηται Ph || **3** Hom. A 141 || **5** ἐν (pro ἂν) Pc || **7** τέσσαρα — βήσομεν om. Pc || **8** Thuc. 1, 11 | οὐκ (om. ἡ) Ac Ph; οὐχὶ (om. ἡ) Vδ | ἀχρη⌊ματ m. po.; ex στ?⌋ία Sf || **10** Dem. 19, 8 | cf. Π. ἰδ. 300, 23. 301, 2 | ἂν om. Vc Sf Ph | ἐλέγξω Sf | τοῦτο νικᾶν Ph | ἀληθ⌊ὲ ex ῶ⌋ς Sf || **11** ἐπηγγελκότα Pah || **11-12** ἀν$\overset{\alpha}{\eta}$λωκότα Pa; ἀναλωκότα Pc || **14** καὶ ὥσπερ τὰ παρὰ τῶι Vc Ac Ph, (om. τὰ) Sf || **16-17** contraria similibus verbis Diodor. XII 53, 4 || **17** κ⌊ε⌋νῶς Pa Vc || **18** Plat. Gorg. 467 B | Plat. Symp. 185 C | cf. Π. ἰδ. 302, 4 || **19** μὲν γὰρ ἴσα Ph || **20-21** Hom. B 758 | cf. Π. ἰδ. 304, 9 || **21** Dem. 19, 248 || **23** supr. Pa Vc Sf, mg. Pch; πῶς γίνεται ὑπερβατόν mg. Ac | mg. ι̅β̅ Ac, ι̅γ̅ **P** || **25** 226, 25: cf. Π. ἰδ. 232, 1; 305, 16

it, and, whatever words are used, each in itself designates something by itself. This escapes notice when spoken but is discovered when repeatedly read; for example (*Iliad* 1.141–144):

> But come now, let us drag a black ship into the bright sea, and let us collect the right number of rowers, and let us put on board a hecatomb and let us embark on it the fair-cheeked daughter of Chryses herself.

Here there are four "equals": "let us drag, let us collect, let us put, let us embark." And Thucydides says (1.11), "The cause was not scarcity of men so much as lack of money, for because of the want of food, | they brought a smaller army." And Demosthenes says (19.8), "If then I shall clearly convict the defendant Aeschines of having brought back a report that was untrue and of having prevented the people from hearing the truth from me and having wasted time and having taken gifts and pay for doing all these things." [429]

They are epideictic whenever there are many agonistic figures that are learnedly developed for the modest pleasure of the hearing, as especially the "equals" in passages of advice in Isocrates.[31]

Those are sophistic—something that is now praised but was ridiculed by the ancients—that flatter the ear in a shameful and empty way. Plato criticizes them (*Gorgias* 467b): "O *lōiste Pōle*,[32] to address you in your own style," and (*Symposium* 185c): "When Pausanias had paused, for the sophists are teaching me to speak equals in this way." Demosthenes and Homer made such things agonistic: "Swift (*thoos*) Prothoos was captain" (*Iliad* 2.758), playing on his name and quality, and (Dem. 19.248), "He bade a long farewell to the wise (*sophos*) Sophocles."

## CHAPTER 14: ON HYPERBATON

Modern writers think that *hyperbaton* is an interweaving of expression and a period that has been ornamented, but they do not understand what a hyperbaton is. Hyperbaton not only is not | [430]

[31] Probably the author is thinking of the many moral injunctions in *To Demonicus* and *To Nicocles*.

[32] "O most agreeable Polus."

[430] οὐ μόνον οὐκ ἔστι | καλὸν σχῆμα, ἀλλὰ καὶ ἀναγκαῖον· γίνεται δέ, ὅταν τὴν αἰτίαν τοῦ λεγομένου, ἣν μέλλει ποθεῖν ὁ ἀκροατής, μέσην ὁ λέγων τάξῃ· καὶ οὕτως γίνεται σαφηνείας ὄργανον τὸ ὑπερβατόν, οἷον

«ὦ φίλοι, οὐ γάρ τ᾽ ἴδμεν, ὅπῃ ζόφος οὐδ᾽ ὅπῃ ἠώς,
οὐδ᾽ ὅπῃ ἠέλιος φαεσίμβροτος εἶσ᾽ ὑπὸ γαῖαν,
οὐδ᾽ ὅπῃ ἀννεῖται· ἀλλὰ φραζώμεθα θᾶσσον»·

εἰ γὰρ εἰρήκει «ὦ φίλοι, φραζώμεθα θᾶσσον», ἐτάραξεν ἂν αὐτοὺς καὶ ἐποίησεν ἐρωτῆσαι, τί γέγονε· διὰ τοῦτο διὰ μέσου τὰς αἰτίας τοῦ φράζεσθαι θᾶσσον ἔταξε. καὶ Θουκυδίδης «οἱ δὲ Ἀθηναῖοι ἐφοβήθησαν, μὴ πολέμιαι ἦσαν αἱ νῆες» διὰ τί; ὁ Θουκυδίδης ἔταξε διὰ μέσου τὴν αἰτίαν τοῦ φόβου «ἦν γὰρ νύξ»· διὰ τοῦτο καὶ ὁ τὴν αἰτίαν σημαίνων σύνδεσμος προηγεῖται, ὁ γάρ.

Μακρὸν δὲ γίνεται ὑπερβατόν, ὁπόταν ἡ αἰτία ἑτέρας αἰτίας χρείαν ἔχῃ, οἷον «ἐπειδὴ δὲ οἵ τε Ἀθηναίων τύραννοι καὶ οἱ ἐκ τῆς ἄλλης Ἑλλάδος ἐπὶ πολὺ καὶ πρὶν τυραννευθείσης οἱ πλεῖστοι καὶ τελευταῖοι πλὴν τῶν ἐν Σικελίᾳ ὑπὸ Λακεδαιμονίων κατελύθησαν» πῶς, ὦ Θουκυδίδη; «ἡ γὰρ Λακεδαίμων μετὰ τὴν κτίσιν τῶν νῦν ἐνοικούντων ἐν αὐτῇ Δωριέων ἐπὶ πλεῖστον χρόνον στασιάσασα ὅμως ἐκ παλαιτάτου
[431] καὶ | εὐνομήθη καὶ ἀεὶ ἀτυράννευτος ἦν»· αἰτίαν τῆς αἰτίας ἀποδίδωσιν «ἔτη γάρ ἐστι μάλιστα τετρακόσια, ἃ Λακεδαιμόνιοι τῇ αὐτῇ πολιτείᾳ χρῶνται, καὶ δι᾽ αὐτὸ δυνάμενοι καὶ τὰ ἐν ταῖς ἄλλαις πόλεσι καθιστᾶν»· εἶτα ἐπανέρχεται ἐπὶ τὴν ἀρχὴν «μετὰ δὲ τὴν τῶν τυράννων κατάλυσιν».

Τὸ δὲ παρ᾽ Ὁμήρῳ

«αὐτὰρ ἐπεὶ διά τε σκόλοπας καὶ τάφρον ἔβησαν
φεύγοντες»

1 οὐ μόνον om. Ph (etiam in argumento mg.) | ⌊οὐ μόνο⌉ν ⌊οὐκ er.⌉ἔστι Pa || 3 οἷον om. Vc Ac Sf Ph || 4 Hom. κ 190 | ⌊τ᾽⌉ Vc; ποτ᾽ Sf || 6 ἀννεῖται Ph; ἀ⌊I⌉νεῖται Vc; ἀνεῖται **P** Ac Sf || 7 φρασώμεθα **P** || 7-8 ἐτάραξεν ⌊γὰρ m. 1 supr.⌉ ἂν αὐτοὺς και ἐποίησεν ἐρωτῆσαι τί γέγονεν εἰ εἴρηκεν ὦ φίλοι φρασώμεθα θᾶσσον διατοῦτο Pc || 7 ἂν om. Ph || 8 ἔταξε ante τοῦ Vc Sf, (ἐξέταξε) Ph || 9 cf. Theon II 82, 20 Sp. | οἱ δὲ Κερκυραῖοι et ὦσιν Thuc. 1, 51 | δέ, γὰρ supr. (m. 2 ?), Vc || 10 ἔταξε post μέσου Vc Sf Ph, post αἰτίαν Ac || 11 ὁ om. Ph || 13 ἑτέρας om. Vc || 14 Thuc. 1, 18 || 17-18 ἐν αὐτῆι οἰκούντων Pc || 18 παλαιοτάτου Sf, (ο er.) Vc Ph || 19 εἰς ἀεὶ Ac || 21-22 καθίστασαν Thuc. || 22 γὰρ (pro δὲ) Ac || 25 Hom. O 1 | τάφον Ph

an ornamental figure but it is even a necessary thing. It occurs whenever a speaker puts in the middle (*of a sentence*) the reason for what is being said,[33] something the hearer is going to want. Thus hyperbaton becomes a tool of clarity; for example (*Odyssey* 10.190–193):

> O Friends, for know we not where lies the underworld, nor
> where the dawn nor where the sun, the light for men, goes
> under the earth nor where he rises; but we soon shall tell.

If he had said "O friends, we soon shall tell," he would have confused them and made them ask what is going on. For this reason he hastened to put the cause of telling in the middle. And Thucydides (1.51): "The Athenians were frightened, lest the ships be those of the enemy." Why? Thucydides put the cause of the fear in the middle: "For it was night." It is for this reason that he introduces the connective indicating the cause: *ho gar*.

A hyperbaton becomes long whenever the cause has need of another cause; for example (Thucydides 1.18), "When the Athenians' tyrants and those from the rest of Greece, for the most part having earlier been ruled by tyrants, the most and last of them except for those in Sicily, were put down by the Lacedaimonians." How was that, Thucydides? "For although after the settlement of the Dorians who now inhabit it Lacedaimon was troubled by strife for a long time, yet from an early date | it was well governed and [431]
always was free from tyranny," and he gives the cause of this cause, "for the Lacedaimonians have used the same form of government for over four hundred years and as a result been able to arrange affairs in the other cities." Then he goes back to the beginning: "after the deposition of the tyrants..."

The following line in Homer (*Iliad* 14.1), however, is not a hyperbaton, as it seems to be to some: "But when through palisades and trench they went in flight." No reason is placed in the

[33] This meaning of hyperbaton is not found in earlier texts; otherwise it refers to placing a word in an unusual position in a phrase, clause, or sentence; cf. Alexander, *On Figures* 2.14 and Phoebammon 1.4.

*οὐκ ἔστιν, ὡς δοκεῖ τισίν, ὑπερβατόν· οὐδεμία γὰρ αἰτία μέση κεῖται, ἀλλ᾽ ὡς ἐγένετο ἡ δυσκολία τῆς ὁδοῦ διὰ σκολόπων καὶ τάφρου, εἶτα ὁμαλὴ ἔξοδος ἐν τῇ φυγῇ, οὕτω καὶ ἡ ἑρμηνεία ἔχει, τὸ πάθος τῶν φευγόντων τῆς λέξεως μιμουμένης.*

## *Περὶ ἀντιθέτου.*

*Τὸ ἀντίθετον σχῆμα ἀναντίρρητόν ἐστι· γίνεται γὰρ διὰ τῶν ὁμολογουμένων. ἔστι δὲ διανοήματι διανόημα ἀντικείμενον. ἁπλούστατον δὲ ὂν ἰσχυρόν ἐστιν, οἷον «ἐδίδασκες γράμματα, ἐγὼ δ᾽ ἐφοίτων· ἐτέλεις, ἐγὼ δ᾽ ἐτελούμην· ἐτριταγωνίστεις, ἐγὼ δ᾽ ἐθεώρουν· ἐγραμμάτευες, ἐγὼ δ᾽ ἐκκλησίαζον· ἐξέπιπτες, ἐγὼ δ᾽ ἐσύριττον».*

[432] *Τοῦτο δὲ τὸ ἀντίθετον ὁ Δημοσθένης ἐποίησε κακό|ηθες, τὸ μὲν πρᾶγμα ἀληθὲς λαμβάνων, τὸ δὲ ἀντικείμενον ψευδὲς ὄν· ὡς ἐν τῷ Περὶ τῆς παραπρεσβείας εἰσάγει συμπόσιον Φιλίππου καὶ τῶν Ὀλύμπια νενικηκότων καὶ διάλογον Σατύρου τοῦ κωμικοῦ ὑποκριτοῦ, οὕτω δὲ ψυχαγωγεῖ τοὺς ἀκούοντας, ὥστε οἰηθῆναι ἐν συμποσίῳ εἶναι· εἶτα ἀντιτίθησι συμπόσιον ἕτερον ὡς γενόμενον Αἰσχίνῃ ψευδόμενος μηδέποτε γενόμενον, ἵνα ἐψυχαγωγημένοι διὰ τῶν προτέρων λόγων οἱ δικασταὶ πιστεύωσι καὶ τοῖς ἐπιφερομένοις ὡς ὁμοίως ἀληθέσι. τοῦτο κακόηθες ἀντίθετον.*

## *Περὶ παρίσου καὶ πῶς γίνεται.*

*Πάρισον σχῆμα ἔστι τε καὶ λέγεται, ὅταν τὸ αὐτὸ ὄνομα ἄλλην καὶ ἄλλην προσλαβὸν συλλαβὴν διαφερούσας διανοίας ἔχῃ. παρὰ*

**1** τισίν: cf. schol. Ven. A (ὑπερβατὸν γὰρ ὁ τρόπος) || **2** τάφρων (ου supra) Ac; τάφων Ph || **5** supr. Vc Sf; mg. **P**, (τοῦ ἀντ.) Ac, (add. τί ἐστι καὶ οἷον) Ph | mg. ιγ Ac Ph, ιδ **P** || **6** cf. p. 140 || **7** ⌊circ. IX⌉ἀντικείμενον Vc || **9** post ἐτελούμην add. Vc: καὶ σὺ μὲν ἐχόρευες ἐγὼ δ᾽ ἐχορήγουν, quod explicat etiam Diac. || **9-10** ordo mutatus est, cf. Dem. 18, 265 || **11** δὲ om. Ac Ph || **11-12** τὸ μὲν — ὄν om. Vδ || **12** ψεῦδος Ac Sf Ph | ὅς? cf. 218, 1 || **12-13** τῶι παρὰ τῆς πρεσβείας Ph | περὶ om. Vc Sf; περὶ τῆς om. Ac | Dem. 19, 192, 196 || **13** εἰσάγει λόγωι Vc; εἰσάγει γὰρ Vδ | ὀλυμπίαι Ac; γρ´ ἐν ὀλυμπία Pc || **14** τοῦ om. Ph | post ὑποκριτοῦ add. Sf: αἰτουμένου τὴν θυγατέρα ἀπολλωφάνους; repetunt Vc Ph: και φιλίππου καὶ τῶν ὀλ. νενικηκότων | οὕτω δὲ **P** Ac; καὶ οὕτω Vc Sf Ph || **16** αἰσχίνῃ (ου supra), m. 1 **P**; αἰσχίνου Vc Ac Sf Ph || **18** πιστεύσωσι Vc Ac Sf || **20** sic mg. **P** Pπ, (καὶ om.) supr. Vc Sf; mg. περὶ παρίσου (om. cet.) Ph (παρίσων) Ac | mg. ιδ Ac Ph, ⸌ιε Pa

middle of anything, but as it happened, the difficult path through the palisades and the trench, then a level opening for their flight, is there in the expression, the wording imitating the suffering of those fleeing.

## CHAPTER 15: ON ANTITHETON

The figure *antitheton* is not open to contradiction, for it derives from things that have been agreed upon.[34] It is thought balanced against thought. It is strong although very simple; for example (cf. Dem. 18.265): "You taught letters; I went to school. You conducted initiations; I was initiated. You played the third part in plays; I was a spectator. You were a clerk; I was a member of the assembly. You were driven from the stage; I hissed." Demosthenes created this malicious antitheton | by opposing a true [432]
fact to a lie.[35] Similarly, in *On the False Embassy* (19.192–195) he brings in an account of a drinking party attended by Philip and the Olympic victors and a conversation with Satyrus the comic actor, and he so leads the listeners on that they think they are at the party. Then (196–198) he contrasts this with another party that never happened, falsely claiming that Aeschines attended it, in order that the jurymen, having been enchanted by his previous words, may believe what is added as equally true.[36] This is a malicious antitheton.

## CHAPTER 16: ON PARISON AND HOW IT OCCURS

It is the figure called *parison*[37] whenever the same word acquires different meanings by compounding with different syllables. For

34 Contrast the discussion of antitheton in *On Invention* 4.2 above.

35 The author regards the statements about Aeschines as false. Some or all probably are based on facts, but the antitheton makes the passage invidious.

36 At this second party, in Macedonia, Demosthenes claims Aeschines, when drunk, was involved in mistreatment of a respectable woman; Aeschines denies the charge (2.156).

37 As the scholia note (Walz 7.2:1262–63), parison, also called parisosis, was originally used to refer to clauses or phrases with an equal number of syllables; Aristotle used both terms in this sense in *Rhetoric* 3.9.9. Aquila Romanus (23–24) distinguished parison from isocolon on the ground that in isocolon the number of words in the clauses or phrases are the same, whereas parison is an

*μὲν Ἰσοκράτει οὕτως «ἐὰν ᾖς φιλομαθής, ἔσῃ πολυμαθής»· τὸ γὰρ μανθάνειν ἐν ἀμφοτέροις ἐστίν, ἀλλ' ὅπου μὲν τὸ πολυ πρόσκειται καὶ σημαίνει τὸν πολλὰ εἰδότα, ὅπου δὲ τὸ φιλο πρόςκειται καὶ ἔστιν ὁ ἡδέως μανθάνων. καὶ παρὰ τῷ Θουκυδίδῃ «καὶ προεπιβουλεύειν αὐτοῖς μᾶλλον ἢ ἀντεπιβουλεύειν»· τὸ γὰρ ἐπιβουλεύειν ἐν ἀμφοτέροις*
[433] *εἴρη|ται, ἀλλ' ὅπου μὲν πρόσκειται προ καὶ σημαίνει τὸ φθάνειν ἐπιβουλεύοντα, ὅπου δὲ ἀντι πρόθεσις καὶ δηλοῖ τὸ ἀμύνεσθαι δεύτερον.*

## *Περὶ προσποιήσεως.*

*Πότε ῥήτωρ προσποιήσεται σχεδιάζειν; τριῶν οὐσῶν ἰδεῶν ῥητορικῆς ἐν τῇ συμβουλευτικῇ μάλιστα δεῖ καὶ ὁμολογεῖν, ὅτι ἐβουλεύσατο· οὐ γὰρ ἀνέχεται ὁ συμβουλευόμενος τὰ ἐπιόντα λέγοντος τοῦ συμβουλεύοντος, τοὐναντίον δὲ χρὴ ἐσκέφθαι ὁμολογεῖν καὶ πεφροντικέναι, ὡς ὁ Δημοσθένης «ἀλλ' ὡς ἔοικεν ὁ καιρὸς ἐκεῖνος οὐ μόνον εὔνουν ἡμῖν καὶ πλούσιον ἄνδρα ἐκάλει, ἀλλὰ καὶ παρηκολουθηκότα ἐξ ἀρχῆς τοῖς πράγμασι»· μάλιστα γὰρ τοῦτο δεῖ προσεῖναι τῷ συμβούλῳ, ἐμπειρίαν πραγμάτων.*

*Ἐν δὲ τῇ δικανικῇ, κἂν ἐσκεμμένος ἥκῃς, προσποιοῦ αὐτόθεν λέγειν, ὅπερ ποιοῦσι πάντες οἱ παλαιοί· γράψαντες γὰρ πάντες ὑποκρίνονται σχεδιάζειν διὰ τί; ὅτι ὁ δικαστὴς ὑποπτεύει τὸν ῥήτορα καὶ δέδοικε, μὴ ἐξαπατηθῇ τῇ δυνάμει τῆς ῥητορικῆς. αὐτὸ τοίνυν τοῦτό ἐστι τέχνη τοῦ ῥήτορος τὸ δοκεῖν αὐτόθεν λέγειν, ἵνα καὶ οὕτως ὁ δι-*
[434] *καστὴς παραχθῇ· καὶ προοίμια ὡς | αὐτόθεν εὑρίσκοντες λέγουσι πάλαι*

1 Isocr. 1, 18 | ᾗς ⌊ὁ er.⌋ Pa || **2** καὶ om. Sf || **3** φιλο Sf Ph; φιλῶ Vc; φίλον Pc Ac; φίλτρον (cr. ex φίλτερον?) Pa | pr. καὶ om. Sf || **4** Thuc. 1, 33 || **5** τὸ γὰρ ἐπιβουλεύειν om. Ph | γὰρ om. Sf || **6** τὸ προ Vc AC | καὶ om. Sf || **7** ἡ ἀντι Ma | προτίθεται? | καὶ om. Sf | δεύτερον om. m. 1 Ma || **8** supr. Vc Sf, mg. **P** Ac Ph | σχεδιασμοῦ add. Portus | mg. ιε Ac Ph, ις **P** || **13** Dem. 18, 172 || **15** μάλιστα γὰρ τοῦτο scripsit Rabe; μάλιστα τοῦτο Ph; μάλιστα· τοῦτο γὰρ Pa Ac Sf, (γὰρ supr., m. 1?) Vc, (δὲ m. po. supr. post μάλιστα·) Pc || **17** ἐσκεμμένως Ph || **17** cf. Dem. 21, 191 c. schol. || **18** ἐσκεμμένος — αὐτόθεν: cf. Π. ἰδ. 358, 16 || **19** ὁ om. Ph || **20** τοίνυν καὶ Vc Ac Sf Ph || **21** ἔστω Sf Ph | τέχνη τοῦ Ph, v.l. **P**; τεχνίτου **P** Vc Ac Sf | cf. Alex. III 14, 10 Sp. || **22** παραχθῆι Ac, (π m. 1 ex τ) Sf v.l. Diac.; ταραχθῇ **P** Vc Ph, v.l. m. 2 Sf | καὶ om. Ph, add. (m. 2?) Vc

example, in Isocrates (1.18): "If you are *philomathēs* ('a lover of learning'), you will be *polymathēs* ('learned in many things')." "To learn" is a part of both, but when *poly* is added it signifies one who knows many things, and when *philo* is added it means one who enjoys learning. And in Thucydides (1.33): "*proepibouleuein* ('to make plans against them ahead of time') rather than *antepibouleuein* ('to defeat the plans made against us')," for *epibouleuein* is said in both, | but when *pro* is prefixed it signifies anticipating [433]
one who is plotting against us, and when *anti* is prefixed it indicates defensive action in response to an attack.

## CHAPTER 17: ON PRETENCE (OF EXTEMPORANEITY)

When will an orator pretend (*prospoiēsetai*) to speak impromptu? Among the three species of rhetoric, it is in deliberative oratory that there is most need even to acknowledge that one has made a plan, for someone offering advice is not suffered to advise on the basis of what suddenly occurs to him, but quite the opposite: he must acknowledge that he has considered the matter and thought it out, as did Demosthenes (18.172): "But, as it seems, that occasion was calling out not only for a man of goodwill toward you and wealthy but one who had followed the course of events from the beginning." The quality that most should belong to a deliberative orator is experience in public affairs.

But in judicial oratory, even if you have come to court with your speech thought out, pretend to speak off the cuff, which all the ancients do,[38] for although having written their speeches, they all affect to speak extemporaneously. Why is that? Because the juryman is suspicious of the speaker and is afraid that he may be deceived by the power of rhetoric. This, then, is the art of the orator, to seem to speak extemporaneously, in order that in this way the juryman may be led astray. And having constructed prooemia

approximate parallelism allowing for a differing number of words; cf. Alexander, *On Figures* 2.26. What the author of *On Method* calls parison is sometimes called paromoiosis (similarity of sound); see Quintilian 9.3.56; Patillon, *Théorie du discours*, 320–21.

[38] Cf. Quintilian 10.6.6. Many "ancient" judicial speeches were prepared in advance by logographers (Lysias, Isaeus, Demosthenes, et al.) and delivered by the litigant, who affected extemporaneity.

*σκεψάμενοι καὶ κεφάλαια ὡς μεταξὺ ἀναμνησθέντες κατὰ πάσας τὰς δίκας.*

*Ἐν δέ γε ἐγκωμιαστικῇ ἰδέᾳ οὐ κωλύει ἀμφοτέροις χρῆσθαί ποτε, καὶ ὁμολογίᾳ γραφῆς καὶ προσποιήσει σχεδίου.*

### Περὶ αὐξήσεως, πότε χρηστέον ἐν δίκαις εὐκαίρως.

*Πότε ῥήτωρ αὐξήσει χρήσεται ἐν δίκαις, εἶτα τότε ταῖς ἀποδείξεσι; δύο δὴ καιροὶ τῆς χρήσεως καὶ μέθοδοι, ὅταν τὸ πρᾶγμα ἀμελῆται ἢ τὸ πρόσωπον τὸ κρινόμενον ἔνδοξον ᾖ. ταύτῃ τῇ τέχνῃ χρῆται Αἰσχίνης ἐν τῷ Κατὰ Τιμάρχου καὶ ἐν τῷ Κατὰ Κτησιφῶντος. ἐν μὲν γὰρ τῷ Κατὰ Τιμάρχου καὶ τὸ πρᾶγμα ἀμελεῖται λοιδορία γὰρ δοκεῖ ἡ ἑταίρησις εἶναι καὶ σκῶμμα ταπεινότερον, καὶ τὸ πρόσωπον τὸ κρινόμενον ἔνδοξόν ἐστιν ὁ γὰρ Τίμαρχος τιμᾶται καὶ λελειτούργηκε καὶ ἀρχὰς ἦρξε καὶ ἔστι περὶ μέσην ἡλικίαν . καὶ ἐν τῷ Κατὰ Κτησιφῶντος ἡ τῶν παρανόμων γραφὴ ἀμελεῖται διὰ τὰς συμφορὰς τῆς πόλεως τό τε πρόσωπον τιμᾶται, Δημοσθένης, καὶ ἀξίωμα ἔχει. διὰ τοῦτο πρότερον αὔξει, εἶτα τότε ἀποδείκνυσιν, ἵνα ἐπιστρέψῃ καὶ ἀναγκάσῃ προσέχειν τοὺς δικαστὰς καὶ μήτε τιμῇ τοῦ προσώπου μήτε καταφρονήσει τοῦ*
[435] *πράγματος μὴ θέλωσιν ἀκούειν. αὕτη ἡ αἰτία τοῦ καὶ τῇ | αὐτῇ τάξει ἐν ἀμφοτέροις τοῖς βιβλίοις τὰ περὶ τῶν πολιτειῶν διεξελθεῖν.*

1 καὶ om. Ph; supr. Vc || **3** γε om. Vc, add. (m. 1 ?) Ph || **5** supr. Vc Sf; mg. **P** Ph, (om. πότε — εὐκαίρως) Ac | mg. ις̅ Ac Ph, ιζ̅ **P** || **6-10** cf. Π. ἰδ. 377, 19 (283, 19) || **6** <πρότερον> αὐξήσει ? | τότε **P** Ac Sf Ph; πότε m. 1 Vc, v.l. m. po. Pa || **7** δὲ Sf Ph, ?m. 1 Vc | αἱ (pro καὶ) Ph, m. 1 Vc || **8** καὶ (pro ἢ) Sf || **10** γὰρ om. Vc || **14** τὰς etiam ante τῆς Vc Ac Sf Ph || **15** δημοσθένους Ph, (-ης, ου supra) Ac; del. ? | cf. Π. ἰδ. 290, 3 || **16** ἵνα ⌊II er.; μὴ ?] Pc || **18** πράγμα⌊τ (ο supra) μὴ m. po. ex τος] Pc | θέλουσιν Ph | τοῦ om. Ph | Aesch. 1, 4; 3, 6

| as though on the spot, (*speakers*) also deliver arguments thought out long before as spontaneous, recalling them (*as needed*) in every trial. [434]

In the encomiastic kind of rhetoric there is nothing to prevent using both approaches at times, both an admission of writing and a pretence of extemporaneity.

## CHAPTER 18: ON AMPLIFICATION: WHEN CAN IT BE OPPORTUNELY USED IN TRIALS?

When will an orator use amplification (*auxēsis*) in trials and then follow it with proofs?[39] There are two occasions and methods of its use: whenever the action is little regarded[40] or the person being tried is well respected. Aeschines uses this technique in *Against Timarchus* and in *Against Ctesiphon*. In *Against Timarchus* the subject is little regarded—for a charge of prostitution seems slanderous and a rather low blow—and the person being tried is honorable—for Timarchus is respected and has performed a liturgy and held offices and is in middle age. Also in *Against Ctesiphon* the indictment for contravening the law is little regarded because of the disasters of the city, and the person, Demosthenes, is honored and has a good reputation. For this reason, Aeschines uses amplification early in the speech (3.6), then offers proofs, in order to deflect criticism and force the jury to pay attention and not refuse to listen out of respect for the person or contempt for the matter. This is the reason for his | following the same order [435]
in the account of constitutions in both books.[41]

[39] The author thinks of amplification as a kind of digression or excursus, inserted early in a speech to forestall some possible objections, an unusual view. Elsewhere amplification is often regarded as a feature of the epilogue; cf., e.g., Anonymous Seguerianus §230.

[40] I.e., the charge might be dismissed as frivolous, malicious, or inappropriate.

[41] I.e., both speeches, as found in two papyrus rolls. See Aeschines 1.4 and 3.6.

## *Περὶ ἐγνωσμένου ψεύσματος, πότε χρηστέον αὐτῷ.*

*Πότε ῥήτωρ ψεύσεται συνειδότων τῶν ἀκροατῶν, ὅτι ψεύδεται; ὅταν τὸ ψεῦδος συμφέρῃ τοῖς ἀκούουσι· διὰ γὰρ τὸ οἰκεῖον λυσιτελὲς οὐκ ἐλέγχουσι τὸν ῥήτορα. οὕτω Δημοσθένης ἐψεύσατο ἐν τῷ Περὶ τοῦ στεφάνου· Αἰσχίνου γὰρ λέγοντος, ὅτι οἱ Ἀθηναῖοι ὑπὸ τὸν αὐτὸν καιρὸν πρέσβεις πρὸς Φίλιππον ἔπεμψαν περὶ εἰρήνης καὶ πρὸς τοὺς συμμάχους περὶ συμμαχίας κατὰ Φιλίππου, καὶ τοῦτο πεποιηκότων Ἀθηναίων, φησὶν ὅτι «καὶ διαβάλλει τὰ μέγιστα τὴν πόλιν, ἐν οἷς ψεύδεται· εἰ γὰρ ὑμεῖς ἅμα τοὺς μὲν Ἕλληνας εἰς πόλεμον παρεκαλεῖτε, αὐτοὶ δὲ περὶ εἰρήνης πρὸς Φίλιππον πρέσβεις ἐπέμπετε, Εὐρυβάτου πρᾶγμα, οὐ πόλεως ἔργον οὐδὲ χρηστῶν ἀνθρώπων διεπράττεσθε».*

## *Περὶ ὅρκου, ποῖον οὐκ ὀμεῖται καὶ ποῖον ὀμεῖται.*

*Πότε ῥήτωρ ὀμόσει καὶ ὅρκῳ χρήσεται; οὐδέποτε ἐπὶ πράγματος ὀμεῖται, οἷον «ἐποίησεν οὗτος φόνον ἢ προδοσίαν ἢ τόδε τι», ἀλλ' ἐπὶ* [436] *ἤθους βεβαιώσει, ὡς ὁ Δη|μοσθένης «ὡς μὲν ἐμοὶ δοκεῖ, δι' ἀμφότερα, ὦ Ἀθηναῖοι, νὴ τοὺς θεούς, κἀμὲ νομίζοντες δεινὰ πεπονθέναι» καὶ πάλιν «πολλὰς δὲ δεήσεις καὶ νὴ Δία ἀπειλὰς ὑπομείνας». ἐκ τούτου δηλοῦται, ὅτι ῥήτωρ πραγματικὸν ὅρκον οὐκ ὄμνυσιν ἀλλ' ἠθικόν.*

*Πρῶτος δὲ ὅρκον ἠθικὸν Ὅμηρος ὤμοσεν, εἶτα Πλάτων ἐμιμήσατο, εἶτα Δημοσθένης ἐκληρονόμησε Πλάτωνος· ἠθικὸν δ' ἕκαστος*

1 mg. **P**, (καὶ πότε) Ph; supr. (καὶ πότε) Vc Sf; περὶ ἐγνωσμένων πότε χρηστέον αὐτοῖς supr. Ac | χρήσεται **P**π | mg. ιζ̄ Ac Ph, ιη̄ **P** || 2 ὁ ῥήτωρ Ac || 5 τοῦ om. Ph | Aesch. 3, 68 | οἱ om. Pc | ὑπ[ὸ ex ἐρ] Vc || 7 τοῦ φιλίππου Ac || 8 φασὶν Ph | Dem. 18, 24 | καὶ om. Pc | τὴν πόλιν τὰ μέγιστα οἷς Vc | τὴν om. Ph || 9 παρακαλεῖτε Ac Ph || 10 πέμπετε Vc; ἀπεπέμπετε Ac; ἔπεμπον Ph || 12 supr. Vc Sf; (καὶ om.) mg. Ph; om. **P**; περὶ ὅρκου πῶς ὀμεῖται ῥήτωρ (om. cet.) supr. Ac | mg. ιη̄ Ac Ph, ιθ̄ **P** || 13 πότε — χρήσεται Vc Sf (ὁ ῥήτωρ) Vδ, (ὁ er.) Ph; mg. **P**; om. Ac | πράγματι Diac. || 14 προδίδωσιν Vc Sf Ph | cf. Π. ἰδ. 326, 24 || 15 Dem. 21, 2 | ὦ (om. Ἀθηναῖοι) Ph || 16 νομίζοντες (α supra ε) Pa || 17 Dem. 21, 3 | δὲ om. Vc Sf Ph || 18 ἀλλ' ἠθικόν: cf. Π. ἰδ. 327, 4 sq. || 19 ὅμηρος ὅρκον ἠθικὸν Ac || 20 ὁ δημοσθένης Ph | Πλάτωνος scripsit Rabe; πάντων codd.; Quint. XII 10, 24: *non illud iusiurandum «per caesos in Marathone ac Salamine propugnatores reipublicae» satis manifesto docet praeceptorem eius Demosthenis Platonem fuisse?* || 20-238.1 ἑκάστου Ph

### CHAPTER 19: ON A PATENT LIE: WHEN OUGHT ONE TO USE IT?

When will an orator tell a lie, his hearers knowing that he is lying? Whenever the lie is expedient for the hearers, for they will not criticize the orator because of what is to their own advantage. This is how Demosthenes lied in *On the Crown*; for Aeschines says (3.68) that the Athenians, about the same time, sent envoys to Philip about a peace treaty and to their allies about an alliance against Philip, and although the Athenians had done this, (Demosthenes) says (18.24) that "(Aeschines) is slandering the city to the greatest extent in the lies he tells, for if you were at one and the same time summoning the Greeks to war when you were sending envoys to Philip about peace, you were doing the deed of a Eurybates,[42] not the act of a city-state nor of honest men."

### CHAPTER 20: ON OATH: WHAT IS NOT SWORN AND WHAT IS SWORN

When will an orator swear and use an oath? He will never swear to an act; for example, (*he will not swear,*) "This man did murder or treason or some such thing," but he will swear an oath to strengthen moral character, as does | Demosthenes (21.2): "(*I* [436]
*brought Meidias to trial,*) it seems to me, for two reasons, Athenians, by the gods, since you thought me to have suffered serious wrongs," and again (21.3), "having had to withstand many appeals and, by Zeus, threats." From this it is clear that the orator is not swearing to a fact but swearing an ethical oath.

Homer was the first to swear an ethical oath, then Plato imitated him, then Demosthenes continued the tradition from Plato.[43] Each swore an ethical oath, and each used a special form of character, Homer in tragic style (*Odyssey* 20.339), "No Aglaeus,

[42] A proverbial deceiver; according to a scholion on this passage, derived from Ephorus (frg. 58), he was given money by Croesus to recruit mercenaries and absconded to Cyrus.

[43] Oddly stated, since the oaths in Homer and in Plato are, of course, attributed to speakers in epic and dialogue and are not the oaths of the writers. On Demosthenes' imitation of Plato, cf. Quintilian 12.10.24.

*ὀμόσας καὶ ἰδίᾳ ἕκαστος ἰδέᾳ τοῦ ἤθους ἐχρήσατο, Ὅμηρος μὲν τραγικὸν*

*«οὔ, μὰ Ζῆν', Ἀγέλαε, καὶ ἄλγεα πατρὸς ἐμεῖο»,*

*τὰς συμφορὰς τοῦ πατρὸς ὅρκον ἐποιήσατο, Πλάτων δὲ ἠθικὸν μὲν ὁμοίως, ἠθικὸν δ' ἐκ τοῦ ἐναντίου ἤθους «οὔ, μὰ τὸν Ζῆν', ὦ Καλλίκλεις», Δημοσθένης δὲ ἠθικὸν πολιτικὸν «οὔ, μὰ τοὺς ἐν Μαραθῶνι προκινδυνεύσαντας καὶ τοὺς ἐν Σαλαμῖνι παραταξαμένους».*

## *Περὶ συνηγόρων, τίσι δοτέον.*

*Πότε ἐν τοῖς προβλήμασι ῥήτωρ μέρεσί τισι συνηγόρους δώσει*
[437] *καὶ κατὰ πόσους τρόπους; τέσσαρας· ἢ διὰ | φύσιν, εἰ γυνή τίς ἐστι, συνήγορον δώσομεν· ἢ δι' ἡλικίαν, εἰ παιδίον ἐστὶν ἢ ὑπέργηρως καὶ ἀσθενής· ἢ διὰ τύχην, εἰ δοῦλός ἐστιν ἢ ἄτιμος, ὥσπερ ἐν τῷ Κατὰ Μειδίου Δημοσθένης Στράτωνι συναγορεύει· ἢ εἰ δι' εὐπρέπειαν κατέγνωσταί τις, καὶ τούτῳ δώσομεν συνήγορον.*

## *Περὶ τοῦ ἐναντία λέγοντα κατορθοῦν ἐναντία.*

*Τίς μέθοδος τοῦ ἐναντία λέγοντα, οἷς βούλεται γενέσθαι, κατορθοῦν, ὃ βούλεται, μὴ δοκοῦντα ἐναντία οἷς θέλει λέγειν; ἡ κακία ἡ ἐν λόγοις ἐνταῦθα ἀρετὴ φαίνεται. τίς δέ ἐστι κακία ἐν λόγοις; εὐδιάλυτα λέγειν καὶ ἐναντία καὶ στρεφόμενα. ταῦτα ἐν τούτῳ τῷ σχήματι τῶν λόγων ἀρετὴ γίνεται.*

**1** ἰδέαι τοῦ ἤθους Pc Vc; τοῦ ἤθους ἰδέα Pa Ac Sf, (τοῦ ex τὸ) Ph | ἐχρήσατο **P** Ac; χρησάμενος Vc Sf Ph || **3** Hom. υ 339 | ἐμοῖο Sf || **5** μὰ τὸν Ζῆθον, om. οὐ, Plat. Gorg. 489 E; Diac.: σφάλμα ἐστὶ γραφικὸν <τὸ οὐ W VII 1282, 9> μὰ τὸν Ζῆνα· παρὰ πᾶσι (ἐν ἅπασι W VII) γὰρ τοῖς <Πλατωνικοῖς W VII> βιβλίοις μὰ (om. W VII) τὸν Ζῆθον ἔχει (ἀπόμνυσιν W VII) || **6** Dem. 18, 203 | cf. Π. ἰδ. 327, 15 sq. || **8** supr. Vc Sf, (om. τίσι δοτέον) Ac; mg. **P** Ph | mg. $\overline{\iota\theta}$ Ac Ph, $\overline{\kappa}$ **P** || **9** ὁ ῥήτωρ Pc || **11** συνηγόρ⌊ους ex ων ?⌉ Pa | καὶ **P** Ac, (postea add. m. 1) Sf; εἰ Ph; η (καὶ supra), utrumque m. po., Vc || **12** ἀσθενής ἐστιν ἢ Vc Sf Ph | ἔστι τις Ph | ἢ **P** Ac Sf Ph; εἰ Vc | ἄτιμός ἐστιν Vc Sf Ph || **13** Dem. 21, 83 sq. || **13-14** Diac.: τουτέστιν ὁ ἠταιρηκώς || **13** συνηγορεύει Pa | εἰ om. Ph || **14** τούτου **P** || **15** supr. Vc Sf, mg. **P** Ph; τίς ἡ ἐν λόγοις κακία supr. Ac | mg. $\overline{\kappa}$ Ac Ph, $\overline{\kappa\alpha}$ **P** || **16** λέγοντος . . . δοκοῦντα Sf, (ος m. 1 supr.) **P** || **16-17** cf. [Dion.] II 1 p. 296, 15 sq. Us. || **17** ἐναντίον Ph | alt. ἡ om. Vc || **17-18** sq. cf. [Dion.] II 1 p. 327, 19 sq. 328, 25 sq. 322, 4 cet. Us. [Plut.] De vita et poesi Hom. 166

by Zeus and by my father's sufferings," where (Telemachus) made an oath on his father's sufferings. And Plato similarly swore an ethical oath, but from the opposite ethos (*Gorgias* 489e): "By Zeus, no, Callicles." And Demosthenes swore an ethical oath in a political style (18.208): "No, by those who stood in the front lines at Marathon and those drawn up in ranks at Salamis."

## CHAPTER 21: ON ADVOCATES: TO WHOM SHOULD THEY BE GIVEN?

When in problems (*of declamation*) shall we grant advocates (*synēgoroi*)[44] to some of the parties and in how many ways? In four. Either because of | gender, we shall grant an advocate if the client [437]
is a woman; or because of age, if a child or very elderly or ill; or because of lot in life, if he is a slave or deprived of civic rights, as Demosthenes speaks on behalf of Straton in *Against Meidias* (cf. Dem. 21.87); or if someone is being prosecuted because of good looks,[45] and then we shall grant this person an advocate.

## CHAPTER 22: ON SUCCESSFULLY ACCOMPLISHING OPPOSITES BY SAYING OPPOSITES

What is the method of success in saying the opposite of what one wants to be the case in order to accomplish what one wants without seeming to say the opposite of what one wants?[46] Here the fault in speaking seems a virtue. But what is a fault in speaking? To say what is easily refuted and contradictory and turned against one. In this figure of speech these things become a virtue.

Homer has done it.[47] Agamemnon is making trial of the Greek force and wants them to remain while saying that they

[44] I.e., when will a declaimer speak in the role of an advocate or spokesman? Ordinarily the speaker is imagined to be a principal in the case.

[45] Understood by the commentators to refer to a male prostitute who has lost the right to speak in person.

[46] The reference is to figured problems as discussed, e.g., in *On Invention* 4.13.

[47] Cf. Pseudo-Dionysius, *Art of Rhetoric* (vol. 2, pp. 327–28 Usener-Radermacher), where the author argues that Agamemnon is intentionally goading the men to oppose what he seems to be ordering; see also Pseudo-Plutarch, *On the Life and Poetry of Homer* 166.

*Ὅμηρος αὐτὸ πεποίηκεν· Ἀγαμέμνων ἐστὶν ὁ ἀποπειρώμενος τοῦ Ἑλληνικοῦ καὶ βουλόμενος αὐτοὺς μένειν λέγων δεῖν μὴ μένειν ἀλλὰ φεύγειν, καὶ δι' ὅλης τῆς δημηγορίας εὐδιάλυτα λέγει καὶ στρεφόμενα, διδοὺς ἀντιλαβὰς τοῖς ἐναντιουμένοις, ἐπὶ τέλει δὲ καὶ ἐναντιώματα λέγων· τὸ γὰρ φάναι*

*«καὶ δὴ δοῦρα σέσηπε νεῶν καὶ σπάρτα λέλυνται»*

[438] | *δηλονότι ἐναντίον ἐστὶ φανερῶς τῷ «φεύγωμεν»· πῶς γὰρ φεύξονται ναῦς οὐκ ἔχοντες; τοῦτο δ' ἂν εἶπε καὶ κωλύων τις αὐτοὺς ἀποπλεῖν, οὐ κελεύων δὲ μένειν τοῖς λόγοις.*

*Ἐν δὲ ταῖς σχολικαῖς ὑποθέσεσιν ἔστι καὶ ἄλλη τις τέχνη, ἣ βοηθεῖ ταῖς τοῦ ἀντιδίκου προτάσεσι καὶ διὰ μακρῶν προβάλλεται καὶ διὰ μαρτυριῶν ἔσθ' ὅτε. ἀλλὰ ἀντιλέγειν προσποιοῦ· οὕτω γὰρ λέγων οὐχ ὑποπτευθήσῃ, καὶ ὃ βούλει, σοὶ ἔσται. ἐν γὰρ τῷ τοιούτῳ σχήματι τῶν λόγων τὸ μὲν νικῆσαι λέγοντα ἡττηθῆναί ἐστι, τὸ δὲ ἡττηθῆναι λέγοντα νικῆσαί ἐστι· γέγονε γάρ, ὃ βουλόμεθα.*

## *Περὶ τοῦ προτείνειν τὰς τοῦ ἐναντίου προτάσεις.*

*Ὁ κατηγορῶν τὰς τοῦ μέλλοντος ἀποκρίνεσθαι οὐχ ἁπλῶς προτείνει προτάσεις, ἀλλὰ κατὰ τρόπους τρεῖς, ἐπιστήμην, δόξαν, ἀκοήν· ἐπιστήμην μὲν «οἶδα, ὅπερ νὴ Δία ἐρεῖ» καὶ ὅσα τοιαῦτα, δόξαν δὲ οἷον «τάχα τοίνυν ἴσως ἐρεῖ», ὡς ἀμφιβάλλων περὶ τῆς προτάσεως, ἀκοὴν δὲ ὡς ἀκούων περὶ τῆς προτάσεως «πυνθάνομαι τοίνυν μέλλειν αὐτὸν λέγειν».*

[439] | *Τὰ μὲν δὴ σχήματα τῆς προτάσεως τῶν τοῦ ἀπολογουμένου κεφαλαίων ταῦτα· ὁ δὲ καιρὸς ἑκάστου τίς; δεῖ γὰρ εἰδέναι, πότε τῇ*

1 ὁ **P**; ante ἀγαμέμνων Vc Ac Sf Ph || 2 καὶ om. Vc Sf || 4 cf. [Dion.] II 1 p. 321, 1. 330, 6. 7 Us. || 6 Hom. B 135 | νεῶν om. m. 1 Vc | λέλυται Ac || 7 Hom. B 140 c. schol. Ven. B || 8 δ' αὖ εἶπε ⌊καὶ m. 1 supr.⌋ Pc || 9 δὲ om. Vδ | μένειν **P** Vc Sf Ph; ἐν Vh; μόνοις Ac; μόνον Vδ || 10 cf. [Dion.] II 1 p. 329, 14 sq. Us. | ὁ σχολικαῖς Ac || 10-11 βοηθεῖ Vc Ac Sf Ph; βοηθεῖται **P** || 11-12 διὰ μαρτυριῶν **P** Ac; διὰ μαρτυρίας Vc Sf; διὰ μαρτυρίαις Ph, v.l. **P** || 12 γὰρ καὶ Vc Ac Sf Ph | cf. Π. ἰδ. 250, 1 sq. 366, 17 sq. || 14 pr. ἐστὶ om. Ph || 16 supr. Vc Ac Sf, mg. **P** Ph | mg. κα Ac Ph, κβ **P** || 17 cf. [Dion.] II 1 p. 362, 17 sq. Us. | (ὁ γὰρ) — p. 242, 7 laudat Dox. (in Herm. Π. ἰδ. p. 238, 14) | οὐ κατηγοροῦντας τοῦ Ph || 19 <οἷον> οἶδα Spengel | ὅτι (pro ὅπερ) Fuhr; cf. [Dion.] l. 23 | οἷον **P** Sf Ph, Dox.; om. Vc Ac || 20 cf. Dem. 21, 191 | ὡς postea add. Vc (m. 1 ?); om. Sf Ph | τὴν πρότασιν Dox. || 21 ἀκούω ἢ (om. περὶ της προτάσεως) Dox.

should not remain (*at Troy*) but should flee, and through the whole harangue what he says is easily refuted and reversed, giving handles of attack to his opponents and at the end saying contradictory things; for he says (*Iliad* 2.135): "The timbers of the ships are rotten and the tacklings are loose." | Certainly this is clearly an ar- [438]
gument against fleeing. How will they flee if they have no ships? He would have said this to prevent them from sailing off, not in ordering them to do so.

There is another technique used in school hypotheses, which supports the propositions of the opponent and defends them at length and sometimes with witnesses, but you are pretending to speak against them, for in so speaking you will not awaken suspicion and you will get what you want. In such a figure of speech, to win (*the argument*) is for a speaker to be defeated, and to be defeated is for a speaker to win, for what we want has come about.

## CHAPTER 23: ON FORESTALLING THE CLAIMS OF THE OPPOSITION

A prosecutor forestalls the claims of a speaker who is going to answer him not only in one but in three ways: on the basis of knowledge, opinion, hearsay.[48] By knowledge: "I know what he will say, by Zeus," and things like that; by opinion, for example (cf. Dem. 21.191): "Probably then he will say," as it were, conjecturing about the claim; and by hearsay, as though hearing about the claim: "I am told that he is going to say. . ."

| These then are the forms of forestalling the headings of the [439]
defendant. But what is the occasion for each? You should know, therefore, that sometimes we shall use knowledge and sometimes opinion and sometimes hearsay, for an inopportune use often has the opposite effect. Some of the things that are going to be claimed

[48] Cf. Pseudo-Dionysius, *Art of Rhetoric* (vol. 2, pp. 362,21–363,1 Usener-Radermacher).

*ἐπιστήμῃ καὶ τῇ δόξῃ καὶ τῇ ἀκοῇ χρησόμεθα· ἡ γὰρ ἀκαιρία πολλάκις καὶ ἐναντία ποιεῖ. τῶν μελλόντων προτείνεσθαι ὑπὸ τοῦ ἀπολογουμένου [τοῦ οὖν ἀντιδίκου] τὰ μέν ἐστιν ἰσχυρότερα, τὰ δὲ ἀσθενῆ, τὰ δὲ μέσα· τὰ μὲν οὖν ἀσθενῆ τοῦ ἀντιδίκου ὡς εἰδὼς τῇ ἐπιστήμῃ προβαλῇ, τὰ δὲ μέσα τῇ ἕξει ὡς στοχαζόμενος, ὅπερ ἐστὶ τῇ δόξῃ, τὰ δὲ ἰσχυρὰ ὡς πυνθανόμενος. ἵνα δοκῇς ἀκούειν αὐτά, μὴ συνειδέναι δὲ ἰσχυρὰ ὄντα. Οὕτω μὲν δὴ δεῖ προτείνειν.*

*Δημοσθένης δὲ τὰ ἄμικτα ἔμιξεν ἐν τῷ Κατὰ Μειδίου, ἐπιστήμην ὁμοῦ καὶ ἀκοήν, λέγων οὕτως «ἔστι δὲ πρῶτον μὲν ἐκεῖνο οὐκ ἄδηλος ἐρῶν, ἐξ ὧν ἰδίᾳ πρός τινας αὐτὸς διεξιὼν ἀπηγγέλλετό μοι»· διὰ μὲν γὰρ τὴν φύσιν τοῦ πράγματος καὶ τὴν ἰσχὺν τοῦ κεφαλαίου τῇ ἀκοῇ κέχρηται, διὰ δὲ τὴν προσποίησιν τῆς καταφρονήσεως τῇ ἐπιστήμῃ. ἀλλὰ καὶ ἐν τῷ Περὶ τῆς ἀτελείας ἰσχυρότατον προτείνων τοῦ Λεπτίνου κεφάλαιον, τὸ τῆς ἀξίας, τῇ ἐπιστήμῃ προέτεινεν οὕτως «ἔστι δ᾽ οὐκ ἄδηλον τοῦθ᾽, ὅτι Λεπτίνης, κἂν τις ἄλλος ὑπὲρ τοῦ νόμου λέγῃ,*
[440] *δίκαιον μὲν οὐδὲν ἐρεῖ περὶ αὐ|τοῦ, φήσει δὲ ἀναξίους τινὰς εὑρομένους ἀτέλειαν ἐκδεδυκέναι τὰς λειτουργίας». λέγομεν οὖν, ὅτι ὁ Δημοσθένης χρῆται τοῖς σχήμασι καὶ κατὰ φύσιν καὶ παρὰ φύσιν, καὶ ἐνταῦθα τῷ μὲν Λεπτίνῃ ἰσχυρότατόν ἐστι τοῦτο τὸ κεφάλαιον, τῷ δὲ Δημοσθένει εὔλυτον.*

## Περὶ τοῦ λεληθότως τὰ αὐτὰ λέγειν ἢ ἑαυτῷ ἢ ἄλλοις.

*Τοῦ ταὐτὰ λέγοντα ἢ ἑαυτῷ ἢ ἄλλῳ τινὶ μὴ δοκεῖν τὰ αὐτὰ λέγειν διπλῆ μέθοδος· τάξεως μεταβολή, καὶ μήκη καὶ βραχύτητες. ἡ δὲ αὐτὴ καὶ τοῦ παραφράζειν μέθοδος· ἢ γὰρ τὴν τάξιν μεταβάλλεις, ᾗπερ*

**2** τὰ μέλλοντα Dox. | ἐπὶ Dox. || **3** τοῦ οὖν ἀντιδίκου **P** Vc Ac Sf Ph; om. Vδ, Dox. | ἰσχυρὰ Dox. || **4** προβαλεῖ Ac Sf Ph, Dox. || **5** τῇ λέξει Ph; τῇ τάξει, ἕ supr., Vδ; ⌊II⌉τ⌊ῇ m. po. ex ι; I er.⌉έξει Vc; cf. Syr. I p. 35, 6 || **6** δοκῆι Ac Ph, Dox. | αὐτὰ ἀκούειν Sf | συνειδέναι Vc Sf Ph, m. 2 Pc, cf. Syr. I p. 35, 4 (addit τοῖς ἀντιδίκοις), [Dion.] II 1 p. 363, 7 Us. (addit τοῖς ἐναντίοις); συνιέναι **P** Ac, Dox., m. po. Vc | δὲ om. Vc Sf Ph || **7** ⌊εἰπεῖν del.⌉ προτείνειν Ph || **9** ὁμοῦ om. Vδ | Dem. 21, 25 || **10** ἐπηγγέλλετό Ph || **14** ἀξίας (τα supr.) (τα m. 2 ?) Vc | Dem. 20, 1 || **15** τοῦθ᾽ om. Pah Vc Ac || **16** περὶ αὐτοῦ ἐρεῖ Vc | εὑρομένους Ph, m. 1 Vc, (α m. 1 supr.) **P**; εὑραμένους Ac Sf || **18** καὶ παρὰ φύσιν om. **P** Vc Ph; γρ καὶ οὕτως· καὶ κατὰ φύσιν καὶ κατὰ τέχνην. ἢ οὕτως· καὶ κατὰ φύσιν καὶ παρὰ φύσιν Pa; γρ´ καὶ κατὰ τέχνην m. 2 Sf | ὡς καὶ ἐνταῦθα Ac || **21** supr. Ac Sf, (τοῖς ἄλλοις) Vc; mg. Pa, (om. τὰ) Pc, (om. τοῦ) Ph | mg. $\overline{\kappa\beta}$ Vc Ac Ph, $\overline{\kappa\gamma}$ **P** | ἢ τοῖς ἄλλοις Vc; ἢ καὶ ἄλλοις **P**π || **24** μεταβαλεῖς Vδ

by the defendant are rather strong, some weak, some intermediate. Now you counter the weak claims of the opponent by saying you have knowledge (*of them*), and the intermediate claims by saying you conjecture (*what they are likely to be*), which is using opinion, and the strong ones as having learned (*about them*) from inquiry, so that you may seem to be hearing of them but not to recognize that they are strong. This is how to forestall.

In *Against Meidias* (21.25) Demosthenes mixed the pure forms, knowledge and hearsay, together, saying, "First, it is not unclear what he will say from what has been reported to me that he told certain people in private." Because of the nature of the subject and the strength of the argument he has used hearsay, but by the affectation of disdain he has claimed knowledge. And in *On the Immunity* (20.1), forestalling a very strong argument of Leptines, that of the (*lack of*) worthiness (*of some given exemption from liturgies*), he forestalled it by his knowledge, as follows: "This is not unclear, that Leptines, and anyone else who may speak in favor of the law, will say nothing fair about | it but will say that some un- [440]
worthy persons have used their exemption to avoid liturgies." We say, therefore, that Demosthenes uses these figures both in a natural and an unnatural way, and here this argument is very strong for Leptines but easily refuted by Demosthenes.[49]

## CHAPTER 24: ON ESCAPING NOTICE WHILE REPEATING WHAT YOU OR OTHERS HAVE SAID

There are two methods of repeating your own or someone else's words without seeming to do so: change of order, and lengthenings and shortenings.[50] The method is the same as in paraphrasing,[51] for you either change the order the other speaker used or the measure; for if the first version was lengthy, you will say these things compressed into few words, or the opposite.

[49] Since the point is strongly in the opponent's favor, it is "unnatural" to claim knowledge, but since the point is easily refuted, Demosthenes' usage is "natural."

[50] *Mēkē kai brakhtytētes*, elsewhere often referring to long and short syllables in poetic meter (cf., e.g., Plato, *Republic* 400b8) but here meaning amplification or concision.

[51] As taught in progymnasmatic exercises; cf. Theon 15; Aphthonius 3; Pseudo-Hermogenes p.7,13 Rabe.

*ἐκεῖνος ἐχρήσατο, ἢ τὸ μέτρον· εἴπερ γὰρ διὰ μακρῶν ἐκεῖνος, ταῦτα ἐν βραχέσι συνελὼν λέγεις, ἢ τὸ ἐναντίον.*

*Τίς δὲ ἑκατέρου τούτων ὁ καιρός; ἡ μὲν συμβουλευτικὴ μήκη καὶ βραχύτητας ἐπιδέχεται· τῆς γὰρ τάξεως μεταβολὴν οὐ δύναται ἔχειν, ὅτι ἐν συμβουλῇ πάντως πρῶτον τὸ κατεπεῖγον εἶναι δεῖ παρὰ παντὶ συμβουλεύοντι. ἐν δὲ τῇ πανηγυρικῇ νόμος ἐστὶ τῶν κεφαλαίων τῆς τάξεως ἀμετάβλητος ἡ φύσις τῶν πραγμάτων. χρώμεθα οὖν τοῖς μήκεσι καὶ ταῖς βραχύτησιν, ὥσπερ ἐν συμβουλευτικῇ μὲν ἰδέᾳ ἐποίησεν ὁ* [441] *Δημοσθένης ἔν τε τοῖς Ὀλυνθιακοῖς καὶ ἐν τῷ Περὶ τῶν ἐν Χερρο|νήσῳ στρατιωτῶν· τὰ αὐτὰ γὰρ λέγων ἑαυτῷ μάλιστα ἔλαθεν. ἐν δὲ πανηγυρικῇ ἰδέᾳ Πλάτων τὰ αὐτὰ λέγων Θουκυδίδῃ ἐν τῷ Ἐπιταφίῳ οὐ μόνον ἔλαθεν, ἀλλὰ καὶ ἄλλα λέγειν ἔδοξε· τὰ γοῦν περὶ τῶν πολέμων Θουκυδίδης μὲν ἐπιμνησθεὶς παρῆκεν, ὁ Πλάτων δὲ ἐπεξειργάσατο· τοὐναντίον δὲ Πλάτων μὲν παρῆκε τὰ περὶ τῆς πολιτείας, Θουκυδίδης δὲ ἐπεξῆλθεν.*

*Ἐν δὲ τῇ δικανικῇ ἰδέᾳ καὶ ἡ τῆς τάξεως μεταβολὴ χώραν ἔχει, ὥσπερ Δημοσθένης ἐποίησεν ἐν τῷ Περὶ τῆς ἀτελείας· Φορμίωνος γὰρ προκατηγορήσαντος τοῦ νόμου καὶ χρησαμένου τοῖς κεφαλαίοις τῆς διαιρέσεως, τῷ δικαίῳ, τῷ συμφέροντι, τῷ καλῷ, τῷ τῆς ἀξίας, ἀνέστρεψε τὴν τάξιν μεταβάλλων· πῶς δὲ τοῦτο ἐποίησεν, ἐν τοῖς περὶ τοῦ λόγου διεξήλθομεν.*

## *Περὶ τοῦ ἀνεπαχθῶς ἑαυτὸν ἐπαινεῖν.*

*Τοῦ ἑαυτὸν ἐπαινεῖν ἐπαχθοῦς ὄντος καὶ εὐμισήτου, <τοῦ> ἀνεπαχθῶς ποιῆσαι μέθοδοι τρεῖς· κοινότης λόγου, ἀνάγκης προσποίησις, προσώπου ὑπαλλαγή.*

*Τούτων παραδείγματα. ὁ Ἰσοκράτης ἐν τῷ πρώτῳ λόγῳ τῶν παραινέσεων τὸ πρῶτον προοίμιον ἑαυτοῦ ἔπαινον κατεσκεύασε· θέλει*

**1** γὰρ et ἐκεῖνος om. Vc Ac Sf Ph || **3** δὲ om. Vc Ph || **5** ἐν μὲν Vc Ac Sf Ph | πάντων Sf || **5-6** παντὶ τῶι Pc || **8** ὁ om. Vc Sf Ph || **9** τῷ Vδ; τοῖς **P** Vc Ac Sf Ph | ἐπὶ Ph || **10** cf. Theon. II 63, 32 Sp. || **12** ἐπὶ Vc | πολέμων Vc Ac Sf Ph, v.l. Pa, cf. Thuc. 2, 36; πολεμίων **P** || **13** μὲν om. Sf | Plat. Menex. 239 A sq. || **14** τὰ Sf; om. **P** Vc Ac Ph | τῆς om. Ac || **19** ἀντέστρεψε Vc Sf || **20** μεταβάλλων Ph; μεταβαλών **P** Vc Ac Sf | scil. ἐν τοῖς εἰς τοὺς δημοσίους ὑπομνήμασιν, cf. Π. ἰδ. 308, 12 | περὶ αὐτοῦ λόγοις Sf, (τούτου) m. po. Vc || **22** supr. Vc Ac Sf, mg. **P** Ph | mg. $\overline{\kappa\gamma}$ Vc Ac Ph, $\overline{\kappa\delta}$ Pc (er. ? Pa) || **23** cf. Alex. III 4, 13 Sp.; Aristid. II 506, 8 Sp. | ὄντως Ph | addidit Rabe || **26** τὰ παραδείγματα Ac Sf Ph | ὁ om. Ph || **27** ἑαυτοῦ mg. suppl. m. 1 Ph | cf. [Dion.] II 1, p. 24, 19 Us; Plut. De se ipsum laudando c. 1 sq.

What is the occasion for each of these? Deliberative oratory is open to lengthenings and shortenings but cannot accept a change of order (*of the arguments*), because in deliberation there must always first be something urgent for every speaker, while in panegyric the nature of the subject provides an unchangeable law about the order of the headings.[52] Thus, we use lengthenings and shortenings, as Demosthenes did in the deliberative species in the *Olynthiacs* and in *On the Soldiers in Chersonese*. | Although re- [441]
peating himself, he mostly escaped notice. In the panegyric form, Plato escaped notice by saying the same things as Thucydides in his *Epitaphios* but seemed to say other things; at least Thucydides dismissed the subject of the wars after brief mention (2.36), while Plato elaborated it (*Menexenus* 239aff.). On the other hand, Plato passed over the subject of the constitution and Thucydides elaborated it.

In the judicial species change of order has a place, as Demosthenes did in *On the Immunity*, for after Phormio had spoken against the law, using the headings of division—the just, the beneficial, the honorable, the question of worthiness—Demosthenes reversed the order. How he did this we described in our exegesis of the speech.[53]

## CHAPTER 25: ON PRAISING ONESELF WITHOUT OFFENSE[54]

Although praising oneself is offensive and easily detested, there are three methods of doing it without offense; generalization of language, claim of necessity, change of person.

Here are examples of these. Isocrates in the first of his speeches of exhortation (1.1) constructed the first prooemion as praise of himself, for he wants to say that "I am | a man of most [442]
excellent character and the only good friend of your dead father, Demonicus, out of goodwill toward you." How, then, does he do

[52] As the example below indicates, the author is thinking of the conventional order of topics in funeral oratory.

[53] Cf. Hermogenes, *On Ideas*, p. 308 Rabe, where there is a similar reference, but this is not evidence of authorship, since many rhetoricians published studies of orations of Demosthenes.

[54] Cf. Plutarch's essay *On Praising Oneself* (vol. 7 of *Moralia;* trans. P. H. De Lacy and B. Einarson; LCL; Cambridge: Harvard University Press, 1992), 110–67.

[442] *γὰρ εἰπεῖν ὅτι «ἐγὼ ἀνὴρ | εἰμι σπουδαιότατος καὶ μόνος φίλος ἀγαθὸς ἀποθανόντος τοῦ πατρός, ὦ Δημόνικε, σοὶ εὐνοῶν»· πῶς οὖν αὐτὸ ποιεῖ; κοινῷ τῷ λόγῳ χρῆται περί τε σπουδαίων ἀνδρῶν καὶ φαύλων λέγων καὶ διακρίνων ἤθη ἀγαθῶν καὶ πονηρῶν φίλων, οὕτω δὲ φαίνεται αὐτὸς ὢν τῶν ἀγαθῶν ἀνδρῶν. Ὁ δὲ Δημοσθένης ἐν τῷ Περὶ τοῦ στεφάνου μέλλων ἑαυτὸν ἐπαινεῖν καὶ τὴν ἑαυτοῦ πολιτείαν πολλάκις τῇ ἀνάγκῃ χρῆται λέγων «ἐὰν δ᾽ ἐφ᾽ ἃ καὶ πεποίηκα καὶ πεπολίτευμαι βαδίζω, πολλάκις λέγειν ἀναγκασθήσομαι περὶ ἐμαυτοῦ». Ἐπειδὴ δὲ τῇ ἀνάγκῃ πολλάκις χρώμενος ὕποπτός ἐστι, καὶ τῇ τοῦ προσώπου ὑπαλλαγῇ χρῆται. ἔστι δὲ τοῦτο· ὅταν τι μέτριον λέγῃ, τότε πρὸς τοὺς Ἀθηναίους λέγει, ὅταν δὲ ὑπερήφανον καὶ ἐπαχθές, πρὸς Αἰσχίνην· «οὐ λίθοις ἐτείχισα τὴν πόλιν οὐδὲ πλίνθοις ἐγώ, ἀλλὰ τὸν ἐμὸν τειχισμὸν εἰ βούλει σκοπεῖν, εὑρήσεις ὅπλα καὶ πόλεις καὶ συμμάχους», καὶ πάλιν ἀλλαχοῦ «ὧν μέντοι ἐκ τῆς ἰδίας οὐσίας ἐπέδωκα, οὐδεμίαν ἡμέραν ὑπεύθυνος εἶναί φημι. ἀκούεις, Αἰσχίνη;» ἀπέστρεψε τὸν λόγον, ἵνα δοκοίη τὸν ἐχθρὸν λυπεῖν, μὴ Ἀθηναίοις ὀνειδίζειν.*

[443] ## | *Περὶ παλαισμάτων δικαστηρίων, ἃ Δημοσθένης ἐτεχνήσατο.*

*Δύο παλαίσματα δικαστηρίων Δημοσθένης ἐπετεχνήσατο, τό τε οἰκεῖον ἰσχυρόν, κἂν μὴ κρινόμενον ᾖ, εἰς κρίσιν ἀγαγεῖν καὶ τὸ τοῦ ἀντιδίκου ἰσχυρὸν κρινόμενον ἐκβαλεῖν. ταῦτα τοίνυν ἀμφότερα ποιεῖ Δημοσθένης καὶ λανθάνει πράττων· ὅταν γὰρ τὸ οἰκεῖον εἰσάγῃ χαριζόμενος ἑαυτῷ, ἀνάγκην προσποιεῖται, ὅταν δὲ τὸ τοῦ ἀντιδίκου ἐκβάλλῃ πανουργῶν, ἁπλότητα ὑποκρίνεται.*

*Τοῦτο ἐποίησε καὶ ἐν δυσὶ λόγοις, ἔν τε τῷ Περὶ τοῦ στεφάνου καὶ ἐν τῷ Κατὰ Ἀριστοκράτους. ὅταν γὰρ τὸ τῆς πολιτείας καὶ ἀξίας*

**2** εὐνοῶν Pa, (ν m. po. in ras.) Pc; εὐνοῶ Vc Ac Sf Ph || **3** Isocr. 1, 1 sq. | φαύλων· λέγων γὰρ καὶ Sf || **4** δὲ om. Vc Ac Sf Ph || **7** Dem. 18, 4 || **8** ἑαυτοῦ (μ supr.) Ph || **9-16** cf. [Dion.] II 1 p. 336, 11. 13 Us. || **10** λέγει om. Ph || **11** Dem. 18, 299 || **12** ἐτειχήσατο Ph || **13** ἐὰν βούληι Vc Sf Ph, cf. Dem. || **14** Dem. 18, 112 | μὲν τῆς ἐκ τῆς Ph || **15** εἰμι (pro εἶναί φημι) Ph || **16** δοκῆι Ph | ἀθηναίους Ph, (υ ex ι, m. 1 ?) Sf || **17** mg. **P**; supr. (ἐπετεχνάσατο) Ac, (των δικαστηρίων; ἐπετεχνήσατο) Vc Sf; om. Ph | mg. $\overline{κδ}$ Ac Ph, $\overline{κε}$ **P** || **18** δημοσθένους Vc Sf Ph; ἃ δημοσθένους Ac | ἐπετεχνήσατο Pa, (ἐπ supr., m. 1 ?) Pc; ἐπιτεχνηματα Vc Ac Sf Ph; γρ ἐπὶ τέχνη μετὰ δημοσθένην Pa; γρ´ ἐπιτεχνήμα (τ sub.) δημοσθ^έ Pc || **20** καὶ ante κρινόμενον supr. Vδ || **22** ἐκβάλη Sf || **23** καὶ ἁπλότητα Vc Sf Ph || **24** καὶ om. Portus | τοῦ om. Ph || **25** καὶ — ἀριστοκράτους Ac, m. po. Pa Vc Sf; om. **P** Vc Sf Ph | γὰρ **P** Ac; om. Ph; suppl. m. po. Vc, m. 2 Sf

it? He uses general language, speaking about good and bad men and distinguishing the characters of good and evil friends, and thus he seems himself to be one of the good men. Demosthenes in *On the Crown,* when he is going to praise himself and his policy, often excuses it by necessity, saying (for example, 18.4), "If I proceed to what I have done and what my policy has been, I shall often be forced to speak about myself." But since using the excuse of necessity often is suspect, he also uses change of person. This is done as follows: whenever he is saying something modest, he addresses it to the Athenians, but whenever what he is saying is arrogant and offensive, he addresses it to Aeschines; (*for example*, 18:299): "Not with stones did I fortify the city nor with bricks, but if you (*singular*) want to inspect my fortification, you will find arms and cities and allies." And again elsewhere (18.112): "I do not admit for one single day—do you hear, Aeschines?—that I am liable for audit of what I gave from my private funds." He changed the statement to seem to annoy his enemy and not to reproach the Athenians.

## | CHAPTER 26: ON TRICKS DEVISED BY DEMOSTHENES IN THE LAWCOURTS [443]

Demosthenes devised two tricks in the lawcourts: (1) bringing a strong point of his own into the case, even if it was not under judgment; and (2) rejecting the strong point of the opponent that was being judged. Well then, Demosthenes does both of these things and escapes notice in doing them, for whenever he introduces something relating to himself that is in his favor, he alleges necessity, and whenever he deceitfully rejects an argument of the opponent, he affects simplicity.

He did this in two speeches, in *On the Crown* and in *Against Aristocrates*. Whenever he introduces the question of his policy and merit, he represents them as necessary; (*for example,* 18.4): "But if I come to what I have done and what my policy was, I shall often be forced to speak about myself"; but when he evades

*ἐπάγῃ, ἀνάγκην ὑποκρίνεται «ἐὰν δὲ ἐφ' ἃ καὶ πεποίηκα καὶ πεπολίτευμαι βαδίζω, πολλάκις λέγειν ἀναγκασθήσομαι περὶ ἐμαυτοῦ»· ὅταν δὲ τοὺς νόμους κλέπτῃ, ἁπλότητα προσποιεῖται λέγων οὕτως «ἔτι μέντοι καὶ τοὺς νόμους δεικτέον εἶναί μοι δοκεῖ», ὡς παρέργου μνημονεύων τοῦ ἰσχυροῦ τῷ ἀντιδίκῳ. Καὶ πάλιν ἐν τῷ Κατ' Ἀριστοκράτους εἰσάγων* [444] *τὸν περὶ Χερρονήσου λόγον | οὐδὲν προσήκοντα τῷ ἀγῶνι φησὶν «ἀνάγκη δέ ἐστι πρῶτον ἁπάντων δεῖξαι, τί ποτε ἔστι τὸ Χερρόνησον ἀσφαλῶς ἔχειν ἡμᾶς πεποιηκός», εἶτα πανουργῶν καὶ πολίτην ἐργαζόμενος τὸν Χαρίδημον, ἵνα αὐτῷ ἰσχύῃ ὁ περὶ τῶν νόμων λόγος, ἐπιφέρει «θεάσασθε τοίνυν, ὡς δικαίως καὶ ἁπλῶς ποιήσομαι τοὺς λόγους, ὃς εἰς μὲν ταύτην τίθεμαι τὴν τάξιν αὐτόν, ἐν ᾗ πλείστης ἂν τυγχάνοι τιμῆς, ἃ δ' οὐδ' ἡμῖν τοῖς γένει πολίταις ἐστίν, οὐδ' ἐκείνῳ δεῖν οἶμαι γενέσθαι παρὰ τοὺς νόμους».*

## *Περὶ δευτερολογιῶν, διὰ ποίας αἰτίας μερίζεται λόγος, καὶ πῶς γίνονται.*

*Δευτερολογιῶν εἴδη τάδε· ἤτοι γὰρ διὰ μέγεθος τοῦ ἀγῶνος μερίζεται ἡ κατηγορία ἢ ἡ ἀπολογία· ἢ προκατηγορήσαντός τινος καὶ προαγωνισαμένου ὁ δεύτερος λέγων αὐξήσει χρῆται, ὥσπερ οἱ Κατὰ Ἀριστογείτονος λόγοι ἔχουσιν· ἢ τὰ αὐτὰ ὁ δεύτερος λέγων οὐκ αὔξει μέν, προστίθησι δέ τινα ἢ ἀφαιρεῖ, ὥσπερ κατορθῶν τὰ εἰρημένα, ὡς ἔχει ὁ τοῦ Νέστορος λόγος ἐν τῇ δευτέρᾳ ῥαψῳδίᾳ μετὰ τὴν Ὀδυσσέως δημηγορίαν· ἢ προαγωνισαμένου ἑτέρου ὁ δεύτερος λέγων τὰ μέλλοντα δεύτερα λέγεσθαι ὑπὸ τοῦ ἀντιδίκου προκαταλαμβάνει λέγων, ὥσπερ ὁ Κατ' Ἀνδροτίωνος ἔχει, προκατηγορήσαντος γὰρ Εὐκτήμονος, ἃ μέλλει λέγειν Ἀνδροτίων, ὁ Διόδωρος προκαταλαμβάνει. Οὗτοι τέσσαρες τρόποι δευτερολογίας.*

1 ἐπαγάγηι Vc Ph; ἐπεισάγηι Ac | Dem. 18, 4 || 3 ἁπλότητ⌊α ex ι⌉ Vc | 248, 8: cf. [Dion.] II 1 p. 302, 23 Us. (de Demosth. Π. παραπρεσβ.): ἁπλότητος προσχήματι κλέπτων τὴν πανουργίαν τῆς κατασκευῆς | Dem. 18, 58 || 4 πάρεργον Ph || 5-6 καὶ πάλιν λέγων θεάσασθε — τοὺς λόγους (sicut p. 248, 8–9) και πάλιν ἐν Vc, (om. ult. καὶ) Ac Sf Ph || 7 Dem. 23, 8 | τὸ om. Ph || 8 ὑμᾶς Vδ; cf. Π. ἰδ. 235, 22 || 10 Dem. 23, 24 || 11 εἰ Pc | τυγχάνηι Pc || 14 supr. Vc Sf, (δευτερολογίας et γίγνεται) Ac; mg. (γίνεται) **P** Ph || 14-15 mg. $\overline{\kappa\varepsilon}$ Ac Ph, $\overline{\kappa\varsigma}$ **P** || 16 γὰρ om. Vc Sf Ph || 17 ἢ κατηγορία ἢ (om. ἡ) Ph || 19 αὐξήσει (om. οὐκ et μὲν) Ph; ⌊οὐκ m. po. supr.⌉ αὔξ⌊ει μὲν m. po.⌉ Vc || 20 Hom. B 337 || 24 κατηγορήσαντος Vc Ac Ph | γὰρ m. 2 suppl. Sf

the laws, he affects simplicity, saying something like, "Further, it seems to me one ought to show what the laws are," mentioning the strong point of his opponent as though in passing. And again, in *Against Aristocrates*, introducing the passage about the Chersonese | that has nothing to do with the trial, he asserts (23.8), "It is necessary first of all to show what has made you hold the Chersonese securely"; then in a deceitful way making Charidemus a citizen, in order that the passage about the laws may strengthen his case, he adds (23.24), "See, then, how justly and candidly I shall treat the questions by assigning him to the rank in which he gets most honor, but I do not think he ought to have in contravention of the laws rights that do not even belong to us who are citizens by birth." [444]

## CHAPTER 27: ON SECOND SPEECHES: WHY A CASE IS DIVIDED AND HOW THIS IS DONE[55]

The kinds of second speeches (*deuterologiai*) are as follows.[56] Either because of the importance of the trial the prosecution or the defense is divided (*among two or more speakers*); or when one speaker has introduced the prosecution and argued it first, a second speaker amplifies it, as seen in the speeches *Against Aristogeiton* (Pseudo-Dem. 25 and 26); or the second speaker makes (*many of*) the same points and does not amplify them but adds or eliminates some things, as though correcting what has been said, as in the speech of Nestor in the second book (*Iliad* 2.337–368) after the harangue of Odysseus; or after one speaker has begun the argument the second speaker refutes in advance what is going to be said in a second speech by the opponent, speaking as in *Against Androtion*, for Euctemon began the prosecution and Diodorus refutes in advance what Androtion is going to say. These are the four kinds of second speeches.

[55] It is unlikely that second speeches were much practiced in schools of declamation, but the progymnasmatic exercise in commonplace was sometimes regarded as like a second speech; cf. Aphthonius, ch. 7, and the comments of John of Sardis thereon (*Aphthonii progymnasmata* [ed. Hugo Rabe; Bibliotheca scriptorum Graecorum et Romanorum Teubneriana; Rhetores Graeci 10; Leipzig: Teubner, 1926], 94). John identifies four kinds of second speeches, distinguishing them by changes in speaker and subject.

[56] On second speeches, cf. Hermogenes, *On Stases,* p. 52,7 Rabe; Nicolaus, *Progymnasmata*, p. 38,2 Felten.

[445] ## | *Περὶ διηγήσεως.*

*Οἱ παλαιοὶ διηγούμενοι διπλῇ τινι μεθόδῳ χρῶνται, ἀναφορᾷ δι᾽ ἀσφάλειαν καὶ διὰ πίστιν βεβαιώσει, οἷον Ἰσοκράτης «Ζεὺς γὰρ Ἡρακλέα καὶ Τάνταλον γεννήσας, ὡς οἱ μῦθοι λέγουσι καὶ πάντες πιστεύουσι», τὸ μὲν «ὡς οἱ μῦθοι λέγουσιν» ἀναφορά, τὸ δὲ «καὶ πάντες πιστεύουσιν» ἡ βεβαίωσις. καὶ Εὐριπίδης «Ζεύς, ὡς λέλεκται» ἀναφορά, «τῆς ἀληθείας ὕπο» βεβαίωσις. καὶ Ἡρόδοτος «οὕτω δὴ λέγουσι Κορίνθιοι» ἀναφορά, «ὁμολογέουσι δέ σφι Λέσβιοι» βεβαίωσις. καὶ Θουκυδίδης «λέγουσι δέ» ἀναφορά, «καὶ οἱ τὰ σαφέστατα Πελοποννησίων μνήμῃ παρὰ τῶν προτέρων δεδεγμένοι» βεβαίωσις. καὶ Δημοσθένης «ὡς δὲ ἐγὼ τῶν ἐν αὐτῇ τῇ χώρᾳ γεγενημένων τινὸς ἤκουον, ἀνδρὸς οὐδαμῶς οἵου τε ψεύδεσθαι, οὐδένων εἰσὶ βελτίους»· καὶ τοῦτο <παρὰ> Πλάτωνος ἔλαβεν «ὡς ἐγώ του παρὰ βασιλέως ἐλθόντος ἤκουσα, ἀνδρὸς ἀξιοπίστου».*

## *Περὶ κοινῶν διανοημάτων, πῶς αὐτὰ ἰδιώσομεν λέγοντες.*

*Οἱ παλαιοὶ κοινὰ λέγοντες διανοήματα ὁμολογίᾳ τῆς κοινότητος*
[446] *ἴδια αὐτῶν ποιοῦσιν. Ἰσοκράτης «ἅπαντες | μὲν εἰώθασιν οἱ παριόντες ἐνθάδε ταῦτα μέγιστα φάσκειν εἶναι, περὶ ὧν ἂν αὐτοὶ ποιῶνται τοὺς λόγους· οὐ μὴν ἀλλ᾽ εἴ τῳ καὶ ἄλλῳ ταῦτα ἥρμοσε λέγειν, καὶ ἐμοὶ προσήκει», καὶ Δημοσθένης ἐν τῷ Κατὰ Τιμοκράτους «εἰώθασι μὲν οὖν οἱ πολλοί», καὶ Αἰσχίνης ἐν τῷ Κατὰ Τιμάρχου «καὶ ὡς ἔοικεν οἱ εἰωθότες λόγοι λέγεσθαι ἐπὶ τοῖς δημοσίοις ἀγῶσιν οὐκ εἰσι ψευδεῖς· αἱ γὰρ ἴδιαι ἔχθραι πολλὰ πάνυ τῶν κοινῶν ἐπανορθοῦσι», καὶ πάλιν*

1 supr. Vc Sf, (διηγήσεων) Ac; mg. **P** Ph | mg. $\overline{\kappa\varsigma}$ Vc Ac Ph, $\overline{\kappa\zeta}$ **P** || 3 Diac.: τινὲς εἰς τὸ «ἀσφάλειαν» στίζουσιν, εἶτα τὸ ἑξῆς ἀναγιγνώσκουσι «καὶ πίστιν βεβαιώσει» . . . ἔνιοι δὲ «δι᾽ ἀσφάλειαν καὶ πίστιν» ἀναγιγνώσκουσιν, εἶτα τὸ ἑξῆς «βεβαιώσει» | Isocr. 1, 50 || 5 οἱ om. Vc || 6 Eur. fr. 591 N.[2]; *Rhein. Museum* 63, 145 l. 13; 146 l. 1 || 7 καὶ τῆς Vc | ὕπο om. Ph, (m. po. suppl.) Vc | ἡ βεβαίωσις Vc Sf Ph | οὕτω **P** Vc Ac, v.l. m. 2 Sf; τῶι Ph, Her. 1, 23; το Sf || 8 ὁμολογοῦσι Ph | Thuc. 1, 9 || 8-10 καὶ — βεβαίωσις om. Pc || 10 δεδιδαγμένοι m. 2 Sf || 11 Dem. 2, 17 | γεγεννημένων Pa | ἤκουσα τινὸς Vc || 12 καὶ τὸ τοῦ Ph || 12-13 παρὰ add. Ma, cf. Π. ἰδ. 348, 6 || 13 Plat. Alcib. I 123 B | του Pc Vc Ac; που Pa, m. 1 Sf; τῶν Ph || 15 supr. Vc Sf, (ἰδιασόμεθα) Ac; mg. Pa, (νοημάτων) Pc, (καὶ πῶς) Ph | mg. $\overline{\kappa\zeta}$ Vc Ac, $\overline{\kappa\eta}$ **P** || 16 διανοήματα λέγοντες Ac || 17 Isocr. 8, 1 || 18 ποιοῦνται, mg. ὧν, Ph || 20 Dem. 24, 4 || 21 Aesch. 1, 2 || 21-252.1 καὶ — τιμάρχου m. po. suppl. Vc

## | CHAPTER 28: ON NARRATION [445]

The ancients use two different methods in narrating, *anaphora* for reassurance and *bebaiōsis*[57] for proof; for example, Isocrates (1.50): "For Zeus, having begotten Heracles and Tantalus, as the myths say and all believe"; "as the myths say" is an anaphora,[58] while "and all believe" is bebaiōsis. And Euripides (frg. 591 Nauck²): anaphora, "Zeus, as has been said"; bebaiōsis, "by the truth." And Herodotus (1.23): "This is what the Corinthians say," anaphora; "and the Lesbians agree with them," bebaiōsis. And Thucydides (1.9): "They say," anaphora; "those of the Peloponnesians who have received the wisest traditions from their ancestors," bebaiōsis. And Demosthenes (2.17): "As I have heard from one of those born in the same place, a man not of the sort to lie, no better than ours." He took this from Plato (*Alcibiades* 1.123b): "As I have heard from one coming from the king, a man to be believed."

## CHAPTER 29: ON COMMONPLACE THOUGHTS: HOW WE SHALL MAKE THEM OUR OWN WHEN SPEAKING

When the ancients spoke commonplace thoughts they made them their own by acknowledging that they were common. Isocrates: "All those | coming before you here are accustomed to claim that [446] these subjects on which they are themselves speaking are the most important; nevertheless, if to say this was (*ever*) fitting for someone else to say, it is fitting for me (*now*)."[59] And Demosthenes in *Against Timocrates* (24.4): "Now many have become accustomed (*to say that whatever they happen to speak about is most important for you*)." And Aeschines in *Against Timarchus* (1.2): "And it seems that the words usually spoken in public trials are not false, for private enmities correct very many problems of the community."

[57] "Strengthening"; not regarded as a figure by other writers. It is the term for confirmation in the *Rhetoric for Alexander* (36.1142b34ff.).

[58] I.e., it "takes up" (*anaphorein*) what has just been said, an unusual usage of the term, which elsewhere is a verbal figure utilizing a succession of statements beginning with the same word; cf., e.g., Phoebammon 1.3.

[59] A somewhat cumbersome paraphrase of what Isocrates says at the beginning of *On the Peace*.

*Αἰσχίνης ἐν τῷ Κατὰ Τιμάρχου «οὐκ ἀγνοῶ δέ, ὅτι ἃ μέλλω ἐν πρώτοις λέγειν».*

*Ἐν δὲ τοῖς Ὀλυνθιακοῖς Δημοσθένης τῷ πρώτῳ λόγῳ, χρώμενος κοινῷ διανοήματι τῷ ἀντὶ πολλῶν χρημάτων αὐτοὺς αἱρήσεσθαι τὸ κοινῇ συμφέρον, οὐ χρῆται τῇ ὁμολογίᾳ τῆς κοινότητος, διότι πανούργως χρῆται, καὶ παραλείπει τὴν ὁμολογίαν, προκατασκευάζει δὲ διὰ τοῦ προοιμίου τὰ θεωρικὰ χρήματα δεῖν ἀποδοῦναι τοῖς στρατιώταις. εἰ μὲν οὖν ὡμολόγει τὴν κοινότητα, ἔφασκε δὲ λυσιτελεῖν καὶ αὐτῷ εἰπεῖν, ὑπωπτεύετο· νῦν δὲ κοινῷ χρησάμενος διανοήματι καὶ λαθὼν αὐτοὺς ὁμολογοῦντας ὕστερον ἀναμιμνήσκει ἀρνεῖσθαι αἰσχυνομένους περὶ τῶν θεωρικῶν χρημάτων. διὰ τοῦτο καὶ ἐπεσφραγίσατο ἐν ἀρχῇ τὸ διανόημα οὕτως «ὅτε τοίνυν τοῦθ᾽ οὕτως ἔχει». ἔθος δὲ Δημοσθένους ἐστίν, ὅταν τι διοικήσηται ἑαυτῷ χρήσιμον, μὴ πρότερον ἀφίστασθαι,*
[447] *πρὶν ἢ ἐπισφραγίσηται. πε|ποίηκε τοῦτο ἐν τοῖς τέτρασι λόγοις, ἐν τῷ Περὶ τοῦ στεφάνου, ἐν τῷ Κατὰ Μειδίου, ἐν τῷ Κατὰ Ἀριστοκράτους, ἐν τῷ πρώτῳ τῶν Ὀλυνθιακῶν.*

## *Περὶ χρήσεως ἐπῶν ἐν πεζῷ λόγῳ.*

*Κατὰ πόσους τρόπους ἐν πεζῷ λόγῳ χρῆσις ἐπῶν γίνεται; κατὰ δύο, κόλλησιν καὶ παρῳδίαν. καὶ κόλλησις μέν ἐστιν, ὅταν ὁλόκληρον τὸ ἔπος εὐφυῶς κολλήσῃ τῷ λόγῳ, ὥστε συμφωνεῖν δοκεῖν· οἷον παρὰ τῷ Αἰσχίνῃ ἐν τῷ Κατὰ Τιμάρχου ἐπιστᾶσά που ἡ τοῦ Πατρόκλου ψυχὴ καθεύδοντι τῷ Ἀχιλλεῖ ἐπισκήπτει περὶ τοῦ ὁμόταφος αὐτῷ γενέσθαι*

*«οὐ γὰρ ἔτι ζωοί γε φίλων ἀπάνευθεν ἑταίρων*
*βουλὰς ἑζόμενοι βουλεύσομεν»*

*καὶ τὰ ἑξῆς, καὶ πάλιν φησὶν Εὐριπίδης*

1 Aesch. 1, 4 || 3 τῶν Ὀλυνθιακῶν? | δημοσθένης om. Vc Sf Ph | ἐν τῷ vulg. cf. p. 252, 16 || 4 τὸ Ph | νομίζειν add. ante αὐτοὺς Vc Ac Sf Ph, cf. Dem. 1, 1 || 6 προπαρασκευάζει Vc Sf Ph || 10 Dem. 1, 19. 20 | αἰσχυνόμενος Ph || 12 Dem. 1, 1 | δὲ m. po. suppl. Vc | δημοσθένει Vc Ac Sf Ph || 14 ἐπισφραγίσεται **P** Ac Ph | πεποίηται Ph; πεποίηκεν δὲ Vc | τοῖς om. Sf (cf. 246, 24) || 15 τοῦ om. Ph || 16 ὀλυνθιακῶι (om. τῶν) Ph || 17 supr. Vc Ac Sf, mg. **P** Ph | mg. $\overline{\kappa\eta}$ Vc Ac Ph, $\overline{\kappa\theta}$ **P** || 18 καὶ ποίους add. ante ἐν Sf | ἐν τῶι Vc Ac | cf. Π. ἰδ. 336, 15 sq. || 19 alt. καὶ om. Vc Sf Ph || 23 Aesch. 1, 149; Hom. Ψ 77 || 25 ἐφεξῆς Vc Sf Ph | ὅ φησιν Sf; φησὶν ὁ Ph

And Aeschines again in *Against Timarchus* (1.4): "I am not unaware that what I am going to say at first (*is something you will undoubtedly have heard from others*)."

In the *Olynthiacs*, in the first speech, although making use of a common thought—that (*the Athenians*) would prefer what was advantageous to the community to a large amount of money—Demosthenes (1.1) does not make an acknowledgement of the common nature of the thought because he is acting in a deceitful way and omits the acknowledgement but throughout the prooemion is anticipating the need to transfer the theoric moneys to pay soldiers. If he acknowledged the commonplace nature of the thought and claimed that it was profitable for him to speak, he would be viewed with suspicion. But now, by using a commonplace thought and escaping the notice of those agreeing with it, he later reminds them that they denied feeling shame about the theoric moneys. For this reason, at the beginning the thought is given special note (*epesphragisato*): "Since then this is so." It is the custom of Demosthenes, whenever something is arranged in a way useful to him, not to leave it until it has been specially noted. | [447]
He did this in four speeches, in *On the Crown, Against Meidias, Against Aristocrates,* and in the *First Olynthiac*.

## CHAPTER 30: ON USE OF VERSES IN PROSE

In how many ways are verses used in a prose? In two: by quotation and by adaptation. It is quotation (*kollēsis*)[60] whenever one quotes the whole verse gracefully in the speech so that it seems to harmonize with it; for example, in Aeschines, in *Against Timarchus* (1.149), the shade of Patroclus standing, I suppose, over the sleeping Achilles enjoins him about common burial with him (*Iliad* 23.77–78):

> For we no longer as in life, sitting apart from our dear companions, shall lay our plans together,

and so on; and again, Euripides says,

[60] Literally, "gluing."

*«ὁ δ᾽ εἰς τὸ σῶφρον ἐπ᾽ ἀρετήν τ᾽ ἄγων ἔρως*
*ζηλωτὸς ἀνθρώποισιν, ὧν εἴην ἐγώ».*

*Κατὰ παρῳδίαν δέ, ὅταν μέρος εἰπὼν τοῦ ἔπους παρ᾽ αὑτοῦ τὸ λοιπὸν πεζῶς ἑρμηνεύσῃ καὶ πάλιν τοῦ ἔπους εἰπὼν ἕτερον ἐκ τοῦ ἰδίου προσθῇ, ὡς μίαν γενέσθαι τὴν ἰδέαν· οἷον Δημοσθένης ἐν τῷ Πα-*
[448] *ραπρεσβείας «ὅστις δ᾽ ὁμιλῶν ἥδεται ταὐτὰ πρεσβεύων Φιλοκράτει, | οὐπώποτ᾽ ἠρώτησα γινώσκων, ὅτι ἀργύριον εἴληφεν οὗτος, ὥσπερ Φιλοκράτης ὁμολογῶν».*

## *Περὶ τῶν κεκρατηκότων ἐν τοῖς ἀκροαταῖς παθῶν.*

*Πρὸς τὰ κεκρατηκότα πάθη οὐ δεῖ ἀντιτείνειν, ἀλλ᾽ εἴκοντα παραμυθεῖσθαι. Ὅμηρος ἐποίησε, Θουκυδίδης ἐμιμήσατο, Δημοσθένης διεδέξατο, Ἰσοκράτης παρέδωκεν. Ὅμηρος*

*«ἦ μὴν καὶ πόνος ἐστὶν ἀνιηθέντα νέεσθαι·*
*καὶ γάρ τίς θ᾽ ἕνα μῆνα μένων ἀπὸ ἧς ἀλόχοιο*
*ἀσχαλάᾳ σὺν νηὶ πολυζύγῳ».*

*Θουκυδίδης ἐν Περικλέους λόγῳ «δουλοῖ γὰρ φρόνημα τὸ αἰφνίδιον καὶ ἀπροσδόκητον καὶ πλείστῳ παραλόγῳ ξυμβαῖνον». Δημοσθένης «εἰ δέ τις ὑμῶν τὸν Φίλιππον εὐτυχοῦντα ὁρῶν ταύτῃ φοβερὸν προσπολεμῆσαι νομίζει, σώφρονος μὲν ἀνδρὸς λογισμῷ χρῆται· μεγάλη γὰρ ῥοπή». Ἰσοκράτης δὲ σαφῶς οὕτως αὐτὸ παραδίδωσι «μηδὲ πρὸς τὰς τῶν παραπλησιαζόντων ὀργὰς τραχέως ἀπαντῶν, ἀλλὰ θυμουμένοις μὲν αὐτοῖς εἴκων, πεπαυμένοις δὲ τῆς ὀργῆς ἐπιπλήττων».*

1 Aeschinis 1, 151; Eurip. Stheneboeae fr. 672 N.²; *Rhein. Museum* 63, 148 l. 19 | οὐδεὶς (ex ὀυδ᾽ εἰς?) Ph | ἀρετῆι Vc, m. 1 Sf || **2** ὥς Ph | κἀγώ Vc || **3-4** πεζῶς λοιπὸν (om. τὸ) Pc || **4** ἕτερον <μέρος>? || **5-6** περὶ παραπρεσβείας Ac || **6** Dem. 19, 245; Eur. fr. 812 N.² | τὰ αὐτὰ Ac Sf Ph; ταῦτα Pc; καὶ ταῦτα Dem. || **9** mg. Pa, (περὶ om.) Pc; supr. (τῶν om.; ἀκούωσι) Vc Ac Sf; mg. περι κεκρατηκότων, om. cet., Ph | mg. κθ̄ Vc Ac, λ̄ **P** || **10** cf. [Dion.] II 1 p. 281, 8. 9 Us. || **13** Hom. B 291 || **15** ἀσαλάαῖς Ph || **16** Thuc. 2, 61 || **17** Dem. 2, 22 || **18** ταύτη τοι φοβερὸν προσπολεμίσαι νομίσοι Vc || **19** νομίσει Sf || **20** σ°αφῶς Vδ || **20-21** πλησιαζόντων Vc Ac, Isocr. 1, 31 || **21** ἀπαντᾶν Vc Ac || **22** εἴκειν Ac | ἐπιπλήττειν Ac

> There is a love that makes men chaste and virtuous, an envied thing among men, of whom I would be one.

It is adaptation (*parōidia*)[61] whenever, after quoting part of the verse, one in his own words expresses the rest in prose and then quoting another verse adds something of his own, so that it becomes a single idea; for example, Demosthenes in the *False Embassy* (19.254): "'Who on an embassy delights in the company' of Philocrates, | 'I never inquired, knowing'[62] that he took money, [448]
as Philocrates admits he did."

## CHAPTER 31: ON POWERFUL EMOTIONS AMONG THE HEARERS

One should not oppose powerful emotions but should yield and allay them. Homer did this, Thucydides imitated him, Demosthenes took up the tradition, Isocrates passed it on. Homer (*Iliad* 2.291–293):[63]

> Indeed there is pain to return home disheartened, for if one remains even one month apart from his wife he has vexation of heart in his benched ship.

Thucydides in a speech of Pericles (2.61):[64] "For the mind quails before what is sudden and unexpected and least within calculation." Demosthenes (2.22): "If any of you, seeing Philip's good fortune, thinks in this he is a formidable antagonist, he reasons like a prudent man, for (*luck*) is a great weight in the scale." And Isocrates clearly transmits it thus (1.31): "Not harshly opposing the angry moods of your associates but yielding to them when in a passion and rebuking them when their anger has cooled."[65]

[61] Another unusual usage; the word otherwise means "parody," as below in ch. 34.

[62] This is thought to come from Euripides' *Phoenix*; cf. frg. 812 Nauck².

[63] Odysseus is addressing Agamemnon about the morale of the troops.

[64] Pericles is defending himself to the citizens after the second invasion by the Spartans.

[65] The author may not realize that Isocrates' speech of advice to Demonicus antedates Demosthenes' *Olynthiacs* by about twenty-five years.

## *Περὶ ὁμολογουμένων ἀδικημάτων.*

*Τῶν ὁμολογουμένων ἀδικημάτων μία παραμυθία ἡ ὁμολογία καὶ*
[449] *ἀπολογία. Ὅμηρος τοῦτο ἐδίδαξεν, Ἡρό|δοτος ἐμιμήσατο. οἷον Ἑλένη*
*τῶν κακῶν αἰτία πᾶσι, καὶ Ἕλλησι καὶ βαρβάροις, καὶ μάλιστα τοῖς Τρωσὶν ὁμολογουμένως κακὸν ἐλήλυθε· τί οὖν ποιεῖ; ὅταν διαλέγηται τῶν Τρώων τινί, ἑαυτῆς κατηγορεῖ καὶ ὁμολογεῖ τὴν ἀδικίαν, καὶ τοῦτο οὐ μόνον αὐτῇ ἀπολογίας, ἀλλὰ καὶ ἐλέου καὶ παραμυθίας αἴτιον γίνεται· αὐτῷ γοῦν τῷ Πριάμῳ διαλεγομένη ἑαυτῆς κατηγορεῖ, ὥστε τὸν γέροντα, εἰ καὶ ἐμίσει αὐτήν, μεταβαλέσθαι καὶ ἐλεεῖν· ἀποκρίνεται οὖν*

*«οὔ τί μοι αἰτίη ἐσσί· θεοί νύ μοι αἴτιοί εἰσι».*

*Καὶ παρ᾽ Ἡροδότῳ ὁ Ἄδραστός ἐστιν, ὑπὸ Κροίσου εὐεργετηθεὶς καὶ καθαρθεὶς καὶ φύλαξ τοῦ παιδὸς αὐτοῦ ἐκπεμφθείς· εἶτα ἀποκτείνας τὸν Ἄτυν ἐν τῇ θήρᾳ καὶ τοῦ Κροίσου βοῶντος καὶ ἀγανακτοῦντος ἑαυτὸν προτείνων, κατηγορεῖ ἑαυτοῦ καὶ ἀποκτεῖναι κελεύει· ὥστε τὸν Κροῖσον παρ᾽ Ἡροδότῳ τὴν τοῦ Πριάμου φωνὴν ἀφιέναι πρὸς τὸν νεανίσκον «εἷς δέ μοι οὐ σὺ τούτων αἴτιος, ἀλλὰ θεῶν κού τις, ὅς μοι προεσήμαινεν ἐν τῷ ὀνείρῳ».*

[450] ## | *Περὶ τοῦ τραγικῶς λέγειν.*

*Τὸ τραγικῶς λέγειν Ὅμηρος μὲν ἐδίδαξε, Δημοσθένης δὲ ἐμιμήσατο. ὅτι μὲν γὰρ τραγῳδὸς καὶ πατὴρ τραγῳδίας Ὅμηρος, Πλάτων μαρτυρεῖ· ὅπως δ᾽ ἐτραγῴδησεν ἐν τῇ ἑαυτοῦ ποιήσει, θεωρητέον.*

1 supr. Vc Ac Sf, mg. **P** ph | mg. $\overline{\lambda}$ Vc Ac Ph, $\overline{\lambda\alpha}$ **P** || **2** sic **P** Sf Ph; ἡ ἀπολογία καὶ ὁμολογία Vc; ἡ ὁμολογία καὶ ἡ κατηγορία Ac || **2-3** Diac.: ἡ δὲ σύνταξις ἔστι τοιαύτη· μία παραμυθία καὶ ἀπολογία τῶν ὁμολογουμένων ἀδικημάτων ἡ ὁμολογία τοῦ ἀδικήματός ἐστιν; cf. [Dion.] II 1 p. 314, 6. 367, 8 Us. (de elocutionis vitiis); Fuhr, Nov. Symb. Joachim. 1907 p. 114 || **5** κακὸν Ac; κακῶς **P** Vc Sf Ph (κακὸν ἤλυθε de Achille Φ 39, de Ulixe γ 306) || **6** τοῦτο om. Ph || **7** ἀπολογία Ac Sf, (ex cr. m. po.) Vc; ὁμολογία Ph, ?Vc m. 1 || **8** [Dion.] II 1 p. 314, 6. 334, 4. 14 Us. || **9** μεταβάλλεσθαι Ac Ph | γοῦν Vδ || **10** Hom. Γ 164 || **11** Her. 1, 35 sq. || **12** εἶτα αὐτὸς ἀποκτείνας Vc Sf Ph || **13-14** παρεδίδου ἑαυτὸν Κροίσῳ προτεινων τὰς χεῖρας Her. 1, 45 || **16** ἧς Ac | κοῦ **P** Vc Ac Sf; καί Ph; γρ καὶ οὔ τις ἄλλος **P** || **17** προεσήμανεν Vc Ac; προεμήνυσεν Sf || **18** supr. Vc Ac Sf Ph, mg. **P** | mg. $\overline{\lambda\alpha}$ Vc Ac Ph, $\overline{\lambda\beta}$ **P** || **20-21** Plat. Reip. X 598 D || **21** αὐτοῦ Ac

## CHAPTER 32: ON ADMITTED WRONGDOING

The one remedy for admitted wrongdoing is confession and apology. Homer did this, Herodotus | imitated him. For example, [449]
Helen was the cause of evils for all, both Greeks and barbarians, and especially her arrival was admittedly an evil for the Trojans. What then does she do? Whenever she converses with one of the Trojans she denounces herself and confesses her crime, and this becomes not only a source of defense to her but of pity and compassion. Even when conversing with Priam himself she denounces herself so that the old man, even if he was hating her, changes and pities her. Thus, he answers her (*Iliad* 3.164), "You are not, I think, the cause; it is the gods who are the cause." And in Herodotus (1.35ff.) there is Adrastus, favored by Croesus and purified and dispatched as a guard for his son. Then after he killed Atys on the hunt and when Croesus is crying out and in distress, offering himself up, Adrastus denounces himself and demands to be put to death. As a result, according to Herodotus Croesus adapted the words of Priam to the young man: "You are not, I think, the one cause of these things, but some one of the gods is and signified it to me in a dream."

## | CHAPTER 33: ON SPEAKING IN TRAGIC STYLE [450]

Homer taught how to speak tragically, and Demosthenes imitated him. That Homer was a tragedian and the father of tragedy, Plato testifies,[66] but one must examine how he made his poetry tragic.

[66] Cf. *Republic* 10.598d.

Ἰλίου ἅλωσιν οὐκ εἶπε, τέχνῃ παραλιπών· οὐ γὰρ ἥρμοζεν αὐτοῦ τῇ τῆς ποιήσεως τραγῳδίᾳ ἑνὸς πολιχνίου πόρθησις· τί οὖν ποιεῖ; πάσης πόλεως εἶπε πόρθησιν ἐν δυσὶν ἔπεσιν

«ἄνδρας μὲν κτείνουσι, πόλιν δέ τε πῦρ ἀμαθύνει,
τέκνα δέ τ' ἄλλοι ἄγουσι βαθυζώνους τε γυναῖκας».

ἂν δ' Ἕκτωρ ἀποθάνῃ, Ἀνδρομάχη λέγει τι καὶ Ἑκάβη, ἀλλὰ καὶ Ἑλένη καὶ χορὸς Τρῳάδων, καὶ πολλὰ δράματα ὡς εἰπεῖν ἀποπληροῦντα τὴν τραγῳδίαν. τί οὖν ἐκ τούτων τὸν χρηστὸν νομίσομεν Ὅμηρον λέγειν ἡμῖν; τὰ μεγάλα τῇ βραχύτητι τῆς ἑρμηνείας φυλάττει μεγάλα, τῆς συντομίας τὸ μέγεθος αὐτοῖς διασῳζούσης, τὰ δὲ μικρὰ καὶ φαῦλα τῇ περιβολῇ τῶν λόγων μέγεθος προσλαμβάνει.

Ταῦτὰ ποιεῖ Δημοσθένης καὶ οὕτω τραγῳδεῖ Φωκέων ἅλωσιν
[451] ἔθνους ὅλου ἐν ὀλίγοις ῥήμασι λέγων «ἦν | ἰδεῖν οἰκίας κατεσκαμμένας, τείχη περιῃρημένα, χώραν ἔρημον τῶν ἐν ἡλικίᾳ, γύναια δὲ καὶ παιδάρια ὀλίγα καὶ πρεσβύτας ἀνθρώπους οἰκτρούς»· μονονουχὶ παρέφρασε τὸ Ὁμηρικόν. ἐν δὲ τῷ Κατὰ Κόνωνος αἰκίας τῆς ὕβρεως περιήγησιν ἐποίησεν ἀκριβῶς ἕκαστα διηγούμενος, δηλονότι τὴν φαυλότητα τοῦ πράγματος αἴρων εἰς μέγεθος τῇ περιττοτέρᾳ ἑρμηνείᾳ καὶ τὴν ὕβριν τραγῳδῶν.

## Περὶ τοῦ κωμικῶς λέγειν.

Τοῦ κωμικῶς λέγειν ἅμα καὶ σκώπτειν ἀρχαίως τρεῖς μέθοδοι· τὸ κατὰ παρῳδίαν σχῆμα, τὸ παρὰ προσδοκίαν, τὸ ἐναντίας ποιεῖσθαι τὰς εἰκόνας τῇ φύσει τῶν πραγμάτων. τούτων παραδείγματα λάβωμεν τὰ μὲν ἐκ τοῦ κωμικοῦ, τὰ δὲ ἐκ τοῦ βίου, τὰ δὲ ἐκ τοῦ ῥήτορος.

Τὸ μὲν κατὰ παρῳδίαν οὕτως ἔχει

**1** τέχνῃ vix. san.; Laurentius vertit *«artificiose eam relinquens»* | καταλιπών **P** || **3** πόρθησιν εἶπεν Vc Ac Sf Ph || **4** Hom. I 593 || **4-12** cf. Theon II 62, 24; 31. 63, 3 Sp. Aps. I 2 p. 317, 3 Sp.-H. || **4** ⌊Π⌉κτεινουσι⌊ν er.⌉ Vc | ἀμαλθύνει Ph || **5** δ' (om. τ') Ac Ph || **6** Hom. Ω 725. 748. 762 | τ⌊ί καὶ m. po.; ex η⌉ Vc; τι (om. καὶ) Ph || **8** τὸν om. Ph | νομίσωμεν Ph || **8-9** ἡμῖν ante ὅμηρον Vc, ante λέγειν Sf Ph; om. Ac || **9** φυλάττειν Vc Ac Ph || **10** σμικρὰ Pc || **11** παραλαμβάνει Vc Sf; προσλαμβάνειν Ac || **12** οὖτος Sf; οὕτως Vc Ac Ph || **13** Dem. 19, 65 || **15** ὀλίγα om. **P**; γρ γυναῖκα δὲ καὶ παιδάρια ὀλίγα Pa, (γύναια) Pc | μονονουχὶ παραμικρον παρέφρασε Sf || **16** Dem. 54, 3 sq. || **20** supr. Vc Ac Sf Ph, mg. **P** | mg. $\overline{\lambda\beta}$ Vc Ac Ph, $\overline{\lambda\gamma}$ **P** || **21** τὸ Ph || **22** cf. Auct. ad. Her. I 6, 10 || **24** τὰ δὲ ἐκ τοῦ βίου post ῥήτορος Pc; del. Spengel, at cf. 260, 11 sq. | ἀπὸ (pro alt. ἐκ) Ac Sf Ph || **25** τὸ scripsit Rabe; τὰ codd.

He did not describe the taking of Ilium, omitting it artistically, for the sack of one small town did not fit well with the tragic nature of his poetry. What then does he do? He described the sack of every city in two verses (*Iliad* 9.593–594):

> They kill the men, and fire levels the city, and strangers lead away the children and the deep-girdled women.

At the death of Hector, Andromache gives a speech (*Iliad* 24.725ff.) and Hecabe too, but also Helen and a chorus of Trojan women, and there are many dramatic scenes that, so to speak, complete the tragedy. From these examples what useful lesson shall we think that Homer tells us? He keeps great things great by the brevity of what he says, the conciseness preserving their greatness, and he adds greatness to small and trivial things by expansion of what is said.

Demosthenes does the same and in a few words gives a tragic turn to the sack of the Phocians, a whole nation (19.65), saying, | [451] "It was possible to see houses leveled to the ground, walls dismantled, the place empty of men in their prime, only a few women and children and pitiable old men." He all but paraphrased the Homeric passage. And in *Against Conon for Outrage* (54.3ff.) he gave an account of the man's hybris, narrating each action in detail, clearly elevating the foulness of his action to great importance by use of a loftier style and by making the hybris tragic.

## CHAPTER 34: ON SPEAKING IN COMIC STYLE

There are three methods of speaking in the style of comedy and at the same time mocking in the ancient way: the figure by parody; by speaking contrary to expectation; and by creating images contrary to the nature of the subjects.[67] Let us consider examples of these, some from comedy, some from everyday life, and some from the Orator.

The following is an example of parody (Aristophanes, *Wasps* 45):

[67] Cf. *Rhetoric to Herennius* 1.10.

*«ὁλᾷς; Θέωλος τὴν κεφαλὴν κόλακος ἔχει»·*

*θέλων γὰρ εἰπεῖν «τὴν κεφαλὴν κόρακος ἔχει» διὰ τὸ τραυλὸς εἶναι δῆθεν ἁμαρτὼν τῇ φωνῇ διεκωμῴδησε τὸν τρόπον.*

*Τὸ δὲ παρὰ προσδοκίαν τοῦτο*

*«βδελυρὸν μὲν οὖν τὸ πρᾶγμα καὶ οὐκ ἂν ἐβουλόμην*
*λαχεῖν, ἐπειδὴ δὲ ἔλαχον»·*

[452] | *προσδοκᾷ μὲν ὁ ἀκροατὴς ἀκοῦσαι «ὑπομενῶ», φησὶ δὲ «οὐκ ἂν ἐβουλόμην».*

*Τὸ δὲ ἐναντίως χρῆσθαι ταῖς εἰκόσι πρὸς τὰ μεγέθη τῶν πραγμάτων οὕτω γίνεται, ἐὰν μεγάλῳ μικρὸν ἀντιτιθῶμεν καὶ μικρῷ μέγα, οἷον «ἐμαχέσαντο οἱ ὄρτυγες ὡς Αἴας καὶ Ἕκτωρ» καὶ «Ἕκτωρ καὶ Ἀχιλλεὺς ἐμαχέσαντο ὡς ἀλεκτρυόνες».*

*Τούτοις πᾶσι χρῆται Δημοσθένης ἐν τῷ Περὶ τοῦ στεφάνου· ὅθεν δηλοῦται, ὅτι κωμῳδεῖν ἐπίσταται· τῇ μὲν παρῳδίᾳ οὕτως «τὸν μὲν πατέρα ἀντὶ Τρόμητος ἐποίησεν Ἀτρόμητον», τῷ δὲ παρὰ προσδοκίαν οὕτω περὶ Αἰσχίνου λέγων «οὐδὲ γὰρ ὧν ἔτυχεν ἦν, ἀλλ᾽ οἷς ὁ δῆμος καταρᾶται», τῇ δ᾽ ἐναντιώσει τῶν εἰκόνων οὕτως «αὐτοτραγικὸς πίθηκος, ἀρουραῖος Οἰνόμαος».*

## Περὶ ἀμφιβολίας.

*Τοῖς μὲν πολλοῖς δοκεῖ πολλὰς ἐν τοῖς βιβλίοις ἀμφιβολίας γίνεσθαι ὑπὸ τῶν παλαιῶν· ἡμεῖς δὲ φαμέν, ὅτι οὐ δύναται ἔν τῳ παλαιῷ βιβλίῳ ἀμφιβολία εἶναι· ἀνάγκη γὰρ τὴν διάνοιαν εἶναι ἄτοπον τὴν ἑτέραν ἢ τὴν σύνταξιν τῆς λέξεως. τὸ γοῦν παρ᾽ Ὁμήρῳ «θεοῖσι δὲ θῦσαι*

1 Arist. Vesp. 45 | ὁλᾶις θεόδωλος . . . κόλακος Vc | θεόδωλος Ph; θεόδωλον Sf || 2 θέλων — ἔχει om. Vc || 3 τὴν φωνὴν Vc Sf Ph || 4 οὕτω Ald. || 5 Fragm. com. anon. 187. **IV** p. 650 Meineke | τὸ om. Ph | γρ οὐκανεβαλόμην Ac || 6 τυχεῖν Sf || 9 ἐναντίως, in argumento mg. ἐναντιαις, Ph || 9-10 παραδειγμάτων Vc Ph || 10 ἀντιτιθῶμεν Pc; ἀντιτιθῶμεν Pah Vc Ac Sf || 11 ὡς om. Ac Ph | alt. καὶ Ἕκτωρ om. Ac Ph || 11-12 cf. Demetr. De eloc. 160 || 13 ἔνθεν Vδ, (ὅ supr.) Pa || 16 Dem. 18, 130 || 17 (αὐτο om.)τραγικὸς Ph | Dem. 18, 242 || 19 supr. Vc Ac Sf Ph, mg. **P** | mg. λγ Vc Ac Ph, λδ **P** || 20 de controversia simili cf. [Dion.] II 1 p. 323, 6; 295, 3 Us. | cf. Theon II 82, 29 Sp. || 20-21 γενέσθαι Vδ || 22 ἀμφιλογία Ph || 23 δὲ (pro γοῦν) Vc Ac | Hom. I 219

"Do you thee, Theolus hath the head of a *kolax*."[68] Wanting to say "he has the head of a crow," because of his lisp he really mispronounced the word and gave it a comic turn. An example of contrary to expectation (*para prosdokian*) is this: "Now the thing is disgusting, and I would not want to get it, but since I did..."[69] | The hearer expects to hear "I put up with getting it," but he says [452] "I would not want."

Use of opposite images when compared with the magnitude of things occurs if we contrast a small thing with a great one and a great one with a small one; for example, "The quails fought like Ajax and Hector" and "Hector and Achilles fought like cocks." Demosthenes uses all of these in *On the Crown*, from which it is clear that he knew how to speak in a comic style. He uses parody thus (18.130): "(Aeschines) made his father out to be Atrometus (*dauntless*) instead of Trometus (*trembling*)," and paraprosdokia when speaking about Aeschines (18.130), thus: "He was not whatever he happened to be but what the people curse," and the opposition of images thus (18.242): "a tragical ape, a countrified Oenomaus."[70]

## CHAPTER 35: ON AMPHIBOLY

To most people, it seems that there are many amphibolies[71] in the books of the ancients, but we say that it is not possible for an amphiboly to exist in any ancient book,[72] for one or the other of the two meanings or grammatical constructions is absurd.[73] They say

[68] The speaker lisps: "thee" = "see," "hath" = "has." Kolax means a flatterer, but here a lisping pronunciation of *korax*, "crow."

[69] From an unknown comedy; cf. frg. 187 in *Fragmenta Comicorum Anonymorum*, vol. 4 (ed. A. Meineke; Berlin: Reimer, 1841), 650. A better example could have been found.

[70] Oenomaus was the rival of Pelops for the hand of Hippodameia, subject of a play by Sophocles. According to the anonymous life of Aeschines (cf. *Scholia in Aeschinem* 1.7 [ed. M. R. Dilts; Bibliotheca scriptorum Graecorum et Romanorum Teubneriana. Leipzig: Teubner, 1992], 2), Aeschines tripped on stage while playing Oenomaus, probably at the rural Dionysia (hence "countrified").

[71] I.e., ambiguities.

[72] I.e., a competent critic should be able to determine the correct meaning of passages in the classics.

[73] On this chapter, see Patillon, *Théorie du discours*, 311–12.

*ἀνώγει Πάτροκλον, ὃν ἑταῖρον» τοῦτο λέγουσιν εἶναι ἀμφιβολίαν, πό-*
[453] *τερον Πάτροκλον κελεύει | σφαγιασθῆναι ἢ τῷ Πατρόκλῳ προσέταξε τοῖς θεοῖς θῦσαι. καὶ τὸ*

*«ὦ Ζεῦ, γένοιτο καταβαλεῖν τὸν σῦν ἐμέ»*

*ἀμφίβολόν φασιν εἶναι, λέγοντες καὶ τοῦτον εἶναι δύνασθαι τὸν νοῦν εὐχομένου τῷ Διὶ ὑπὸ τοῦ συὸς καταβληθῆναι· οὕτω μὲν δὴ ὁ νοῦς ἄτοπός ἐστιν, ἡ δὲ ἑρμηνεία ἄλογος. τὸν αὐτὸν δὲ τρόπον «στασιάσαντες δὲ ἔτη πολλά, ὡς λέγεται, ἀπὸ πολέμου τινὸς τῶν προσοίκων βαρβάρων ἐφθάρησαν»· ζητοῦσιν, ὑπὸ τίνος ἐφθάρησαν, ὑπὸ τοῦ πολέμου ἢ ὑπὸ τῆς στάσεως. ἀδύνατον ὑπὸ τοῦ πολέμου εἶναι τὴν φθοράν· ὃ δὲ λέγει, τοιοῦτόν ἐστιν «στασιάσαντες ἀπὸ πολέμου, ἐφθάρησαν», ἵνα ἡ μὲν στάσις ᾖ γεγονυῖα ἐκ τοῦ πολέμου, ἡ δὲ φθορὰ ἐκ τῆς στάσεως· οὐ δεῖ γὰρ λέγειν «ἀπὸ πολέμου ἐφθάρησαν». Τοσαῦτα περὶ ἀμφιβολίας.*

## Περὶ ἐργασίας δημηγορίας, διαλόγου, κωμῳδίας, τραγῳδίας, συμποσίων Σωκρατικῶν.

*Δημηγορία, διάλογος, κωμῳδία, τραγῳδία, συμπόσια Σωκρατικὰ διά τινος διπλῆς μεθόδου πάντα πλέκεται.*

[454] *| Ἡ μὲν δημηγορία ἐπιτίμησιν ἔχει καὶ παραμυθίαν, τῆς μὲν ἐπιτιμήσεως κολαζούσης καὶ παιδευούσης τὰς γνώμας τῶν ἀκουόντων, τῆς δὲ παραμυθίας τὸ λυπηρὸν ἐκβαλλούσης ἐκ τῆς ἐπιτιμήσεως. παράδειγμα ταύτης τῆς πλοκῆς πάντες οἱ Φιλιππικοὶ ἀναμὶξ συγκείμενοι.*

*Κωμῳδίας δὲ πλοκὴ πικρὰ καὶ γελοῖα, τῶν μὲν πικρῶν σωφρονιζόντων, τῶν δὲ γελοίων παραμυθουμένων· ὅπερ καὶ ἐξ αὐτῶν τῶν ποιημάτων ἔστι καταμαθεῖν, οὐχ ἥκιστα δὲ ἐν τοῖς Ἀχαρνεῦσιν ὁ Ἀριστοφάνης δηλοῖ λέγων οὕτως*

1 ὃν om. Ac | ἀμφίβολον ? || 2 Πάτροκλον om. Vc || 4 sq. cf. Aristid. II 508, 6 Sp. | adesp. fr. 188 N.[2] | καταλαβεῖν Ph || 5 δύνασθαι καὶ τοῦτον εἶναι Vc Ac Sf Ph || 6 εὐχομένωι Vc; exsp. εὔχομαι | τοῦ om. Pc || 7 καὶ τὸ post τρόπον add. Ac | Thuc. 1, 24 || 8 τινὲς Vc || 9 τίνων Ac || 10 <ἀλλ' ἔστιν> ἀδύνατον ? | ⌊ὑ m. po.⌉πὸ Vc | sq. Diac.: παρόραμα τοῦτο τῷ Ἑρμογένει ἐγένετο || 10-11 ὃ λέγει δὲ τοῦτό ἐστιν Vc Sf Ph || 11-12 ἵνα — στάσεως om. Ac || 12-13 οὐδεὶς γὰρ λέγει (m. po. γρ´ καὶ οὐ δεῖ λέγειν) Vc || 13 γαρ supr. Ph | τοσαῦτα περὶ ἀμφιβολίας om. Vc || 14 supr. Ac Sf, (διαλόγου δημηγορίας) Vc; mg. Ph; περὶ δημηγορίας διαλόγου καὶ τῶν λοιπῶν **P**π, mg. **P** || 14-15 mg. $\overline{\lambda\delta}$ Vc Ac Ph, $\overline{\lambda\epsilon}$ **P** || 18 μὲν γὰρ Vδ | cf. [Dion.] II 1 p. 331, 25 Us. || 18-19 ἐπιτιμίας Vc || 20 ἐκβαλούσης Sf | τὸ ἐκ Vc || 20-21 παραδείγματα Vc || 24 ὁ om. Vc Sf

the Homeric line (*Iliad* 9.219) "to sacrifice to the gods he orders Patroclus, his companion" is an amphiboly. Does he order Patroclus | to be slaughtered, or did he assign to Patroclus to sacrifice [453] to the gods? And the line "O Zeus, let me overcome the boar"[74] they claim is ambiguous and that it is possible for him to be praying to be overcome by the boar. This meaning is absurd and the interpretation unreasonable. In the same way (Thucydides 1.24), "Having had many years of partisan strife, it is said, *apo (by/from)* a war with the neighboring barbarians they were destroyed." The critics want to know by what they were destroyed, by a war or by partisan strife? It is impossible that the destruction was caused by the war, and he says so; that is the meaning of "having had many years of partisan strife from war, they were destroyed"; so the strife came about from the war and the destruction from the strife, for one should not say "they were destroyed by war." So much about amphiboly.

## CHAPTER 36: ON ELABORATION OF PUBLIC SPEAKING, DIALOGUE, COMEDY, TRAGEDY, AND SOCRATIC SYMPOSIA

Public speaking (*dēmēgoria*), dialogue, comedy, tragedy, and Socratic symposia are all constructed by a double method. | [454]

Public speaking includes censuring and reassuring, the censure (*epitimēsis*) chastising and teaching the minds of the hearers, the reassurance (*paramythia*) removing the sting from the censure. All the *Philippics* (of Demosthenes) are an example of this combination, mingled together.

Comedy combines bitter and humorous things, the bitter ones teaching prudence, the humorous ones reassuring. This can be learned from their own poems, and not least in the *Acharnians* Aristophanes exhibits it, saying (line 1), "How much have I

[74] From an unknown tragedy; cf. frg. adesp. 188 Nauck². The reference is probably to the Calydonian boar.

«ὅσα δὴ δέδηγμαι τὴν ἐμαυτοῦ καρδίαν»

τὸ πικρόν,

«ἥσθην δὲ βαιά»

λέγων γελοῖον πάθος.

Τραγῳδίας πλοκὴ οἶκτος καὶ θαῦμα, ὅπερ ἔστι καταμαθεῖν καὶ ἐκ τῶν τραγῳδιῶν, οὐχ ἥκιστα δὲ καὶ ἀπὸ τῶν Ὁμήρου· τοῦτον γὰρ ἔφη ὁ Πλάτων πατέρα τραγῳδίας εἶναι καὶ χορηγόν· εὑρήσομεν οὖν ἐν τοῖς προοιμίοις αὐτοῦ ἀναμὶξ οἶκτον καὶ θαῦμα.

Συμποσίου Σωκρατικοῦ πλοκὴ σπουδαῖα καὶ γελοῖα καὶ πρόσωπα καὶ πράγματα, ὥσπερ καὶ ἐν τῷ Ξενοφῶντος καὶ ἐν τῷ Πλάτωνος Συμποσίῳ. ἀλλὰ καὶ ἐν τῇ Κύρου παιδείᾳ φησὶ Ξενοφῶν «ἀεὶ μὲν οὖν ἐπεμελεῖτο ὁ Κῦρος, ὁπότε συσκηνοῖεν, ὅπως εὐχαριτώτεροί τε λόγοι ῥηθήσονται καὶ παρορμῶντες εἰς ἀρετήν».

[455] | Διαλόγου πλοκὴ ἠθικοὶ λόγοι καὶ ζητητικοί. ὅταν ἀναμίξῃς προσδιαλεγόμενος καὶ ζητῶν, οἱ ἠθικοὶ παρεμβληθέντες λόγοι ἀναπαύουσι τὴν ψυχήν, ὅταν δ᾿ αὖ ἀναπαύσηται, ἐπάγεται ἡ ζήτησις, ὥσπερ ἐν ὀργάνῳ ἡ τάσις καὶ ἄνεσις γίνεται.

## *Περὶ ἀποφάσεως.*

Ἡ ἀπόφασις τῇ καταφάσει ποτὲ μὲν τὸ ἴσον δύναται, ποτὲ δὲ τὸ ἔλαττον, ποτὲ δὲ τὸ πλέον. ἴσον μέν, ὅταν δι᾿ ἐγγύτητα τῆς λέξεως φεύγων τις τὴν ταυτότητα μεταβάλλῃ τὴν λέξιν· οἷον «θύων τε γὰρ φανερὸς ἦν καὶ μαντικῇ χρώμενος οὐκ ἀφανὴς ἦν», ταὐτὸ ἐδήλωσεν. ἔλαττον δὲ καὶ πλέον ἤτοι ὑποστελλομένων ἡμῶν δι᾿ ἀσφάλειαν ἢ ἐπιτεινόντων δι᾿ αὔξησιν κατὰ ἤθους προσθήκην· οἷον

1 Arist.Ach. 1 | δὴ om. Ac || 3 δὲ βαιαὶ Vc; βεβαία Ph || 4 λόγων Ac Sf Ph, (ε ex ο?) Vc | γελοίων Vc Ac Sf Ph || 5 δὲ πλοκὴ Vc Ph || 7 Plat. Reip. X 598 D | εἶναι om. Vc || 8 ἀναμὶξ om. **P** || 11 Xen. Cyrop. II 2, 1 || 12 εὐχαριστότεροί Ac Sf Ph || 13 ῥηθήσωνται Ac Sf; ἐμβληθήσονται Xen. || 14 διαλογου — γίνεται post 454, 14 πάθος Vδ || 14-17 cf. W. Schmid, *Der Atticismus* I 219, 4 || 14 ἀναμίξεις, η supr. (m. 2?), Ph; ἀναμί[Ι]ς Sf || 15 καὶ om. Vc Ph | οἱ γὰρ Sf | λόγοι παρεμβληθέντες Ac || 16 δ᾿ ὀῦν Vc || 17 καὶ ἡ ἄνεσις Sf || 18 mg. **P**; (καὶ καταφάσεως add.) supr. Vc Ac Sf, mg. Ph | mg. λε̅ Vc Ac Ph, λϛ̅ **P** || 19 cf. Π. ἰδ. 306, 8 || 21 μεταβάλη Vc Sf; μεταβάλλ[η ex ει] Pa | Xen. Mem. I 1, 2 || 22 φανερῶς Ph | ταυτὸν Sf; ταὐτὸ γὰρ Ac

gnawed my heart," the bitter, "but I have enjoyed a few things," speaking of a humorous emotion.

In the case of tragedy, pity and wonder are combined, which can be learned from the tragedies but no less also from Homer, for Plato said (*Republic* 10.598d) he was the father and choregus of tragedy. We shall thus find in his prooemia a mixture of pity and wonder.[75]

In Socratic symposia there is a combination of the serious and humorous in regard both to persons and actions, as in the *Symposium* of Xenophon and that of Plato. But in the *Cyropedia* also Xenophon says (2.2.1), "Cyrus always took care, when associating with officers on campaign, that the words he was going to say were genial and promoted virtue."

| In a dialogue the combination is that of ethical and investigative speeches.[76] Whenever you intermingle conversation and inquiry, the ethical speeches that are interspersed refresh the mind, and when one is refreshed, the inquiry is brought in, like the tension and relaxing of an instrument. [455]

## CHAPTER 37: ON NEGATION

Negation (*apophasis*)[77] has sometimes equal force with affirmation, sometimes less, and sometimes more. Equal, whenever one changes the expression to avoid repetition because of a nearby word; for example (Xenophon, *Memorabilia* 1.1.2), "He was openly sacrificing and *not unseen* while using divination," repeating the same thing. It has less or more force when we impose restrictions out of caution or extend *(the thought)* through amplification by addition of an indication of moral character; for example

75 Especially in the opening lines of the *Odyssey*.

76 Conversational remarks, revealing character, and philosophical disquisitions, respectively.

77 Cf. the figure *antenantiōsis* as described by Alexander, *On Figures* 2.23. The modern term is litotes.

*«ὦ ξεῖν᾽, ἐπεὶ οὔτε κακῷ οὔτ᾽ ἄφρονι φωτὶ ἔοικας»·*

*ἐνταῦθα τὸ «οὐ κακῷ καὶ ἄφρονι» ἔλαττόν ἐστι τοῦ «ἀγαθῷ καὶ φρονίμῳ»· οὐ γὰρ δὴ οἶδεν αὐτόν, ἵνα αὐτῷ ταῦτα μαρτυρῇ, ἀλλ᾽ ἱκανὴν φιλοφροσύνην εἶναι νομίζει κακίαν ἀφελεῖν, οὐχὶ ἀρετὴν προσθεῖναι. ὅταν δὲ λέγῃ «ἐπεὶ οὔ μιν ἀφαυρότατος βάλ᾽ Ἀχαιῶν», μεῖζον ἡ ἀπό-*
[456] *φασις δηλοῖ τῆς καταφάσεως· τὸν γὰρ πάνυ | ἰσχυρὸν δεῖξαι θέλει. ὁμοίως δ᾽ ἔχει καὶ τὸ «οὐδ᾽ ἄρα τώ γε ἰδὼν γήθησεν Ἀχιλλεύς»· τὸ γὰρ λίαν λελυπῆσθαι τῇ ἀποφάσει δεδήλωκεν.*

1 ὦ om. Hom. ζ 187; ἠ Ph | ξέν᾽ Vc; ξεῖν᾽ ⌊I⌉ Pa || **2-3** ἀγαθοῦ καὶ φρονίμου **P** Ac || **4** καὶ κακίαν Pc || **5** Hom. Ο 11 || **6** θέλει δεῖξαι Vc Ac Sf Ph || **7** Hom. Α 330 c. schol.; [Plut.] De vita et poesi Homeri 25 || **8** λελυπεῖσθαι Ph; λυπεῖσθαι vulg. | subscr. τέλος τῆς περὶ μέθοδον (sic Pa; μέθο[δ] Pc) δεινότητος **P**; ἑρμογένους περὶ μεθόδου δεινότητος Vc Ph; om. Ac Sf

(*Odyssey* 6.187), "O Stranger, since you seem like *neither a bad nor an ignorant* man. . ." Here "neither bad nor ignorant" is less than "good and wise," for (Odysseus) did not know the man and thus could not testify to this in him, but he thinks him to be sufficiently kind to avoid wickedness, not to acquire virtue. But when (Homer) says (*Iliad* 15.11), "since *not the weakest* of the Acheans hit him," the negation has a stronger sense than an affirmation, for he wants | to show him as very strong. "On seeing the two, [456]
Achilles did not rejoice" (*Iliad* 1.330) has a similar effect, for he has indicated exceeding displeasure by the negative.

End of the Treatise *On Method*

# Glossary and Index of Technical Terms

References are to book and chapter of *On Invention* and, if marked M, to chapters of *On Method*.

For an index of proper names and citations of Greek literature, see Rabe, *Hermogenes*, 457–66. For a complete index verborum (transliterated), see Patillon, *L'Art rhétorique*, 580–622.

epiphonēma (value judgment) 1.5; 4.9
epitimetikē periodos (censorious period) 4.3
ergasia (elaboration) 3.4; 3.7–8
eskhēmatismena problēmata (figured problems) 4.13
gymnasmata (written exercises in composition) 2.3
gnomikē (maxim) 4.3
heuresis (invention) 1.1
horkos (oath) M20
horos (definition) 3.14
hypodiaeresis (subordination) 1.1; 3.10
hyperbaton (change in word order) 4.3; M14
hypomerismos (subordinate part) 3.15
hypophora (proposition of the opponent) 3.4
hypothesis (declamation theme) 1.1
isa skhēmata (a form of amplification) M13
kairos (past occasion) 1.4
kakozēlon (bad taste) 3.15; 4.10; 4.12
kataskeuē (argument, proof) 1.5; 3.2; 3.15
kephalaios (heading of argument) 3.4
khōrion (topic) 3.15
khiasmos (chiasmus) 4.3
kollēsis (quotation) M30
kōlon (clause) 2.7; 4.3–4
komma (phrase) 3.8
kyklos (the same word at the beginning and ending of a grammatical unit) 4.8
lysis (refutation) 3.4; 3.12
makhē (objection) 3.6
metapoiēsis (variation) 3.6; 4.3
paragraphē (suit for illegal prosecution) 3.5
paraleipsis (omission) 2.5; M7
parēkhēsis (two or more words with similar sounds) 4.7
parison (word play, using compounds) M16
paroidia (paraphrase, parody) M30; M34
peribolē (expansion) 1.5
perigraphē (complex sentence) 2.7
periodos (period) 4.3
periousia (superfluity) 1.3
periplokē (circumlocution) M8
peristasis (circumstance) 3.5
perittotēs (abundance) M5
peusis (interrogation) M10
plaston (fictive argument) 3.11
plēthos (fullness)
pneuma (a period delivered in one breath) 4.4
pragmatikē (heading about future effect) 3.4; 3.12; 4.14
probolē (appeal) 3.2
prodiēgēsis (introduction to the narration) 2.1; 2.5; 2.7
proekthesis (preliminary statement of headings) M12
prokataskeuē (introduction to the proof) 3.2
prokatastasis (introduction to the narration) 1.4; 2.1–6; 3.2
protasis (introductory statement) 1.1; 1.5
prosōpopoiia (personification) 3.10
semnon (solemn language) 4.11
skediazein (to speak extemporaneously) M17
skhēma (figure of speech) 4.1
symplokē (interweaving of ideas) 4.3
synēgoros (advocate) M21

Printed in the United States
62390LVS00004B/280-300

9 781589 831216